LAST MAN

6

The Rescue

WITHDRAWN

Balak + Sanlauille + Uiuès

First Second

New York

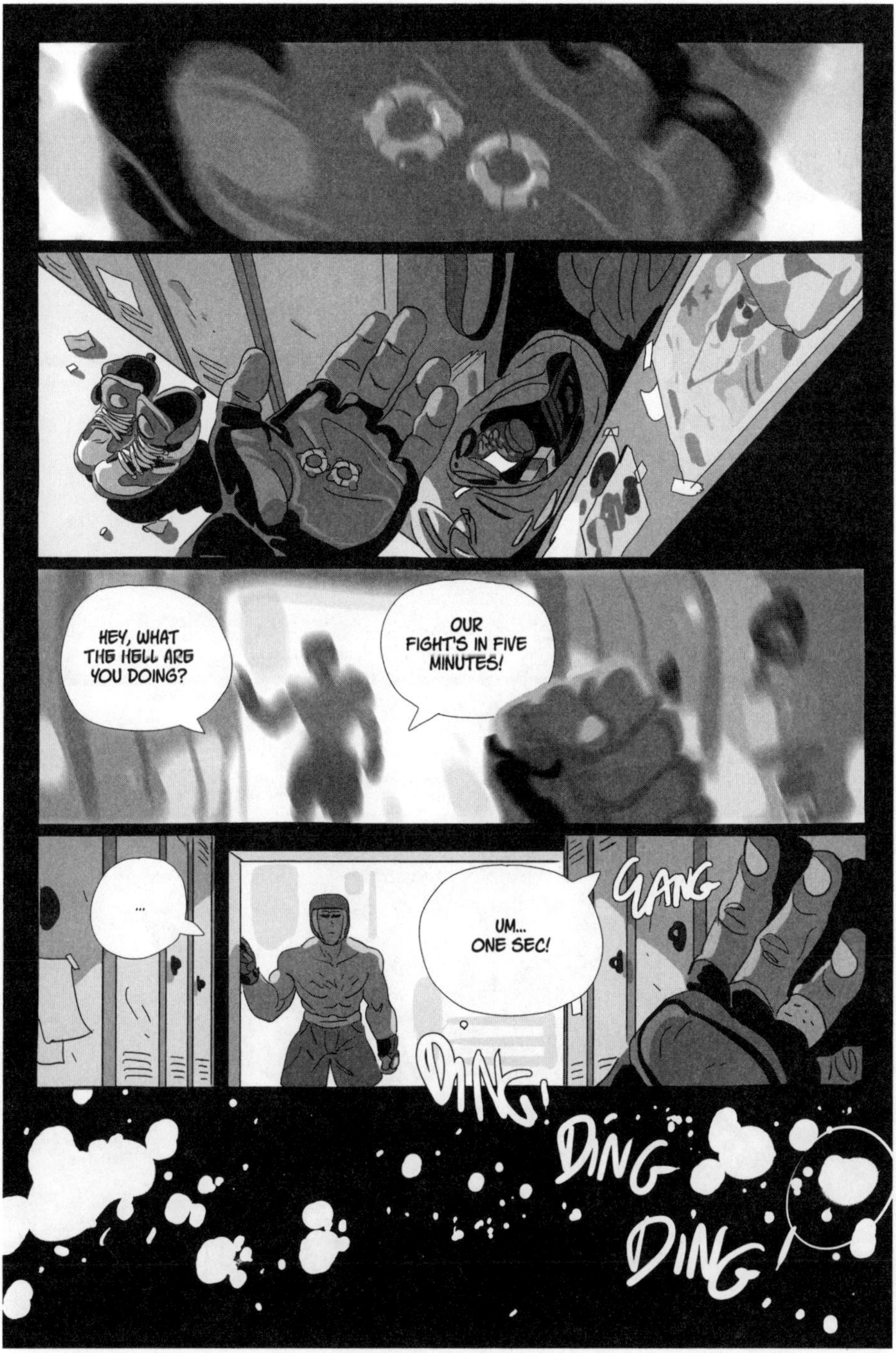

HEY, WHAT THE HELL ARE YOU DOING?
OUR FIGHT'S IN FIVE MINUTES!
...
UM... ONE SEC!
CLANG
DING!
DING
DING!

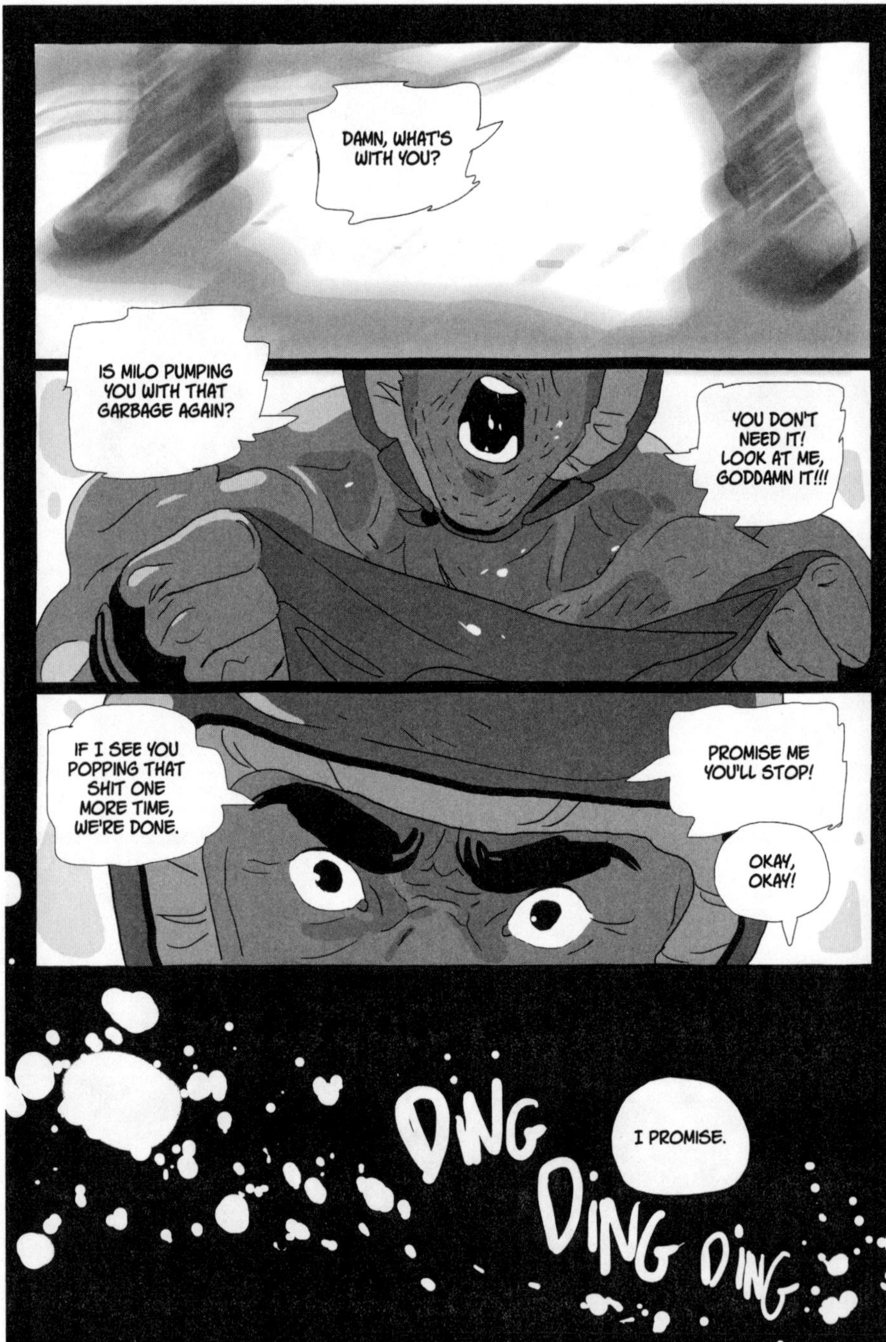
DAMN, WHAT'S WITH YOU?
IS MILO PUMPING YOU WITH THAT GARBAGE AGAIN?
YOU DON'T NEED IT! LOOK AT ME, GODDAMN IT!!!
IF I SEE YOU POPPING THAT SHIT ONE MORE TIME, WE'RE DONE.
PROMISE ME YOU'LL STOP!
OKAY, OKAY!
DING
I PROMISE.
DING DING

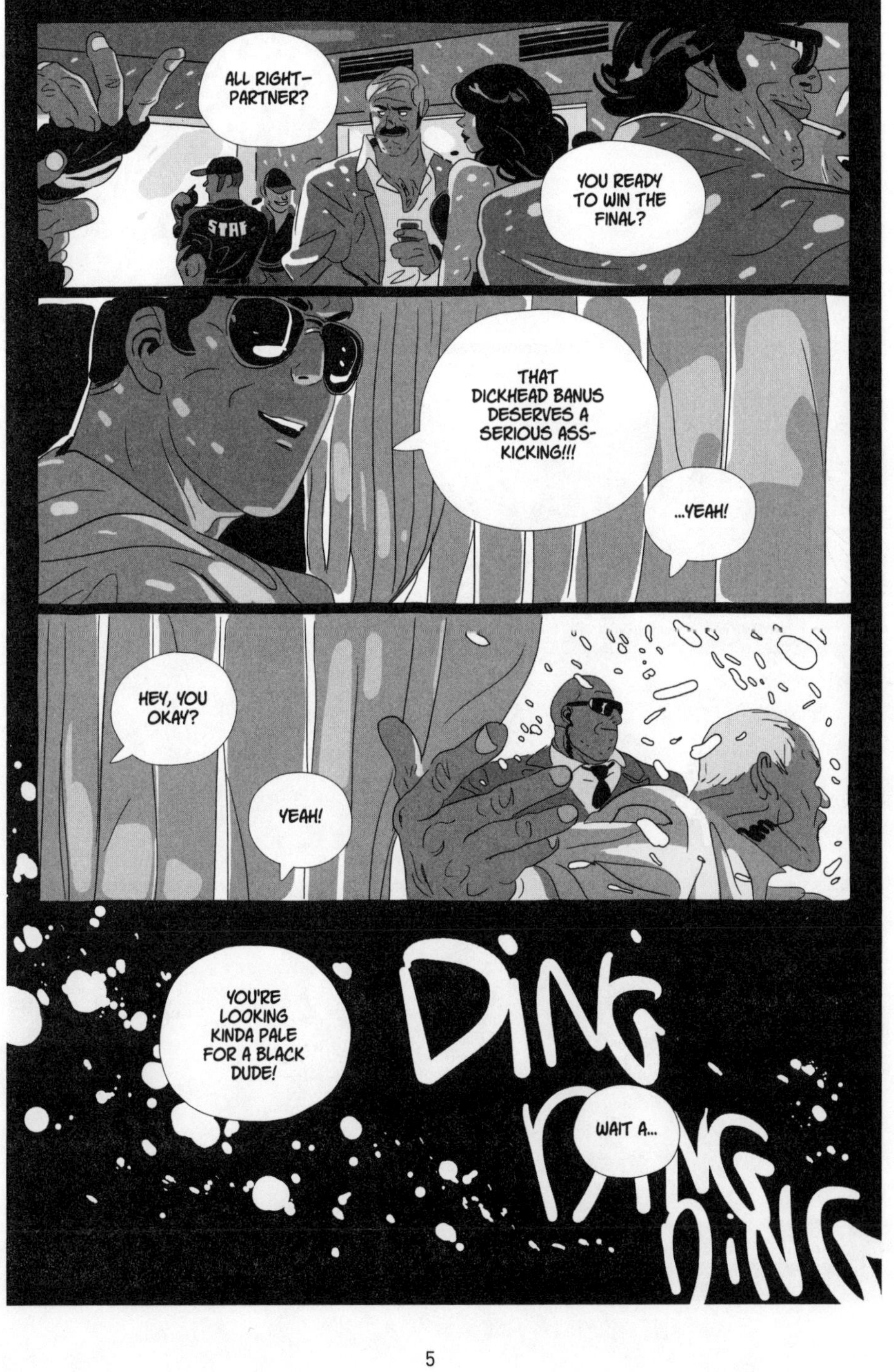
ALL RIGHT—PARTNER?
STAFF
YOU READY TO WIN THE FINAL?
THAT DICKHEAD BANUS DESERVES A SERIOUS ASS-KICKING!!!
...YEAH!
HEY, YOU OKAY?
YEAH!
YOU'RE LOOKING KINDA PALE FOR A BLACK DUDE!
DING
WAIT A...
DING
DING

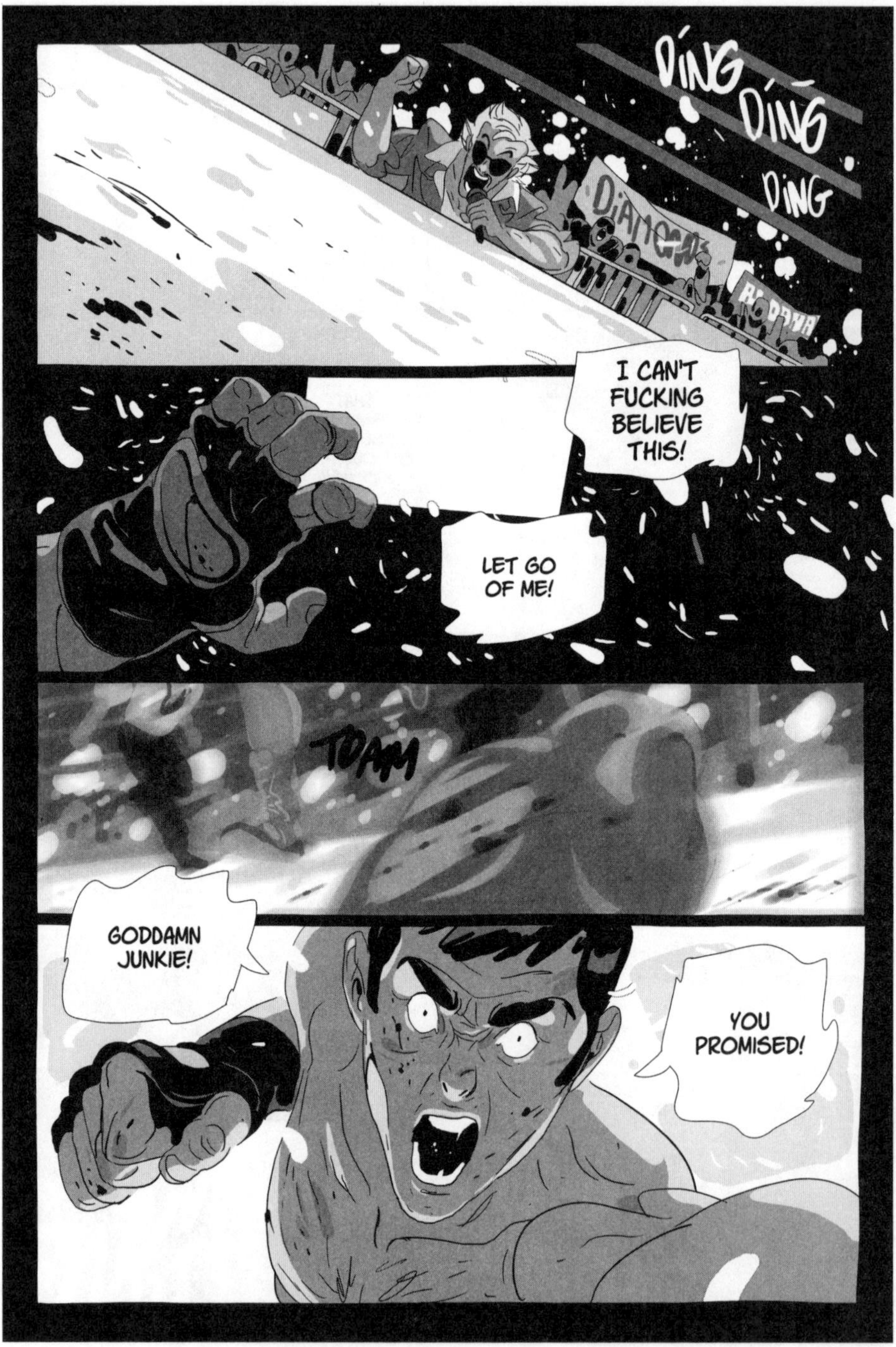
DING DING DING
I CAN'T FUCKING BELIEVE THIS!
LET GO OF ME!
TOAM
GODDAMN JUNKIE!
YOU PROMISED!

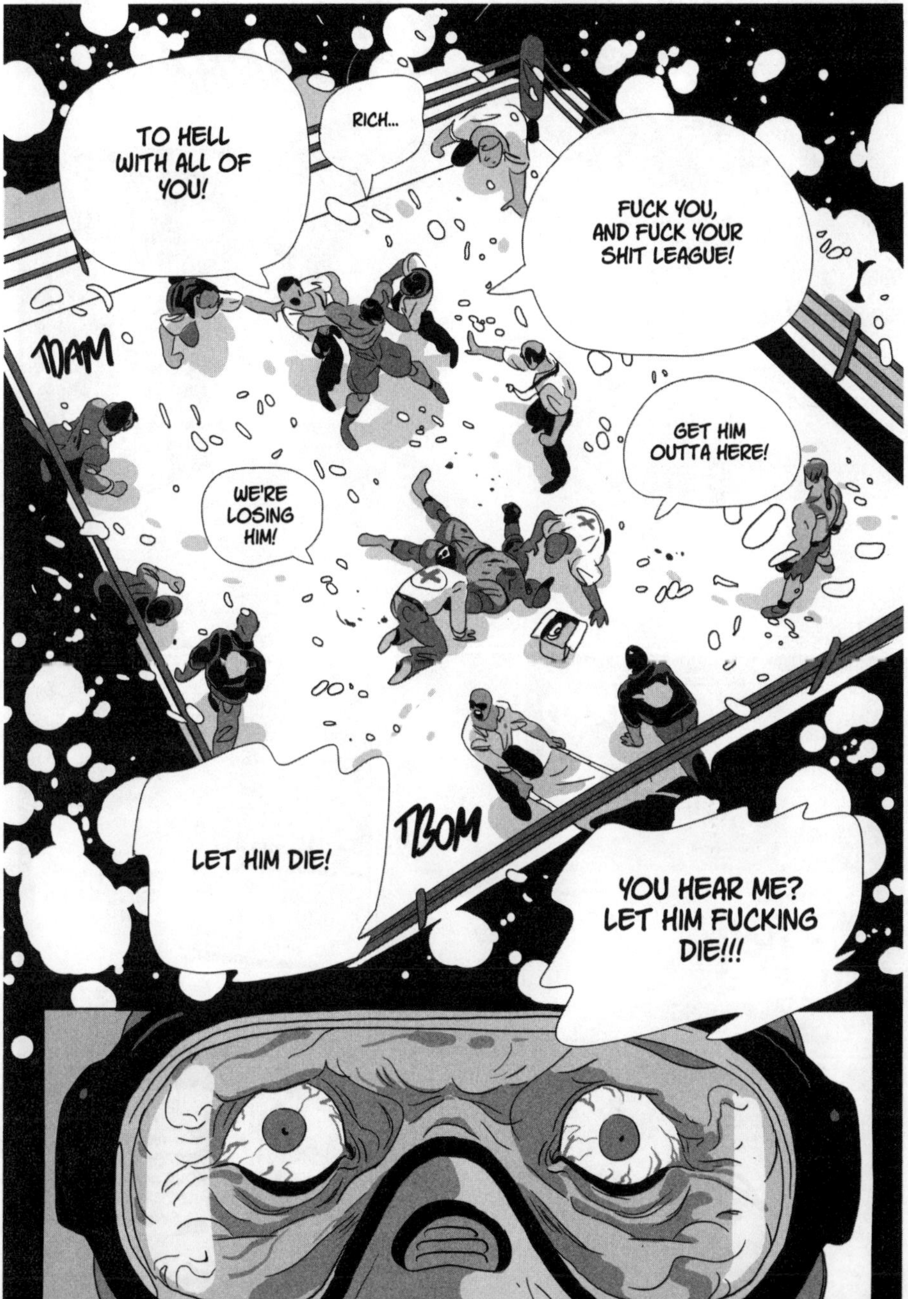
TO HELL WITH ALL OF YOU!
RICH...
FUCK YOU, AND FUCK YOUR SHIT LEAGUE!
TDAM
GET HIM OUTTA HERE!
WE'RE LOSING HIM!
LET HIM DIE!
TBOM
YOU HEAR ME? LET HIM FUCKING DIE!!!

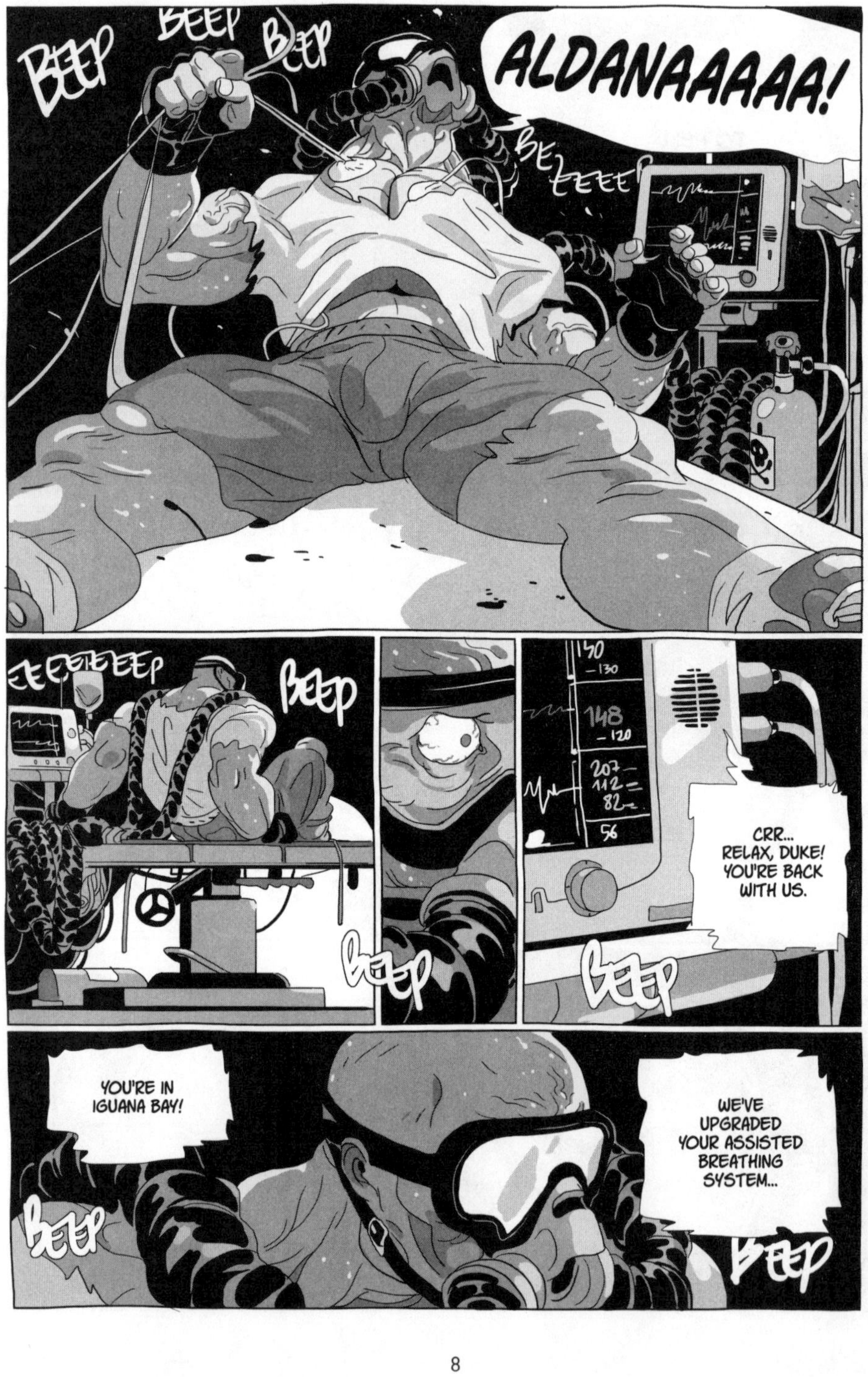
BEEP
BEEP
BEEP
ALDANAAAAAA!
BEEEEEEP
EEEEEEEEP
BEEP
BEEP
130
148
207
112
82
56
CRR... RELAX, DUKE! YOU'RE BACK WITH US.
BEEP
YOU'RE IN IGUANA BAY!
WE'VE UPGRADED YOUR ASSISTED BREATHING SYSTEM...
BEEP
BEEP

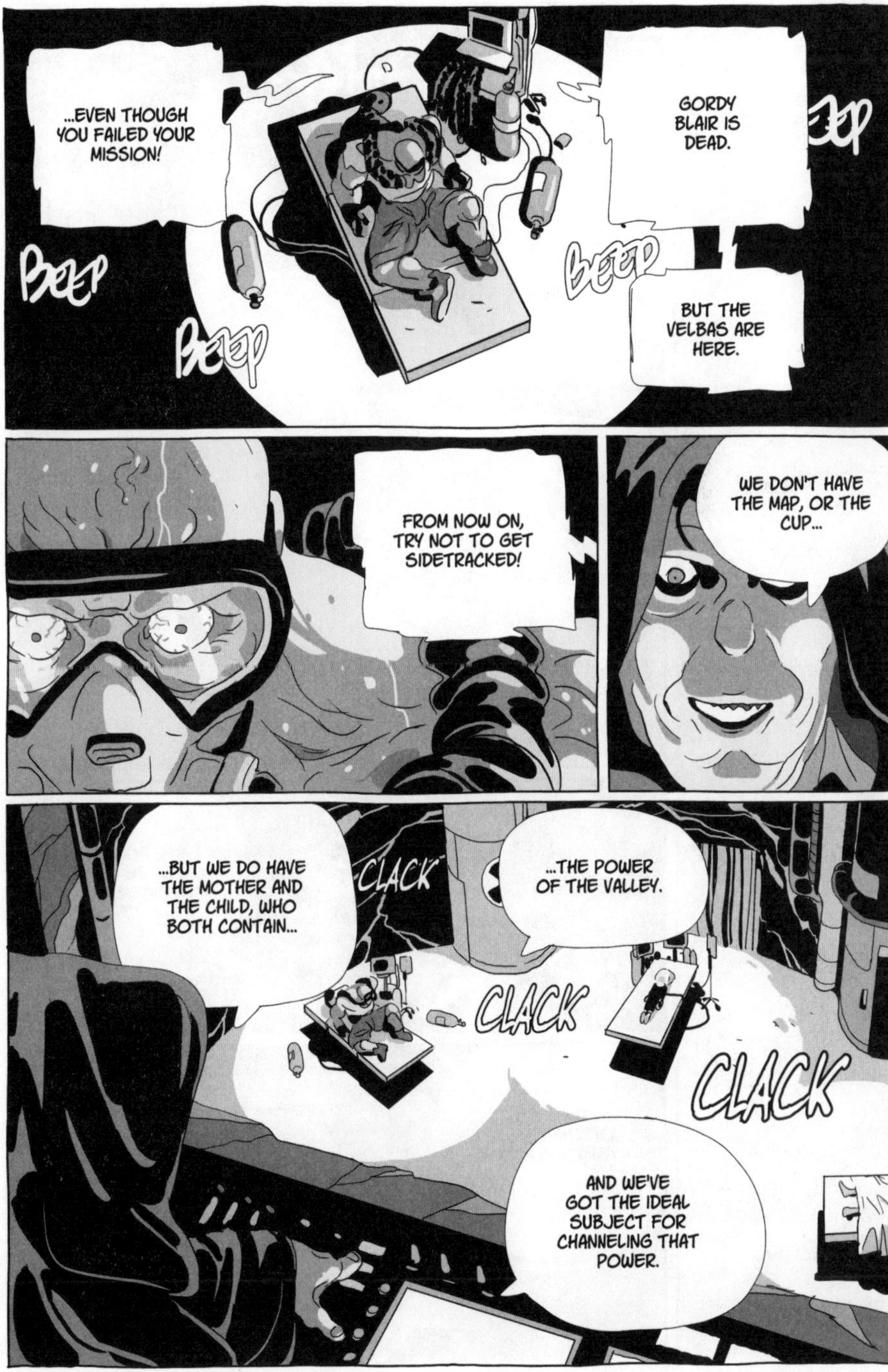
...EVEN THOUGH YOU FAILED YOUR MISSION!
GORDY BLAIR IS DEAD.
BEEP
BEEP
BEEP
BEEP
BUT THE VELBAS ARE HERE.
FROM NOW ON, TRY NOT TO GET SIDETRACKED!
WE DON'T HAVE THE MAP, OR THE CUP...
...BUT WE DO HAVE THE MOTHER AND THE CHILD, WHO BOTH CONTAIN...
CLACK
...THE POWER OF THE VALLEY.
CLACK
CLACK
AND WE'VE GOT THE IDEAL SUBJECT FOR CHANNELING THAT POWER.

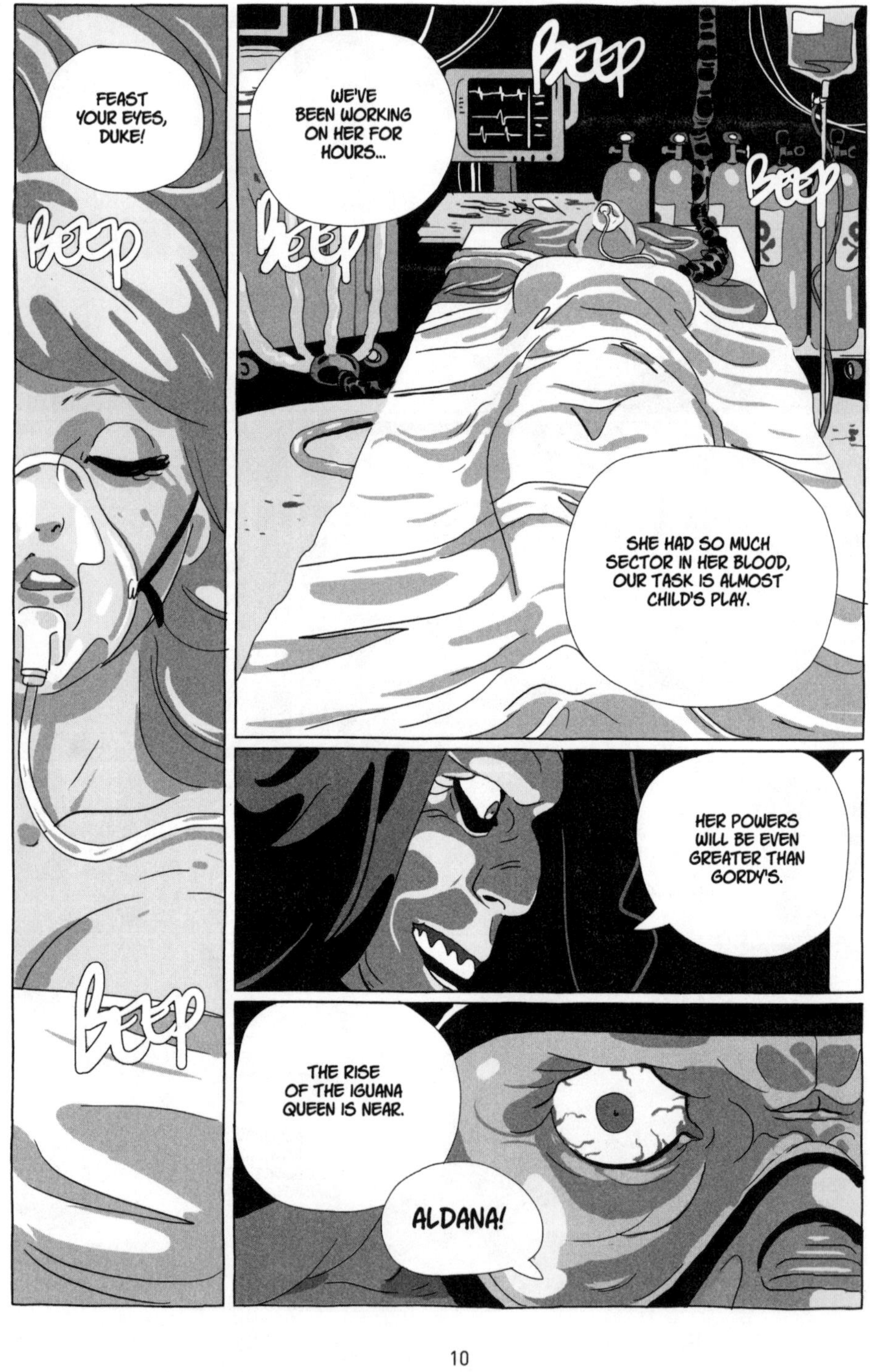

FEAST YOUR EYES, DUKE!
BEEP
BEEP
WE'VE BEEN WORKING ON HER FOR HOURS...
BEEP
BEEP
BEEP
SHE HAD SO MUCH SECTOR IN HER BLOOD, OUR TASK IS ALMOST CHILD'S PLAY.
HER POWERS WILL BE EVEN GREATER THAN GORDY'S.
THE RISE OF THE IGUANA QUEEN IS NEAR.
ALDANA!

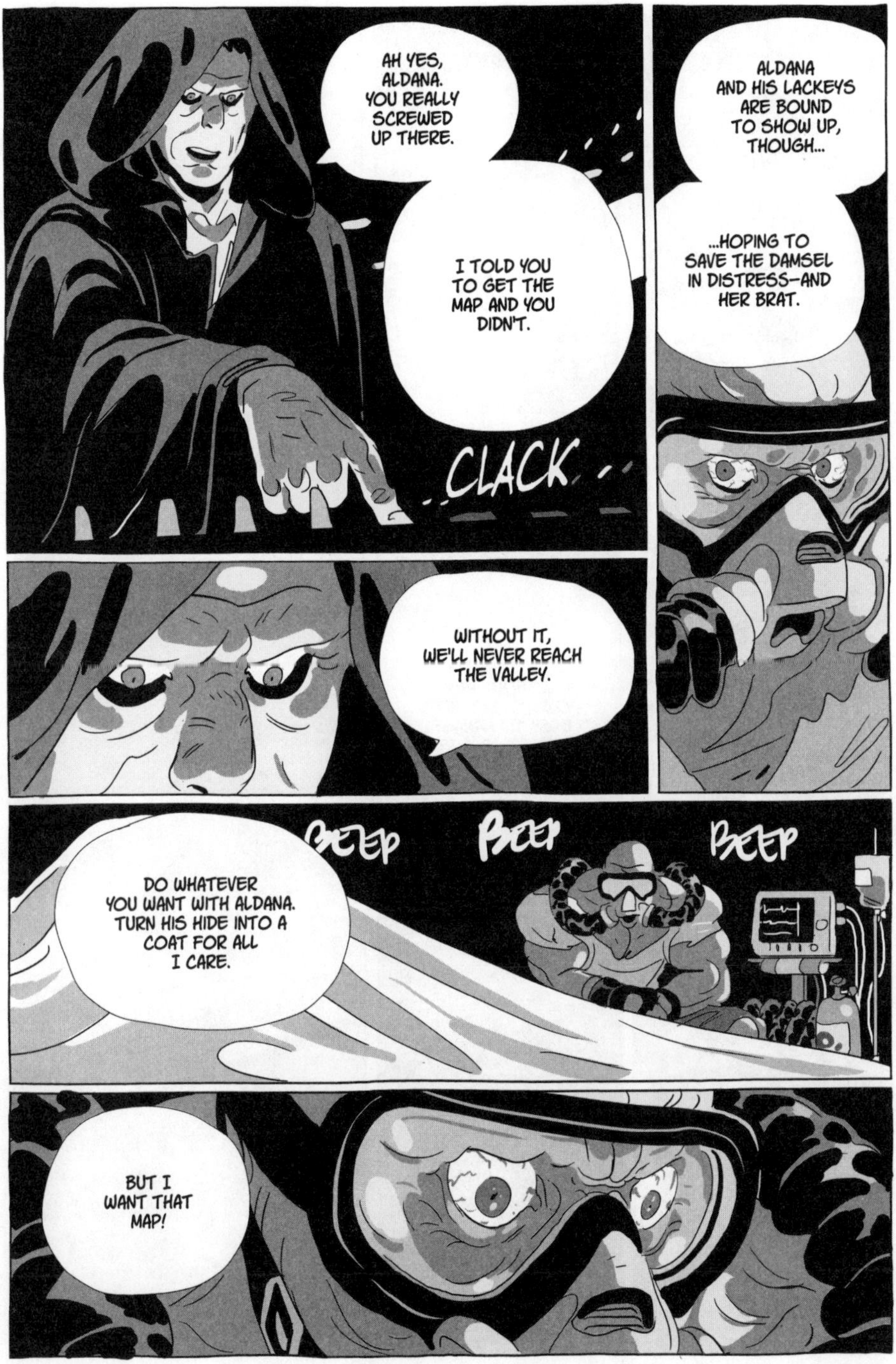

AH YES, ALDANA. YOU REALLY SCREWED UP THERE.
I TOLD YOU TO GET THE MAP AND YOU DIDN'T.
CLACK
ALDANA AND HIS LACKEYS ARE BOUND TO SHOW UP, THOUGH...
...HOPING TO SAVE THE DAMSEL IN DISTRESS—AND HER BRAT.
WITHOUT IT, WE'LL NEVER REACH THE VALLEY.
BEEP
BEEP
BEEP
DO WHATEVER YOU WANT WITH ALDANA. TURN HIS HIDE INTO A COAT FOR ALL I CARE.
BUT I WANT THAT MAP!

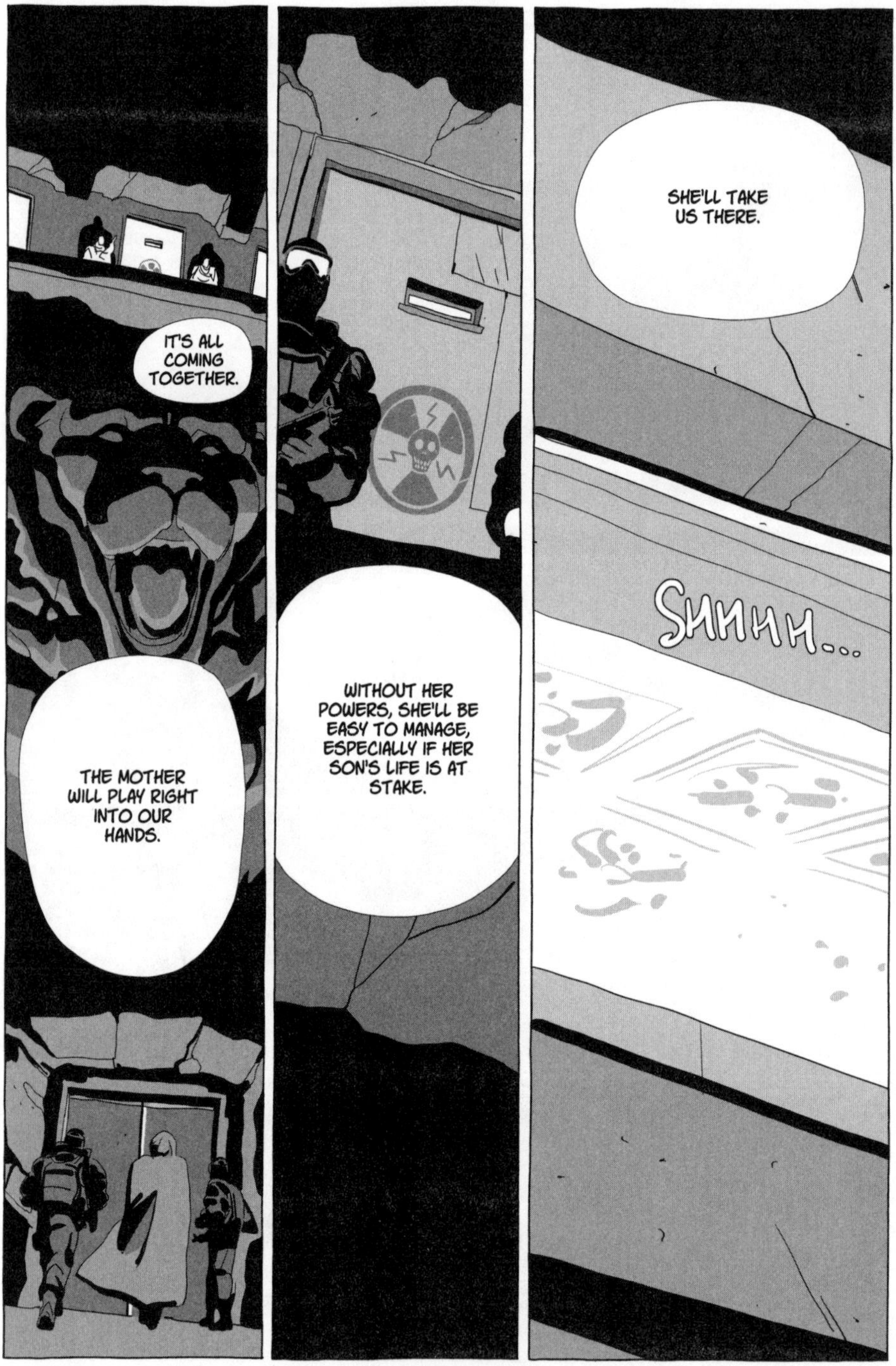
IT'S ALL COMING TOGETHER.
THE MOTHER WILL PLAY RIGHT INTO OUR HANDS.
WITHOUT HER POWERS, SHE'LL BE EASY TO MANAGE, ESPECIALLY IF HER SON'S LIFE IS AT STAKE.
SHE'LL TAKE US THERE.
SHHHH...

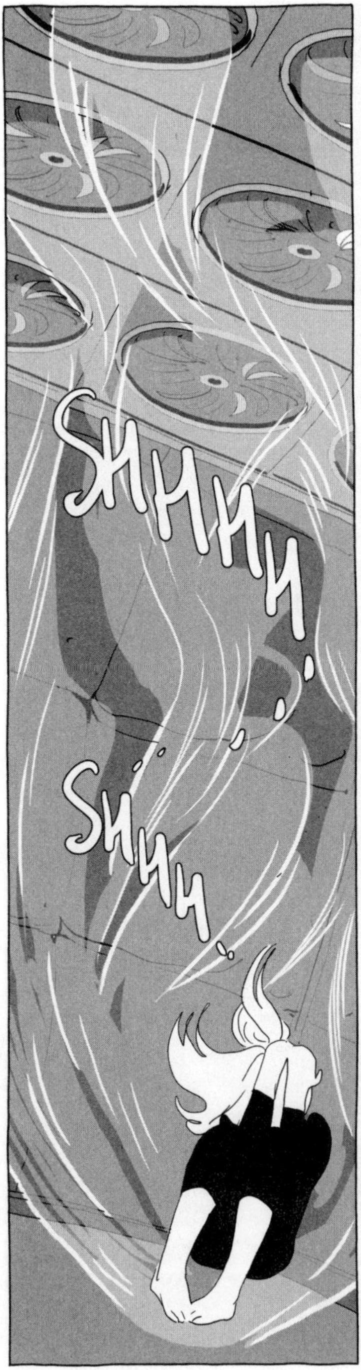
SHHHH...
SHHH...

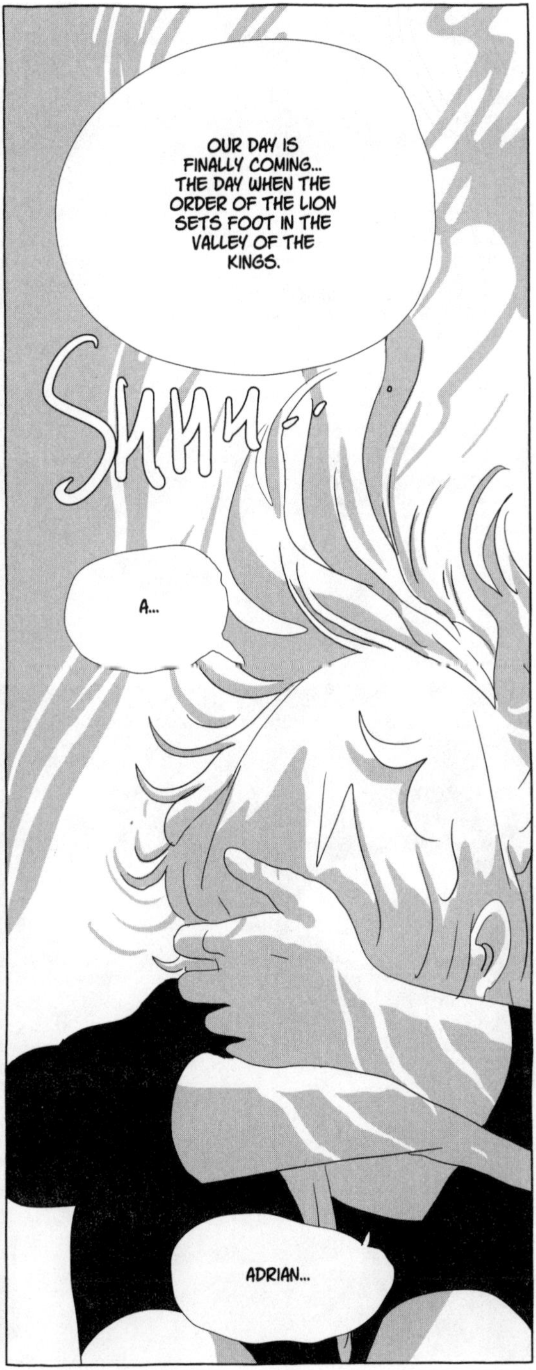
OUR DAY IS FINALLY COMING... THE DAY WHEN THE ORDER OF THE LION SETS FOOT IN THE VALLEY OF THE KINGS.
SHHH...
A...
ADRIAN...

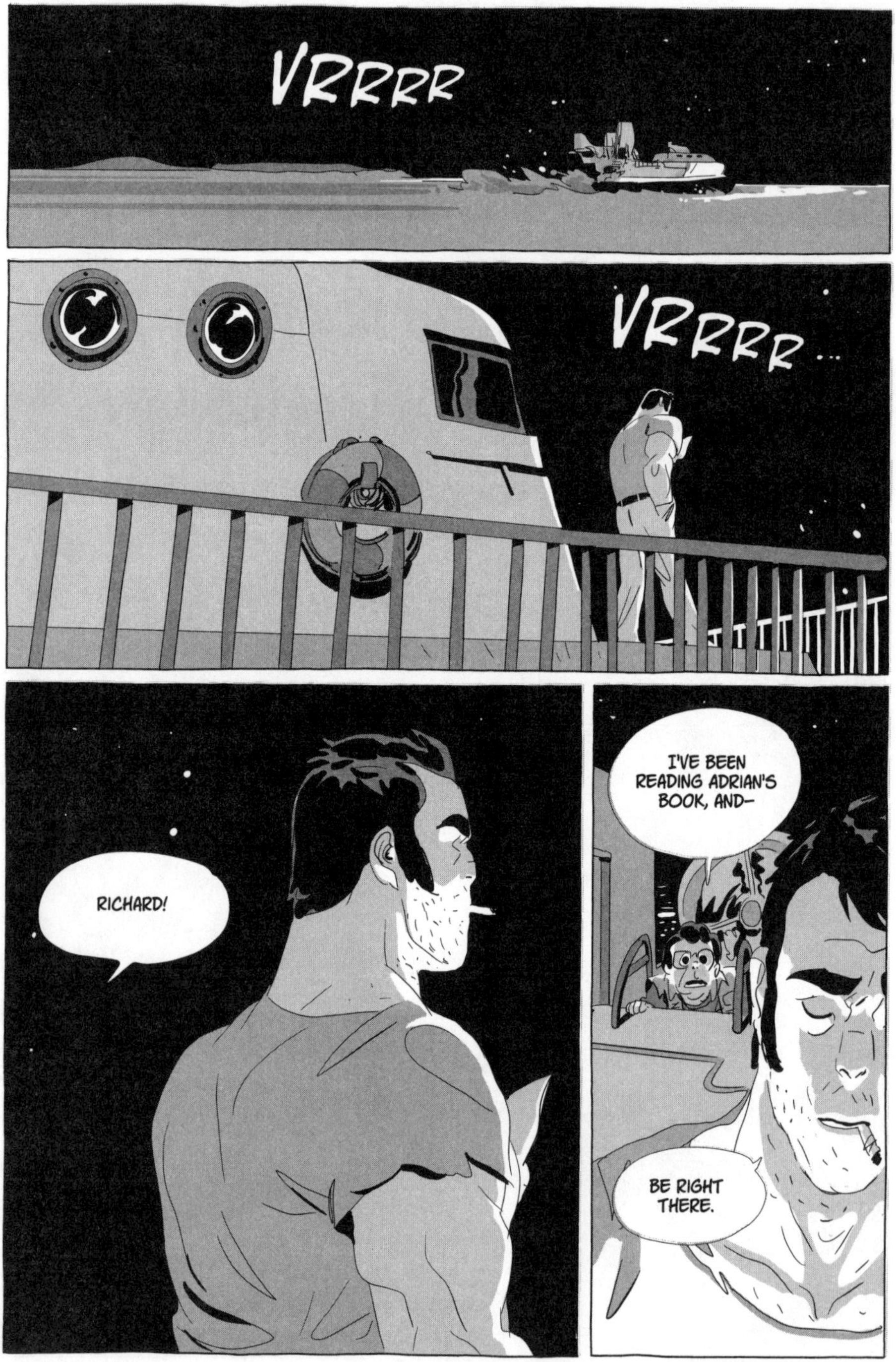
VRRRR
VRRRR...
RICHARD!
I'VE BEEN READING ADRIAN'S BOOK, AND–
BE RIGHT THERE.

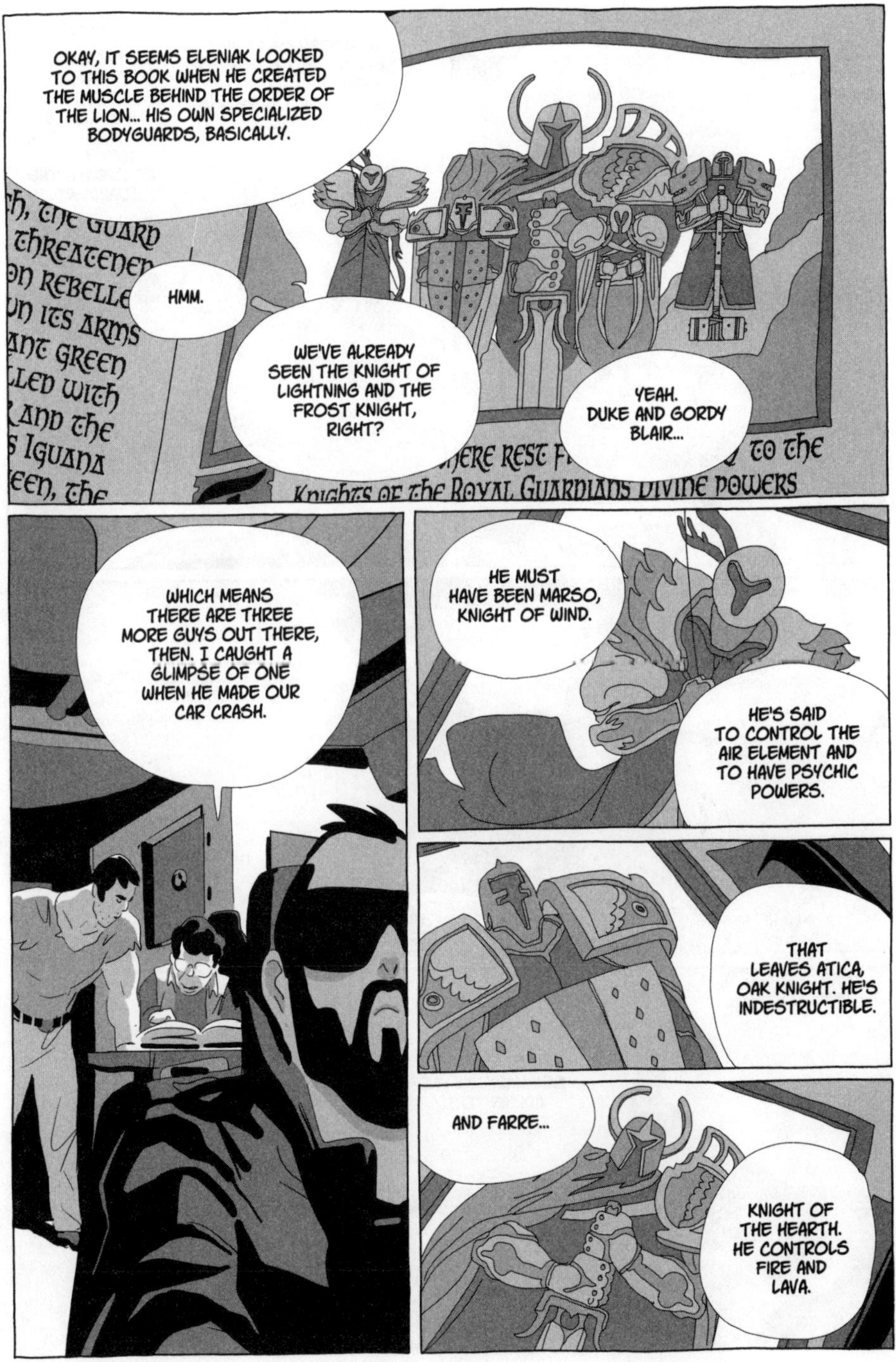
OKAY, IT SEEMS ELENIAK LOOKED TO THIS BOOK WHEN HE CREATED THE MUSCLE BEHIND THE ORDER OF THE LION... HIS OWN SPECIALIZED BODYGUARDS, BASICALLY.
HMM.
WE'VE ALREADY SEEN THE KNIGHT OF LIGHTNING AND THE FROST KNIGHT, RIGHT?
YEAH. DUKE AND GORDY BLAIR...
KNIGHTS OF THE ROYAL GUARDIANS DIVINE POWERS
WHICH MEANS THERE ARE THREE MORE GUYS OUT THERE, THEN. I CAUGHT A GLIMPSE OF ONE WHEN HE MADE OUR CAR CRASH.
HE MUST HAVE BEEN MARSO, KNIGHT OF WIND.
HE'S SAID TO CONTROL THE AIR ELEMENT AND TO HAVE PSYCHIC POWERS.
THAT LEAVES ATICA, OAK KNIGHT. HE'S INDESTRUCTIBLE.
AND FARRE...
KNIGHT OF THE HEARTH. HE CONTROLS FIRE AND LAVA.

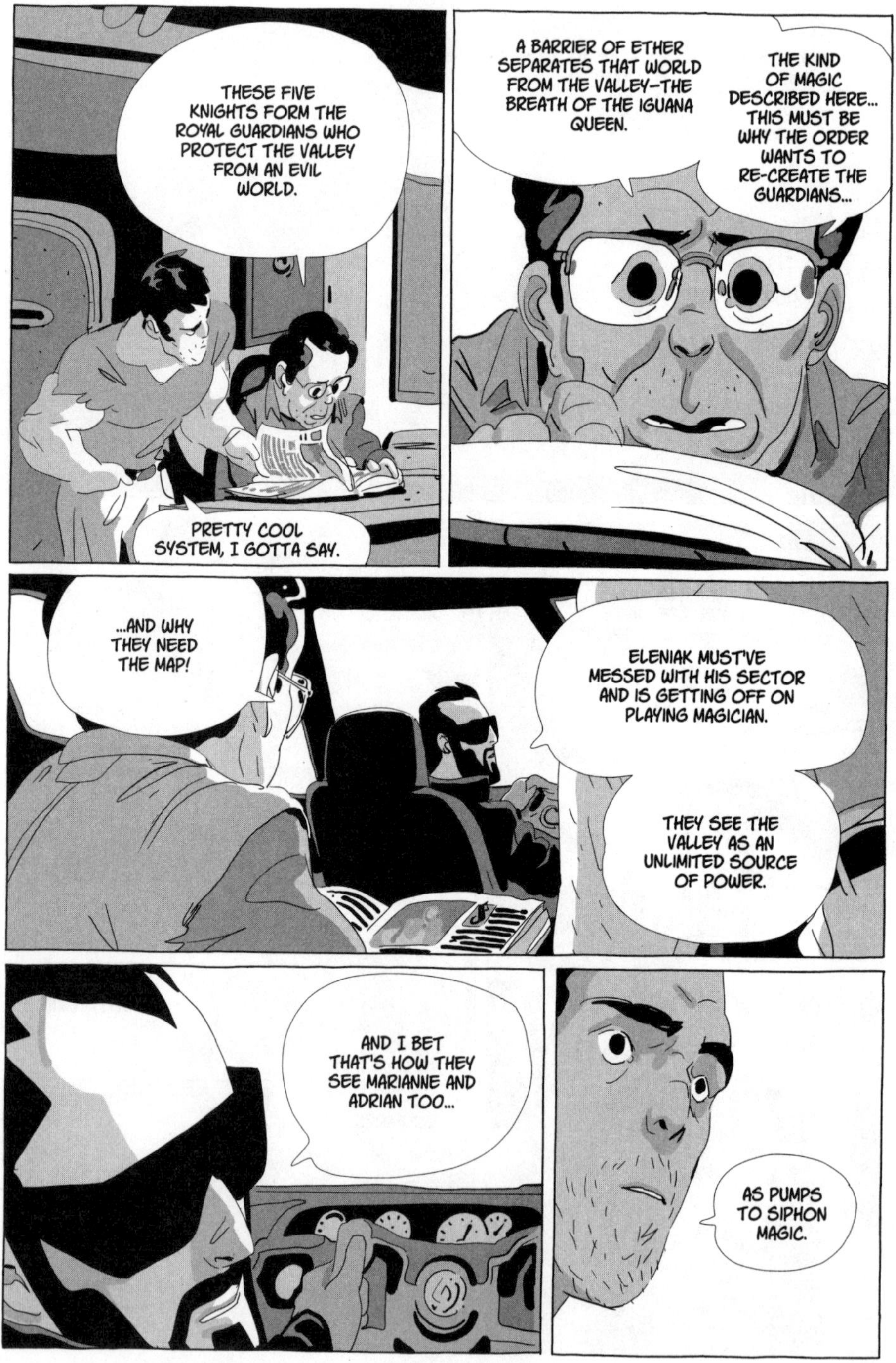
THESE FIVE KNIGHTS FORM THE ROYAL GUARDIANS WHO PROTECT THE VALLEY FROM AN EVIL WORLD.
PRETTY COOL SYSTEM, I GOTTA SAY.
A BARRIER OF ETHER SEPARATES THAT WORLD FROM THE VALLEY—THE BREATH OF THE IGUANA QUEEN.
THE KIND OF MAGIC DESCRIBED HERE... THIS MUST BE WHY THE ORDER WANTS TO RE-CREATE THE GUARDIANS...
...AND WHY THEY NEED THE MAP!
ELENIAK MUST'VE MESSED WITH HIS SECTOR AND IS GETTING OFF ON PLAYING MAGICIAN.
THEY SEE THE VALLEY AS AN UNLIMITED SOURCE OF POWER.
AND I BET THAT'S HOW THEY SEE MARIANNE AND ADRIAN TOO...
AS PUMPS TO SIPHON MAGIC.

SO, UH... WHEN YOU GUYS TALK ABOUT THE VALLEY OF THE KINGS AND MAGIC AND ALL THAT...

...IT'S FICTION, RIGHT?

NOT REAL?

YEAH, DON'T WORRY ABOUT IT. GOT ANYTHING ELSE?

WELL, YES. THE ROYAL GUARDIANS RESTORED PEACE IN THE VALLEY BY FIGHTING OFF DEMONS...

AND AMONG THOSE DEMONS THEY FOUGHT I FOUND THIS...

Kahllo

THE KAHLLOS, A WARRIOR CASTE FROM THE EASTERN LANDS...

THEIR MASKS REMIND ME OF...

...ENT CASTE OF THE EAST THAT
FEARSOME WARRIORS WH...
SO POWERFUL T...
KING T...

HEY, CRISTO! YOU'RE MORE FAMOUS THAN I THOUGHT.

CUTE FAMILY!

YOU GUYS GO CAMPING ON WEEKENDS?

17

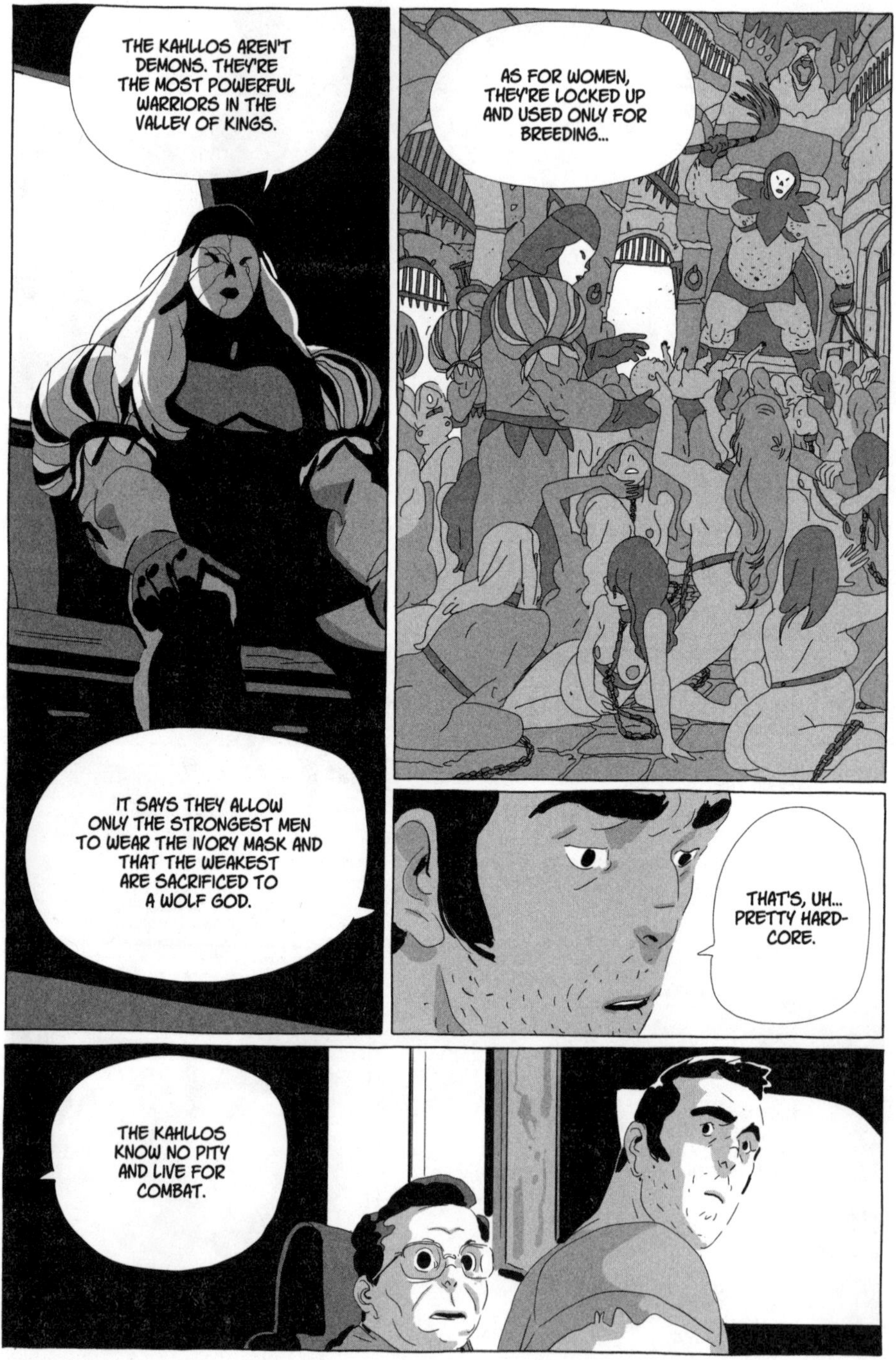
THE KAHLLOS AREN'T DEMONS. THEY'RE THE MOST POWERFUL WARRIORS IN THE VALLEY OF KINGS.
IT SAYS THEY ALLOW ONLY THE STRONGEST MEN TO WEAR THE IVORY MASK AND THAT THE WEAKEST ARE SACRIFICED TO A WOLF GOD.
AS FOR WOMEN, THEY'RE LOCKED UP AND USED ONLY FOR BREEDING...
THAT'S, UH... PRETTY HARD-CORE.
THE KAHLLOS KNOW NO PITY AND LIVE FOR COMBAT.

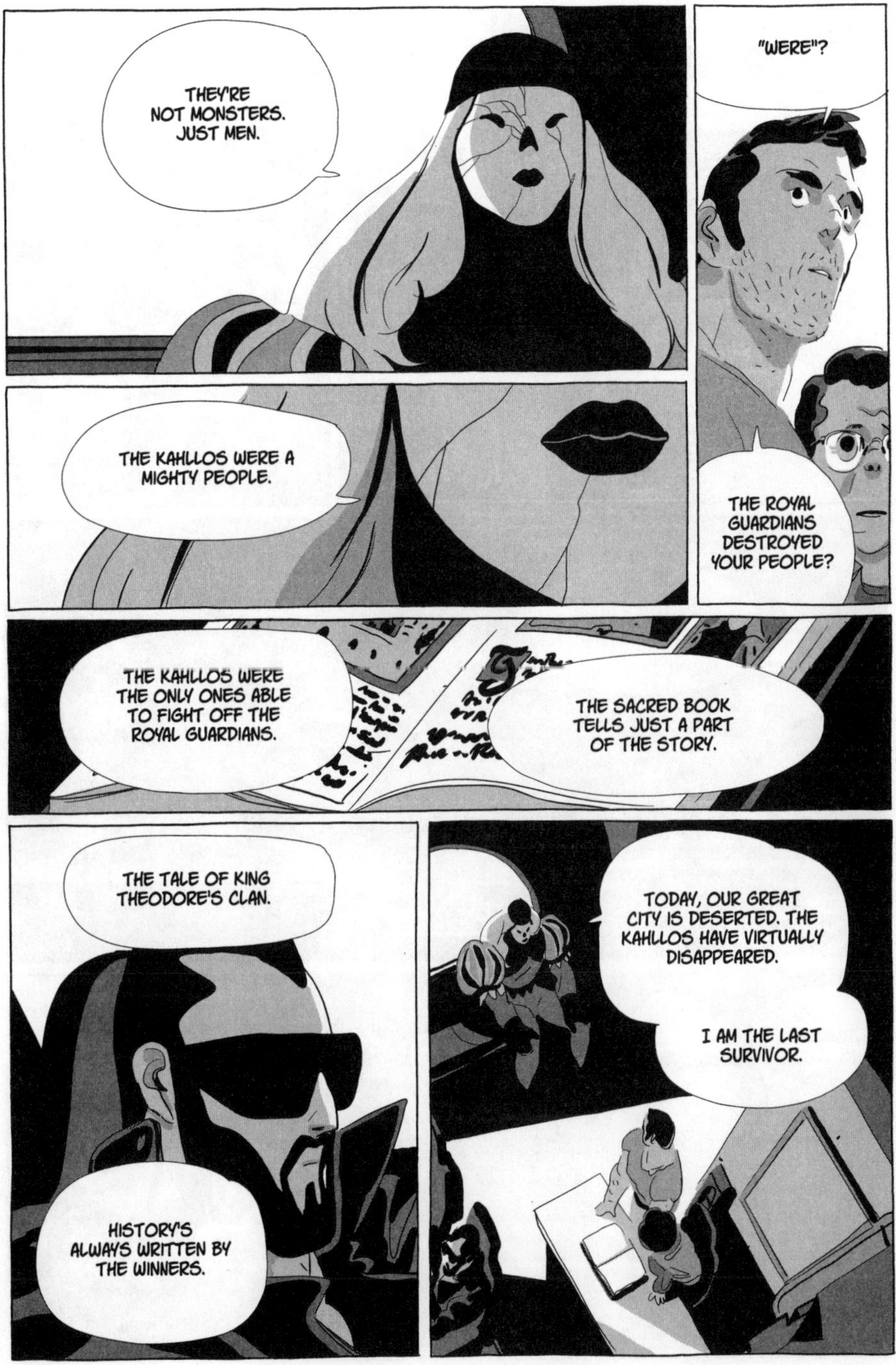
THEY'RE NOT MONSTERS. JUST MEN.
THE KAHLLOS WERE A MIGHTY PEOPLE.
"WERE"?
THE ROYAL GUARDIANS DESTROYED YOUR PEOPLE?
THE KAHLLOS WERE THE ONLY ONES ABLE TO FIGHT OFF THE ROYAL GUARDIANS.
THE SACRED BOOK TELLS JUST A PART OF THE STORY.
THE TALE OF KING THEODORE'S CLAN.
HISTORY'S ALWAYS WRITTEN BY THE WINNERS.
TODAY, OUR GREAT CITY IS DESERTED. THE KAHLLOS HAVE VIRTUALLY DISAPPEARED.
I AM THE LAST SURVIVOR.

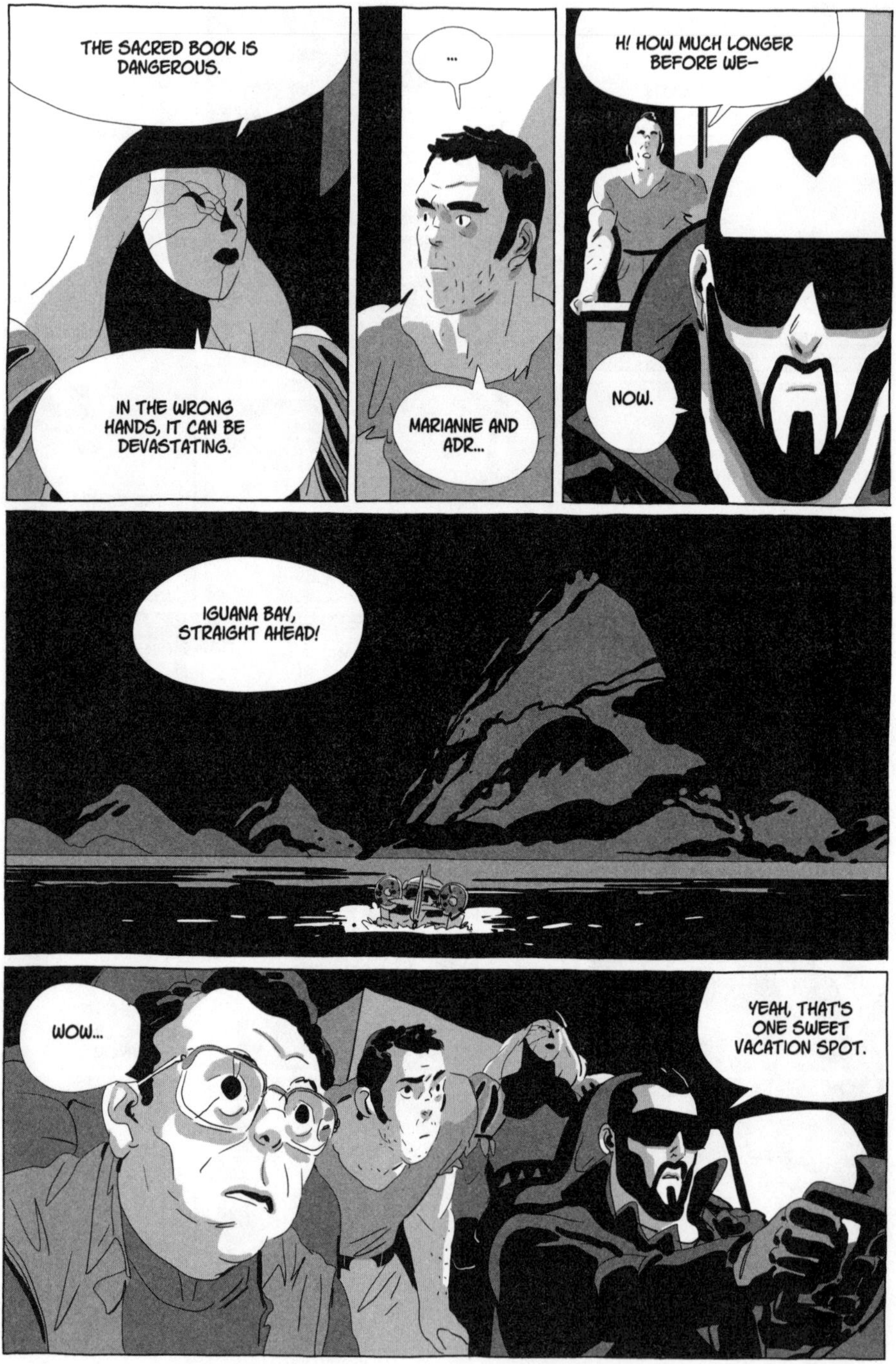
THE SACRED BOOK IS DANGEROUS.
IN THE WRONG HANDS, IT CAN BE DEVASTATING.
...
MARIANNE AND ADR...
H! HOW MUCH LONGER BEFORE WE–
NOW.
IGUANA BAY, STRAIGHT AHEAD!
WOW...
YEAH, THAT'S ONE SWEET VACATION SPOT.

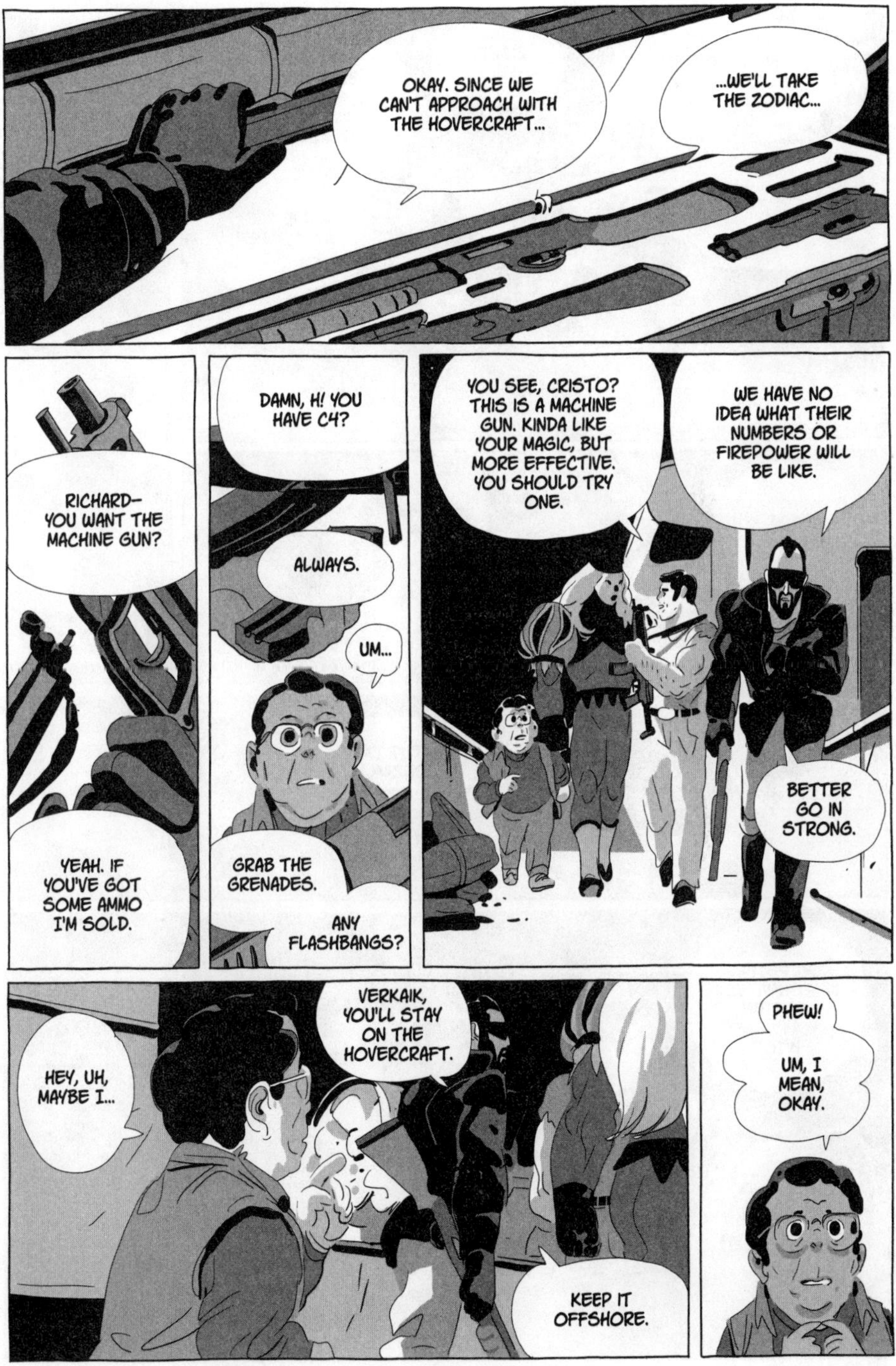
OKAY. SINCE WE CAN'T APPROACH WITH THE HOVERCRAFT...
...WE'LL TAKE THE ZODIAC...
RICHARD— YOU WANT THE MACHINE GUN?
YEAH. IF YOU'VE GOT SOME AMMO I'M SOLD.
DAMN, H! YOU HAVE C4?
ALWAYS.
UM...
GRAB THE GRENADES.
ANY FLASHBANGS?
YOU SEE, CRISTO? THIS IS A MACHINE GUN. KINDA LIKE YOUR MAGIC, BUT MORE EFFECTIVE. YOU SHOULD TRY ONE.
WE HAVE NO IDEA WHAT THEIR NUMBERS OR FIREPOWER WILL BE LIKE.
BETTER GO IN STRONG.
HEY, UH, MAYBE I...
VERKAIK, YOU'LL STAY ON THE HOVERCRAFT.
KEEP IT OFFSHORE.
PHEW!
UM, I MEAN, OKAY.

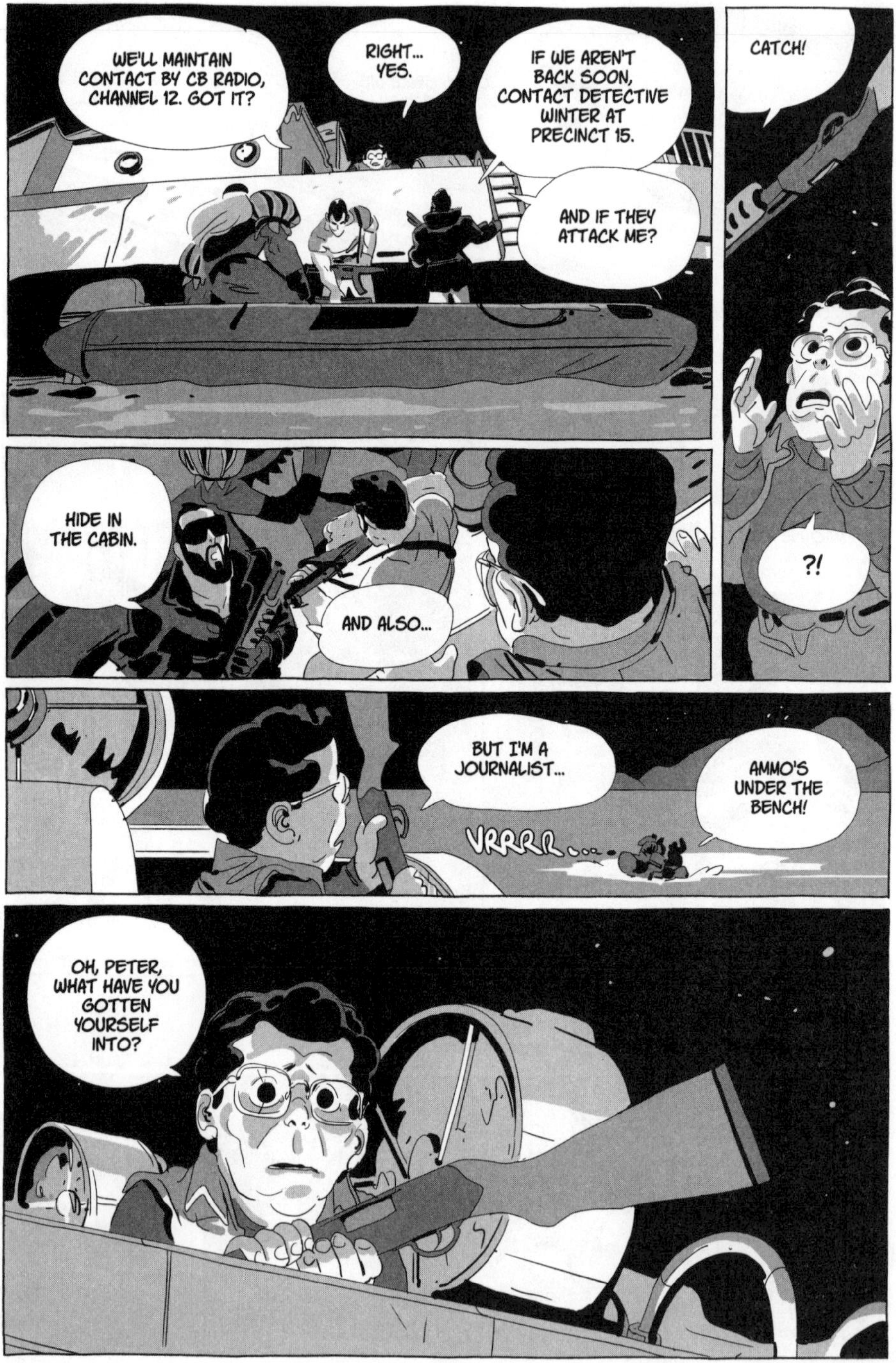
WE'LL MAINTAIN CONTACT BY CB RADIO, CHANNEL 12. GOT IT?
RIGHT... YES.
IF WE AREN'T BACK SOON, CONTACT DETECTIVE WINTER AT PRECINCT 15.
AND IF THEY ATTACK ME?
HIDE IN THE CABIN.
AND ALSO...
CATCH!
?!
BUT I'M A JOURNALIST...
VRRRR...
AMMO'S UNDER THE BENCH!
OH, PETER, WHAT HAVE YOU GOTTEN YOURSELF INTO?

I SEE TWO MEN, BOTH ARMED.
DOESN'T LOOK LIKE THE MAIN ENTRANCE.
GOTTA BE ELENIAK'S GUYS.
SO, EITHER WE WERE RIGHT, OR THIS IS SOME KINDA NAZI BOY SCOUT CAMP.
ONLY TWO GUARDS...
BUT THEY MUST SUSPECT WE'RE COMING. WE'LL HAVE TO PLAY IT SAFE.
CRISTO...

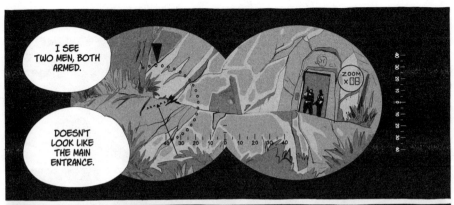

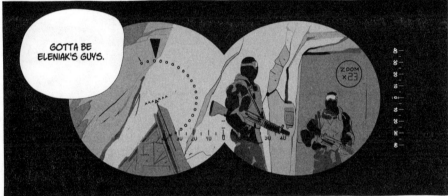

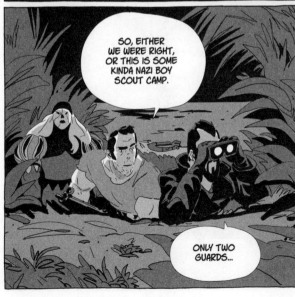

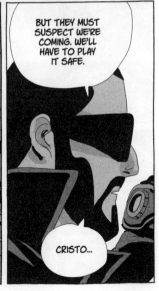

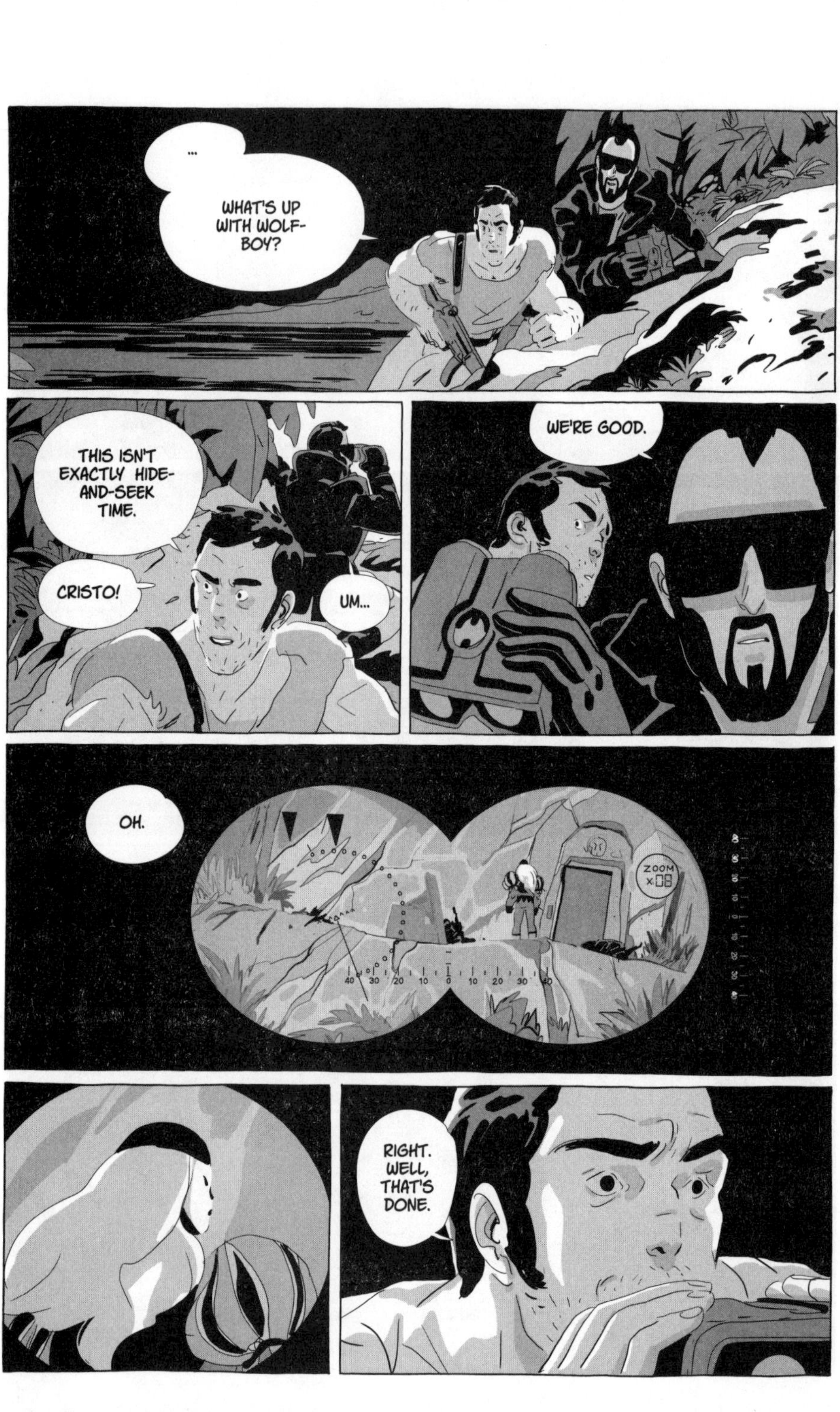
...
WHAT'S UP WITH WOLF-BOY?
THIS ISN'T EXACTLY HIDE-AND-SEEK TIME.
CRISTO!
UM...
WE'RE GOOD.
OH.
RIGHT. WELL, THAT'S DONE.

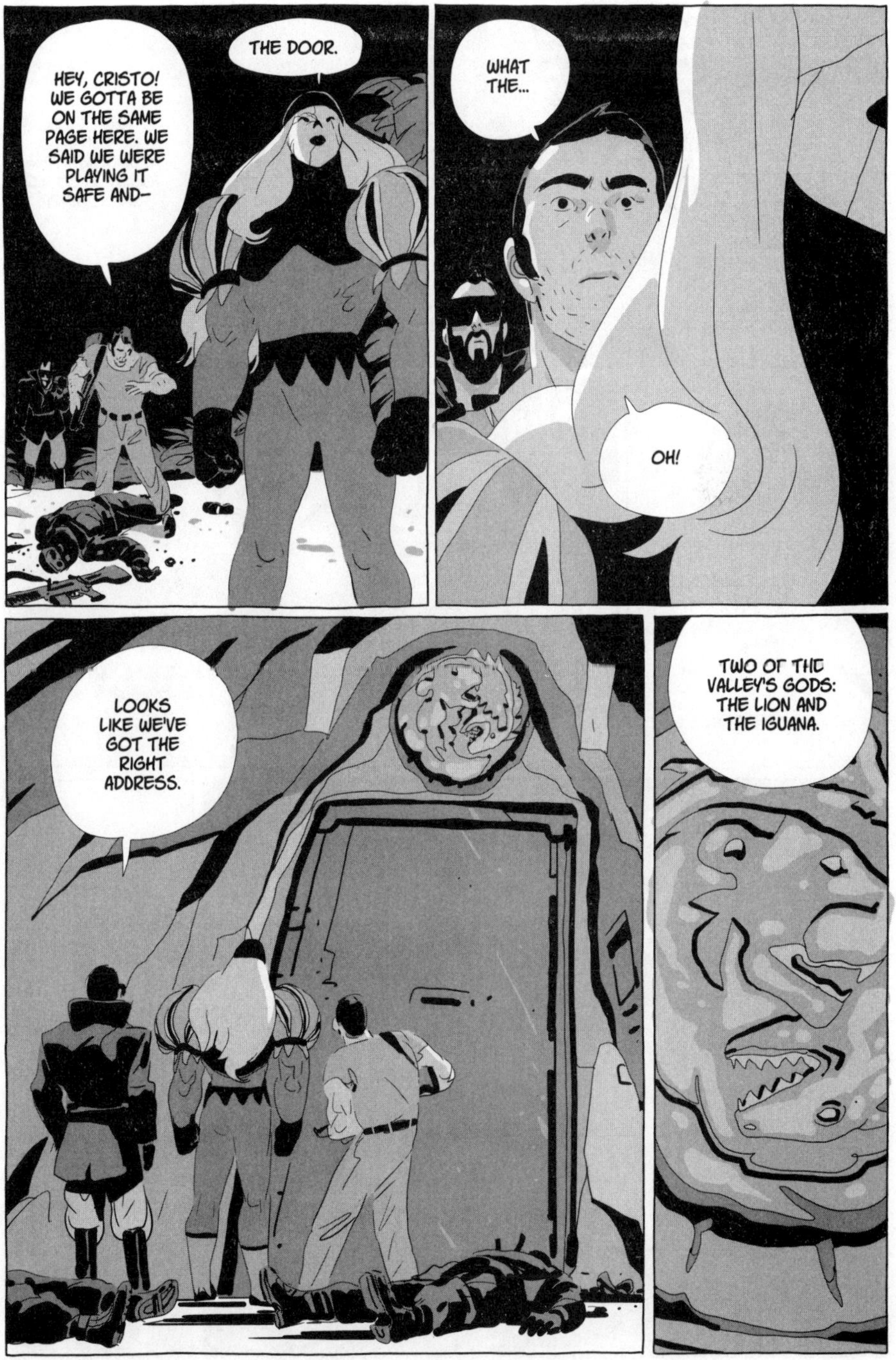
HEY, CRISTO! WE GOTTA BE ON THE SAME PAGE HERE. WE SAID WE WERE PLAYING IT SAFE AND–
THE DOOR.
WHAT THE...
OH!
LOOKS LIKE WE'VE GOT THE RIGHT ADDRESS.
TWO OF THE VALLEY'S GODS: THE LION AND THE IGUANA.

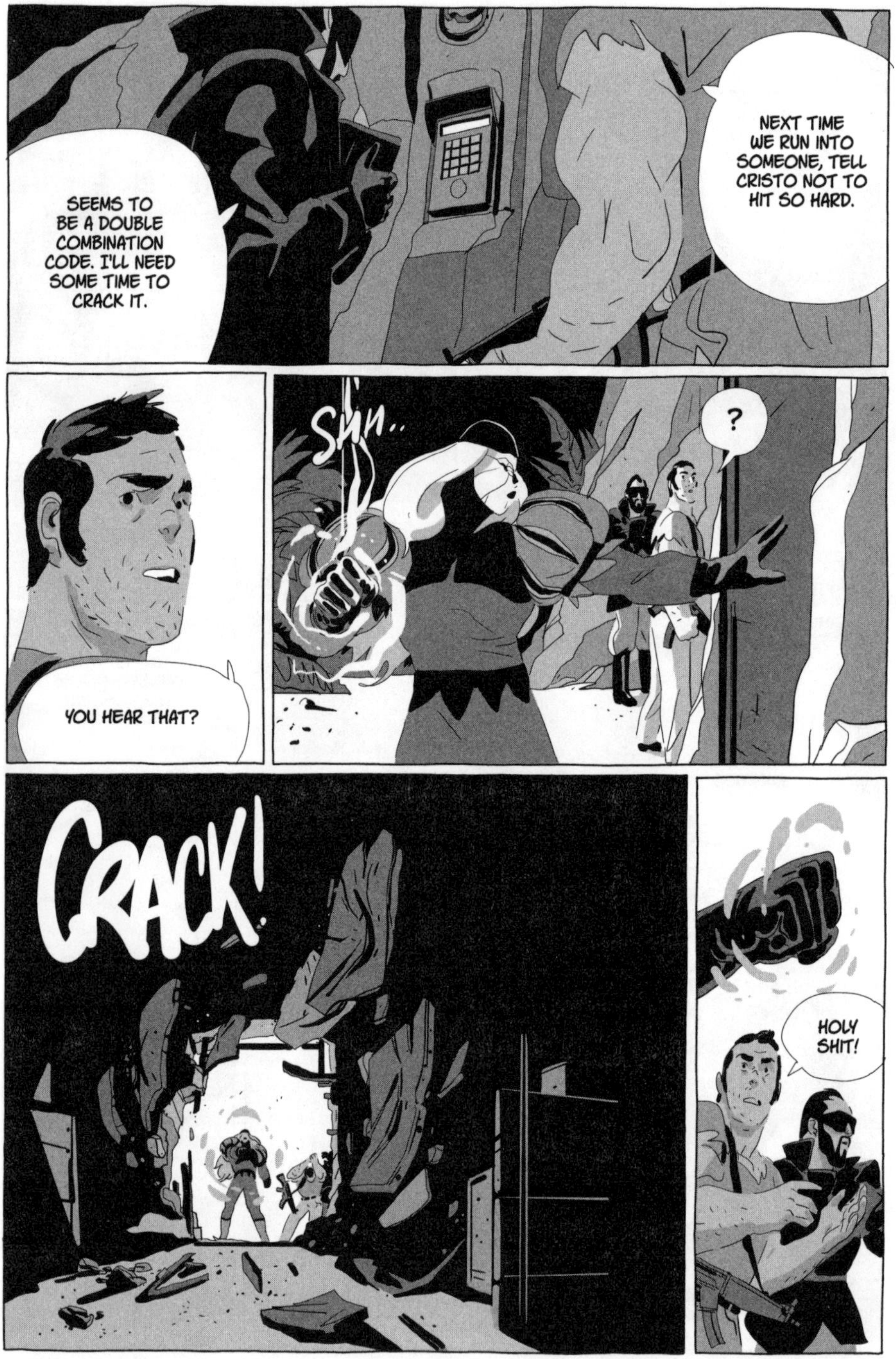
SEEMS TO BE A DOUBLE COMBINATION CODE. I'LL NEED SOME TIME TO CRACK IT.
NEXT TIME WE RUN INTO SOMEONE, TELL CRISTO NOT TO HIT SO HARD.
YOU HEAR THAT?
SHH..
?
CRACK!
HOLY SHIT!

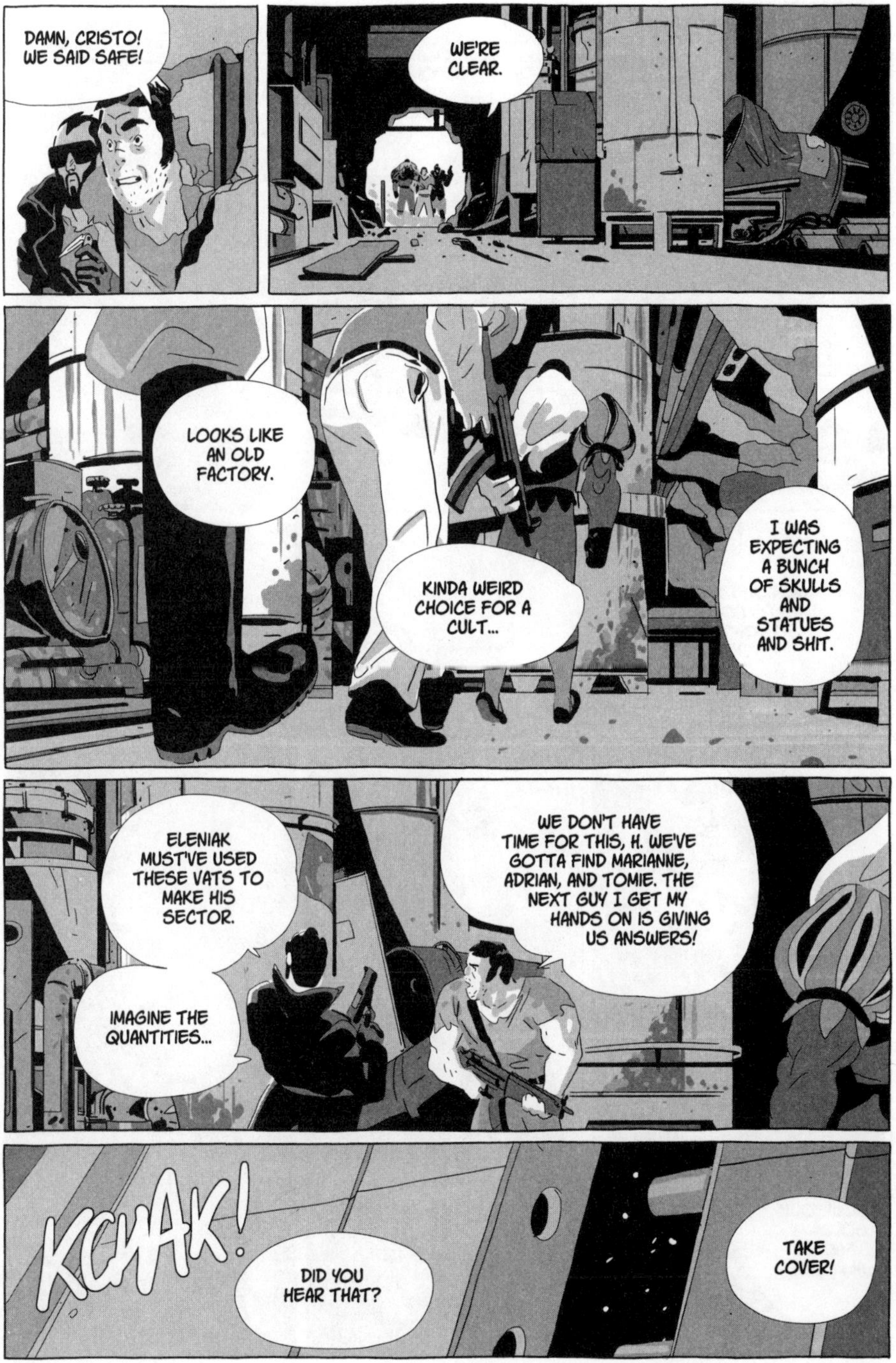
DAMN, CRISTO! WE SAID SAFE!
WE'RE CLEAR.
LOOKS LIKE AN OLD FACTORY.
KINDA WEIRD CHOICE FOR A CULT...
I WAS EXPECTING A BUNCH OF SKULLS AND STATUES AND SHIT.
ELENIAK MUST'VE USED THESE VATS TO MAKE HIS SECTOR.
IMAGINE THE QUANTITIES...
WE DON'T HAVE TIME FOR THIS, H. WE'VE GOTTA FIND MARIANNE, ADRIAN, AND TOMIE. THE NEXT GUY I GET MY HANDS ON IS GIVING US ANSWERS!
KCHAK!
DID YOU HEAR THAT?
TAKE COVER!

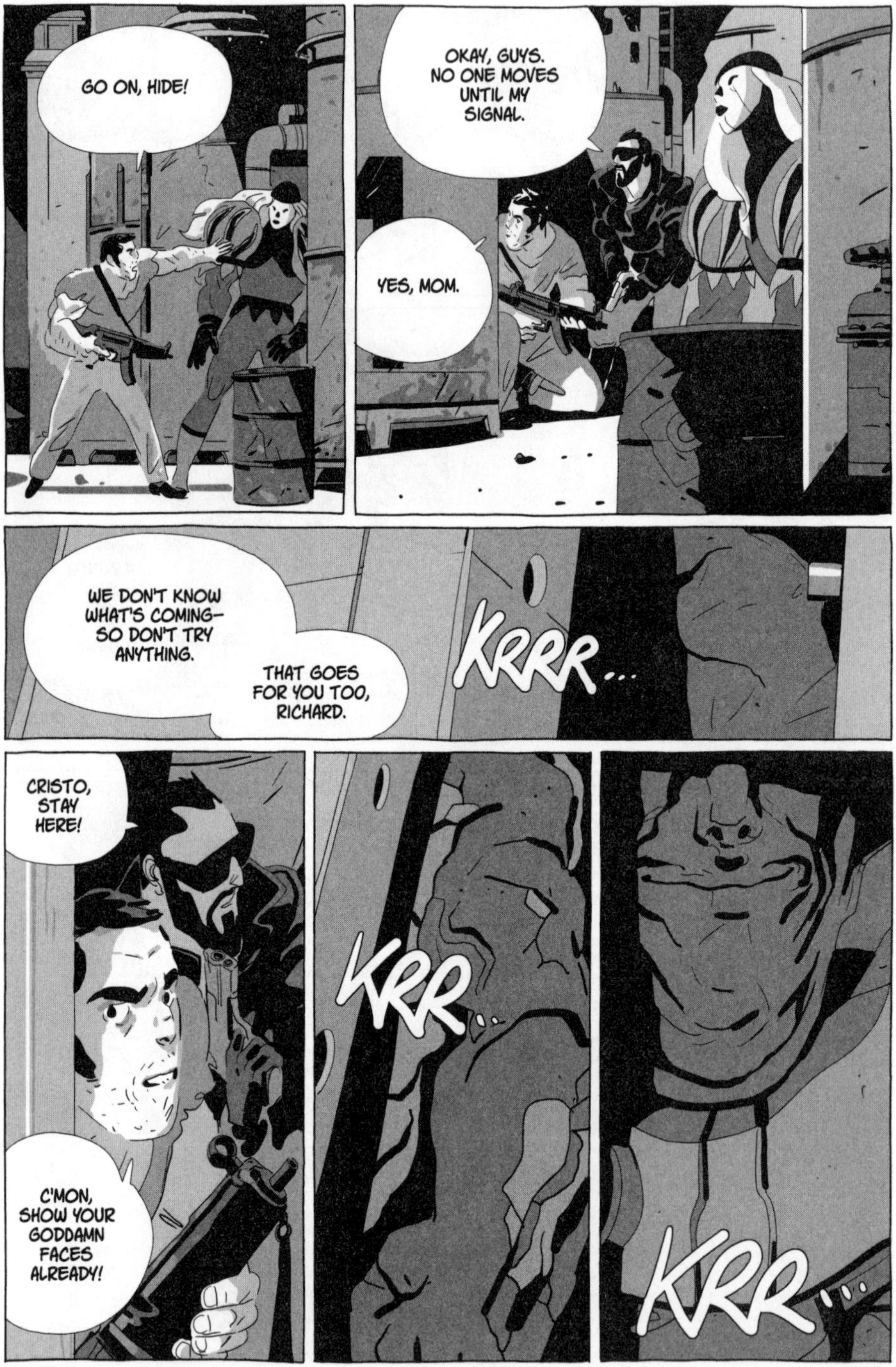
GO ON, HIDE!
OKAY, GUYS. NO ONE MOVES UNTIL MY SIGNAL.
YES, MOM.
WE DON'T KNOW WHAT'S COMING— SO DON'T TRY ANYTHING.
THAT GOES FOR YOU TOO, RICHARD.
KRRR...
CRISTO, STAY HERE!
C'MON, SHOW YOUR GODDAMN FACES ALREADY!
KRR...
KRR...

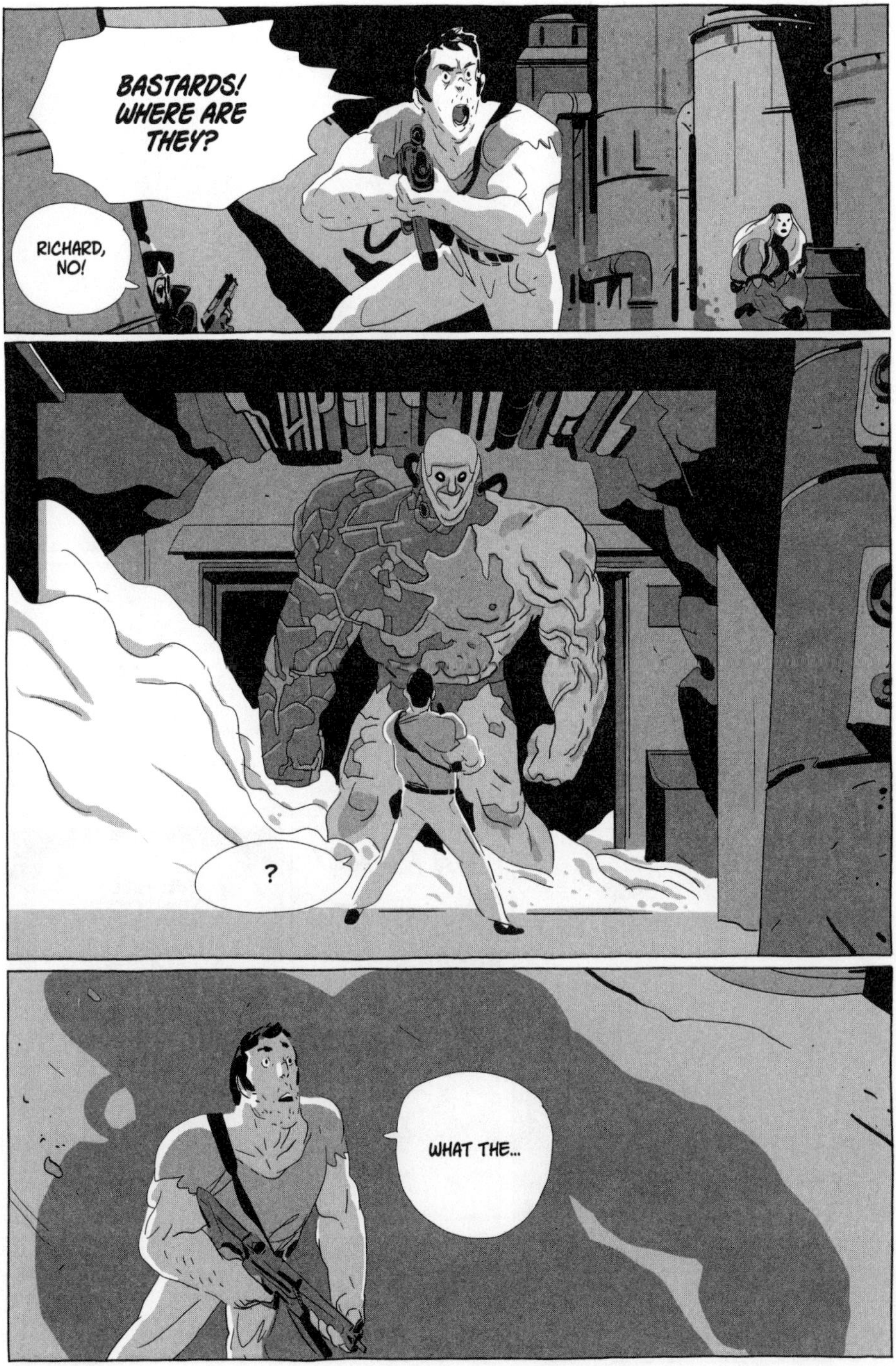

BASTARDS! WHERE ARE THEY?
RICHARD, NO!
?
WHAT THE...

WE WEREN'T EXPECTING YOU SO SOON. I'M—

RATATATA!

SHUT IT, FREAK!

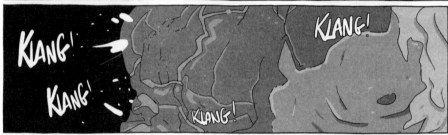

KLANG!

KLANG!

KLANG!

KLANG!

IS IT A ROBOT?

LOOKS MORE LIKE SOME KIND OF ARMOR.

HA HA HA!

I LOVE THAT MOMENT, EVERY TIME!

FEEL FREE TO EMPTY YOUR MAGAZINES— MY SKIN'S INDESTRUCTIBLE. YOU'RE OUT OF LUCK.

KLANG! KLANG!

30

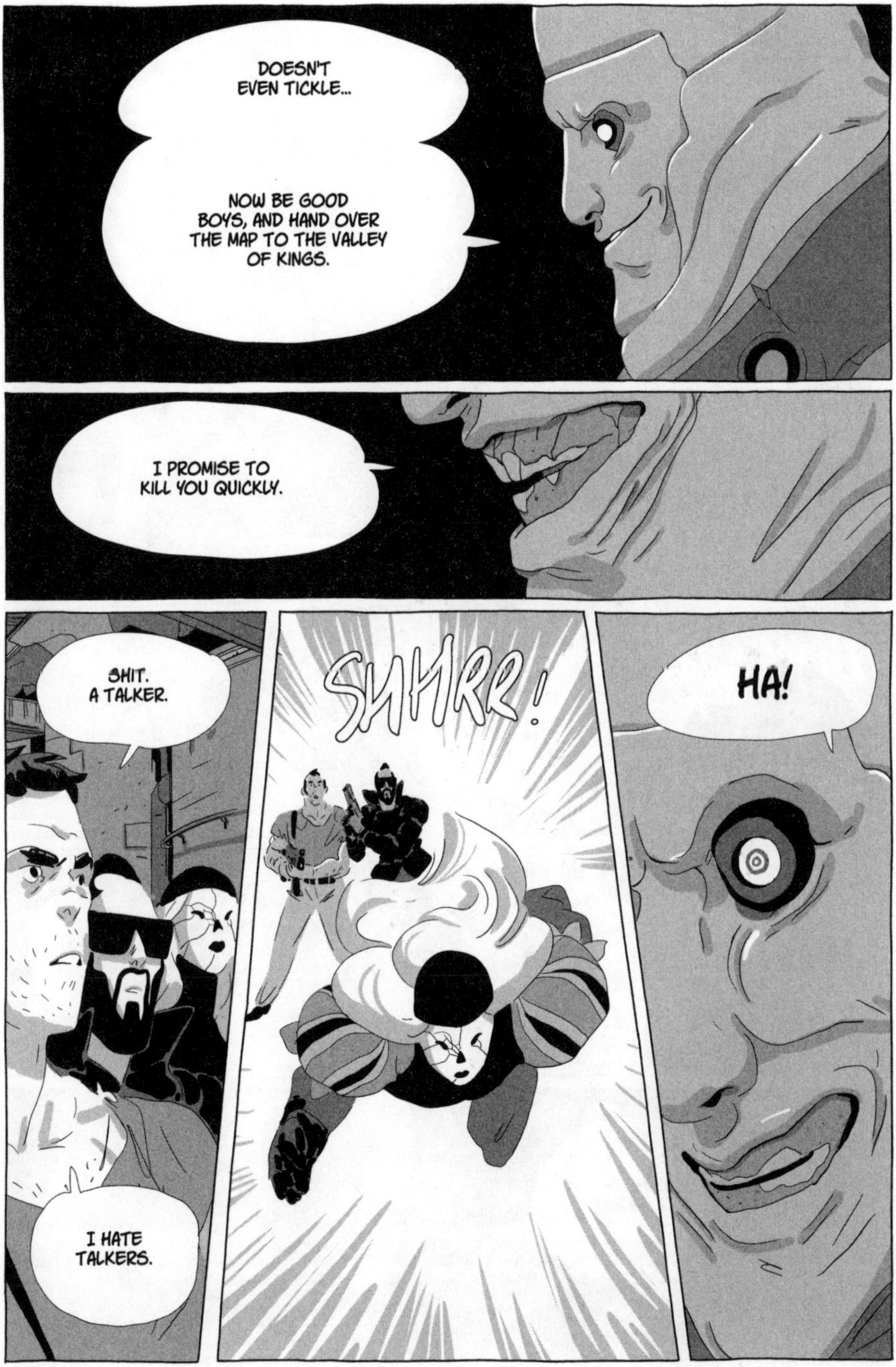
DOESN'T EVEN TICKLE...
NOW BE GOOD BOYS, AND HAND OVER THE MAP TO THE VALLEY OF KINGS.
I PROMISE TO KILL YOU QUICKLY.
SHIT. A TALKER.
I HATE TALKERS.
SHHRR!
HA!

WAA M!!
!!!
SHH..
KLANG!
HA HA HA!
NOT BAD!
GO ON—
TRY AGAIN.

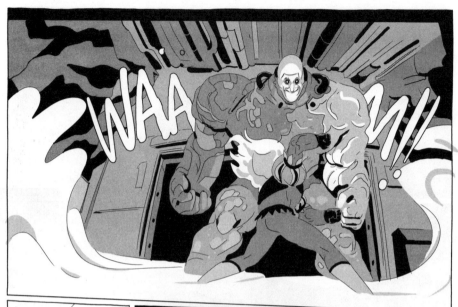

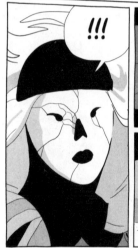

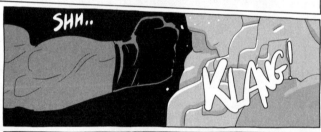

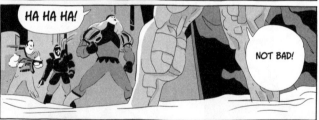

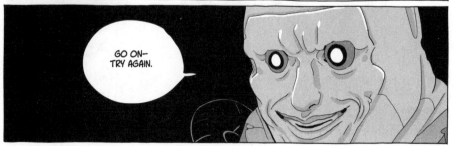

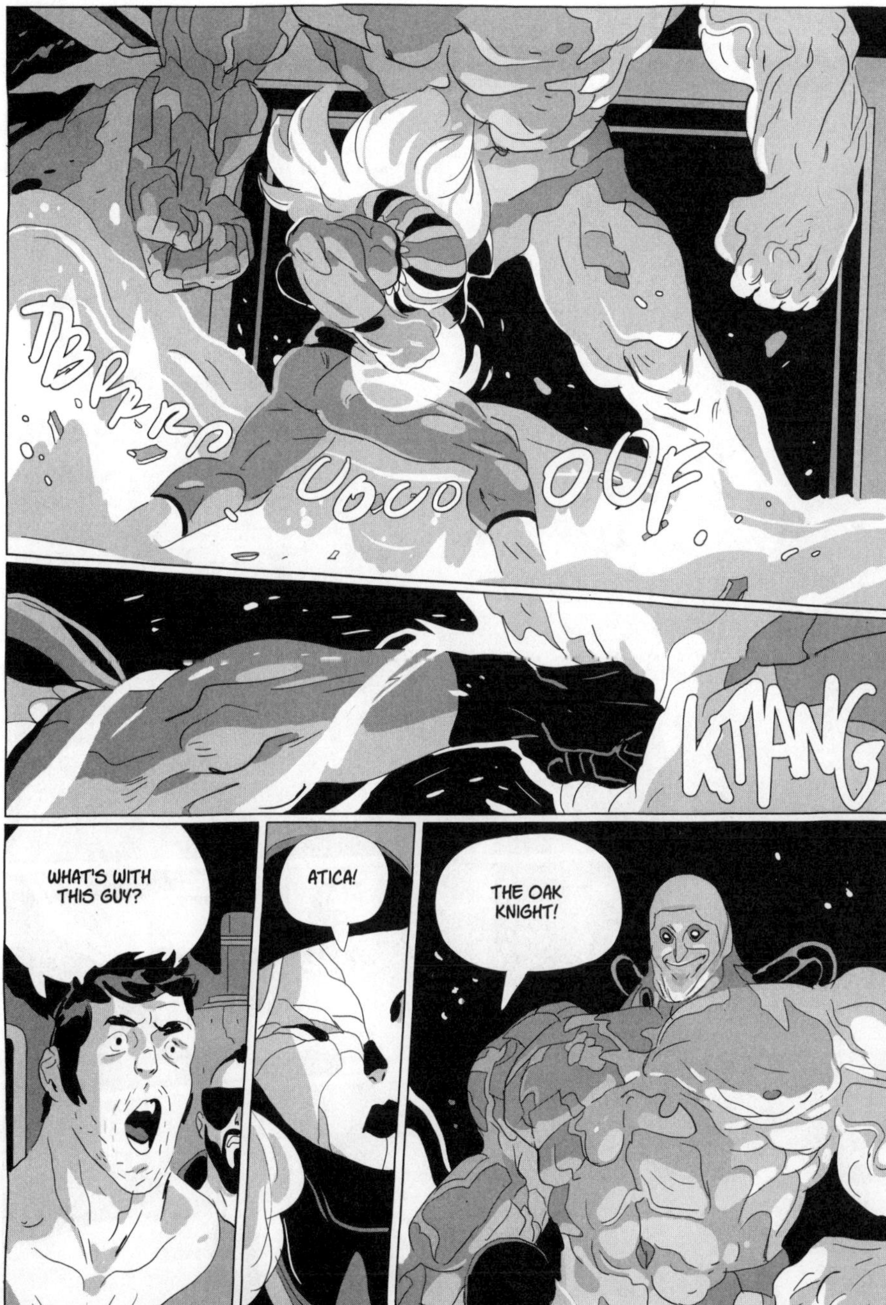
TBRRRRR
UOOO OOF
KTANG
WHAT'S WITH THIS GUY?
ATICA!
THE OAK KNIGHT!

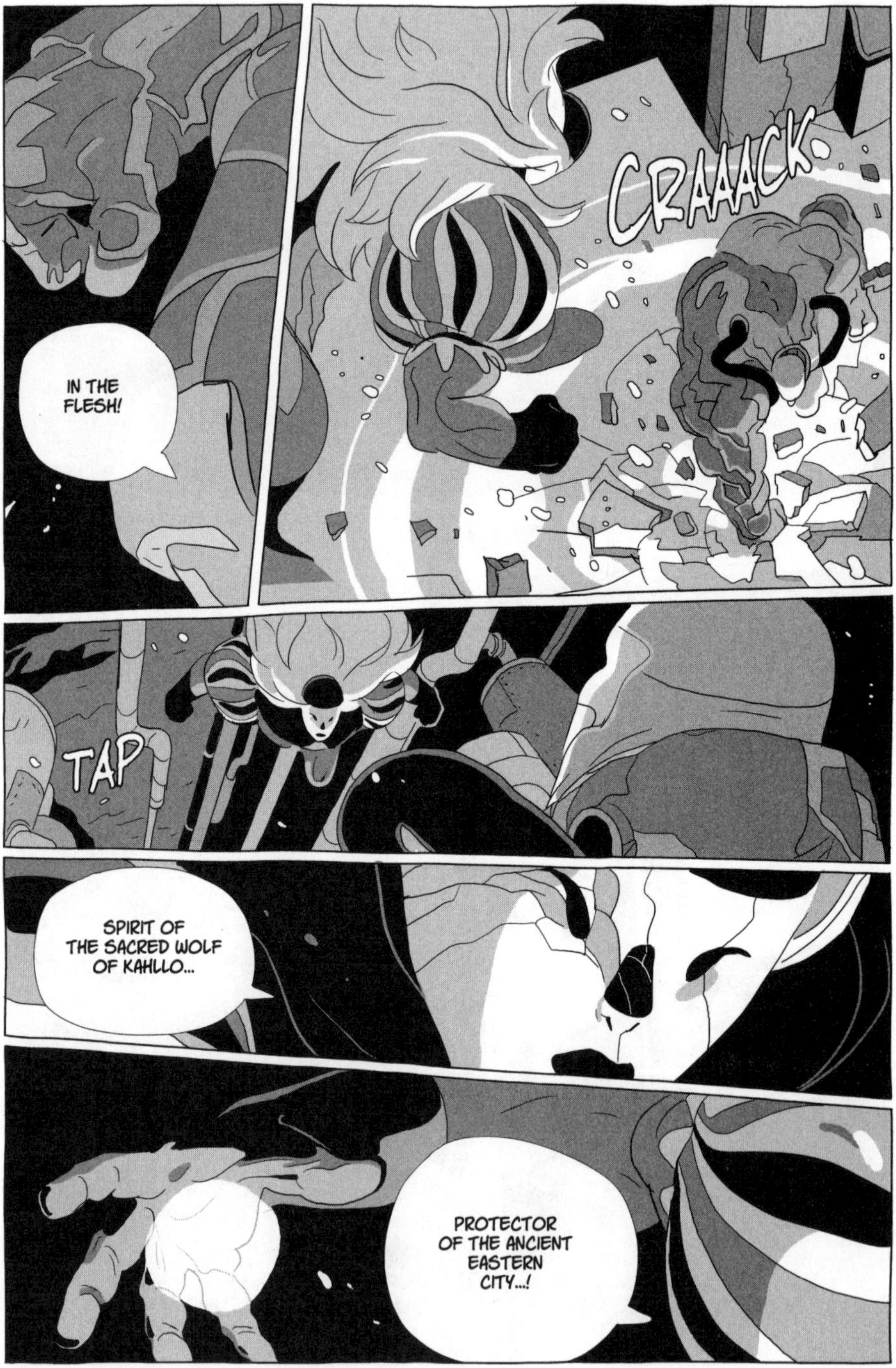
IN THE FLESH!
CRAAACK
TAP
SPIRIT OF THE SACRED WOLF OF KAHLLO...
PROTECTOR OF THE ANCIENT EASTERN CITY...!

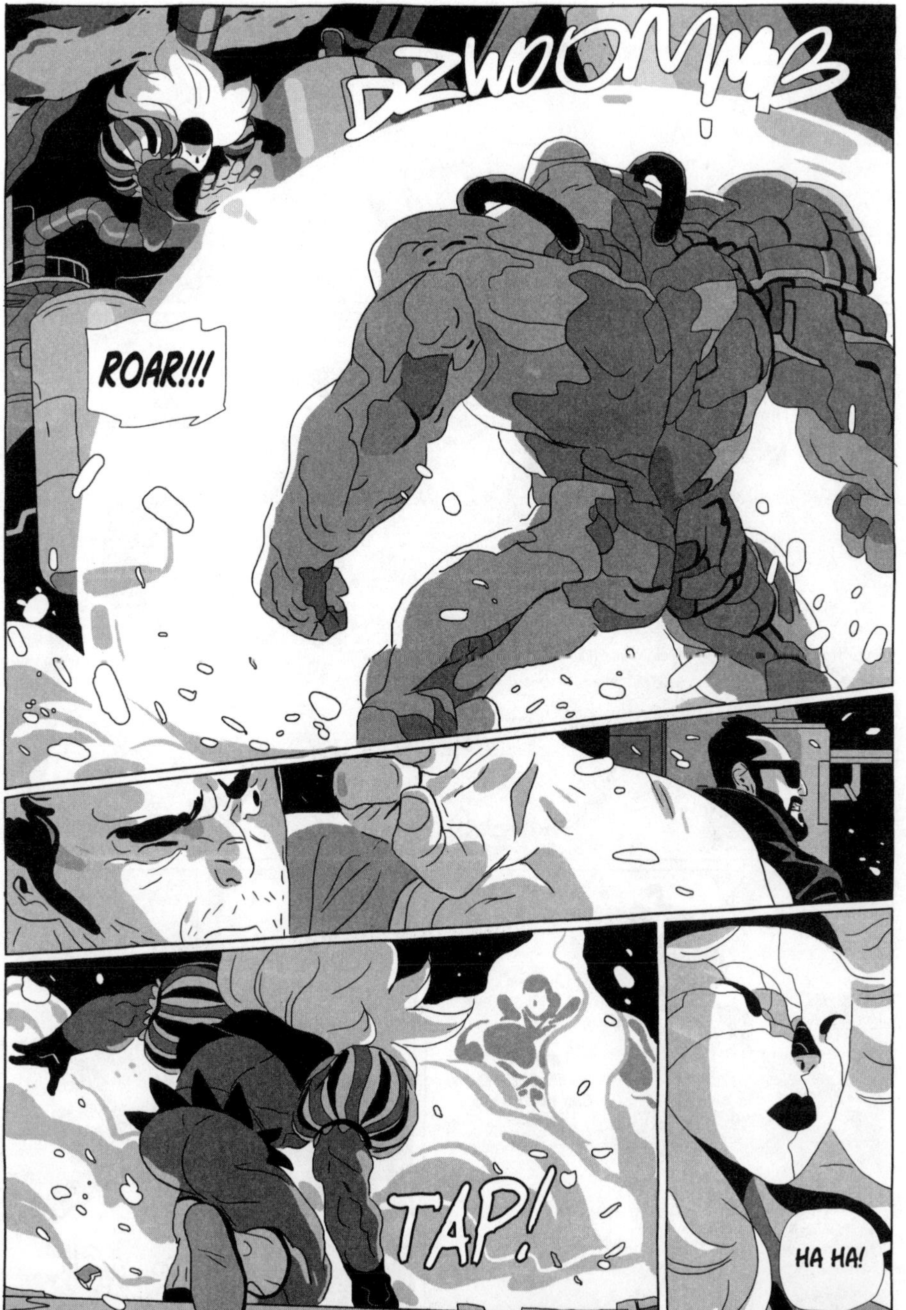
DZWOOMMB
ROAR!!!
TAP!
HA HA!

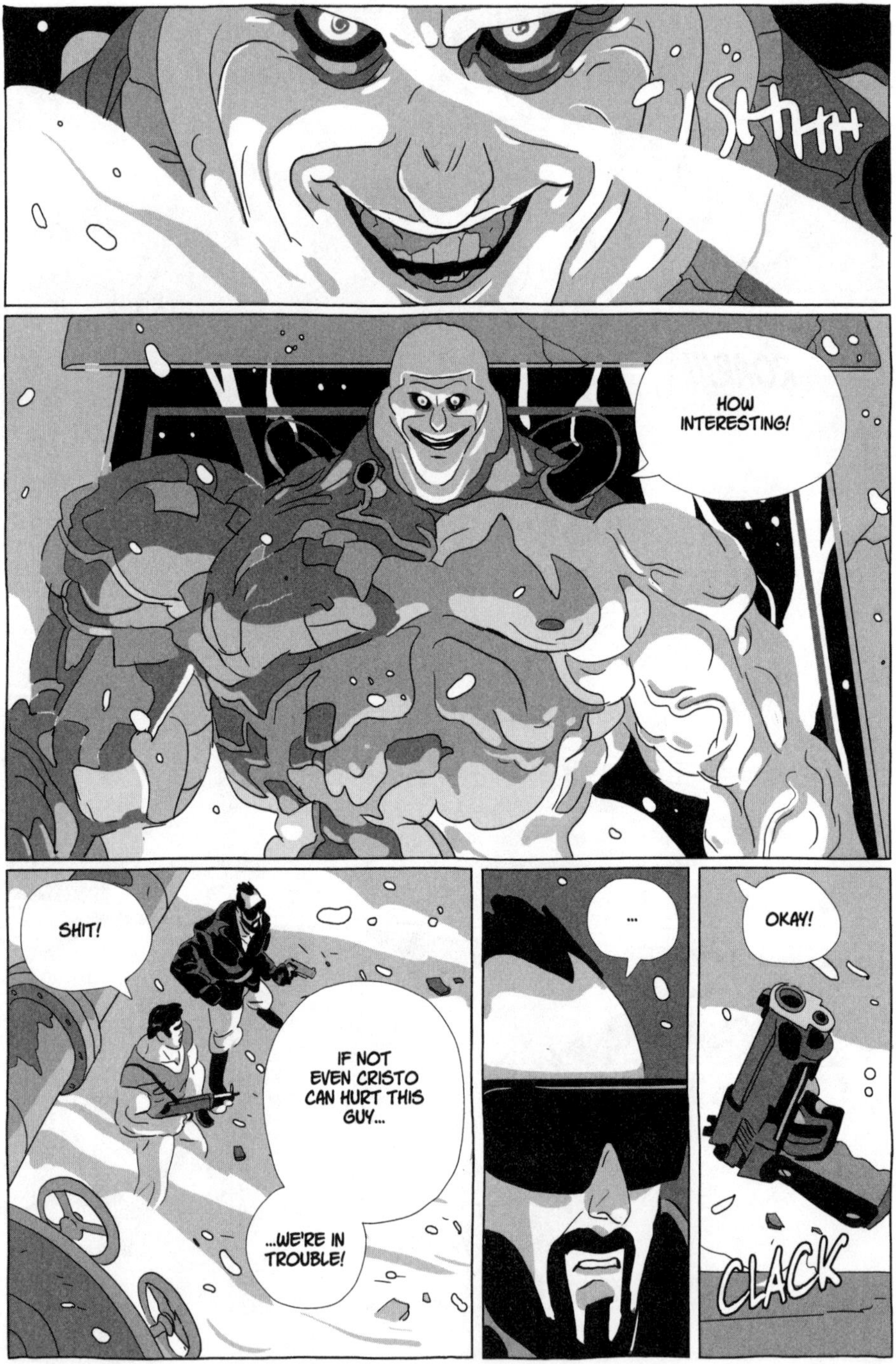
SHHH
HOW INTERESTING!
SHIT!
IF NOT EVEN CRISTO CAN HURT THIS GUY...
...WE'RE IN TROUBLE!
...
OKAY!
CLACK

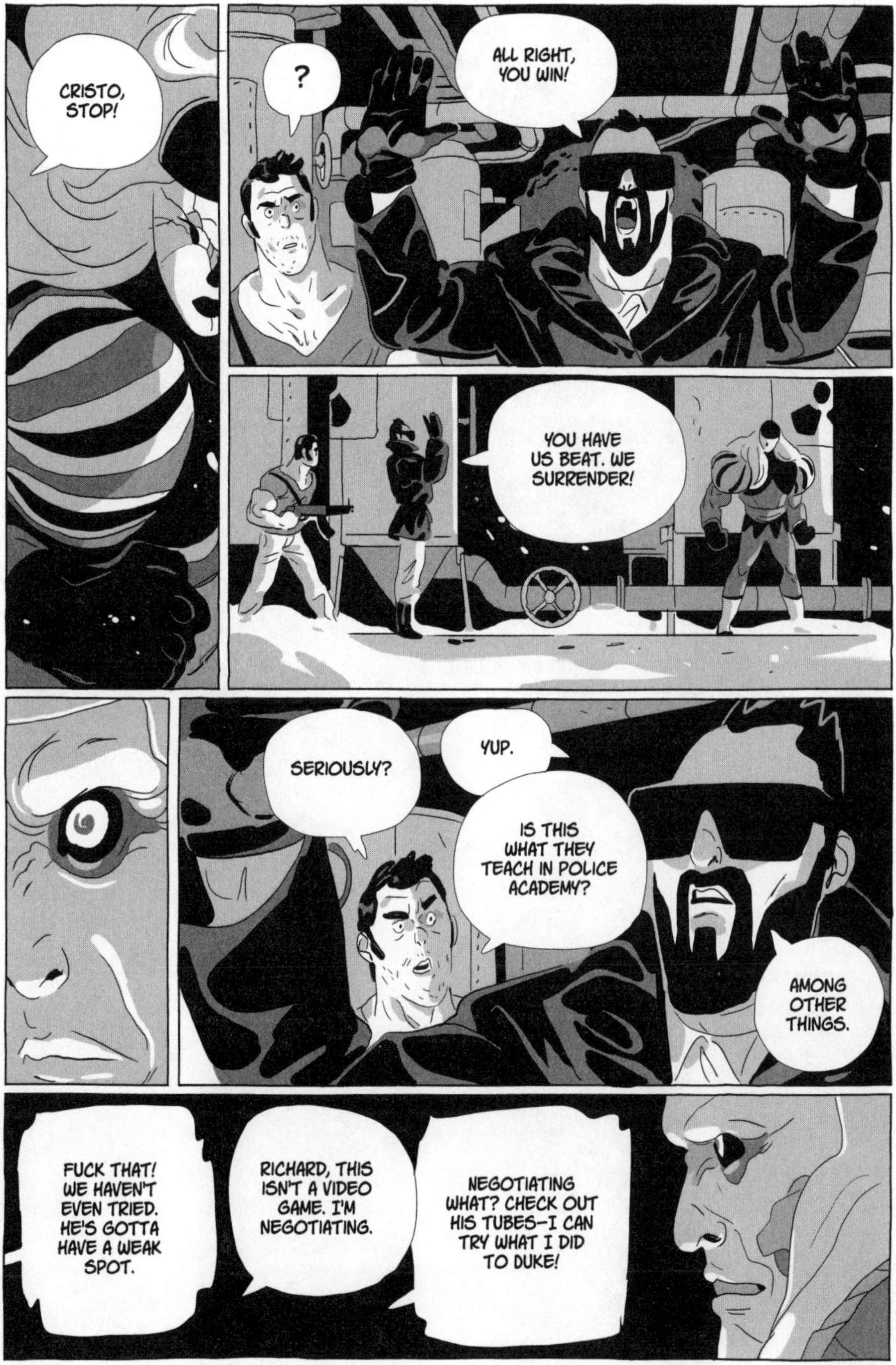
CRISTO, STOP!
?
ALL RIGHT, YOU WIN!
YOU HAVE US BEAT. WE SURRENDER!
SERIOUSLY?
YUP.
IS THIS WHAT THEY TEACH IN POLICE ACADEMY?
AMONG OTHER THINGS.
FUCK THAT! WE HAVEN'T EVEN TRIED. HE'S GOTTA HAVE A WEAK SPOT.
RICHARD, THIS ISN'T A VIDEO GAME. I'M NEGOTIATING.
NEGOTIATING WHAT? CHECK OUT HIS TUBES—I CAN TRY WHAT I DID TO DUKE!

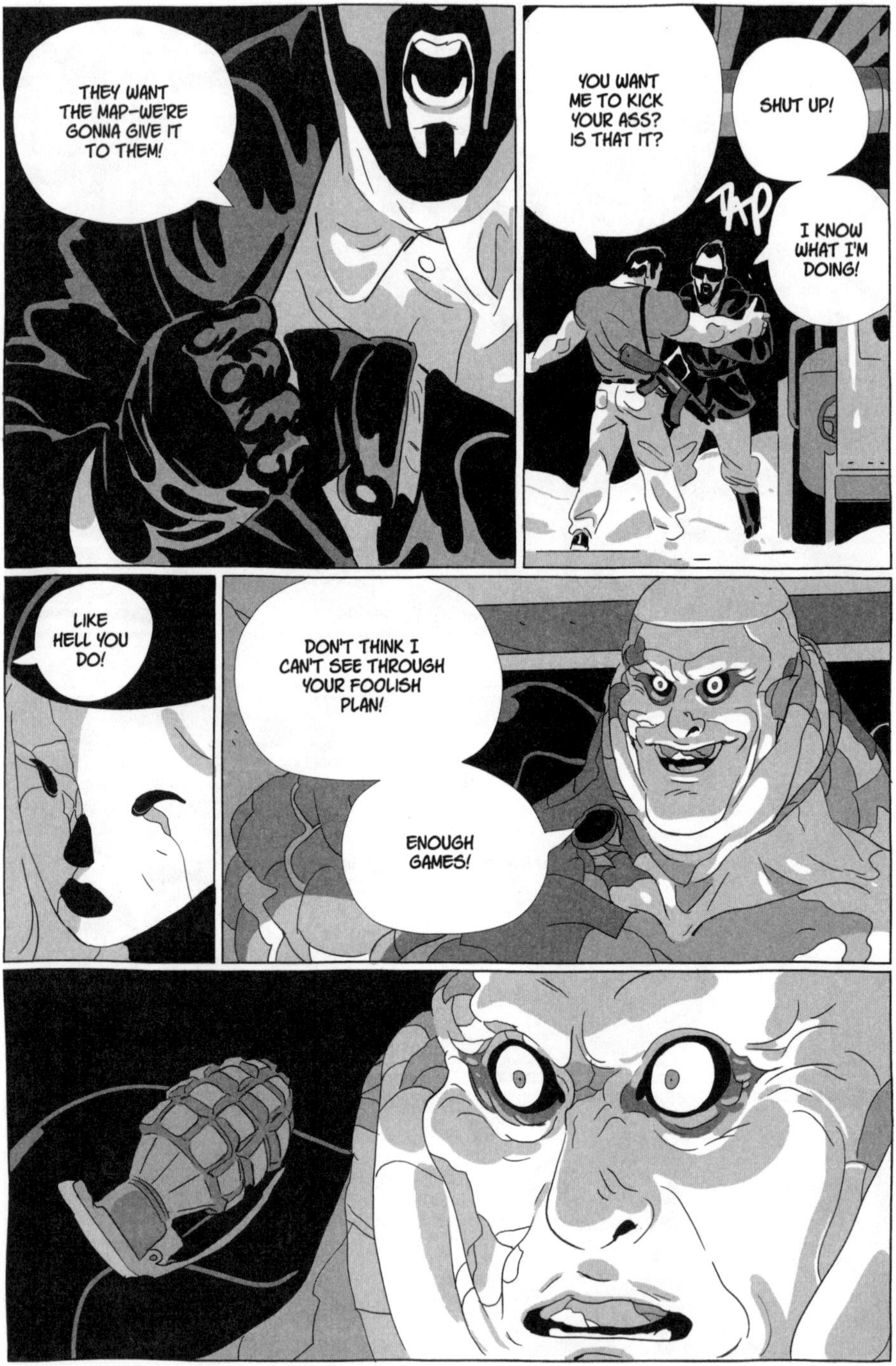
THEY WANT THE MAP—WE'RE GONNA GIVE IT TO THEM!
YOU WANT ME TO KICK YOUR ASS? IS THAT IT?
SHUT UP!
TAP
I KNOW WHAT I'M DOING!
LIKE HELL YOU DO!
DON'T THINK I CAN'T SEE THROUGH YOUR FOOLISH PLAN!
ENOUGH GAMES!

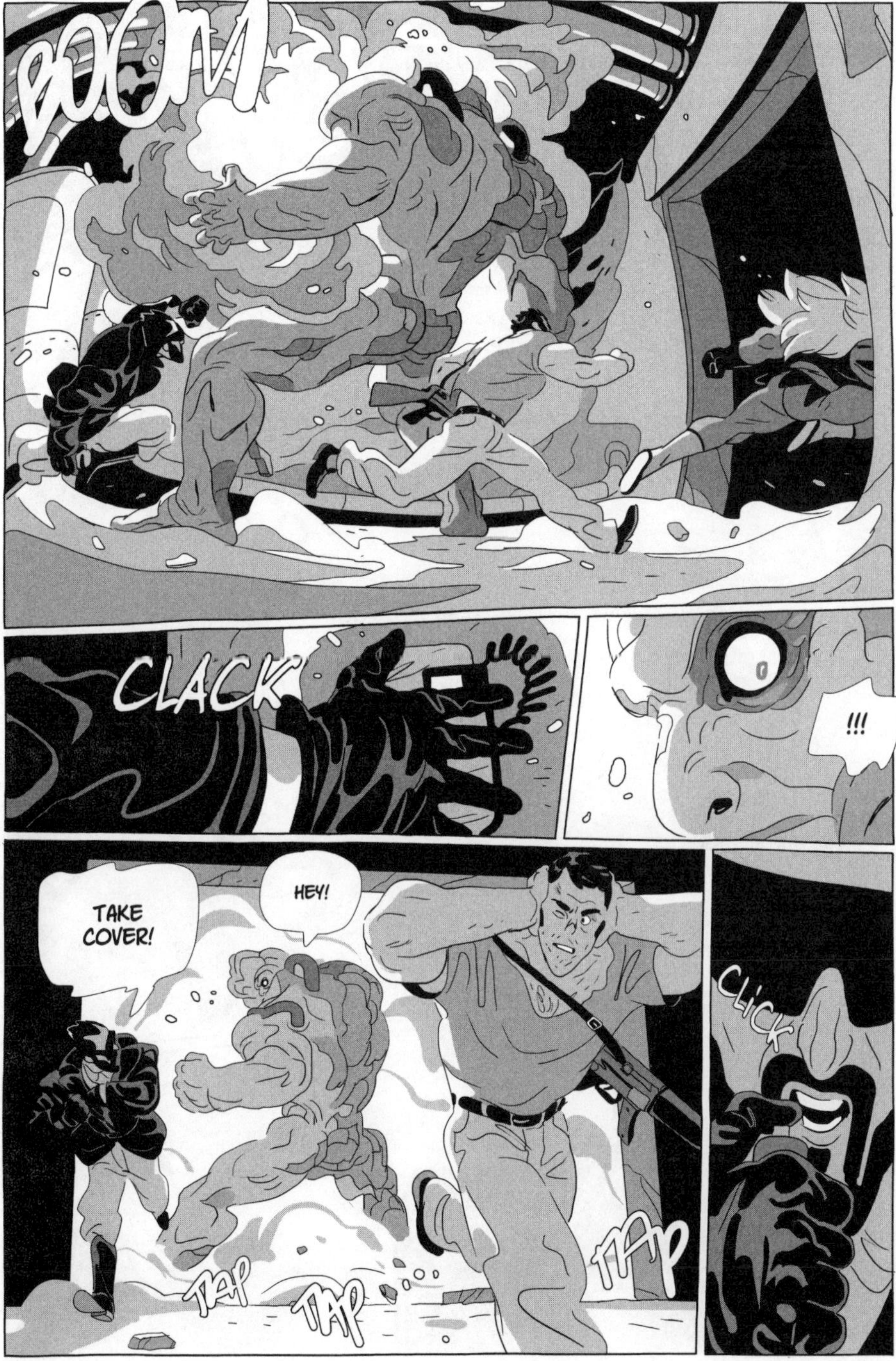
BOOM
CLACK
!!!
TAKE COVER!
HEY!
TAP
TAP
TAP
CLICK

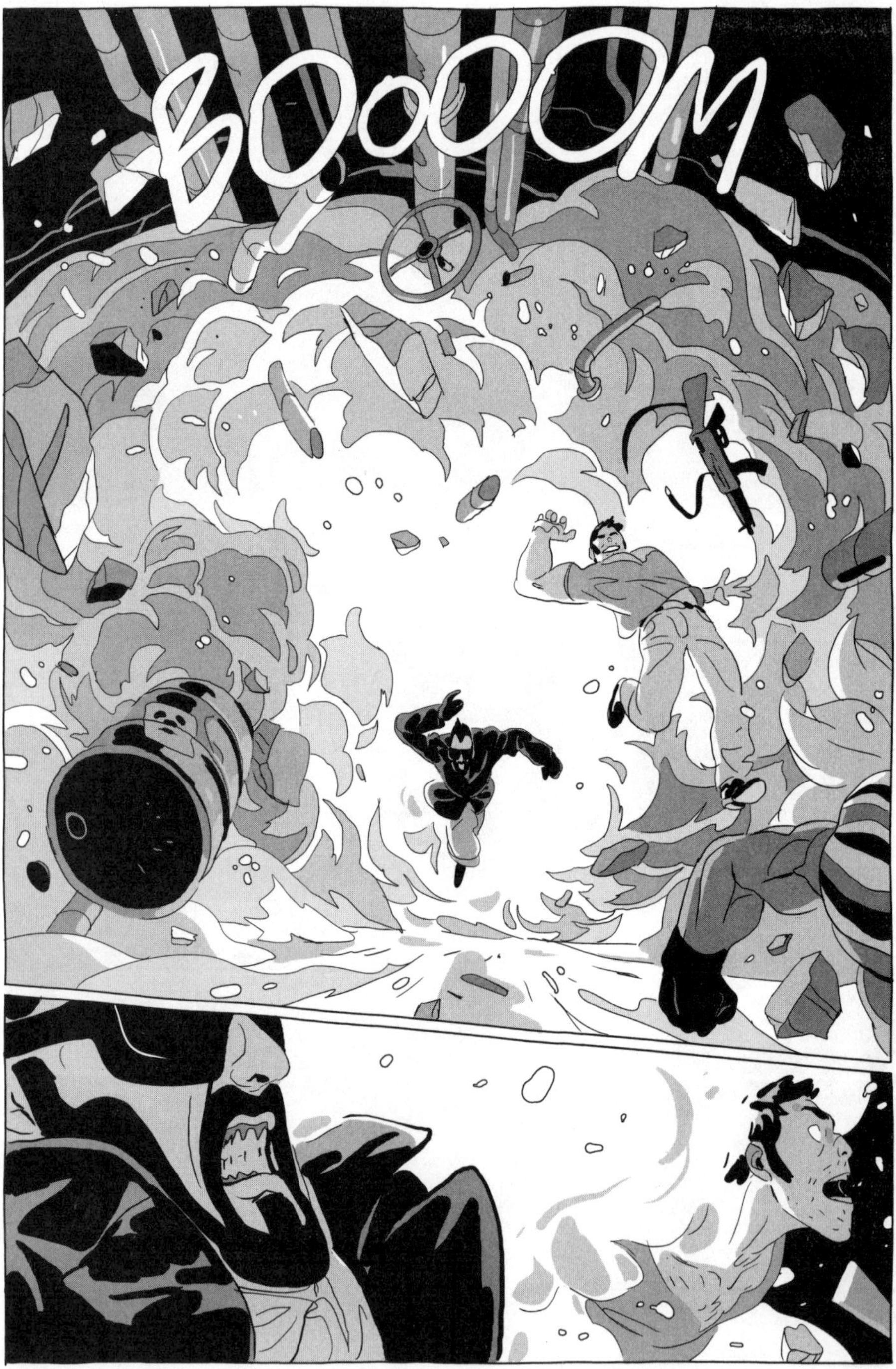
BOOOOM

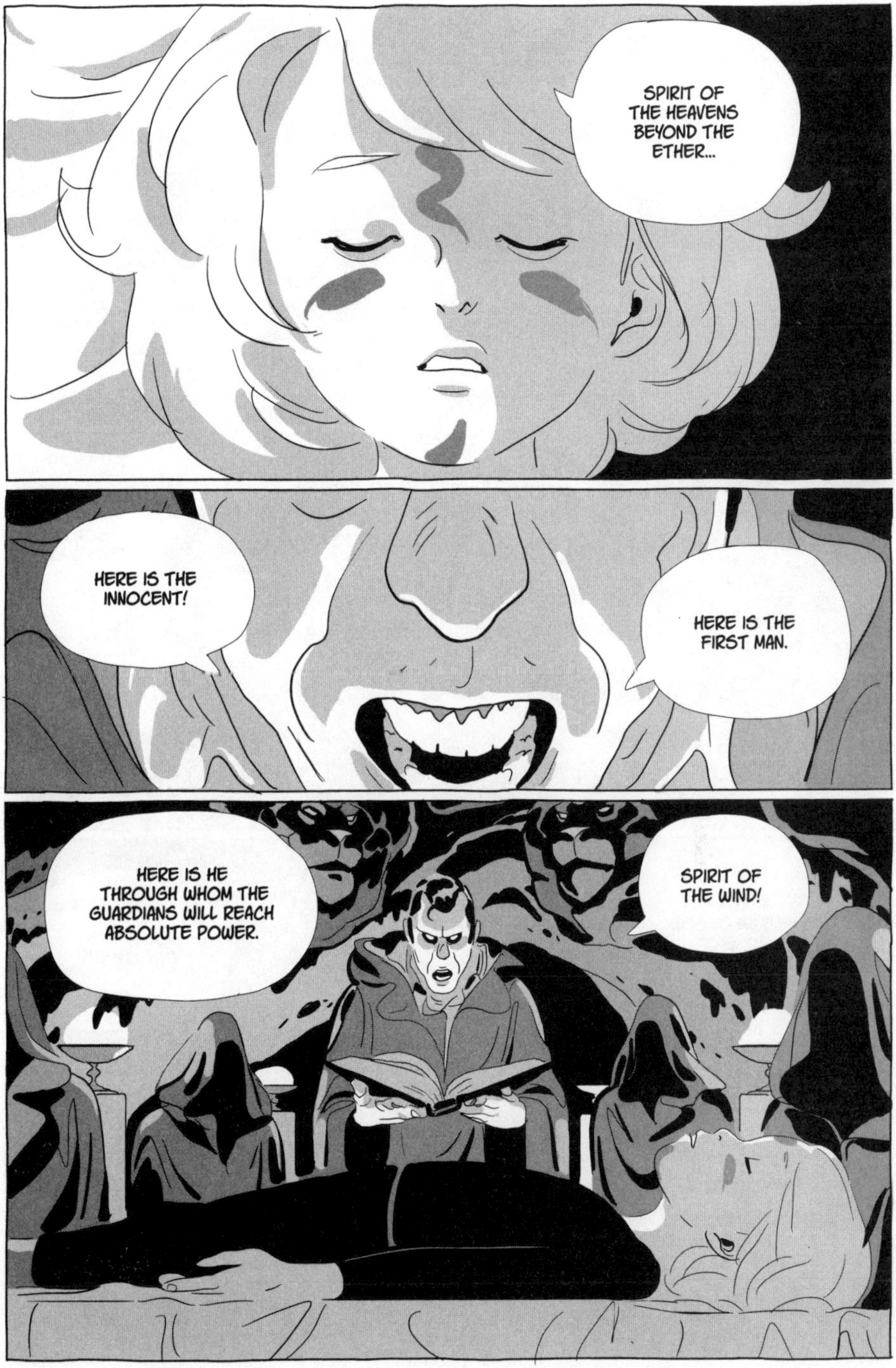
SPIRIT OF THE HEAVENS BEYOND THE ETHER...
HERE IS THE INNOCENT!
HERE IS THE FIRST MAN.
HERE IS HE THROUGH WHOM THE GUARDIANS WILL REACH ABSOLUTE POWER.
SPIRIT OF THE WIND!

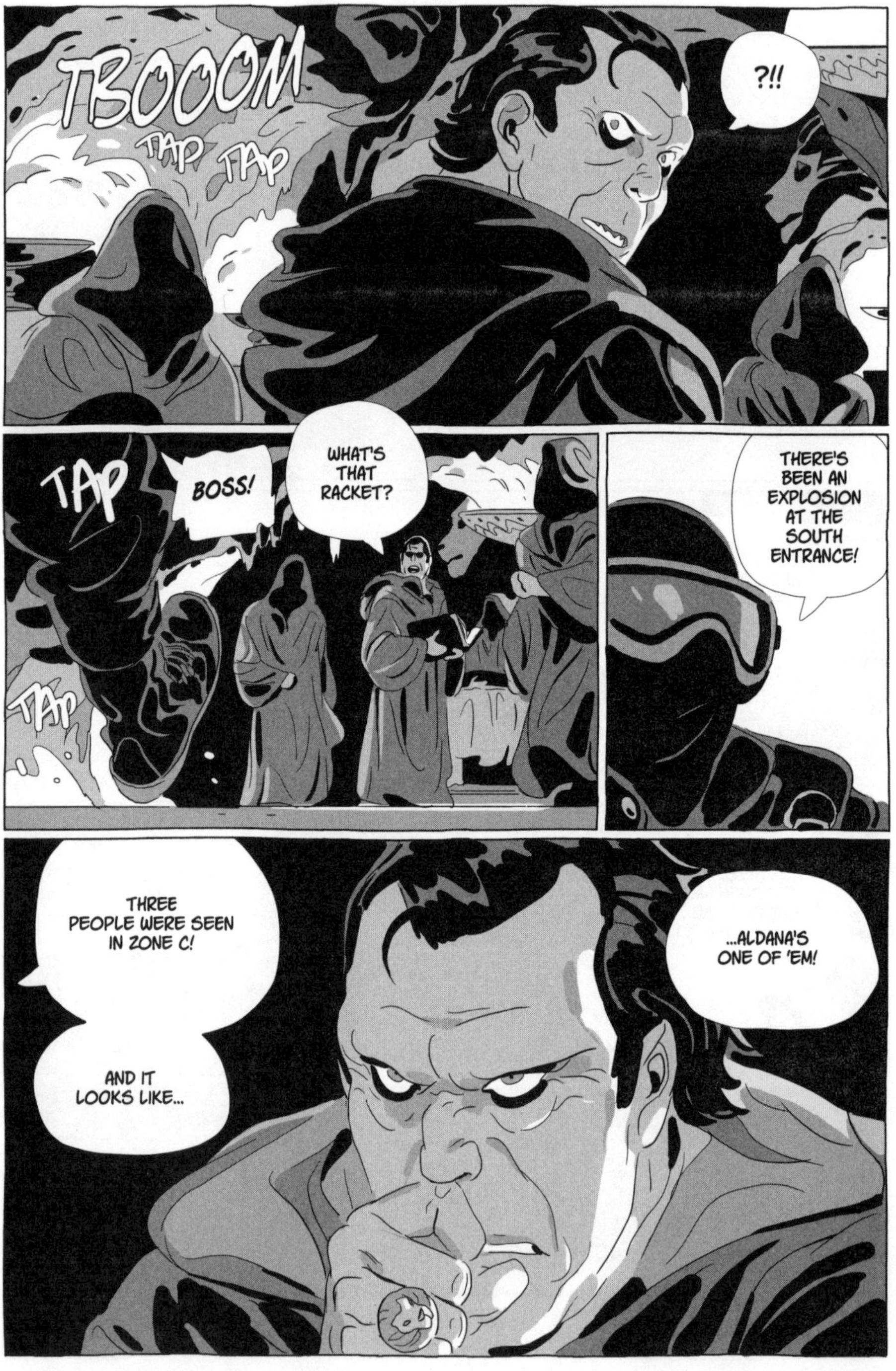
TBOOOM
TAP TAP
?!!
TAP
BOSS!
WHAT'S THAT RACKET?
TAP
THERE'S BEEN AN EXPLOSION AT THE SOUTH ENTRANCE!
THREE PEOPLE WERE SEEN IN ZONE C!
AND IT LOOKS LIKE...
...ALDANA'S ONE OF 'EM!

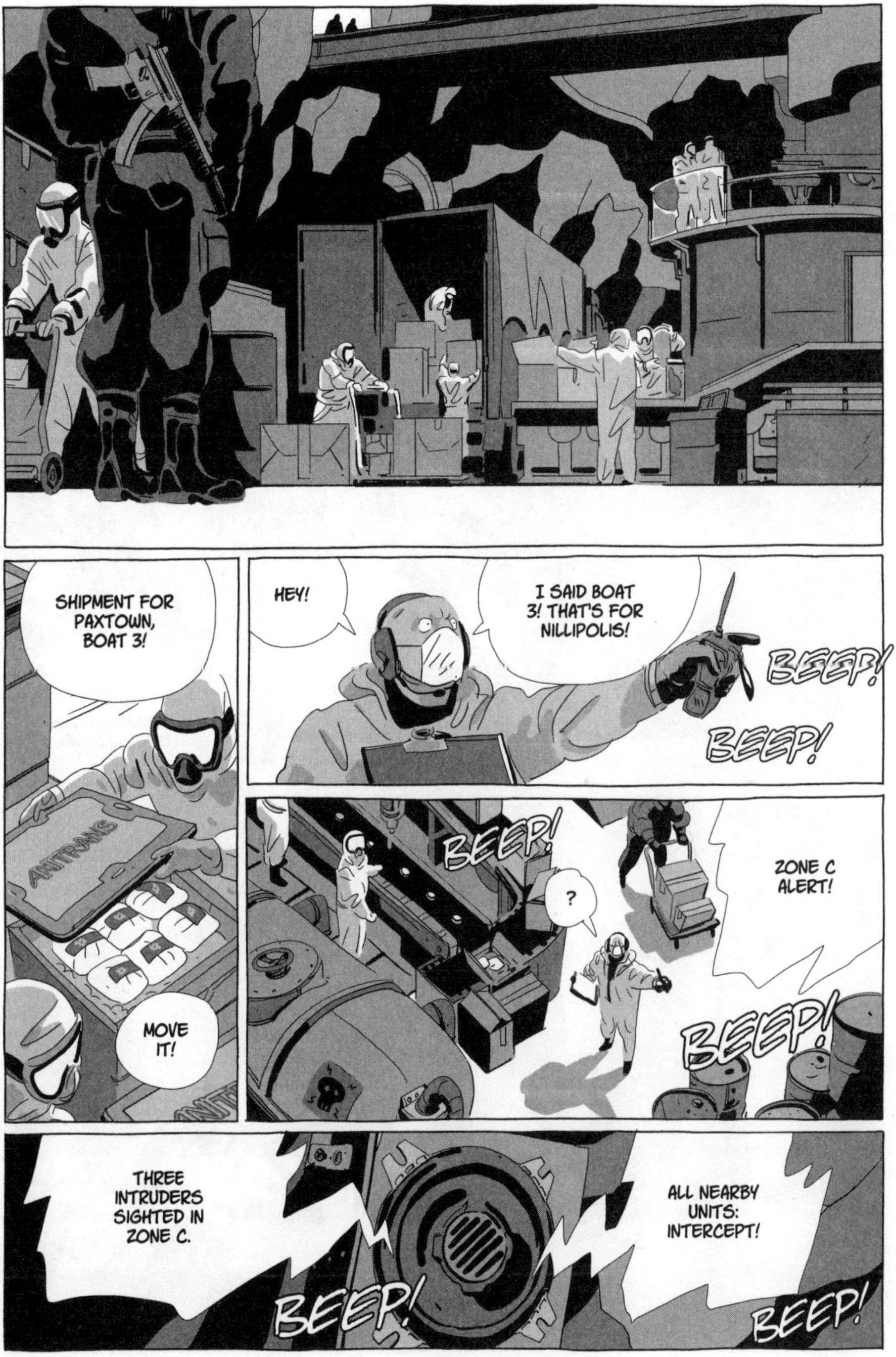
SHIPMENT FOR PAXTOWN, BOAT 3!
ANITRANS
MOVE IT!
HEY!
I SAID BOAT 3! THAT'S FOR NILLIPOLIS!
BEEP!
BEEP!
BEEP!
?
ZONE C ALERT!
BEEP!
THREE INTRUDERS SIGHTED IN ZONE C.
ALL NEARBY UNITS: INTERCEPT!
BEEP!
BEEP!

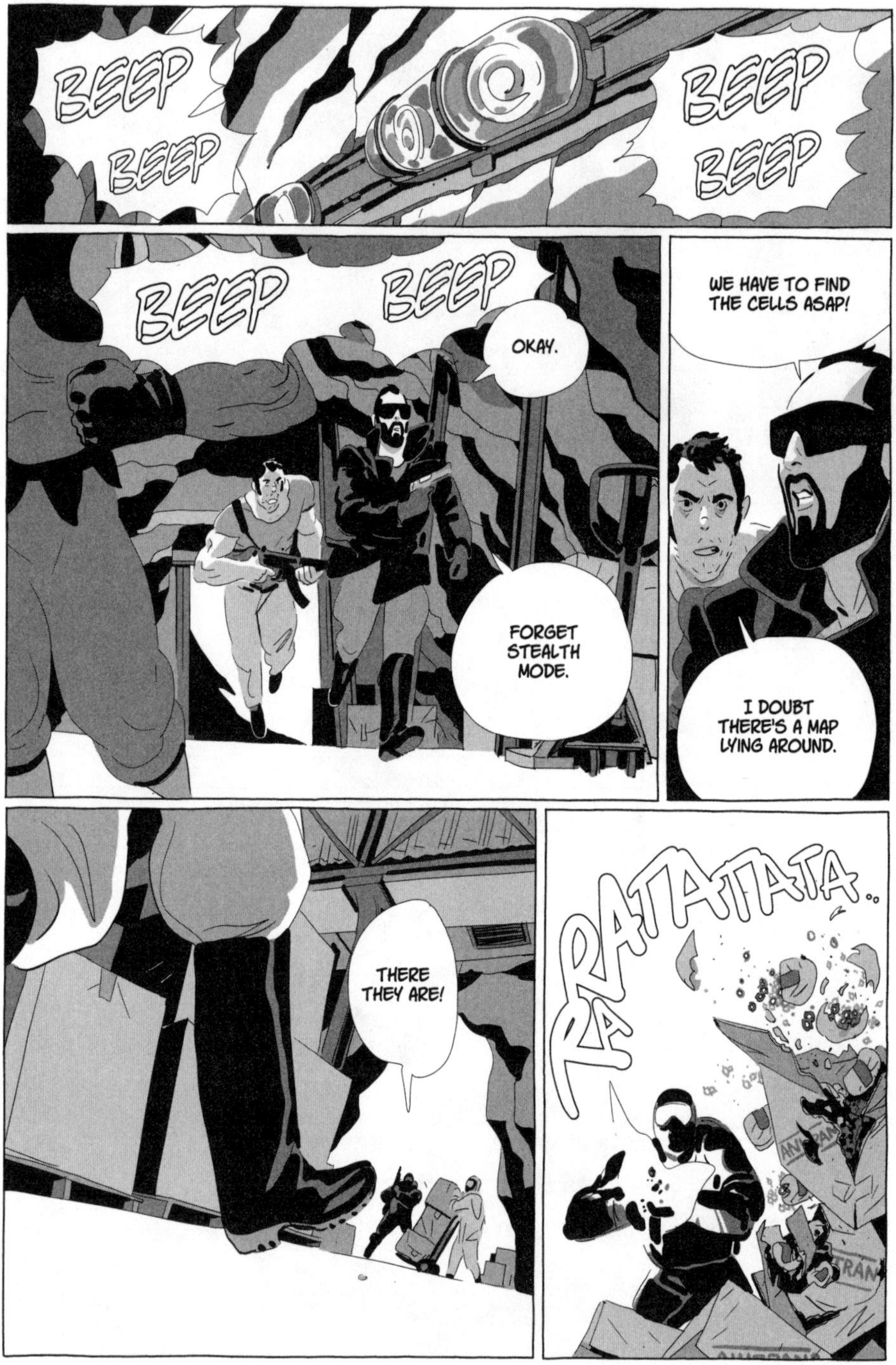
BEEP
BEEP
BEEP
BEEP
BEEP
BEEP
OKAY.
FORGET STEALTH MODE.
WE HAVE TO FIND THE CELLS ASAP!
I DOUBT THERE'S A MAP LYING AROUND.
THERE THEY ARE!
RATATATATA..

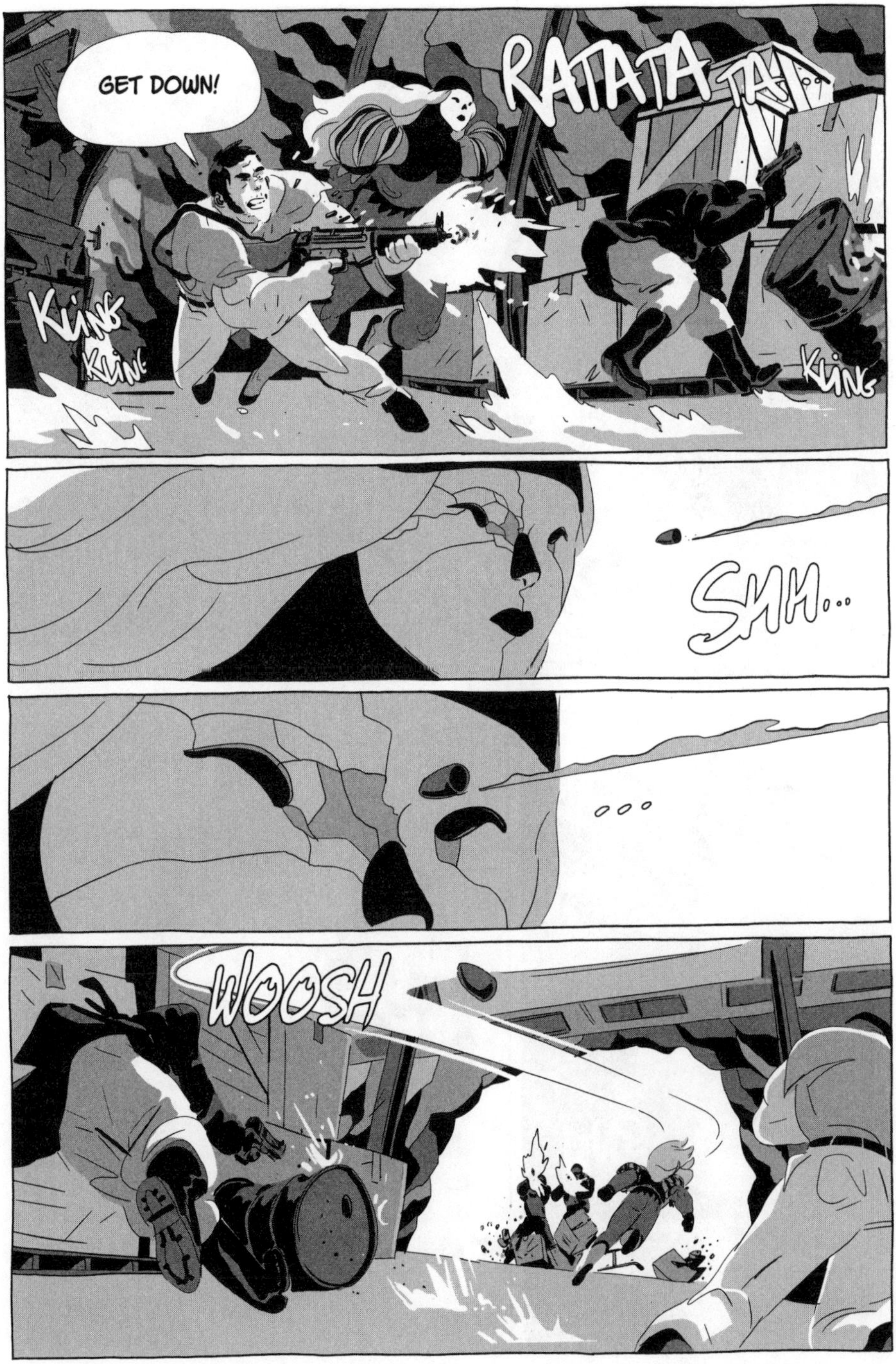

GET DOWN!
RATATA TA!
KLING
KLING
KLING
SHH...
...
WOOSH

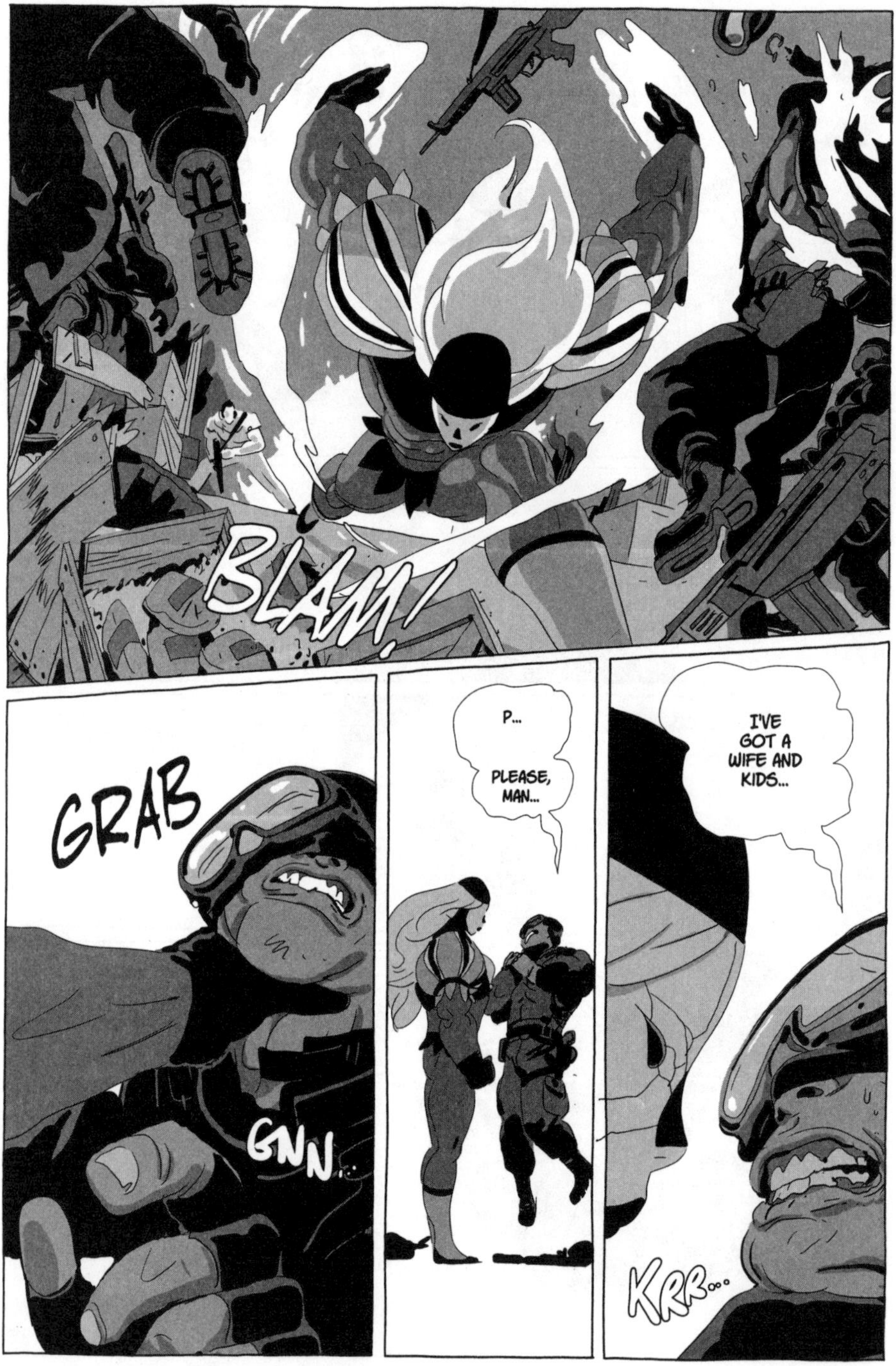
BLAM!
GRAB
GNN...
P...
PLEASE, MAN...
I'VE GOT A WIFE AND KIDS...
KRR...

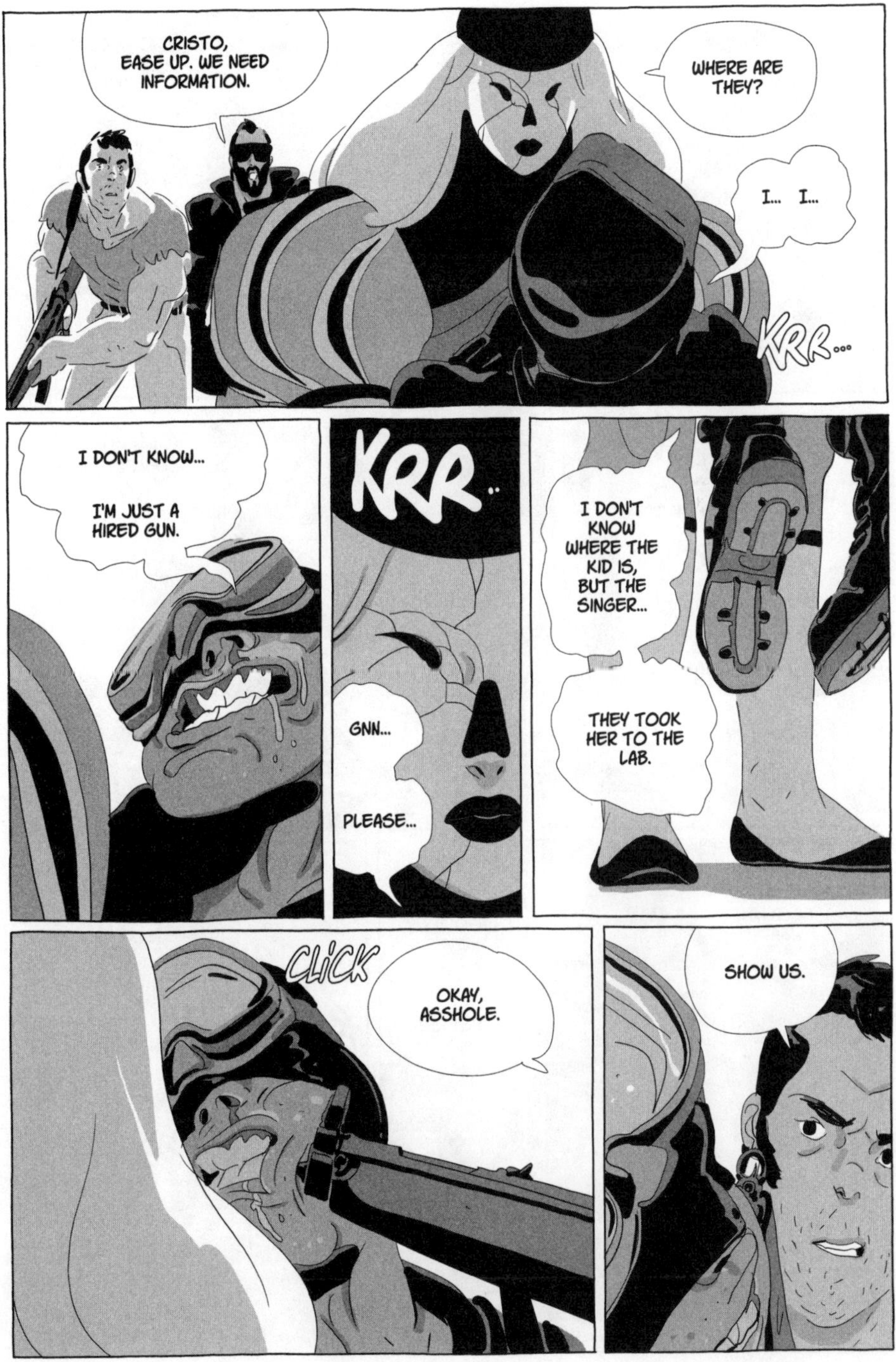
CRISTO, EASE UP. WE NEED INFORMATION.
WHERE ARE THEY?
I... I...
KRR...
I DON'T KNOW...
I'M JUST A HIRED GUN.
KRR..
GNN...
PLEASE...
I DON'T KNOW WHERE THE KID IS, BUT THE SINGER...
THEY TOOK HER TO THE LAB.
CLICK
OKAY, ASSHOLE.
SHOW US.

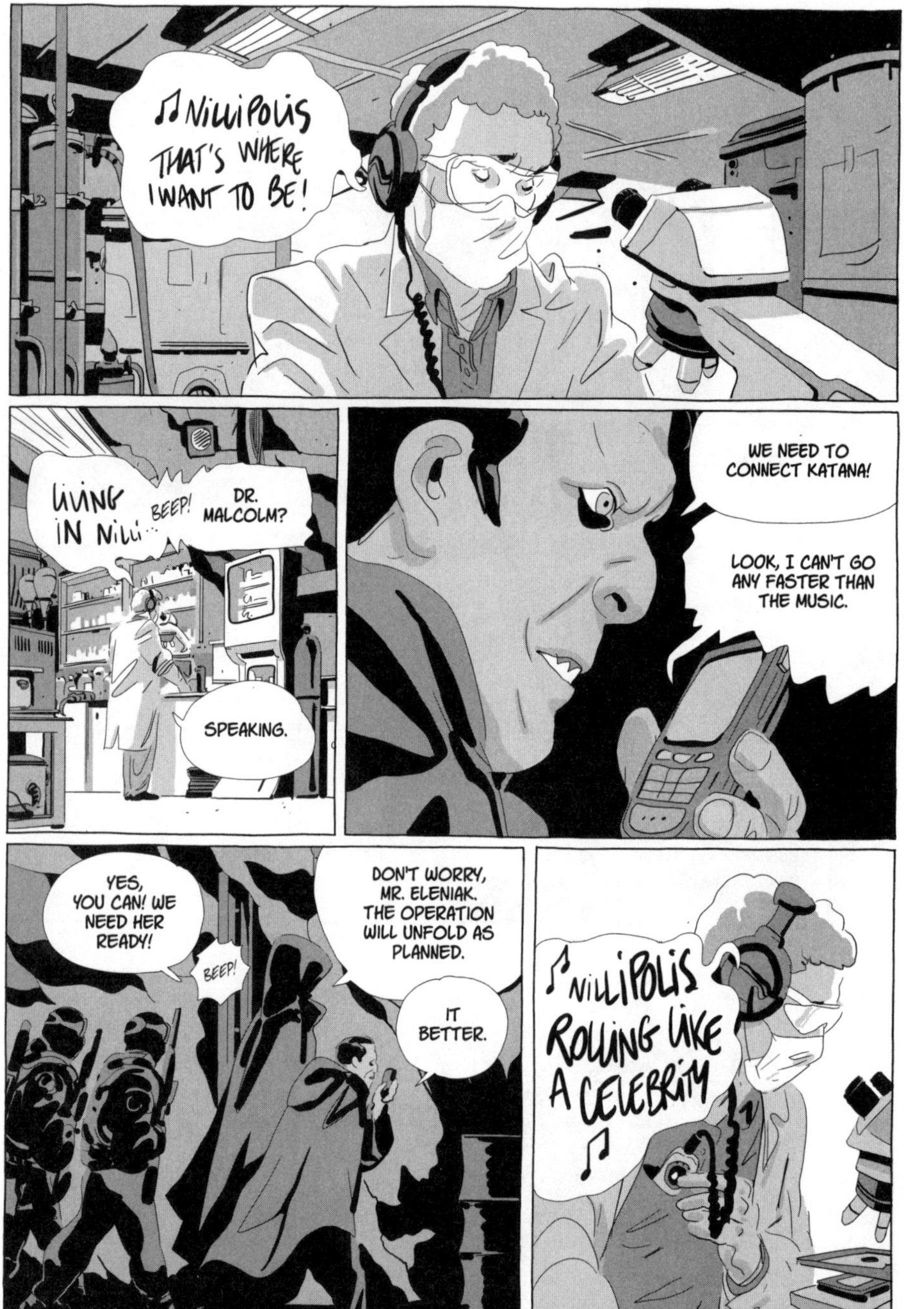
♫ NILLIPOLIS THAT'S WHERE I WANT TO BE!
LIVING IN NILLI...
BEEP!
DR. MALCOLM?
SPEAKING.
WE NEED TO CONNECT KATANA!
LOOK, I CAN'T GO ANY FASTER THAN THE MUSIC.
YES, YOU CAN! WE NEED HER READY!
BEEP!
DON'T WORRY, MR. ELENIAK. THE OPERATION WILL UNFOLD AS PLANNED.
IT BETTER.
♪ NILLIPOLIS ROLLING LIKE A CELEBRITY ♪

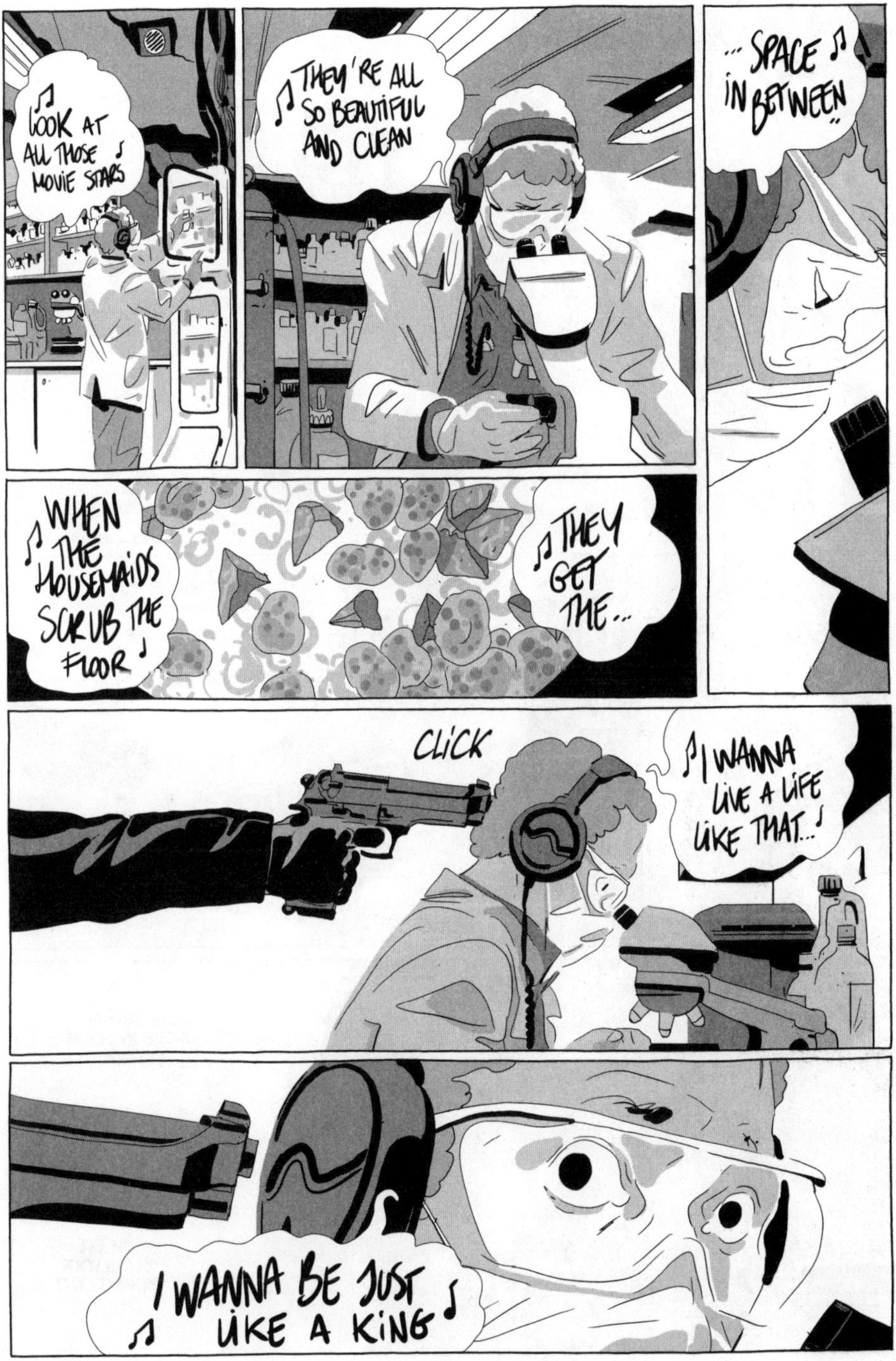
♫ LOOK AT ALL THOSE ♪ MOVIE STARS
♫ THEY'RE ALL SO BEAUTIFUL AND CLEAN
... SPACE ♫ IN BETWEEN
♫ WHEN THE HOUSEMAIDS SCRUB THE FLOOR ♩
♫ THEY GET THE...
CLICK
♫ I WANNA LIVE A LIFE LIKE THAT... ♩
I WANNA BE JUST ♪ ♫ LIKE A KING ♩

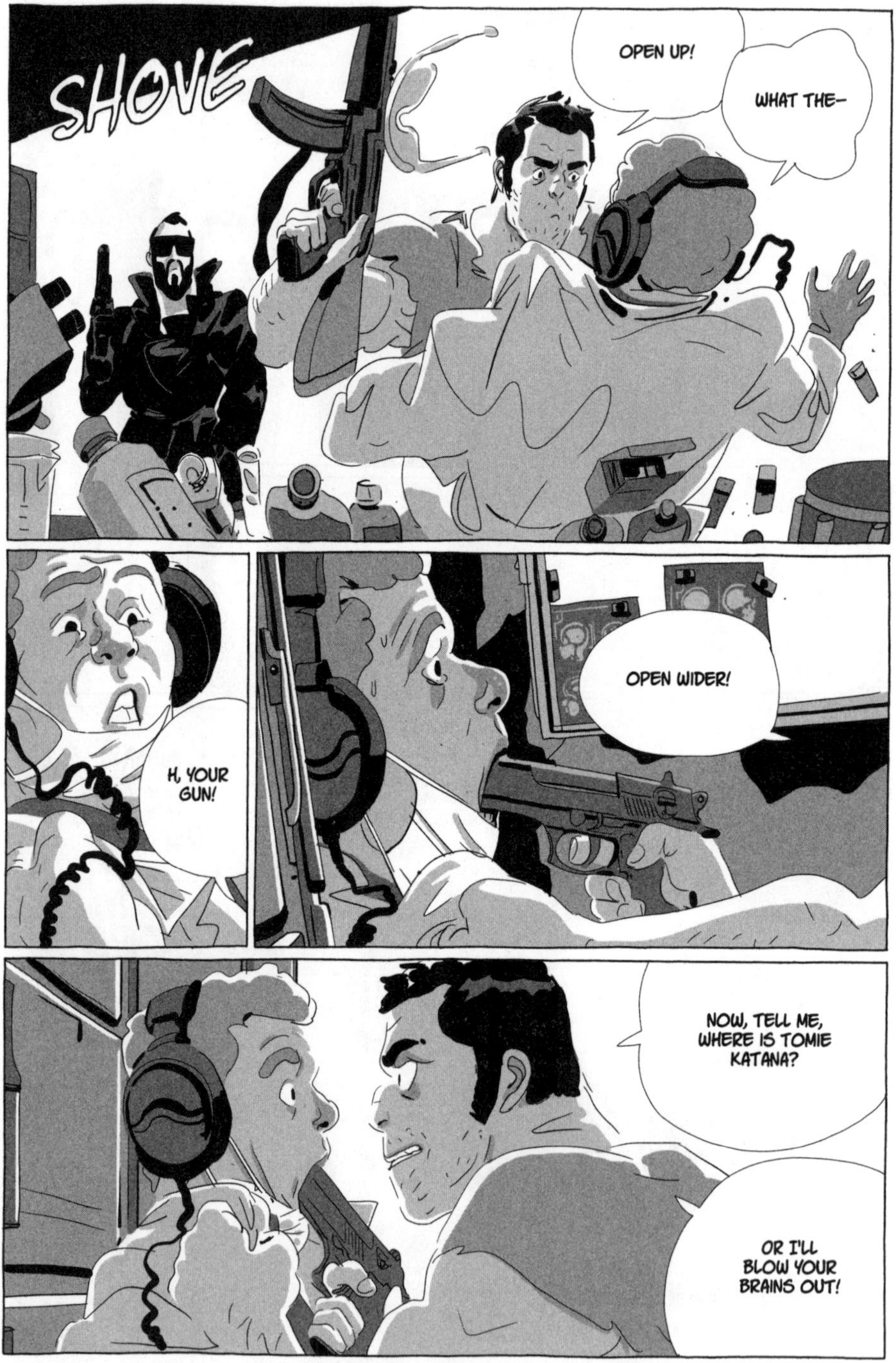
SHOVE
OPEN UP!
WHAT THE-
H, YOUR GUN!
OPEN WIDER!
NOW, TELL ME, WHERE IS TOMIE KATANA?
OR I'LL BLOW YOUR BRAINS OUT!

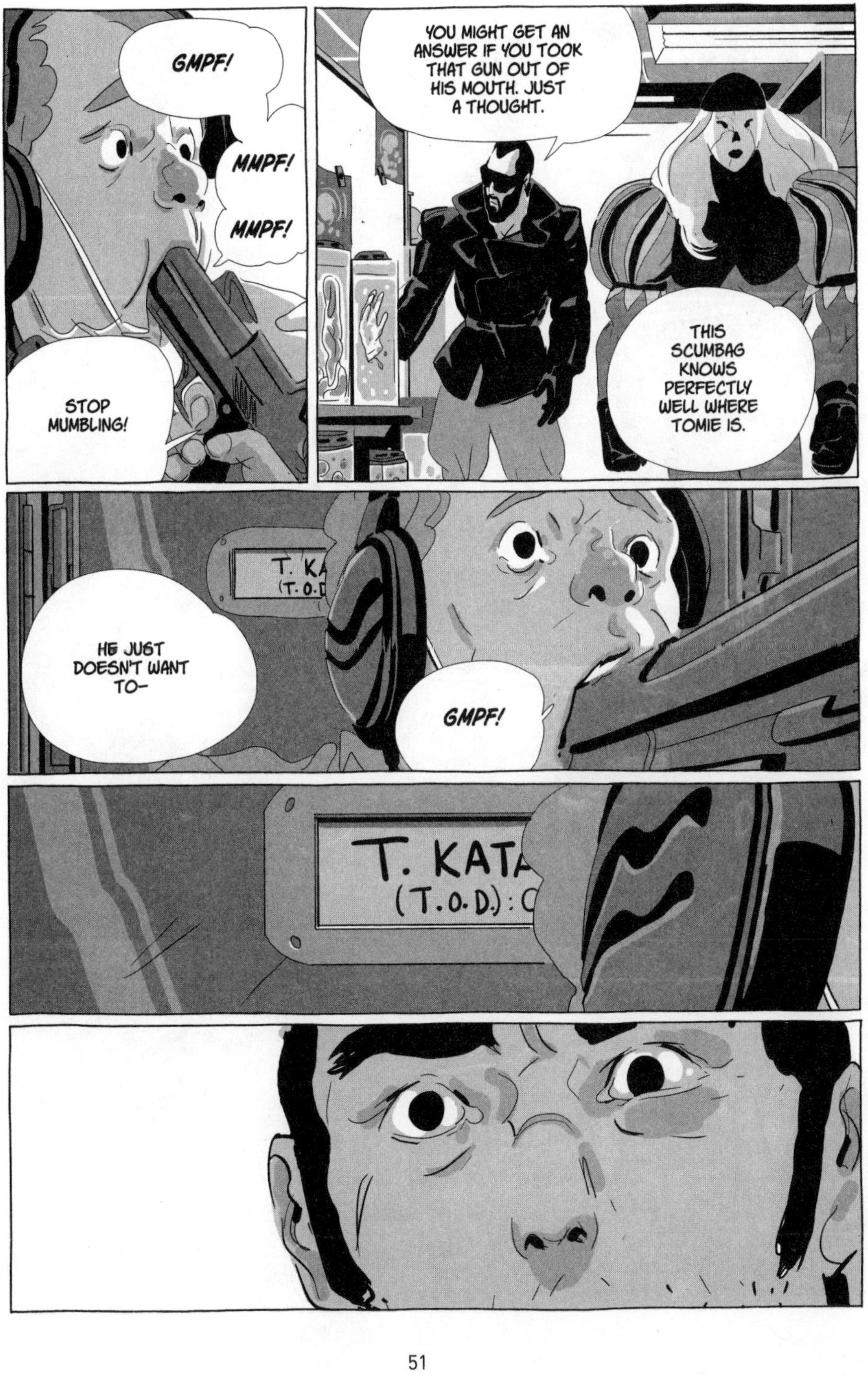
GMPF!
MMPF!
MMPF!
STOP MUMBLING!
YOU MIGHT GET AN ANSWER IF YOU TOOK THAT GUN OUT OF HIS MOUTH. JUST A THOUGHT.
THIS SCUMBAG KNOWS PERFECTLY WELL WHERE TOMIE IS.
HE JUST DOESN'T WANT TO-
GMPF!

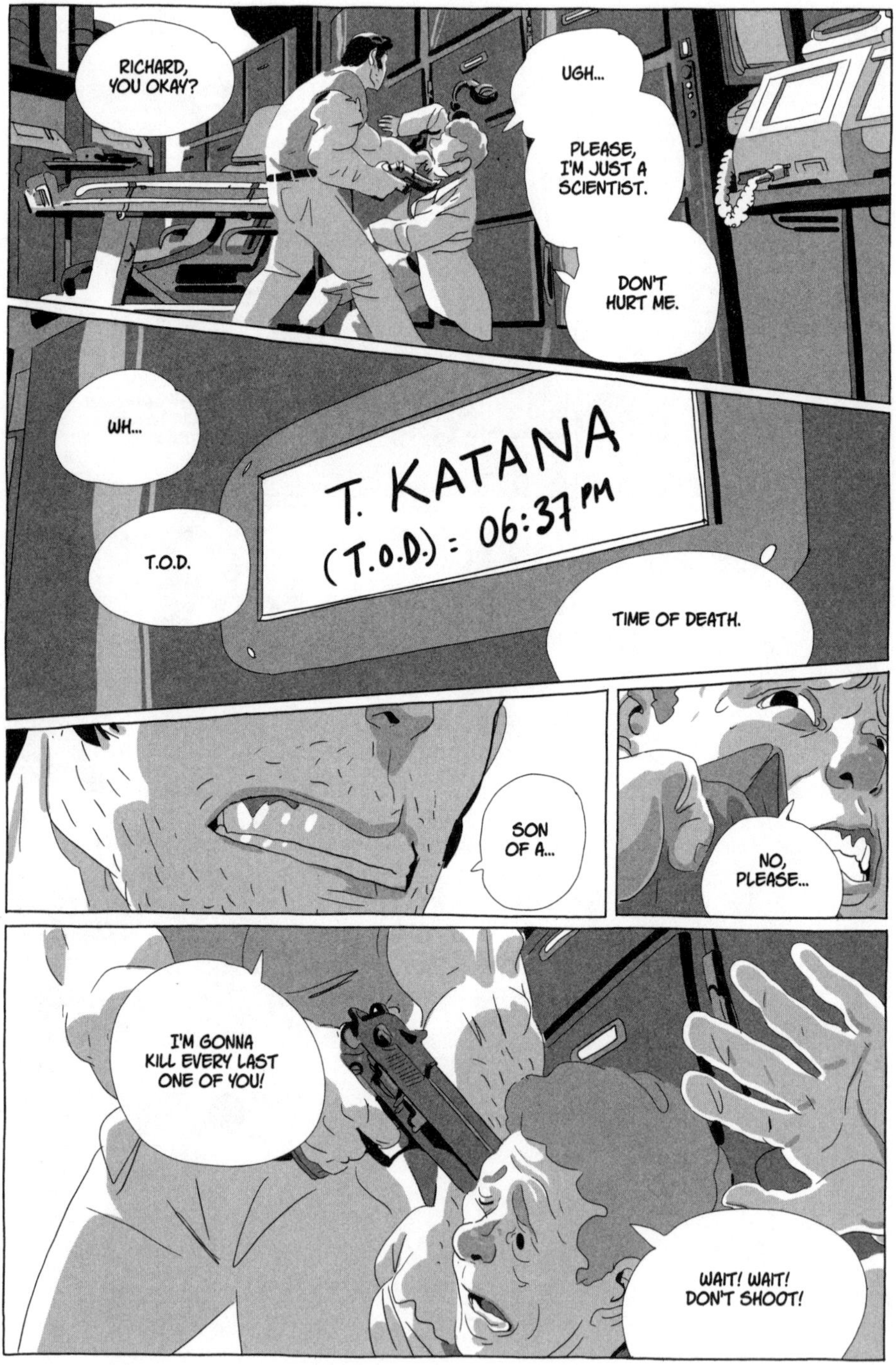
RICHARD, YOU OKAY?
UGH...
PLEASE, I'M JUST A SCIENTIST.
DON'T HURT ME.
WH...
T. KATANA (T.O.D.) = 06:37 PM
T.O.D.
TIME OF DEATH.
SON OF A...
NO, PLEASE...
I'M GONNA KILL EVERY LAST ONE OF YOU!
WAIT! WAIT! DON'T SHOOT!

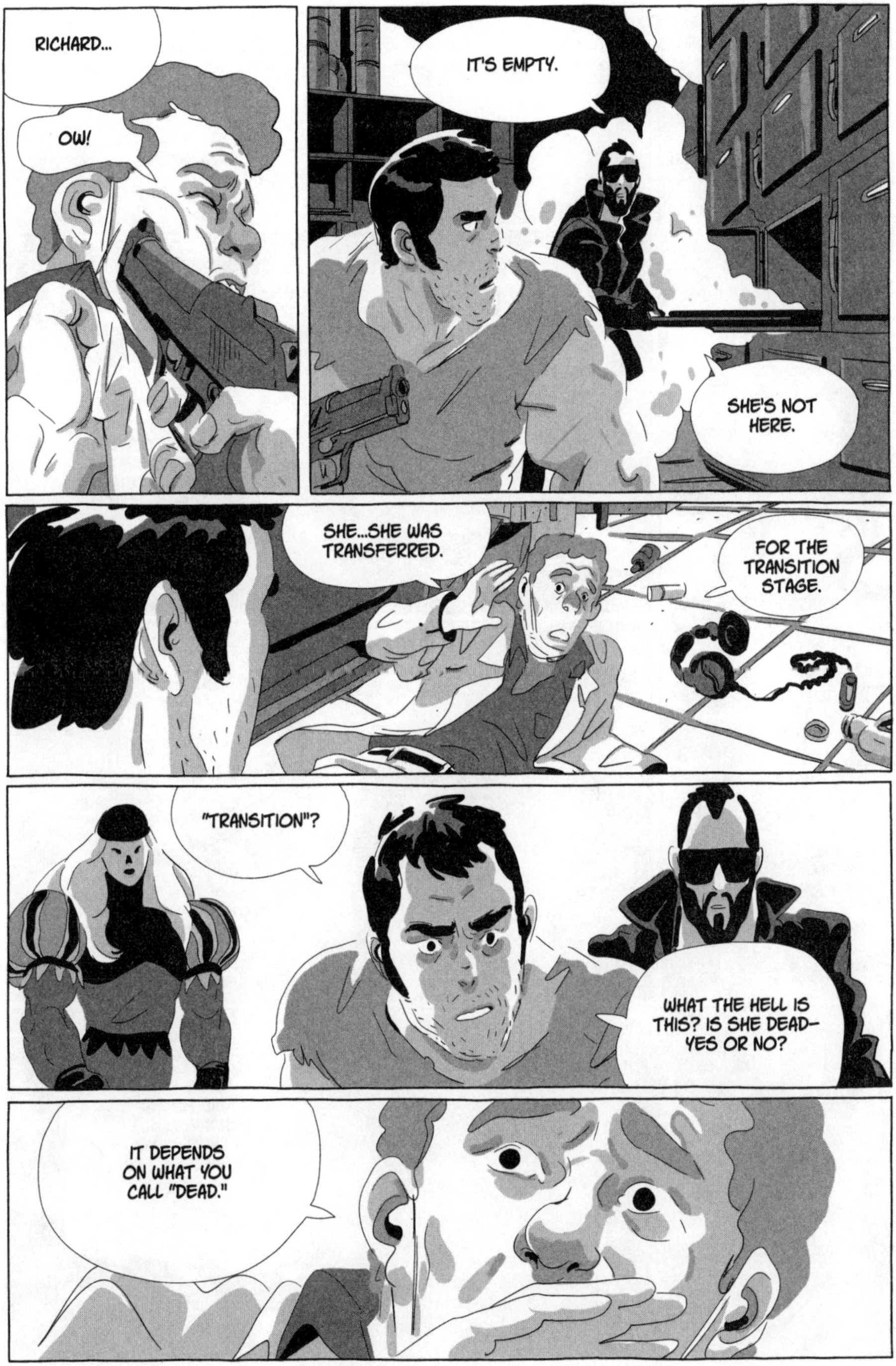
RICHARD...
OW!
IT'S EMPTY.
SHE'S NOT HERE.
SHE...SHE WAS TRANSFERRED.
FOR THE TRANSITION STAGE.
"TRANSITION"?
WHAT THE HELL IS THIS? IS SHE DEAD- YES OR NO?
IT DEPENDS ON WHAT YOU CALL "DEAD."

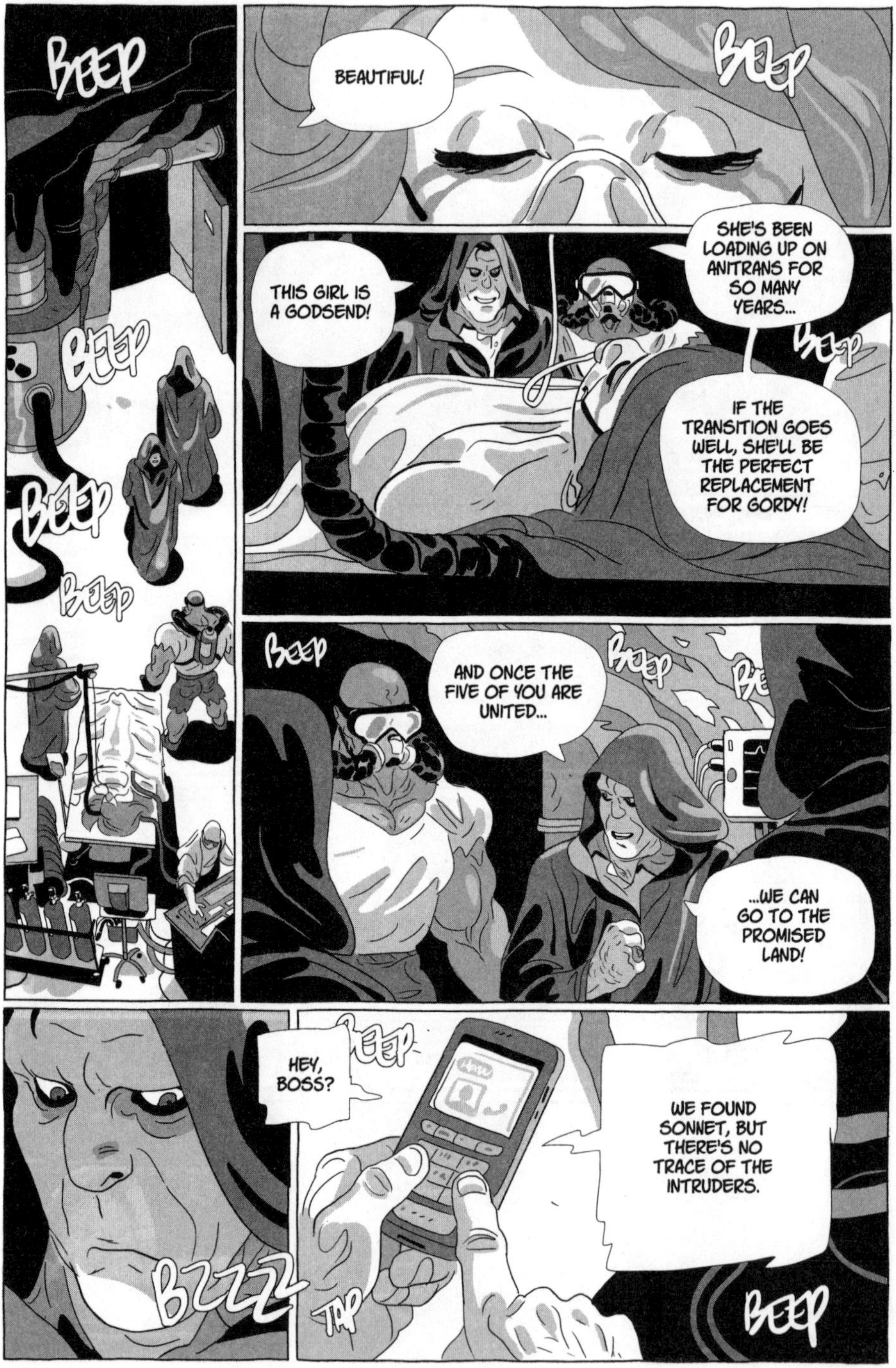
BEEP
BEEP
BEEP
BEEP
BEAUTIFUL!
BEEP
THIS GIRL IS A GODSEND!
SHE'S BEEN LOADING UP ON ANITRANS FOR SO MANY YEARS...
BEEP
IF THE TRANSITION GOES WELL, SHE'LL BE THE PERFECT REPLACEMENT FOR GORDY!
BEEP
AND ONCE THE FIVE OF YOU ARE UNITED...
BEEP
...WE CAN GO TO THE PROMISED LAND!
BZZZZ
HEY, BOSS?
BEEP
WE FOUND SONNET, BUT THERE'S NO TRACE OF THE INTRUDERS.
TAP
BEEP

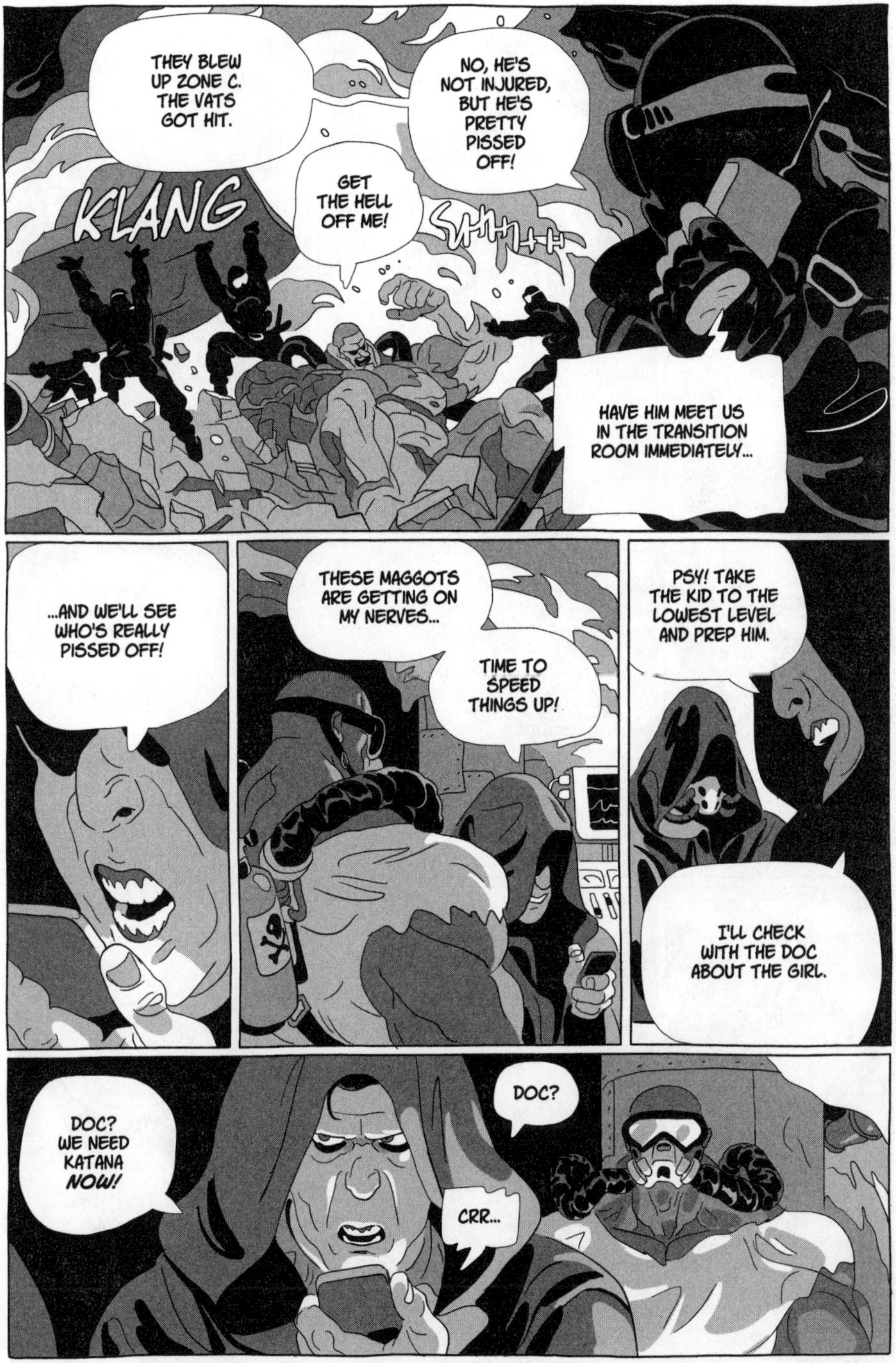
THEY BLEW UP ZONE C. THE VATS GOT HIT.
NO, HE'S NOT INJURED, BUT HE'S PRETTY PISSED OFF!
GET THE HELL OFF ME!
KLANG
HAVE HIM MEET US IN THE TRANSITION ROOM IMMEDIATELY...
...AND WE'LL SEE WHO'S REALLY PISSED OFF!
THESE MAGGOTS ARE GETTING ON MY NERVES...
TIME TO SPEED THINGS UP!
PSY! TAKE THE KID TO THE LOWEST LEVEL AND PREP HIM.
I'LL CHECK WITH THE DOC ABOUT THE GIRL.
DOC? WE NEED KATANA *NOW!*
DOC?
CRR...

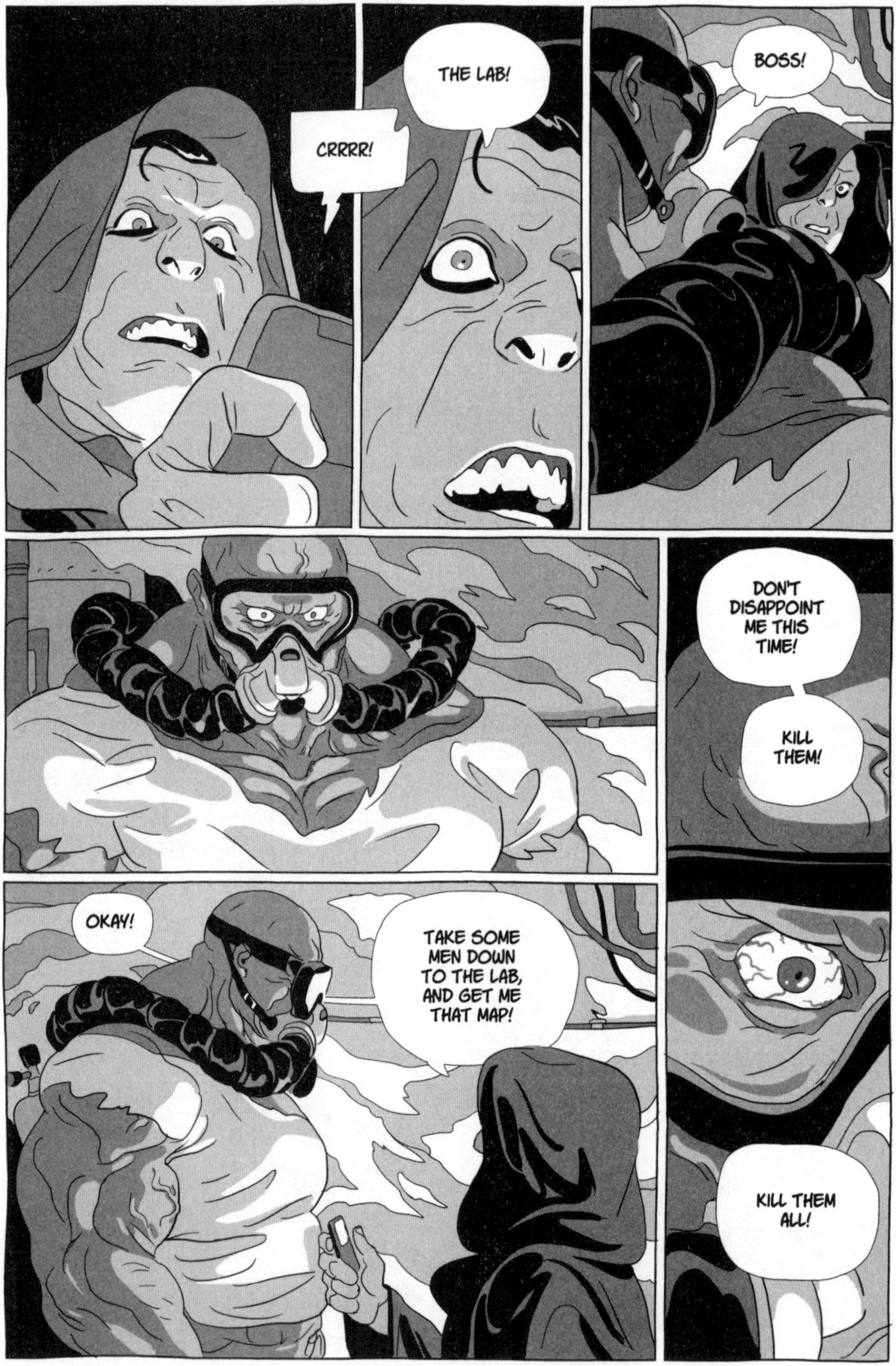
CRRRR!
THE LAB!
BOSS!
DON'T DISAPPOINT ME THIS TIME!
KILL THEM!
OKAY!
TAKE SOME MEN DOWN TO THE LAB, AND GET ME THAT MAP!
KILL THEM ALL!

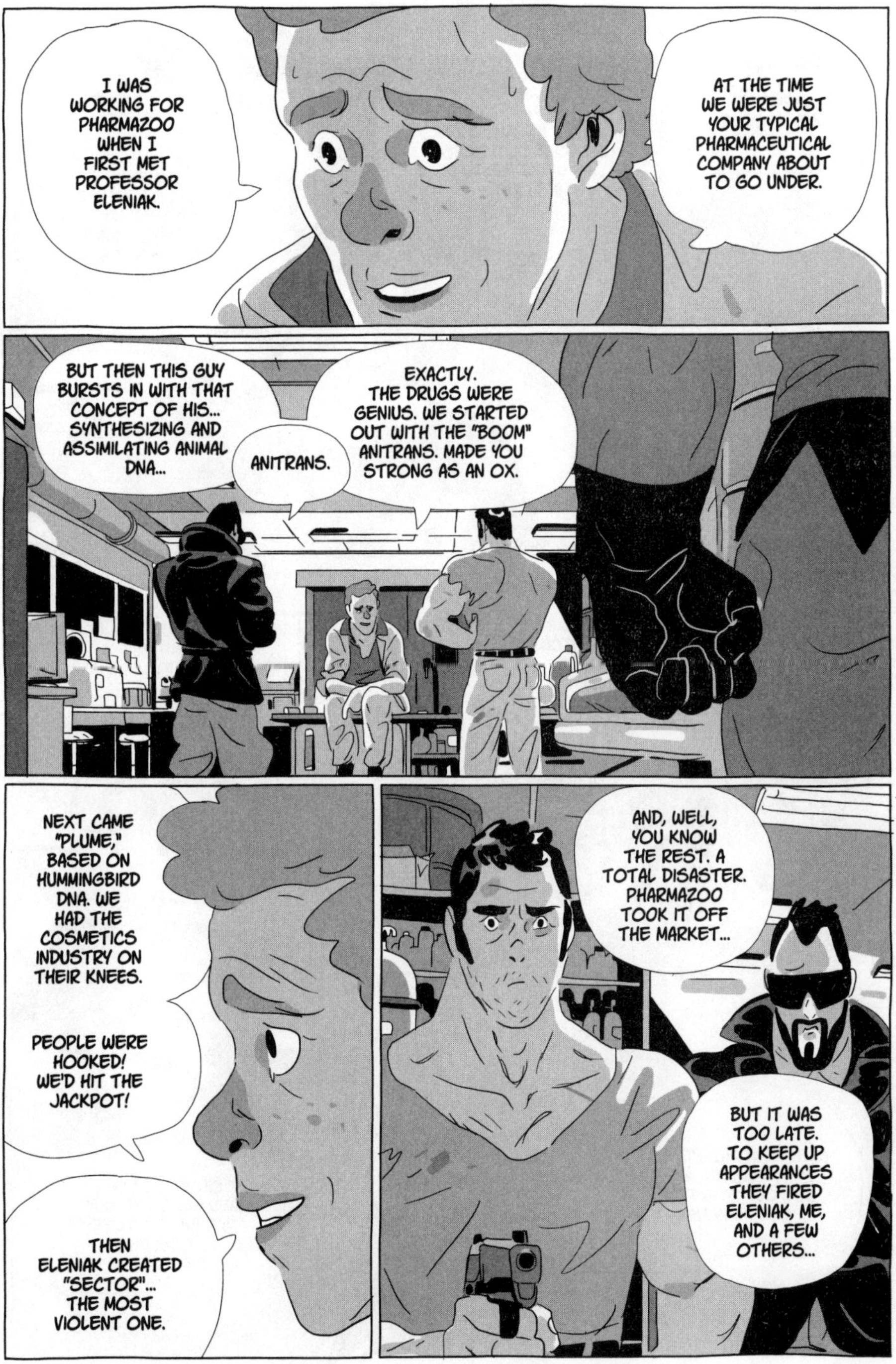
I WAS WORKING FOR PHARMAZOO WHEN I FIRST MET PROFESSOR ELENIAK.
AT THE TIME WE WERE JUST YOUR TYPICAL PHARMACEUTICAL COMPANY ABOUT TO GO UNDER.
BUT THEN THIS GUY BURSTS IN WITH THAT CONCEPT OF HIS... SYNTHESIZING AND ASSIMILATING ANIMAL DNA...
ANITRANS.
EXACTLY. THE DRUGS WERE GENIUS. WE STARTED OUT WITH THE "BOOM" ANITRANS. MADE YOU STRONG AS AN OX.
NEXT CAME "PLUME," BASED ON HUMMINGBIRD DNA. WE HAD THE COSMETICS INDUSTRY ON THEIR KNEES.
PEOPLE WERE HOOKED! WE'D HIT THE JACKPOT!
THEN ELENIAK CREATED "SECTOR"... THE MOST VIOLENT ONE.
AND, WELL, YOU KNOW THE REST. A TOTAL DISASTER. PHARMAZOO TOOK IT OFF THE MARKET...
BUT IT WAS TOO LATE. TO KEEP UP APPEARANCES THEY FIRED ELENIAK, ME, AND A FEW OTHERS...

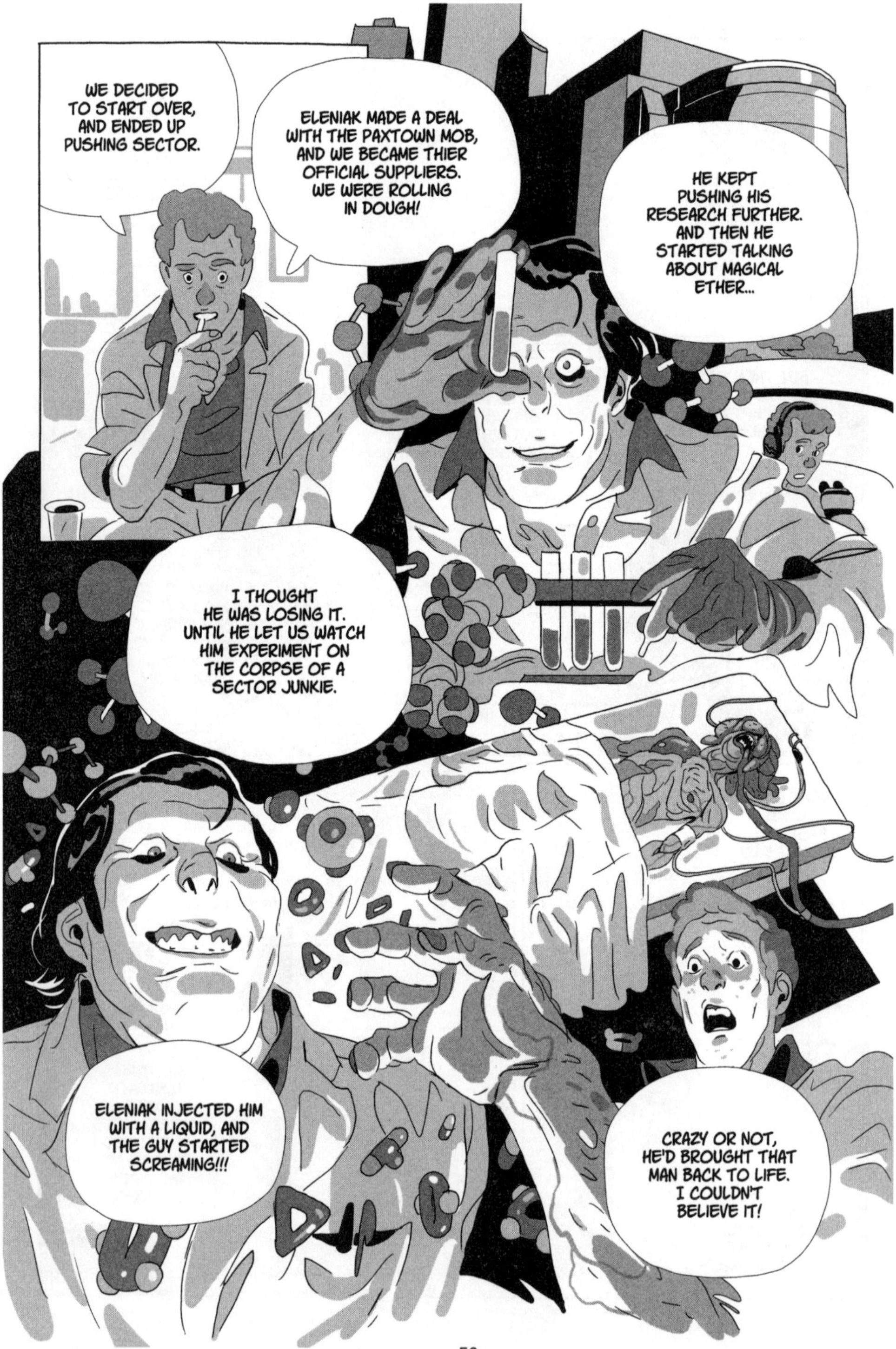
WE DECIDED TO START OVER, AND ENDED UP PUSHING SECTOR.
ELENIAK MADE A DEAL WITH THE PAXTOWN MOB, AND WE BECAME THIER OFFICIAL SUPPLIERS. WE WERE ROLLING IN DOUGH!
HE KEPT PUSHING HIS RESEARCH FURTHER. AND THEN HE STARTED TALKING ABOUT MAGICAL ETHER...
I THOUGHT HE WAS LOSING IT. UNTIL HE LET US WATCH HIM EXPERIMENT ON THE CORPSE OF A SECTOR JUNKIE.
ELENIAK INJECTED HIM WITH A LIQUID, AND THE GUY STARTED SCREAMING!!!
CRAZY OR NOT, HE'D BROUGHT THAT MAN BACK TO LIFE. I COULDN'T BELIEVE IT!

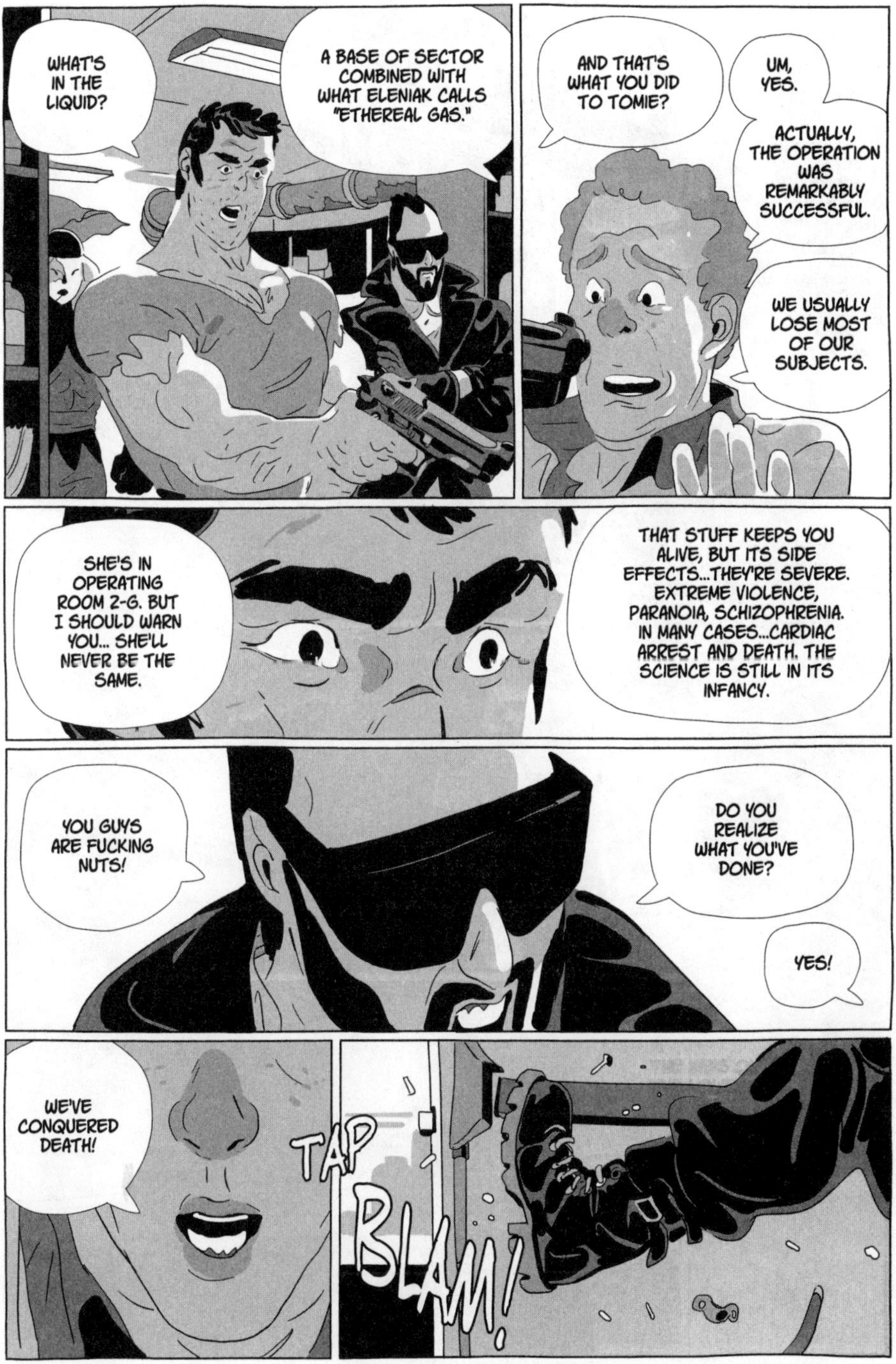
WHAT'S IN THE LIQUID?
A BASE OF SECTOR COMBINED WITH WHAT ELENIAK CALLS "ETHEREAL GAS."
AND THAT'S WHAT YOU DID TO TOMIE?
UM, YES.
ACTUALLY, THE OPERATION WAS REMARKABLY SUCCESSFUL.
WE USUALLY LOSE MOST OF OUR SUBJECTS.
SHE'S IN OPERATING ROOM 2-G. BUT I SHOULD WARN YOU... SHE'LL NEVER BE THE SAME.
THAT STUFF KEEPS YOU ALIVE, BUT ITS SIDE EFFECTS...THEY'RE SEVERE. EXTREME VIOLENCE, PARANOIA, SCHIZOPHRENIA. IN MANY CASES...CARDIAC ARREST AND DEATH. THE SCIENCE IS STILL IN ITS INFANCY.
YOU GUYS ARE FUCKING NUTS!
DO YOU REALIZE WHAT YOU'VE DONE?
YES!
WE'VE CONQUERED DEATH!
TAP
BLAM!

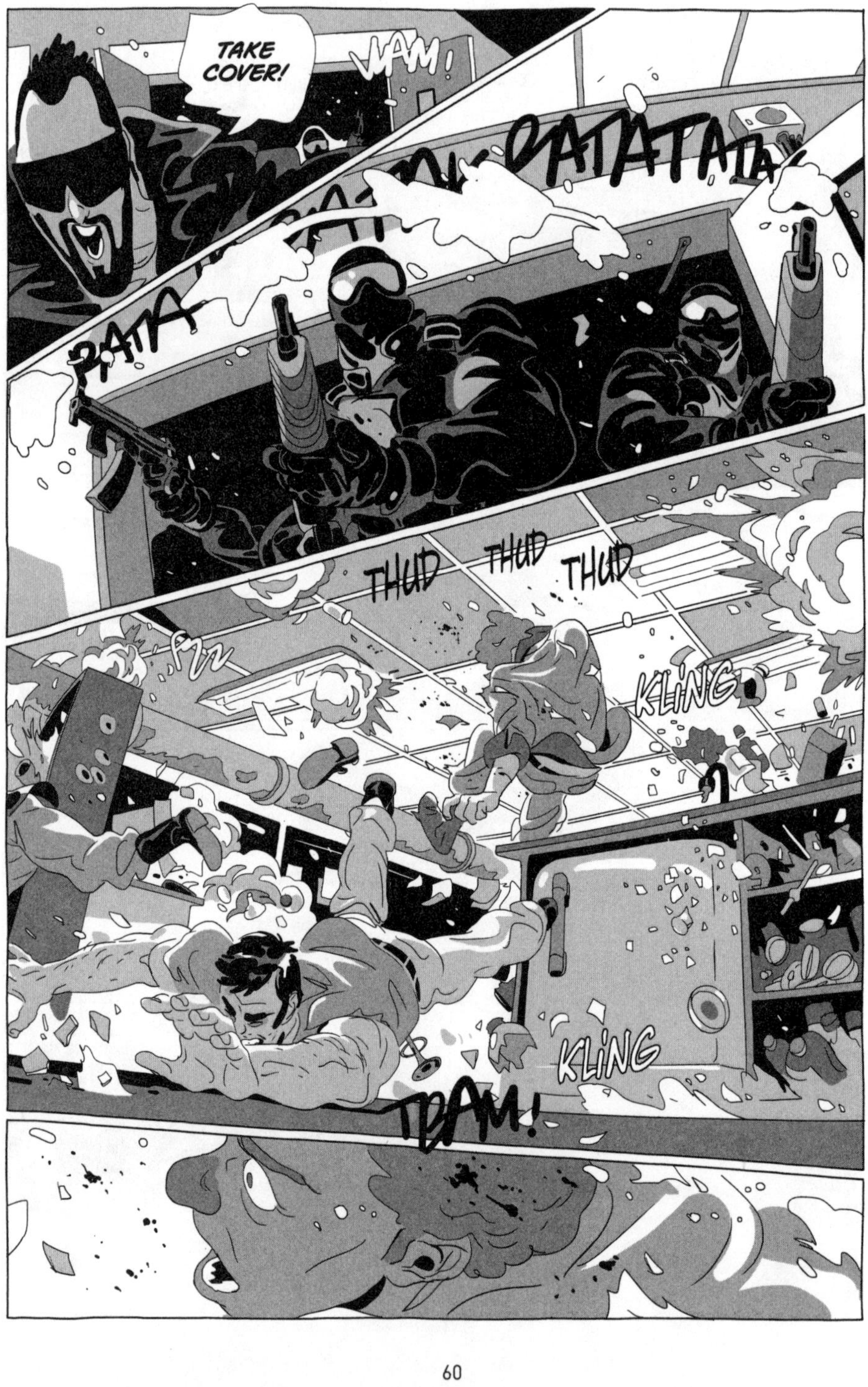
TAKE COVER!
VAM!
RATATATATA
THUD THUD THUD
KLING
KLING
TBAM!

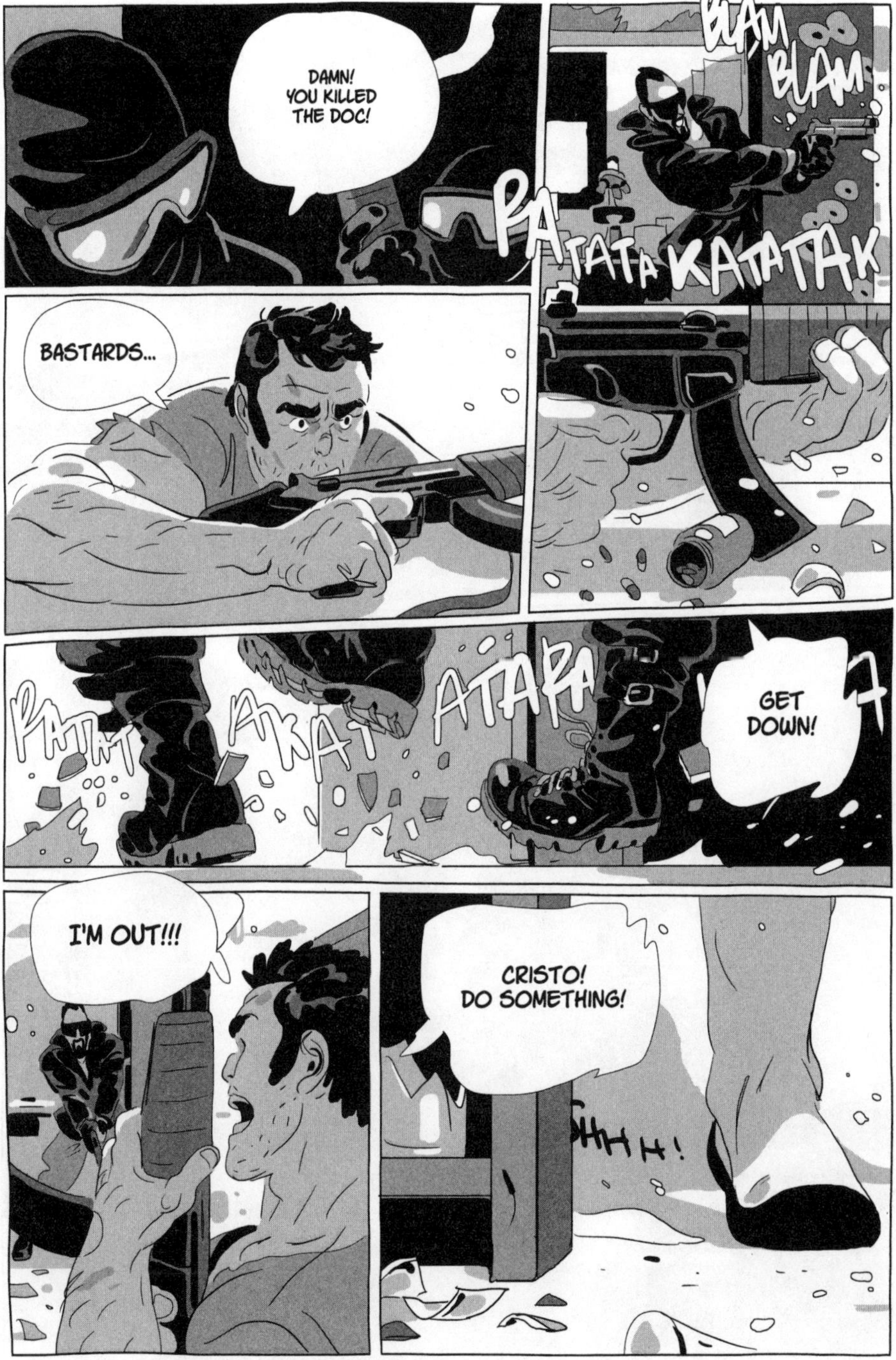
DAMN! YOU KILLED THE DOC!
BLAM BLAM
RATATA KATATAK
BASTARDS...
RATATAT AKAT ATARA
GET DOWN!
I'M OUT!!!
CRISTO! DO SOMETHING!

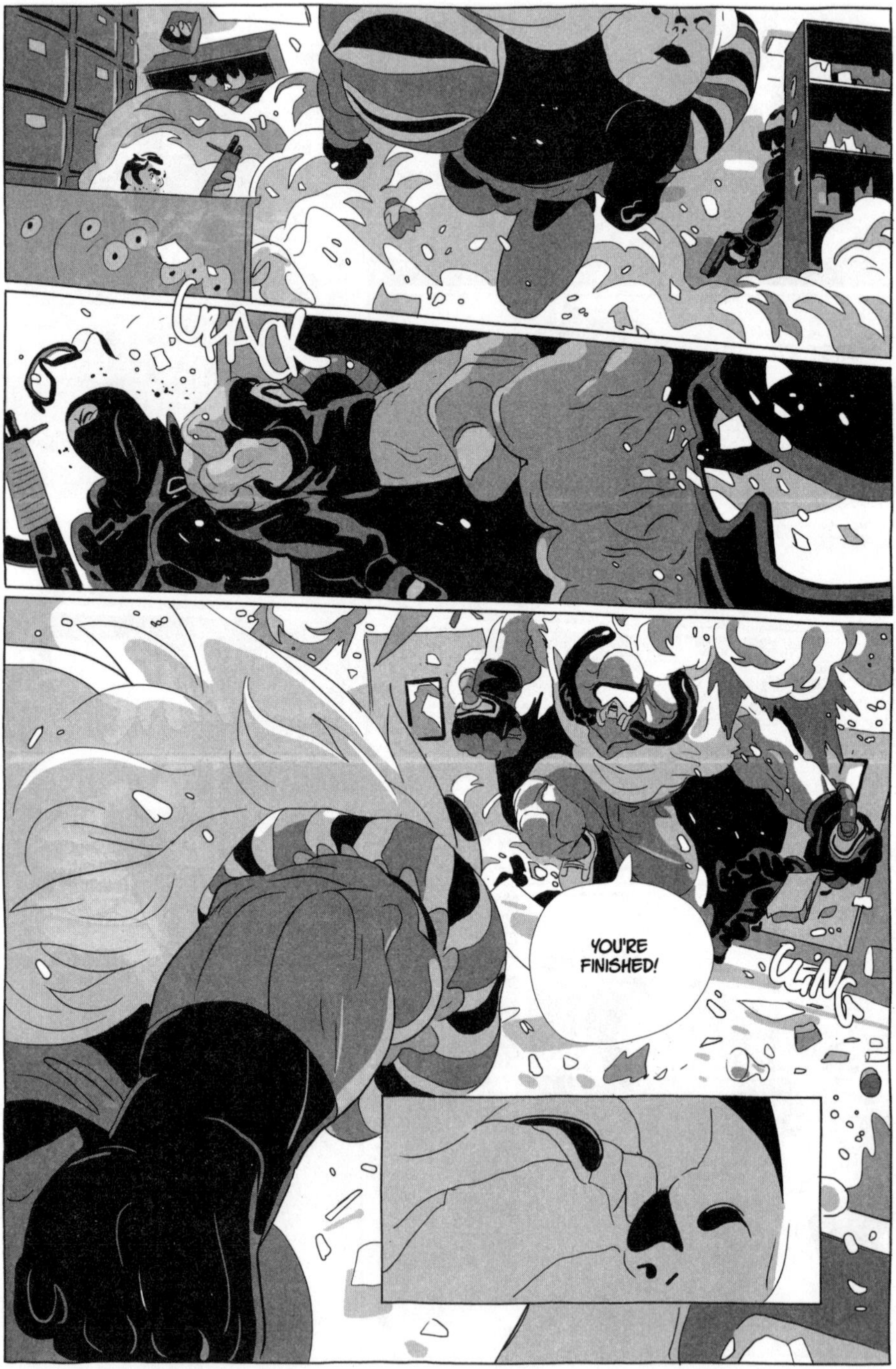
CRACK
YOU'RE FINISHED!
CLING

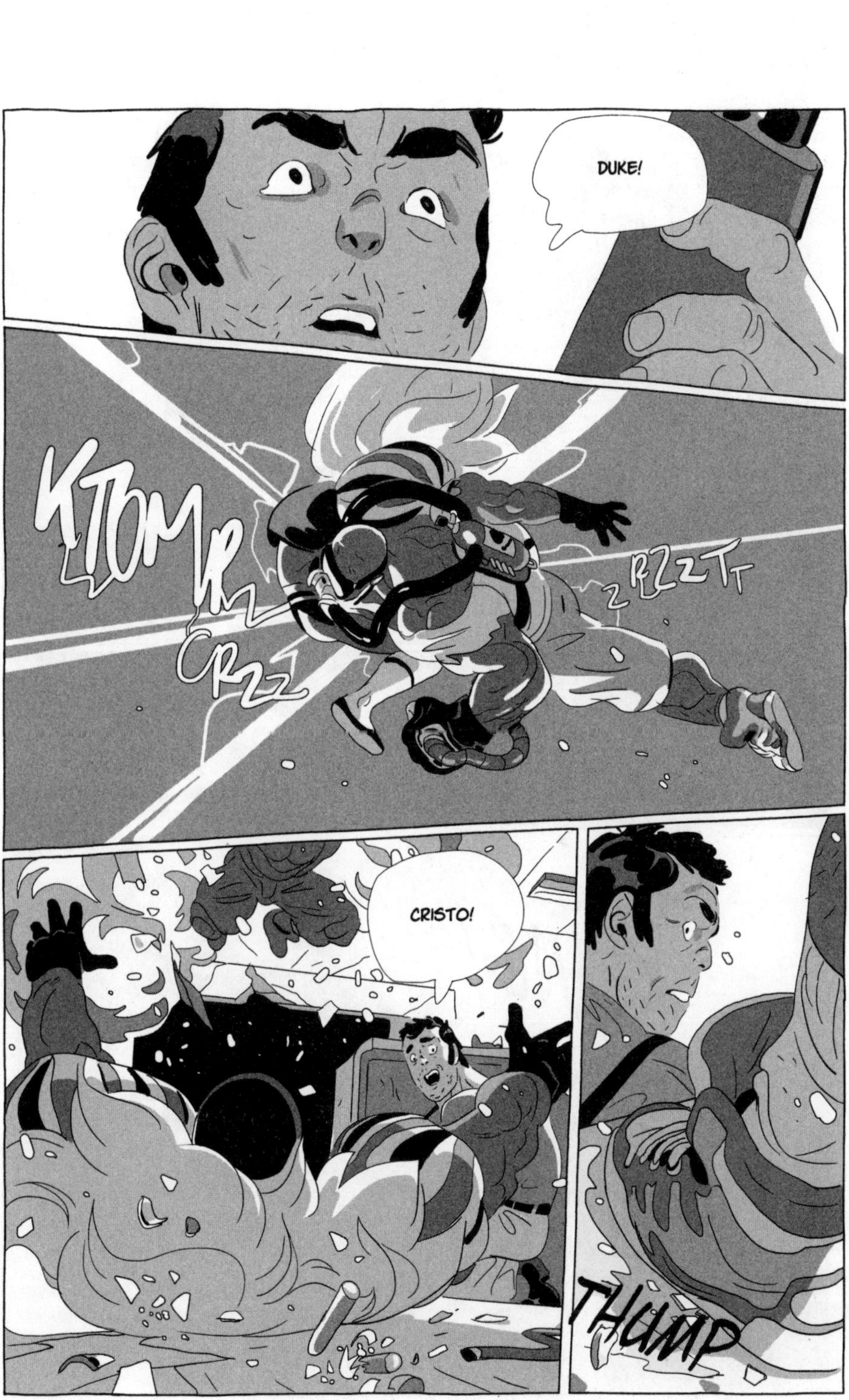
DUKE!
KTOM
VRZZ
CRZZZ
ZRZZTT
CRISTO!
THUMP

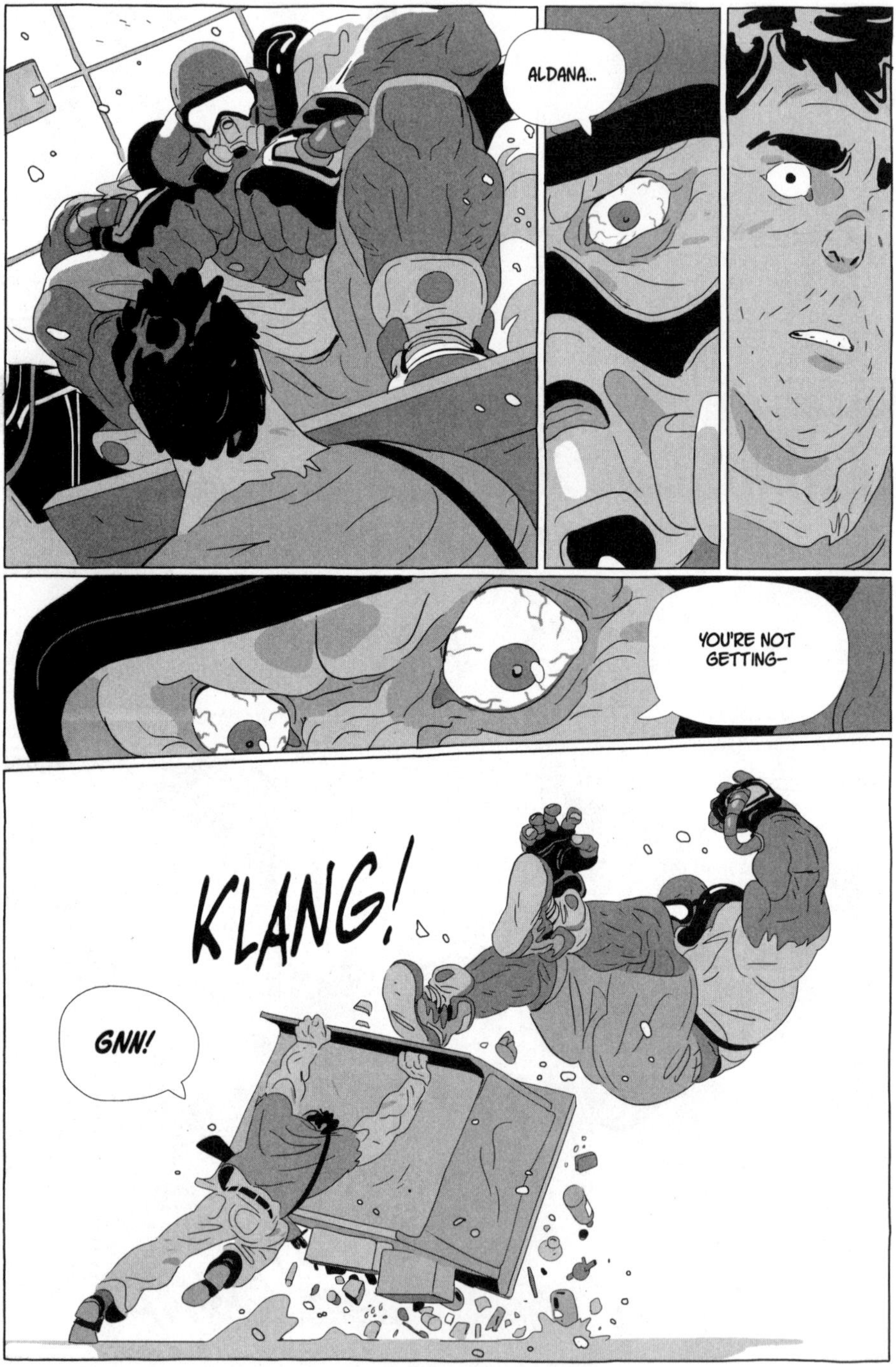
ALDANA...
YOU'RE NOT GETTING–
KLANG!
GNN!

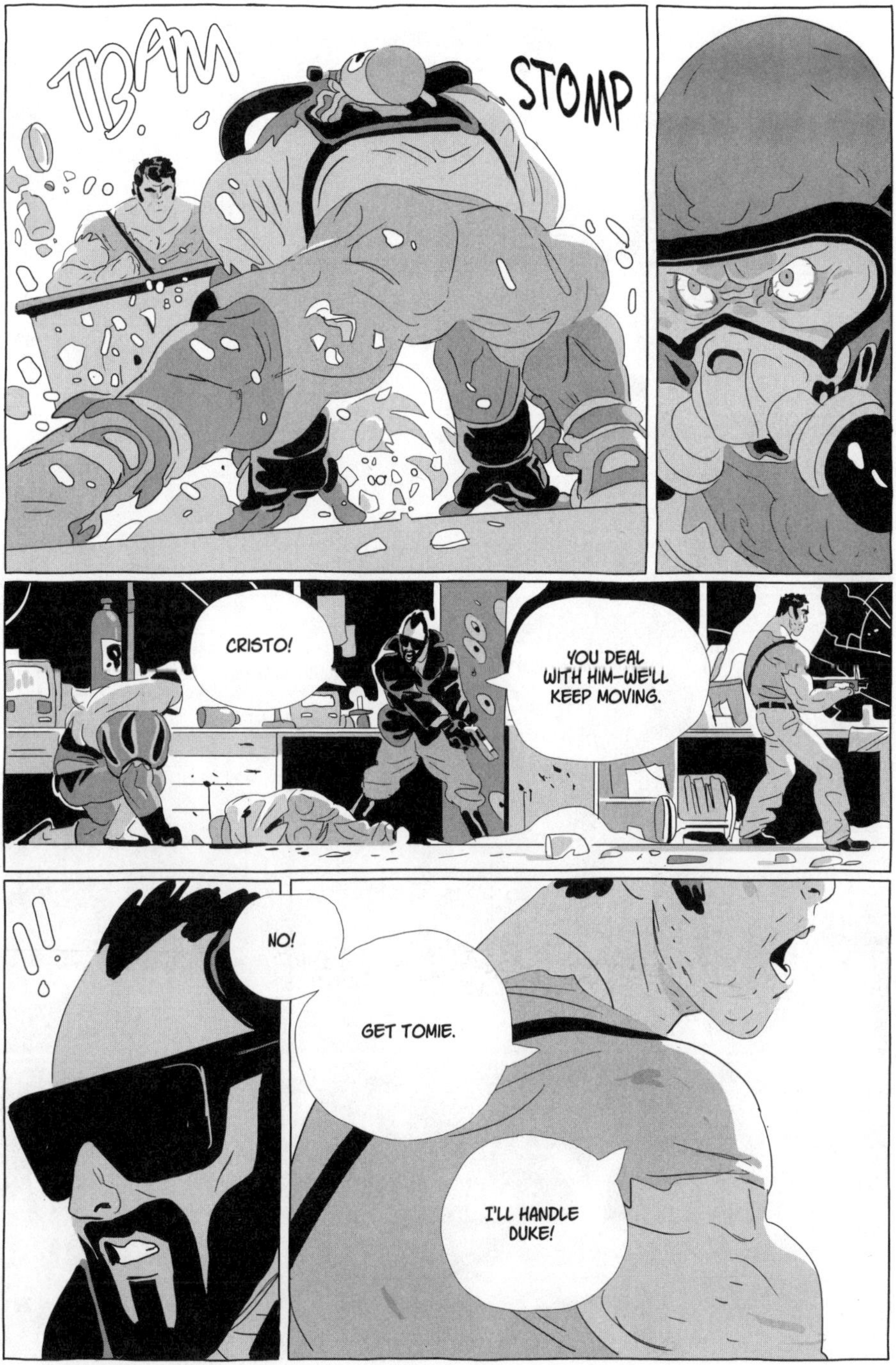
TBAM
STOMP
CRISTO!
YOU DEAL WITH HIM—WE'LL KEEP MOVING.
!!
NO!
GET TOMIE.
I'LL HANDLE DUKE!

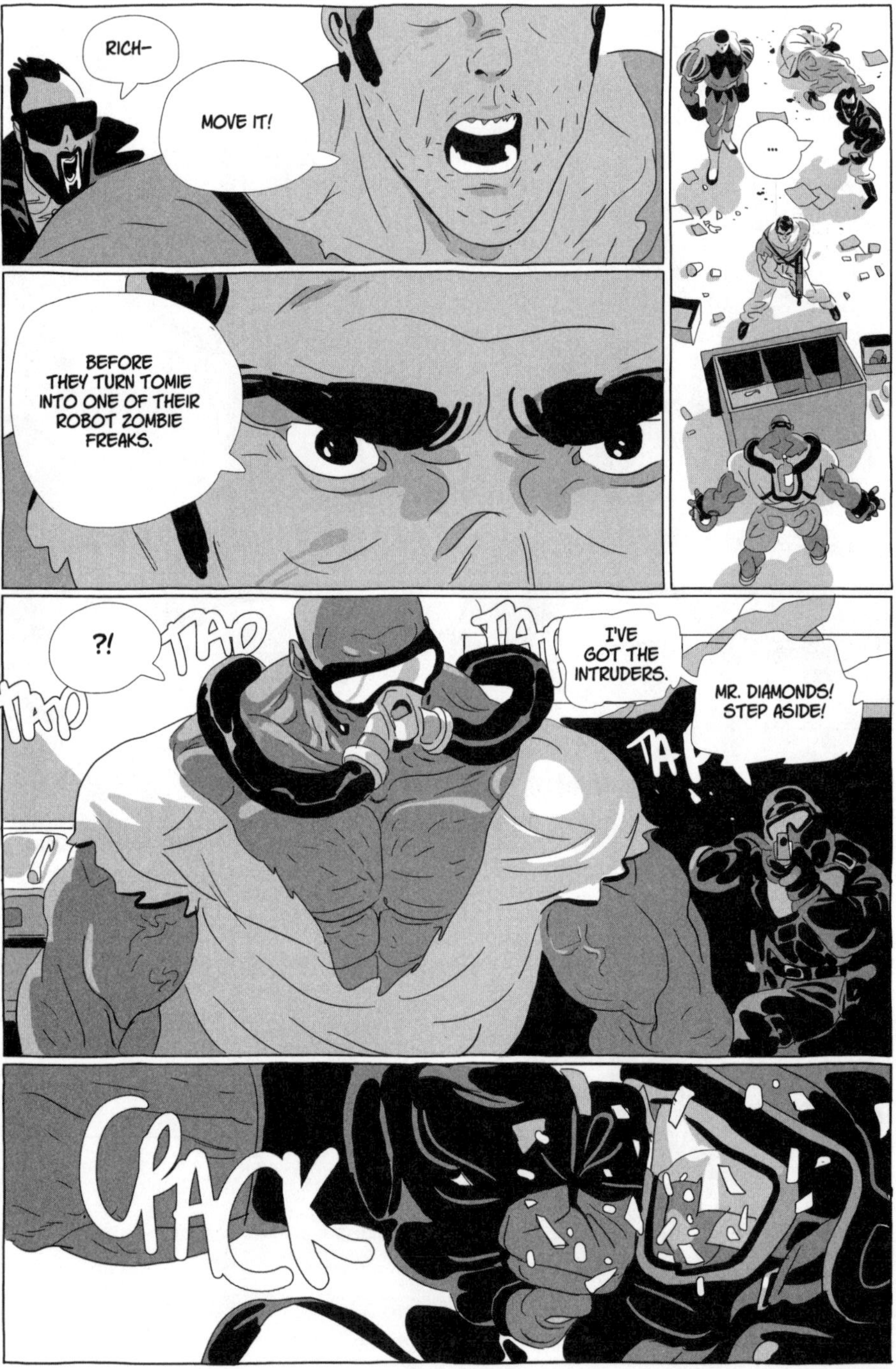
RICH-
MOVE IT!
...
BEFORE THEY TURN TOMIE INTO ONE OF THEIR ROBOT ZOMBIE FREAKS.
?!
TAP TAP
TAP
I'VE GOT THE INTRUDERS.
MR. DIAMONDS! STEP ASIDE!
TAP
CRACK

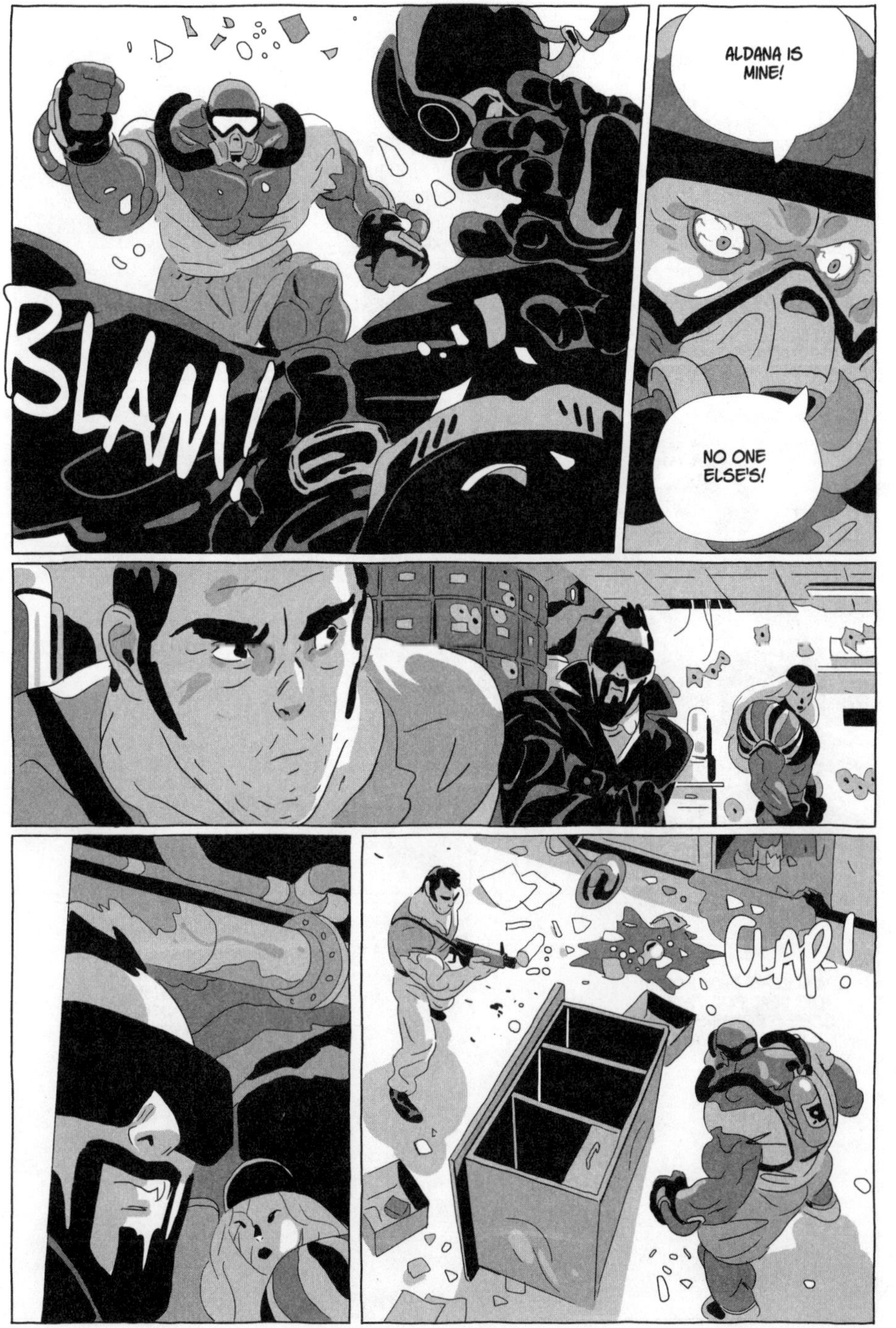
BLAM!
ALDANA IS MINE!
NO ONE ELSE'S!
CLAP!

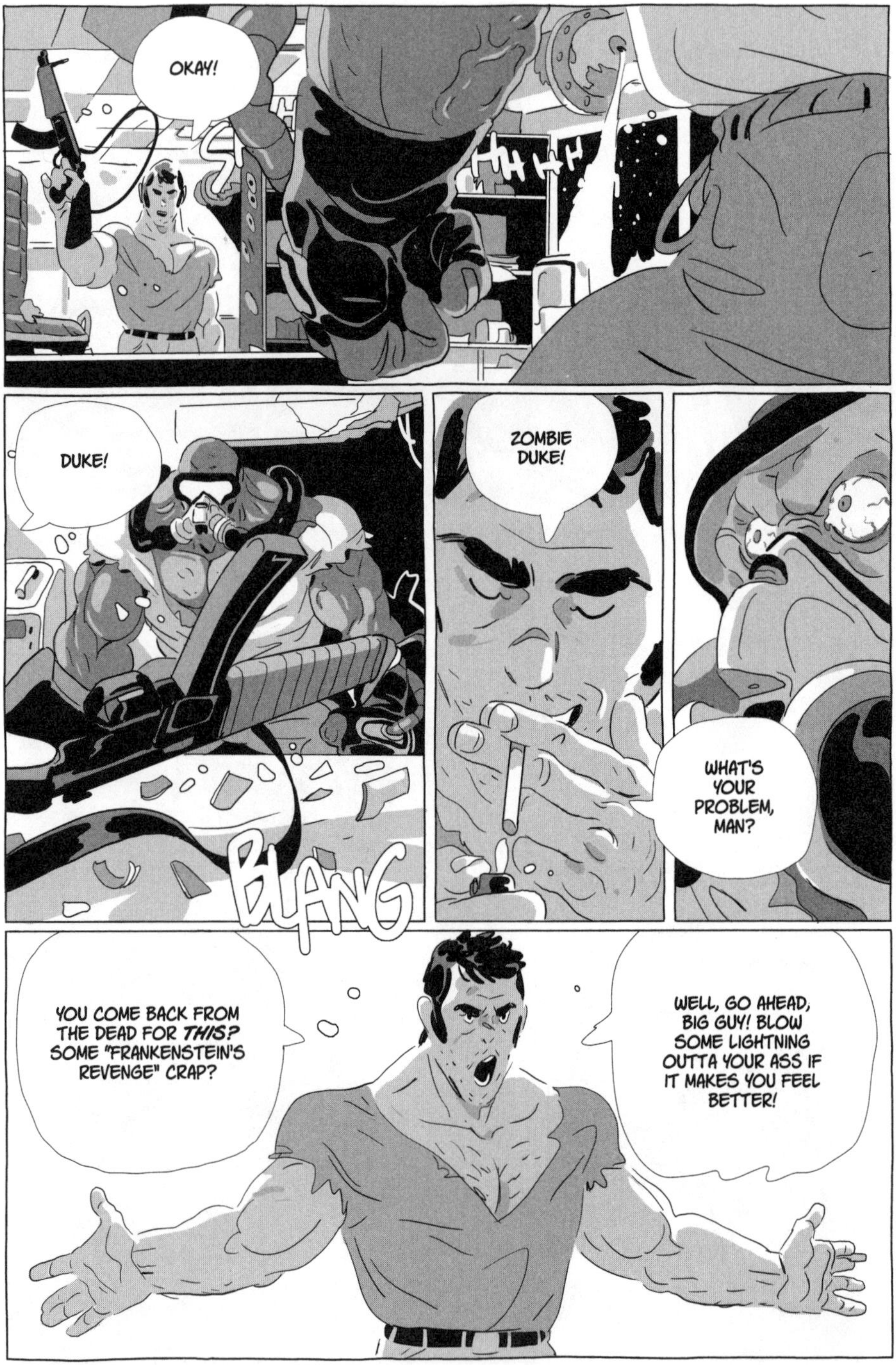
OKAY!
DUKE!
BLANG
ZOMBIE DUKE!
WHAT'S YOUR PROBLEM, MAN?
YOU COME BACK FROM THE DEAD FOR *THIS?* SOME "FRANKENSTEIN'S REVENGE" CRAP?
WELL, GO AHEAD, BIG GUY! BLOW SOME LIGHTNING OUTTA YOUR ASS IF IT MAKES YOU FEEL BETTER!

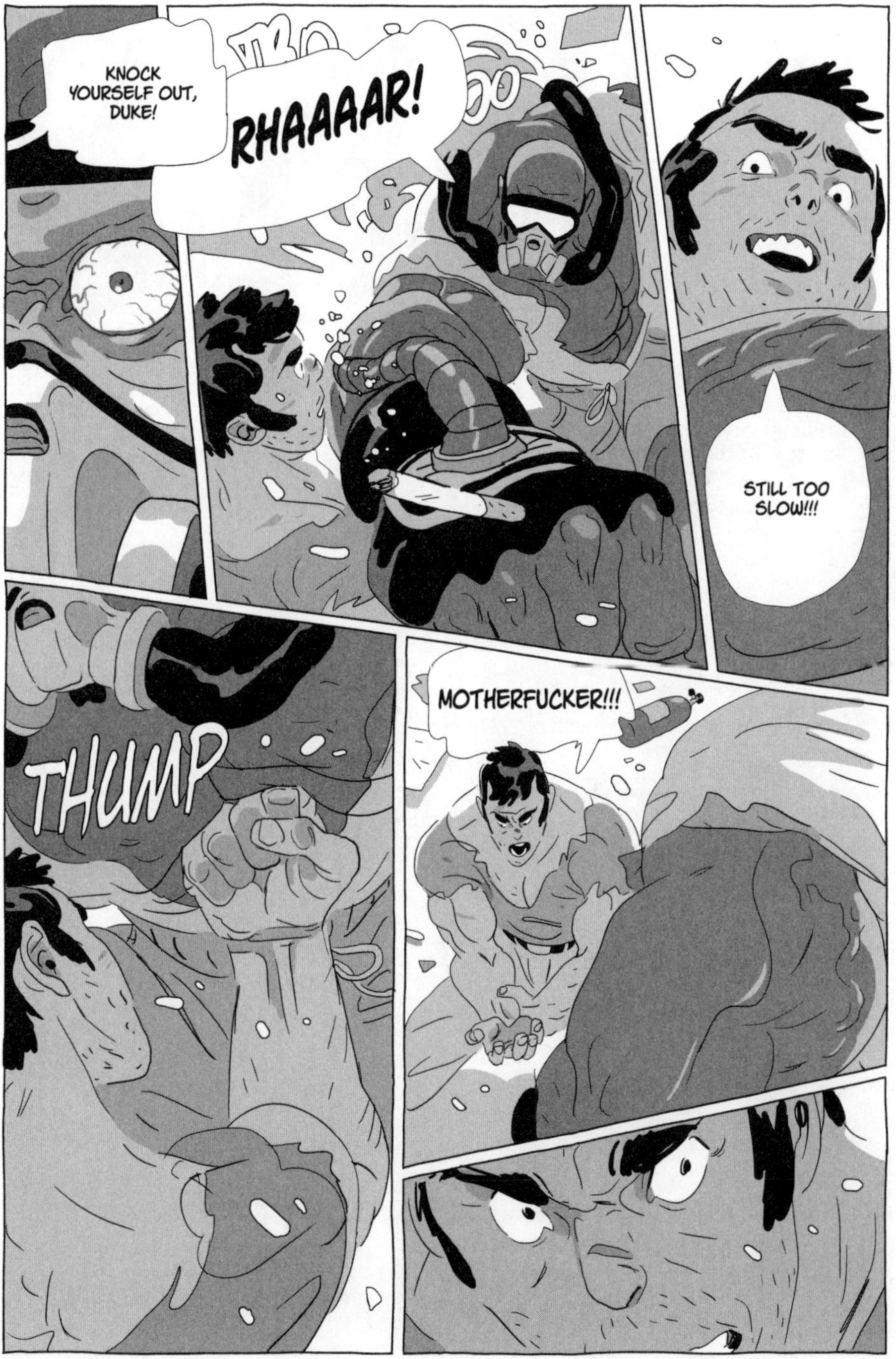
KNOCK YOURSELF OUT, DUKE!
RHAAAAR!
STILL TOO SLOW!!!
THUMP
MOTHERFUCKER!!!

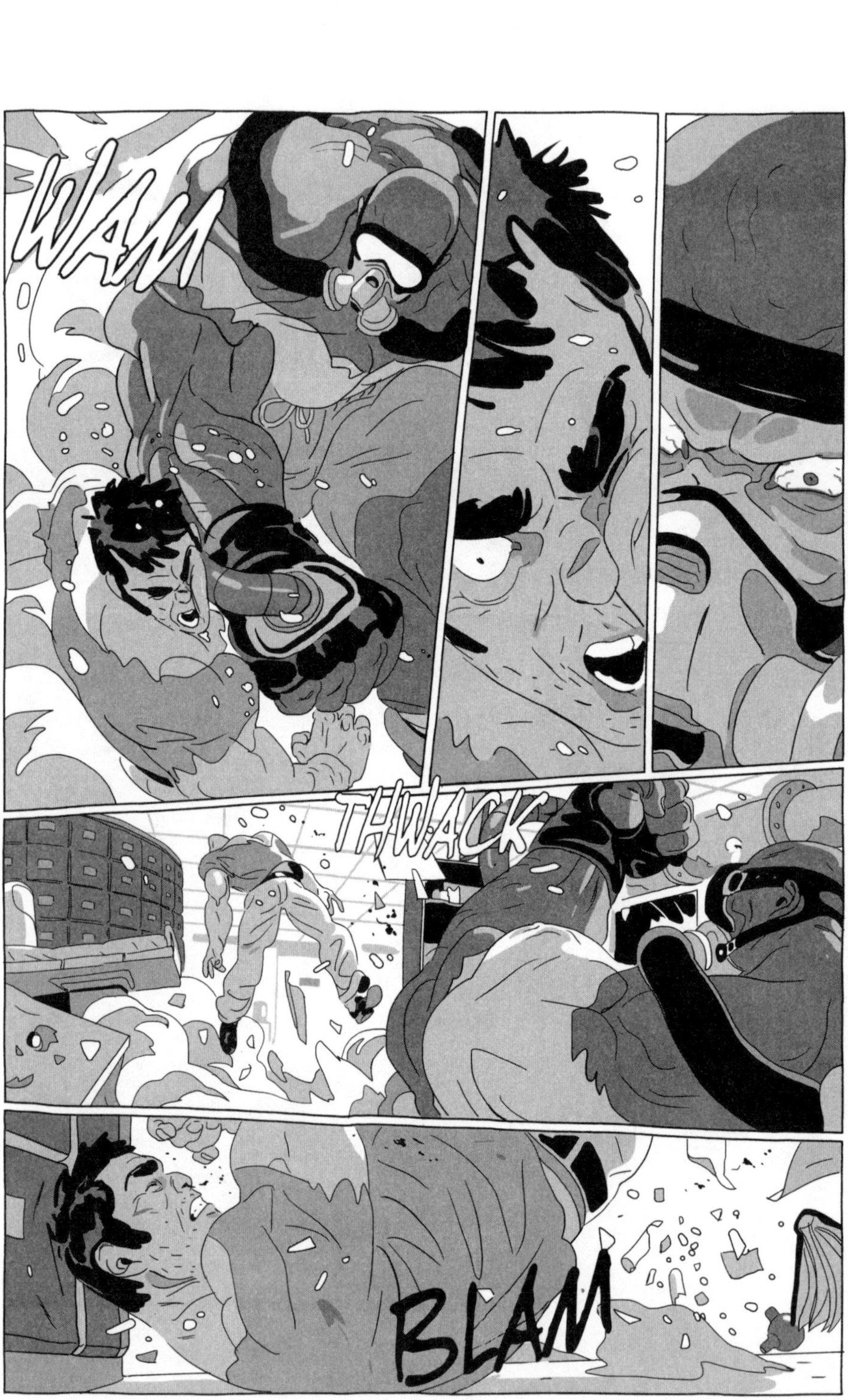
WAM
THWACK
BLAM

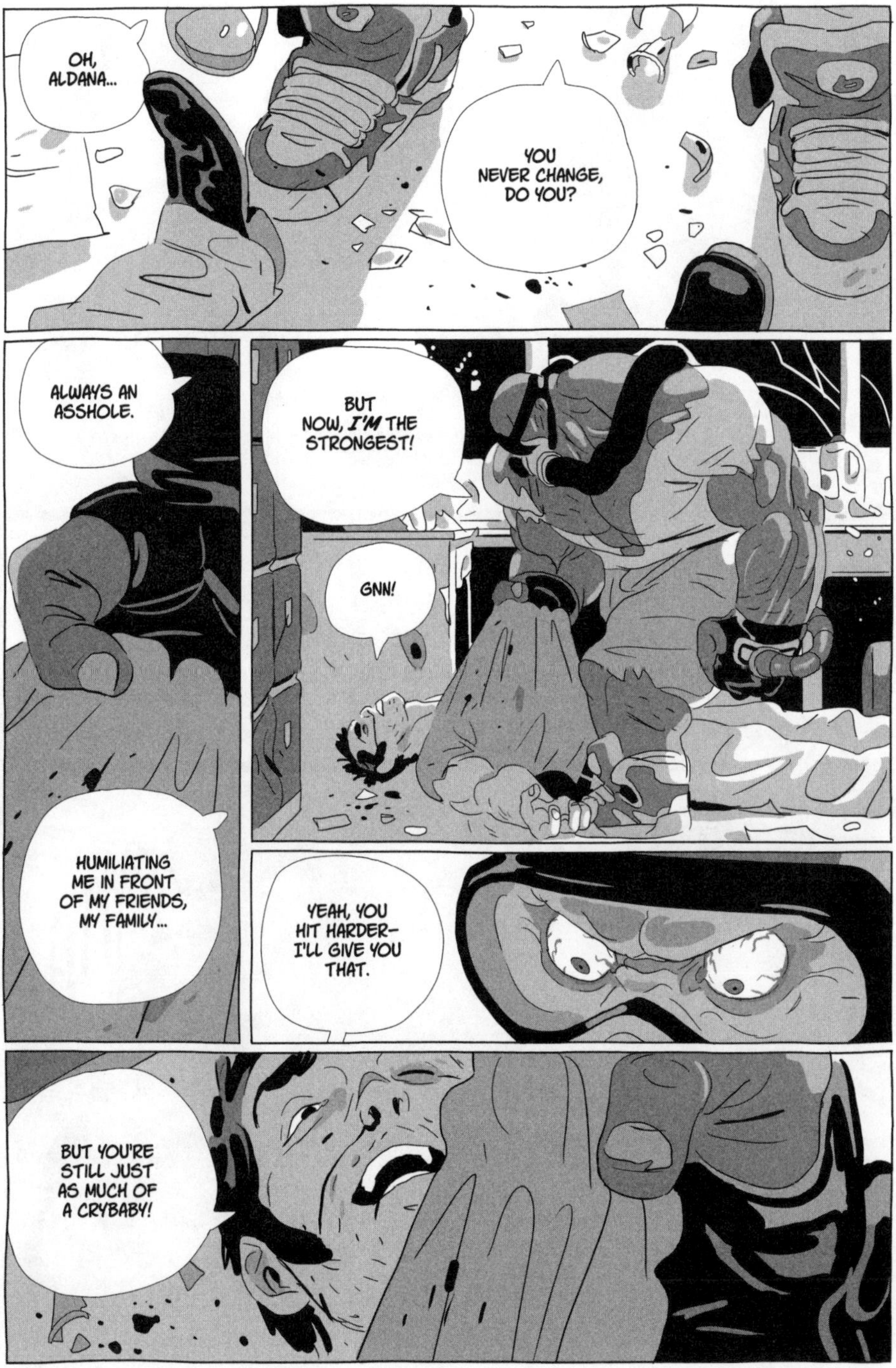
OH, ALDANA...
YOU NEVER CHANGE, DO YOU?
ALWAYS AN ASSHOLE.
HUMILIATING ME IN FRONT OF MY FRIENDS, MY FAMILY...
BUT NOW, *I'M* THE STRONGEST!
GNN!
YEAH, YOU HIT HARDER– I'LL GIVE YOU THAT.
BUT YOU'RE STILL JUST AS MUCH OF A CRYBABY!

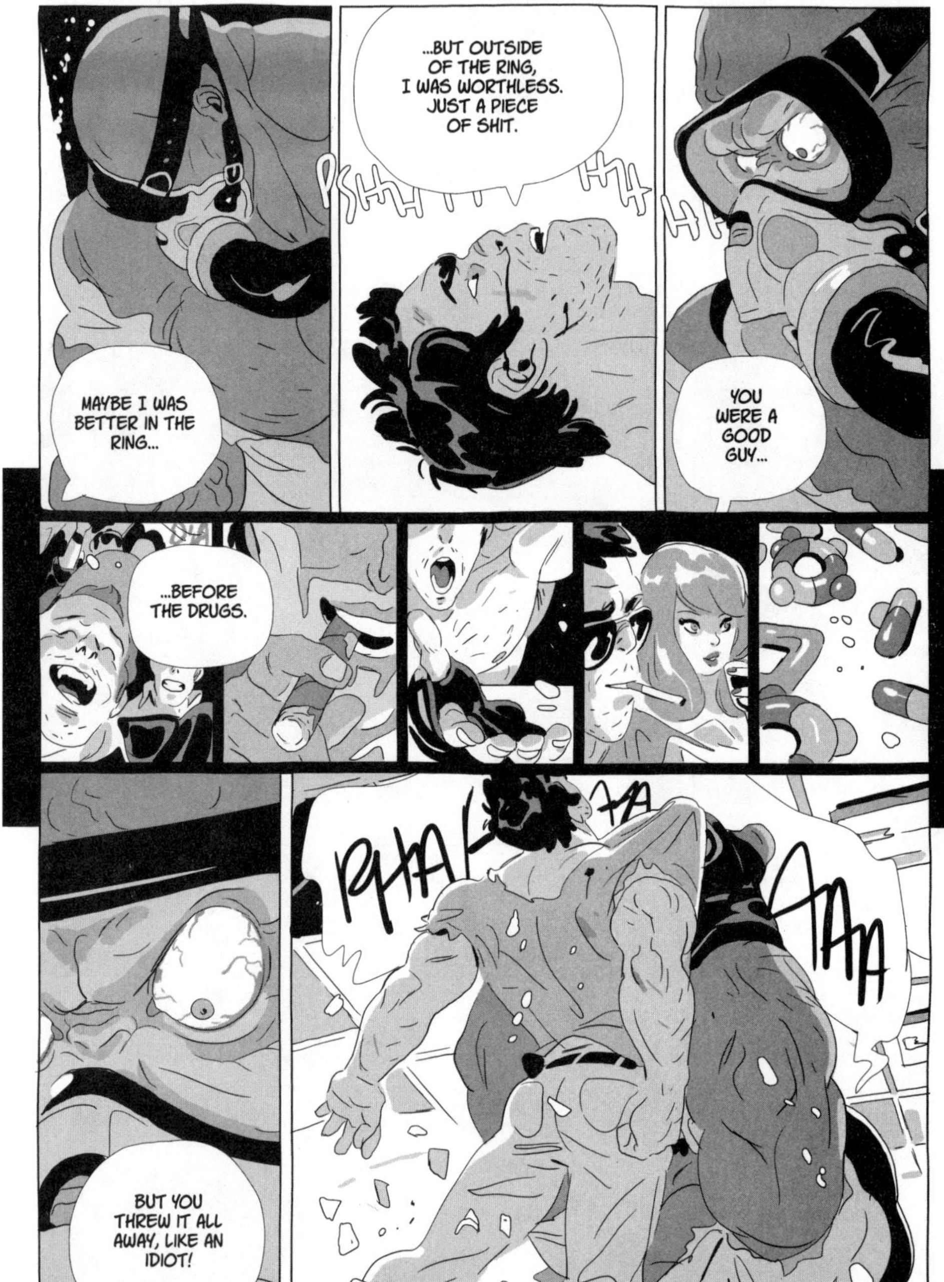
MAYBE I WAS BETTER IN THE RING...
...BUT OUTSIDE OF THE RING, I WAS WORTHLESS. JUST A PIECE OF SHIT.
YOU WERE A GOOD GUY...
...BEFORE THE DRUGS.
BUT YOU THREW IT ALL AWAY, LIKE AN IDIOT!
PHAA

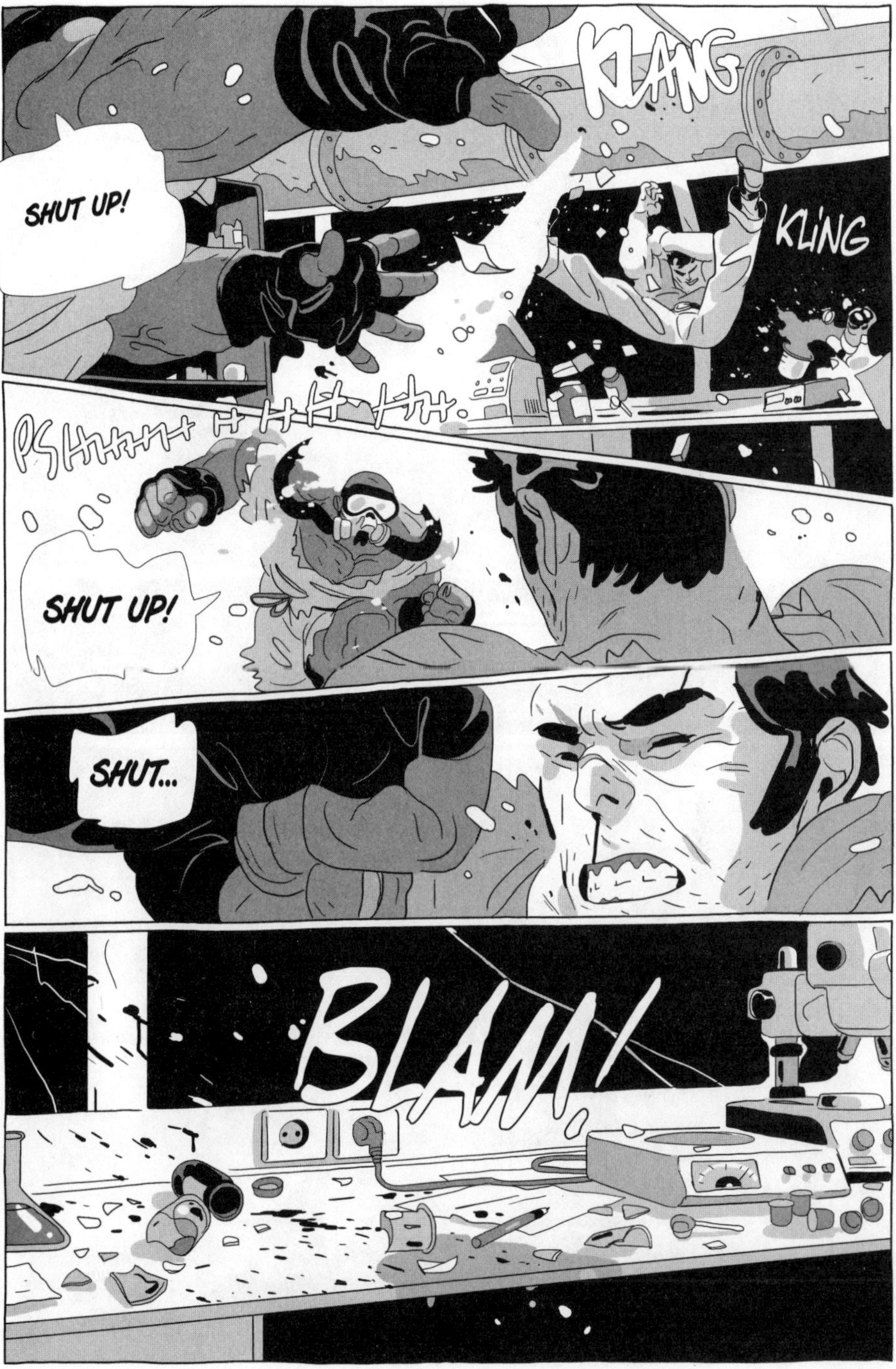
SHUT UP!
KLANG
KLING
PSHHH…
SHUT UP!
SHUT...
BLAM!

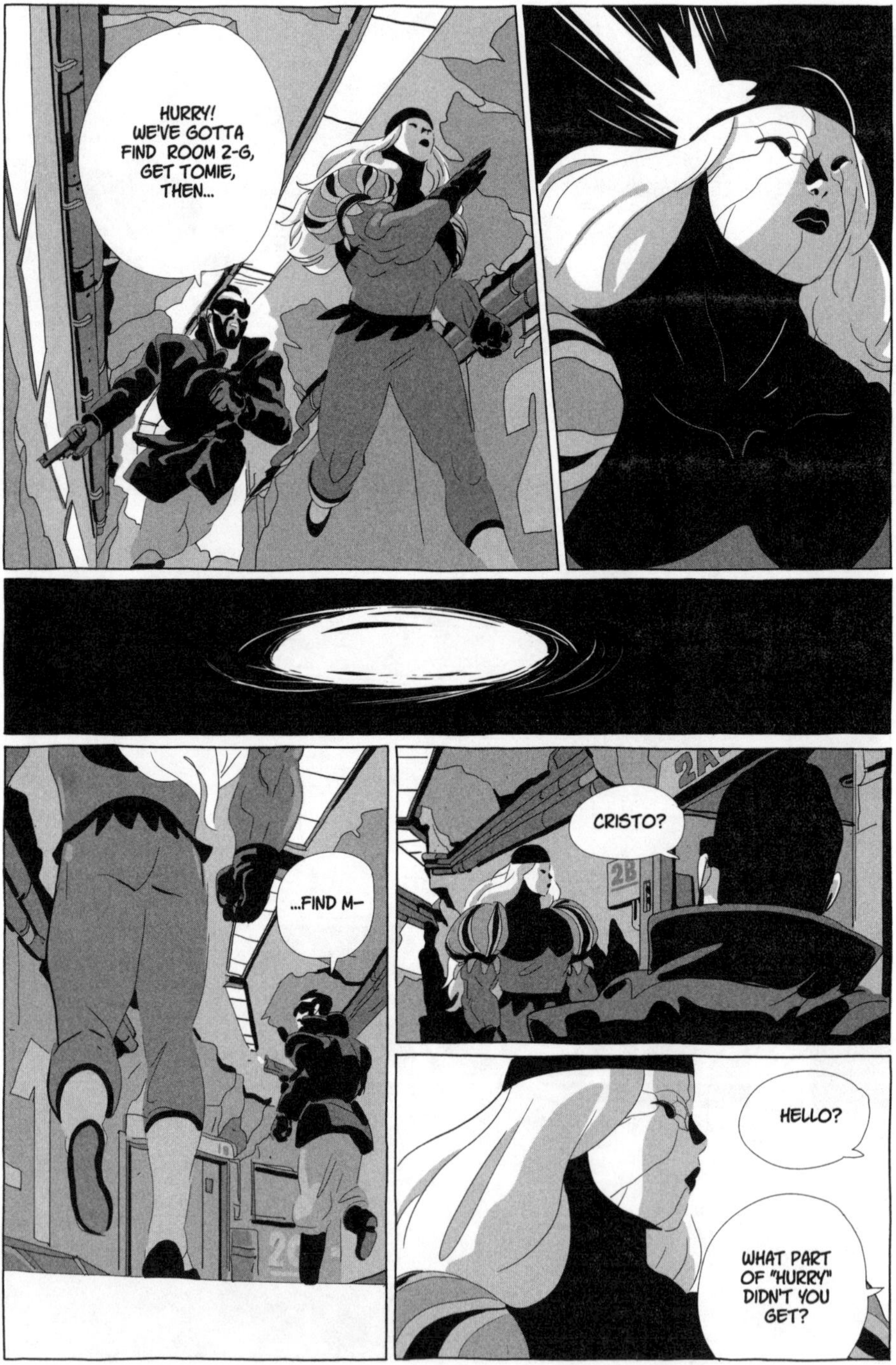
HURRY! WE'VE GOTTA FIND ROOM 2-G, GET TOMIE, THEN...
...FIND M—
CRISTO?
2B
HELLO?
WHAT PART OF "HURRY" DIDN'T YOU GET?

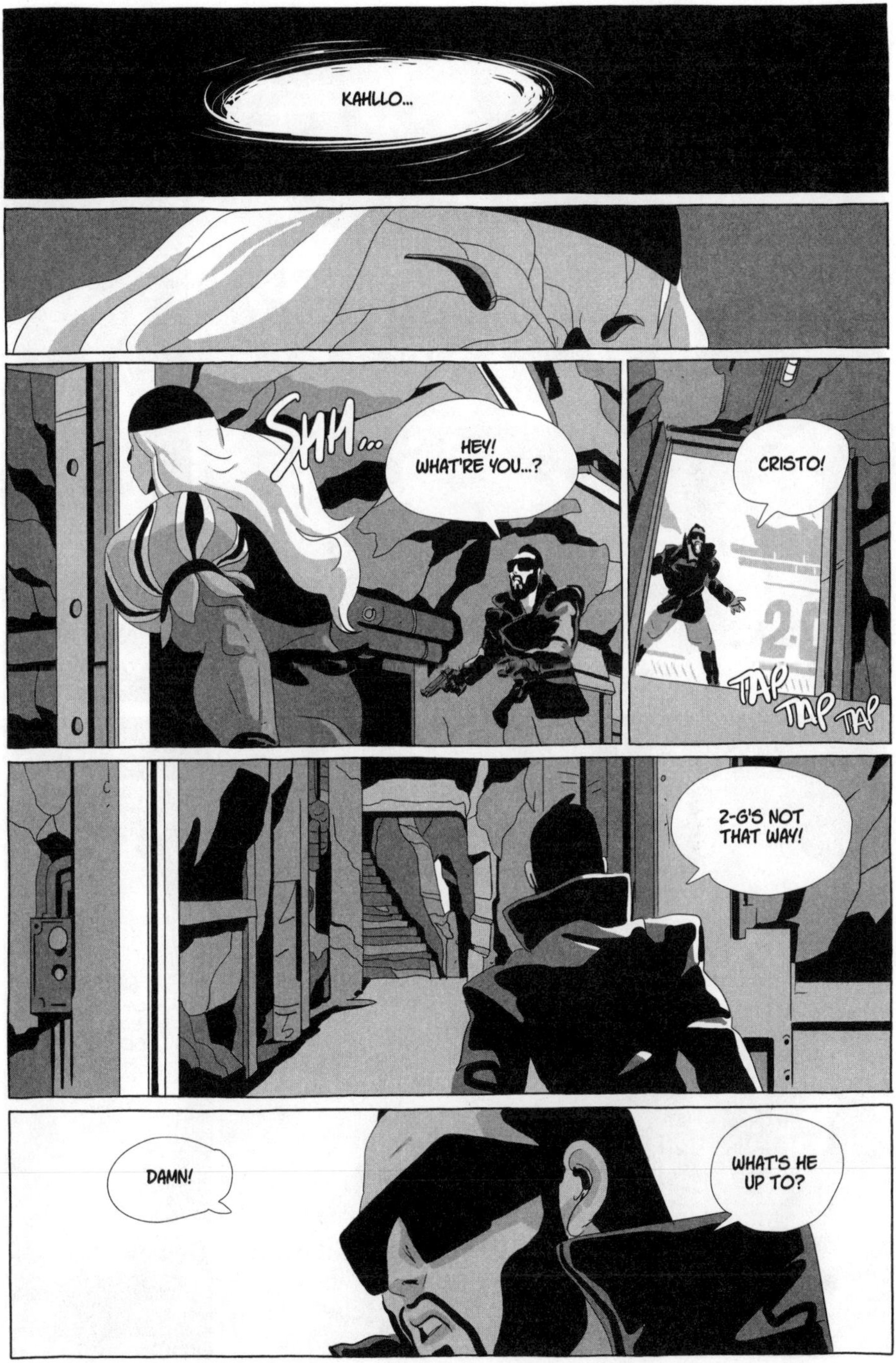

KAHLLO...
SHH...
HEY! WHAT'RE YOU...?
CRISTO!
TAP TAP TAP
2-G'S NOT THAT WAY!
DAMN!
WHAT'S HE UP TO?

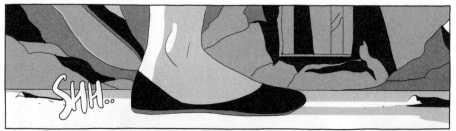

SHH..

TAP   TAP

KAHLLO...

WOLF OF THE EAST... SO FAR FROM YOUR PACK...

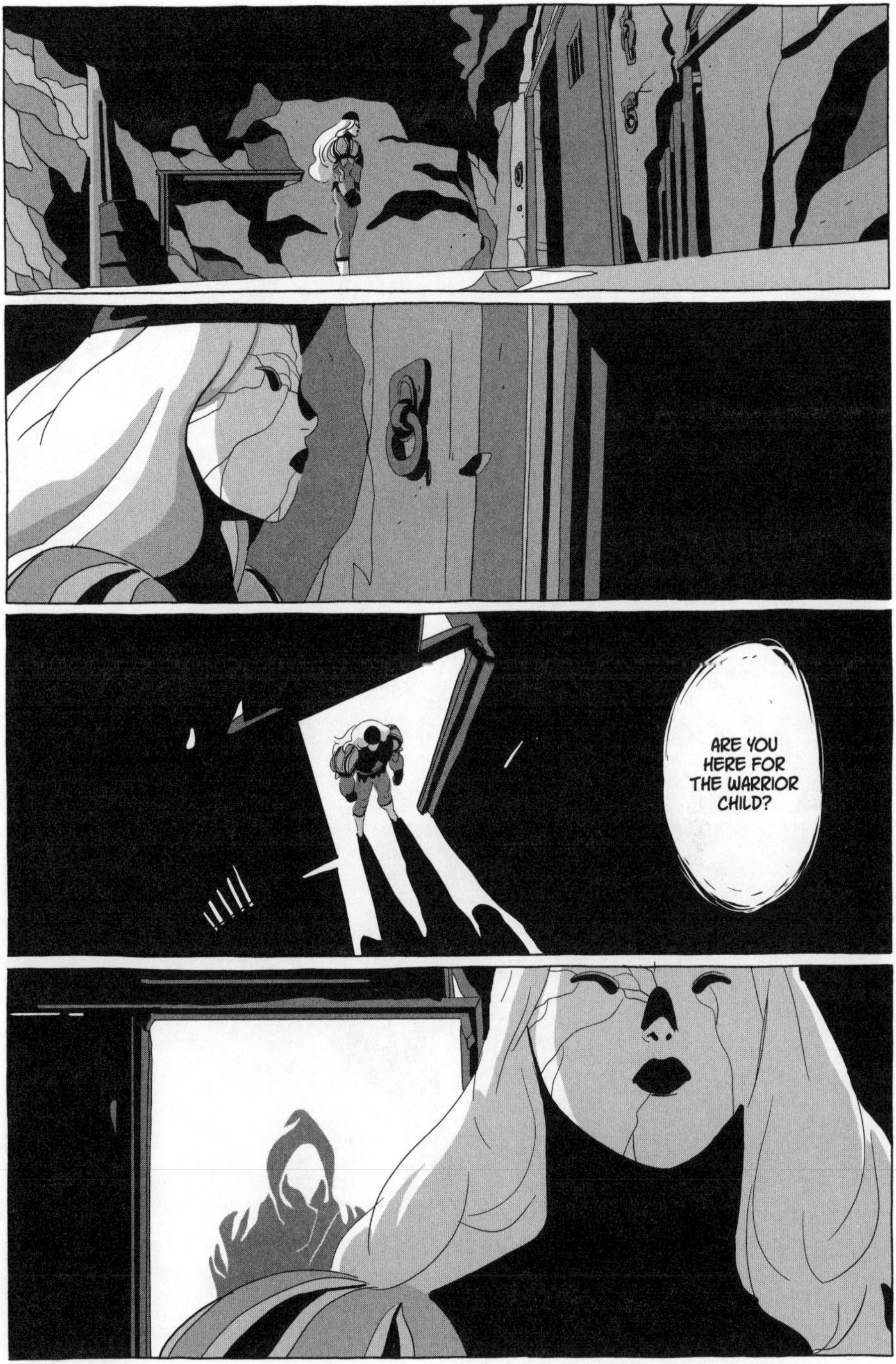
ARE YOU HERE FOR THE WARRIOR CHILD?

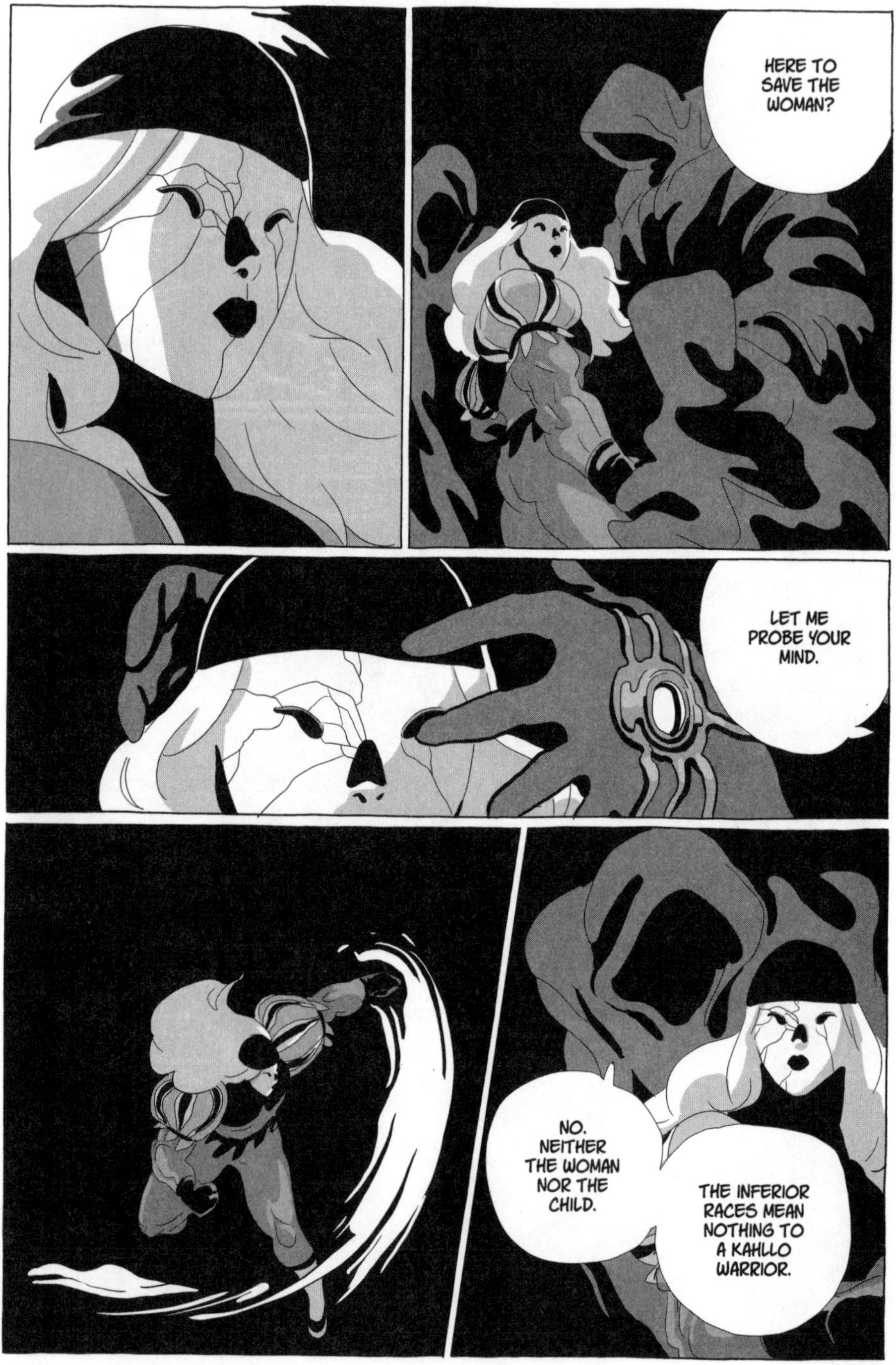
HERE TO SAVE THE WOMAN?
LET ME PROBE YOUR MIND.
NO. NEITHER THE WOMAN NOR THE CHILD.
THE INFERIOR RACES MEAN NOTHING TO A KAHLLO WARRIOR.

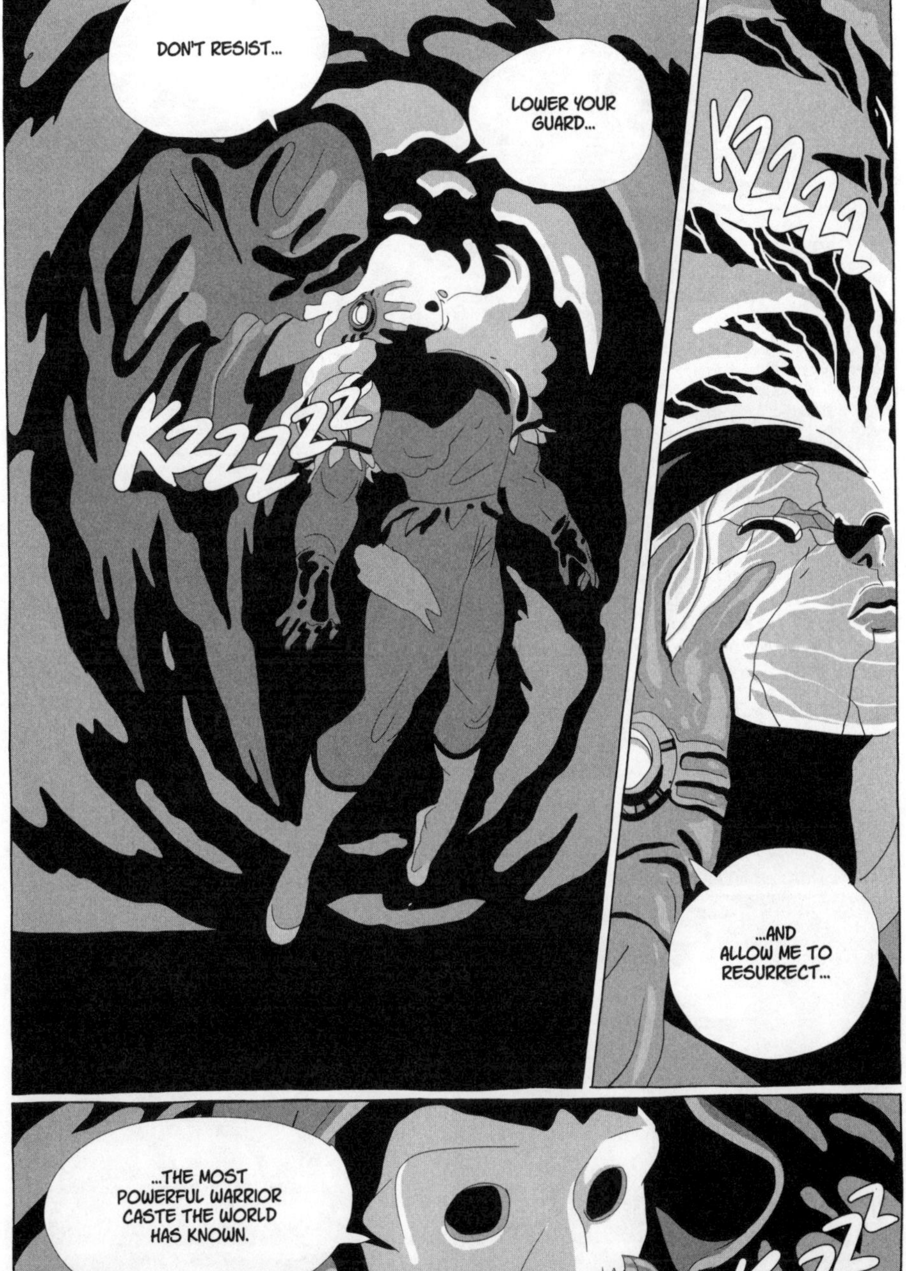
DON'T RESIST...
LOWER YOUR GUARD...
KZZZZZ
KZZZZZ
...AND ALLOW ME TO RESURRECT...
...THE MOST POWERFUL WARRIOR CASTE THE WORLD HAS KNOWN.
KZZZZ

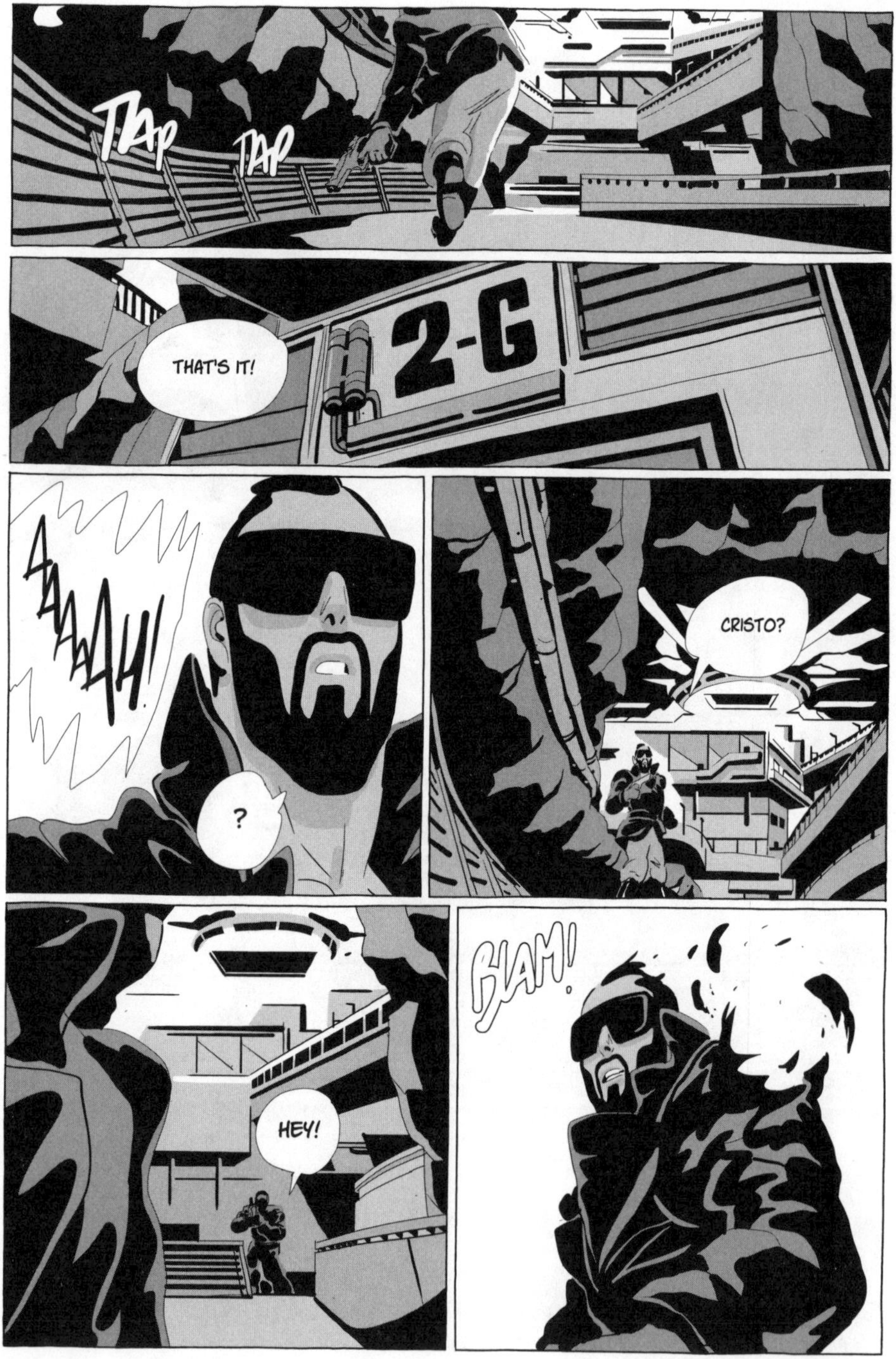
TAP
TAP
THAT'S IT!
2-G
AAAAAH!
?
CRISTO?
HEY!
BLAM!

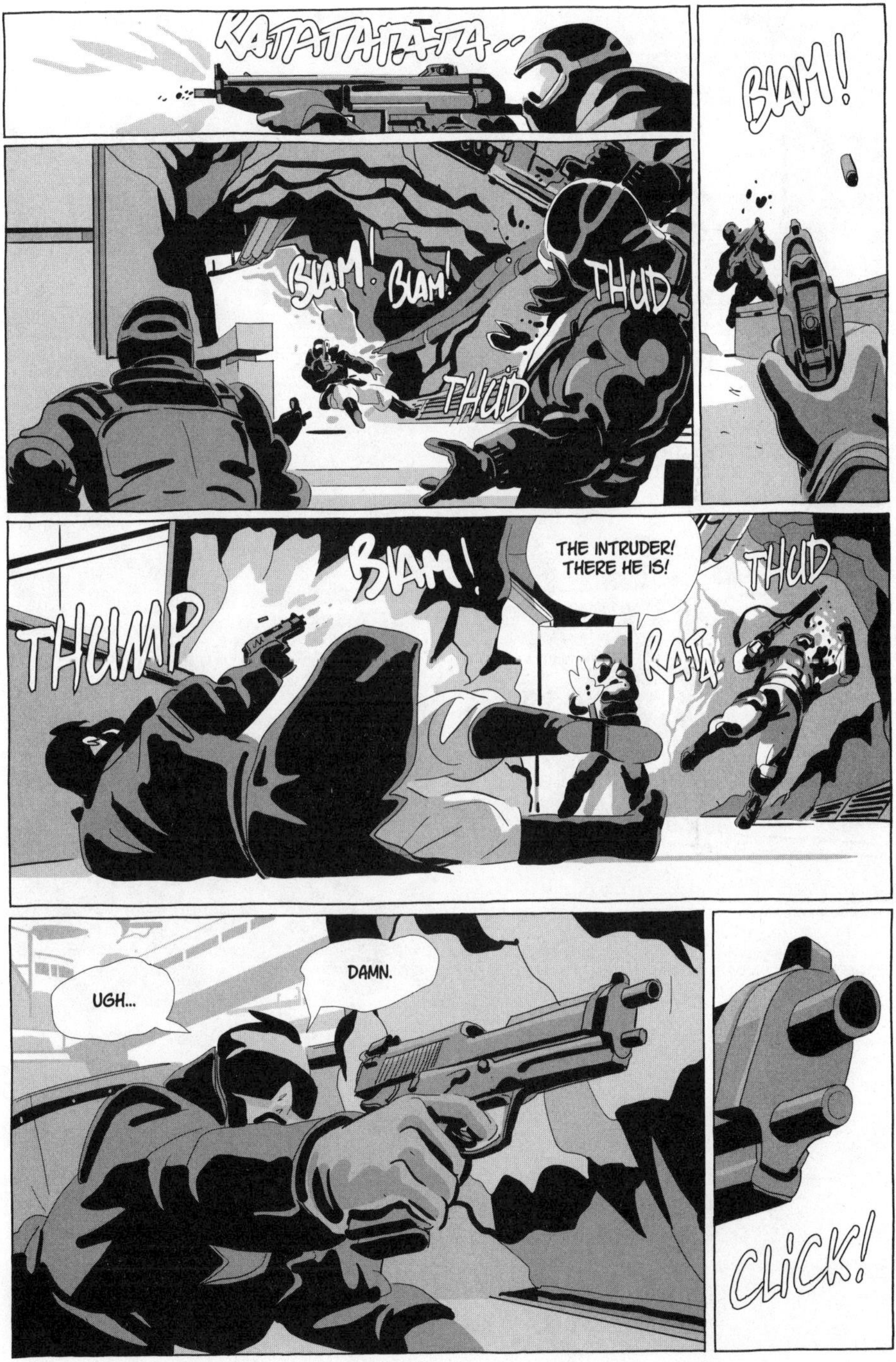
KATATATATATA..
BIAM!
BIAM!
THUD
THUD
BIAM!
THUMP
BIAM!
THE INTRUDER! THERE HE IS!
RATA.
THUD
UGH...
DAMN.
CLICK!

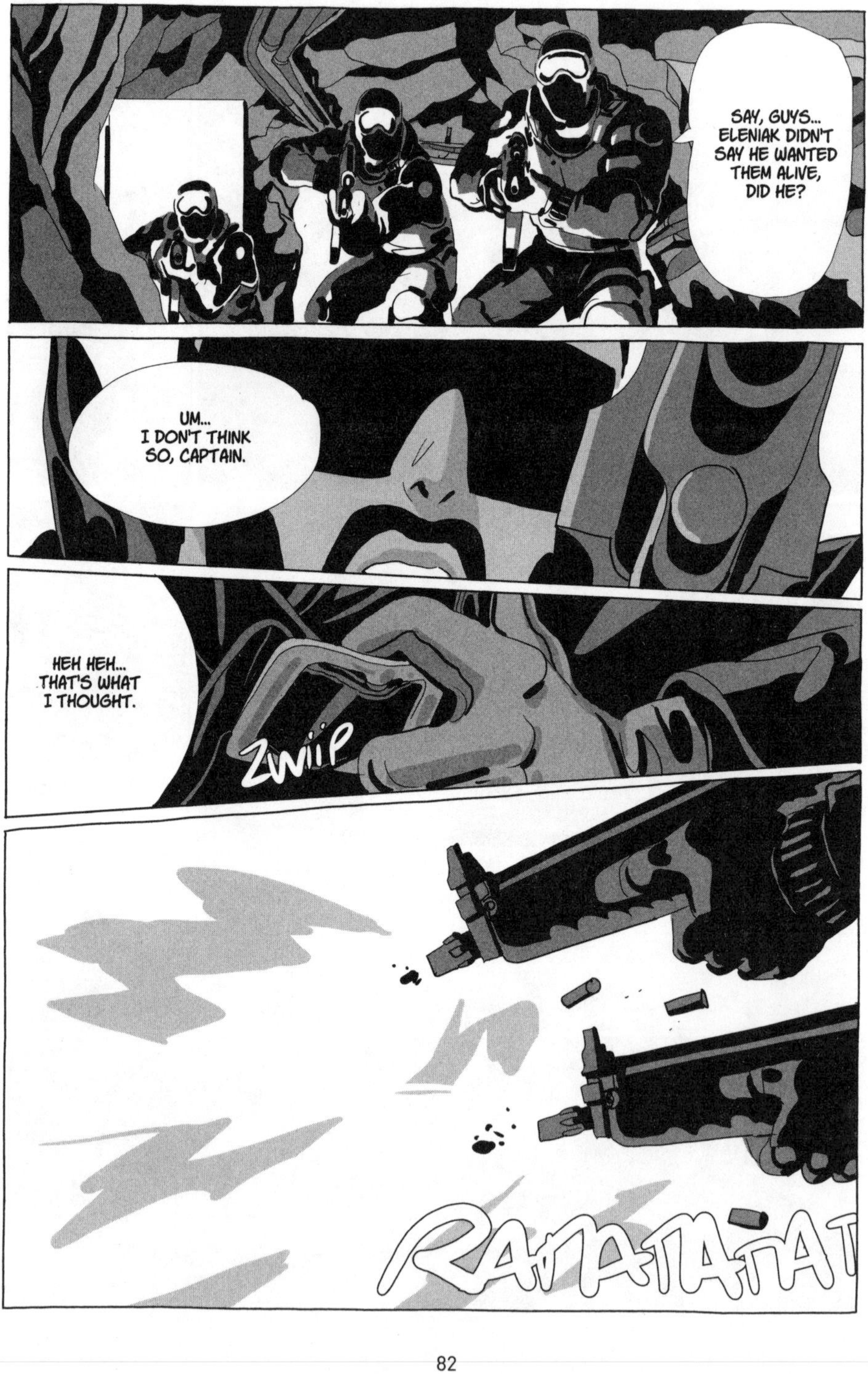
SAY, GUYS... ELENIAK DIDN'T SAY HE WANTED THEM ALIVE, DID HE?
UM... I DON'T THINK SO, CAPTAIN.
HEH HEH... THAT'S WHAT I THOUGHT.
ZWIIP
RATATATAT

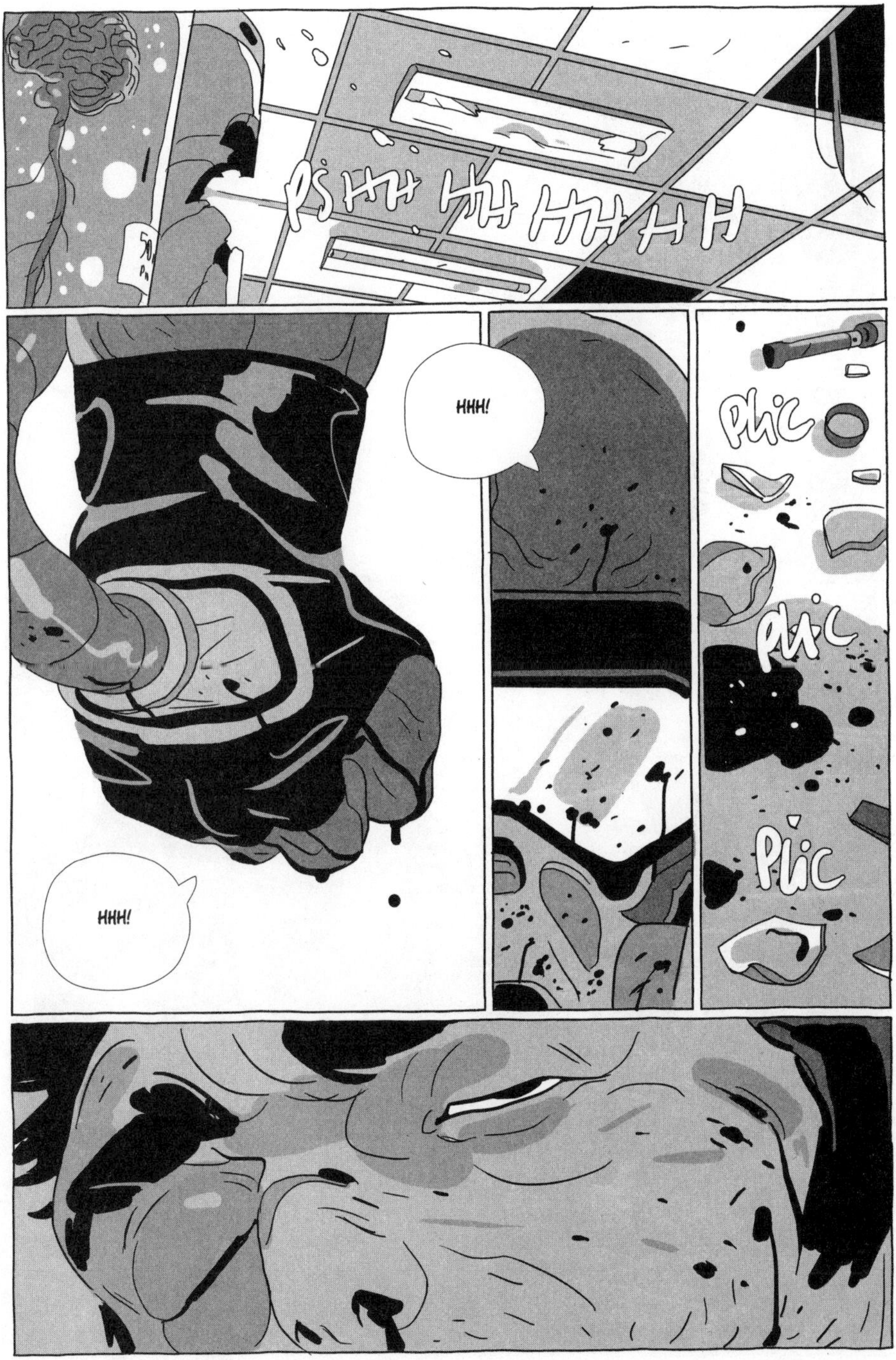
PSHH HHH HHHH H H
HHH!
HHH!
Plic
Plic
Plic

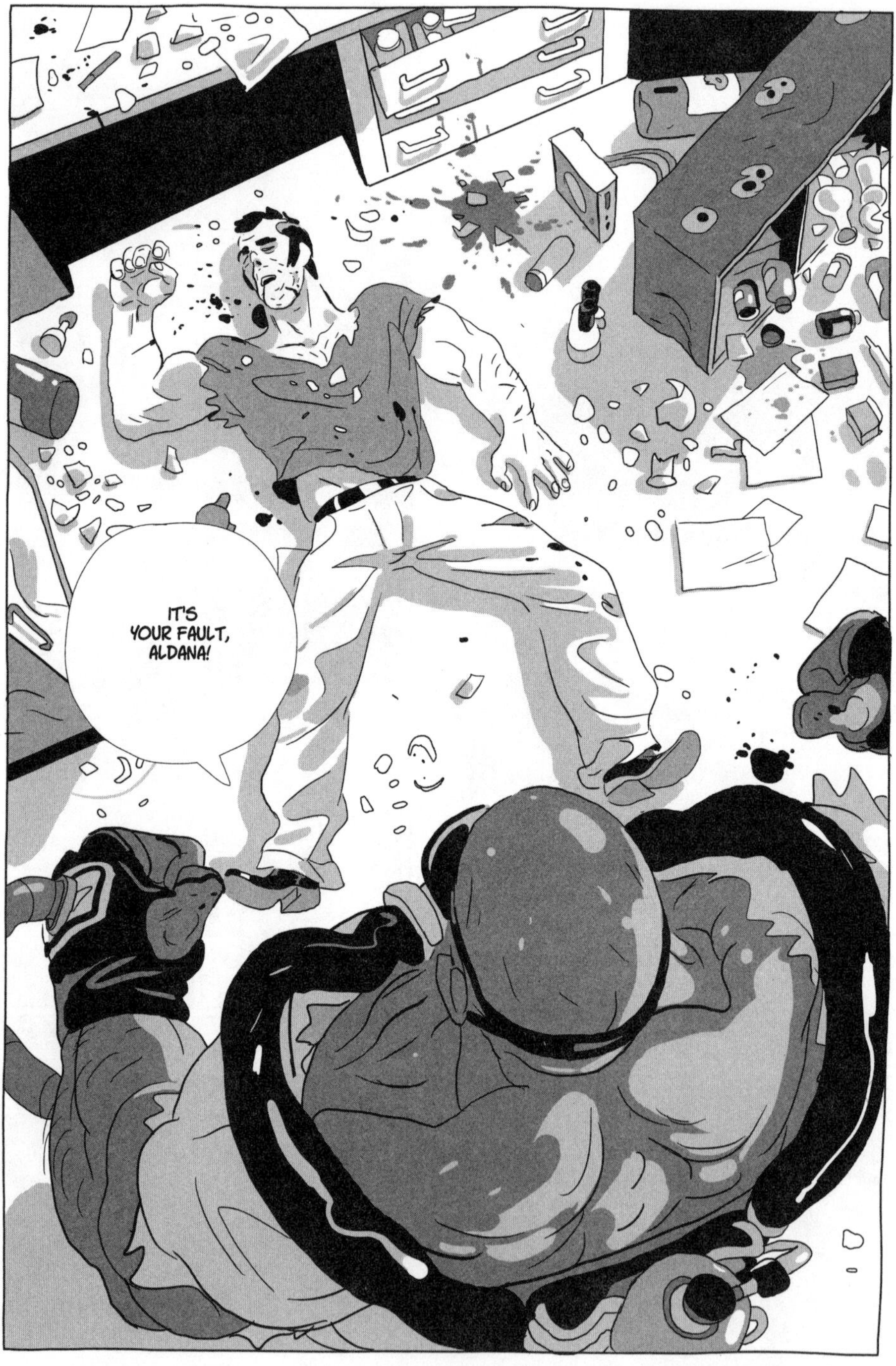
IT'S YOUR FAULT, ALDANA!

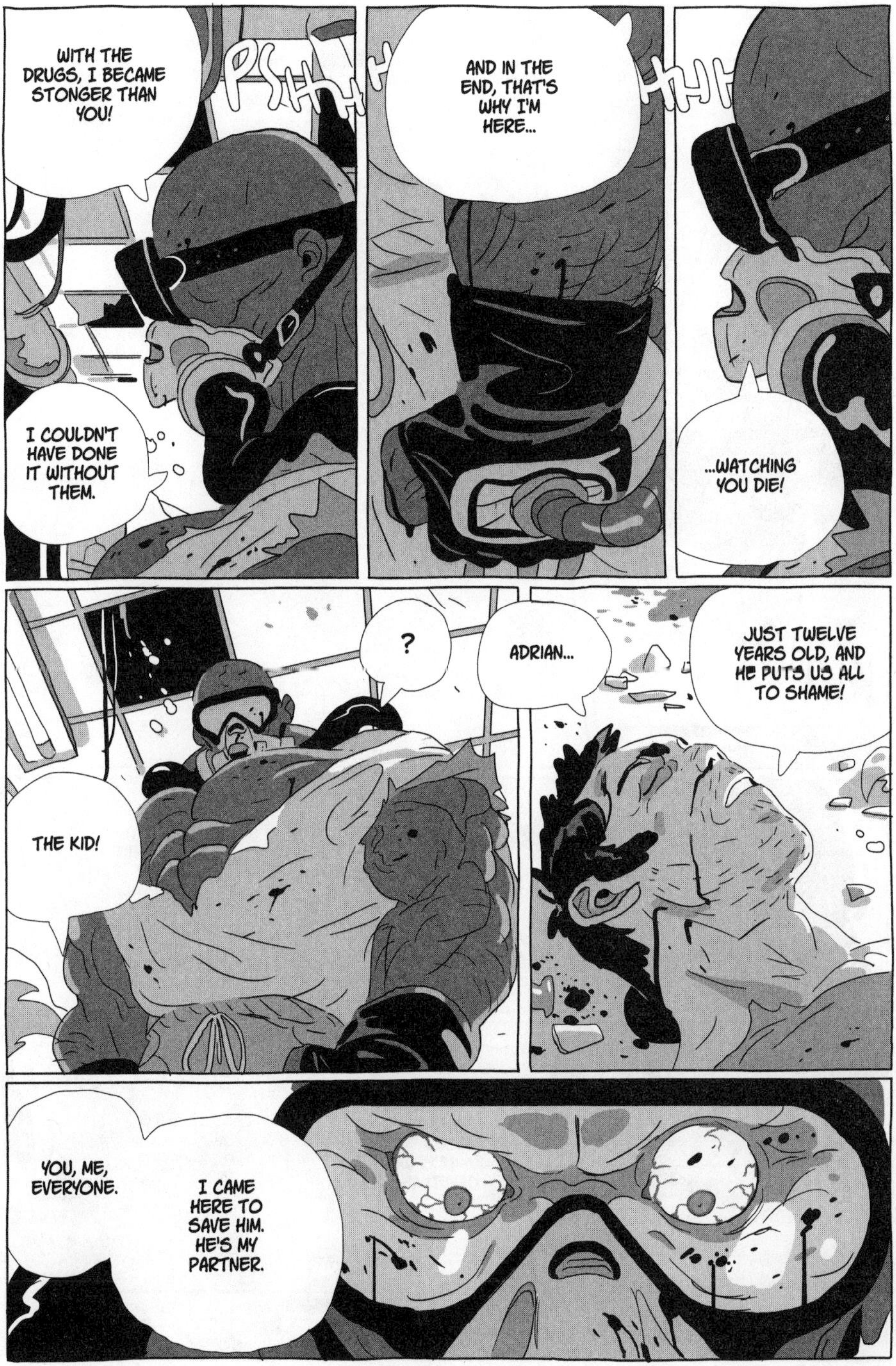

WITH THE DRUGS, I BECAME STONGER THAN YOU!
I COULDN'T HAVE DONE IT WITHOUT THEM.
PSHHHHHHHHH
AND IN THE END, THAT'S WHY I'M HERE...
...WATCHING YOU DIE!
?
THE KID!
ADRIAN...
JUST TWELVE YEARS OLD, AND HE PUTS US ALL TO SHAME!
YOU, ME, EVERYONE.
I CAME HERE TO SAVE HIM. HE'S MY PARTNER.

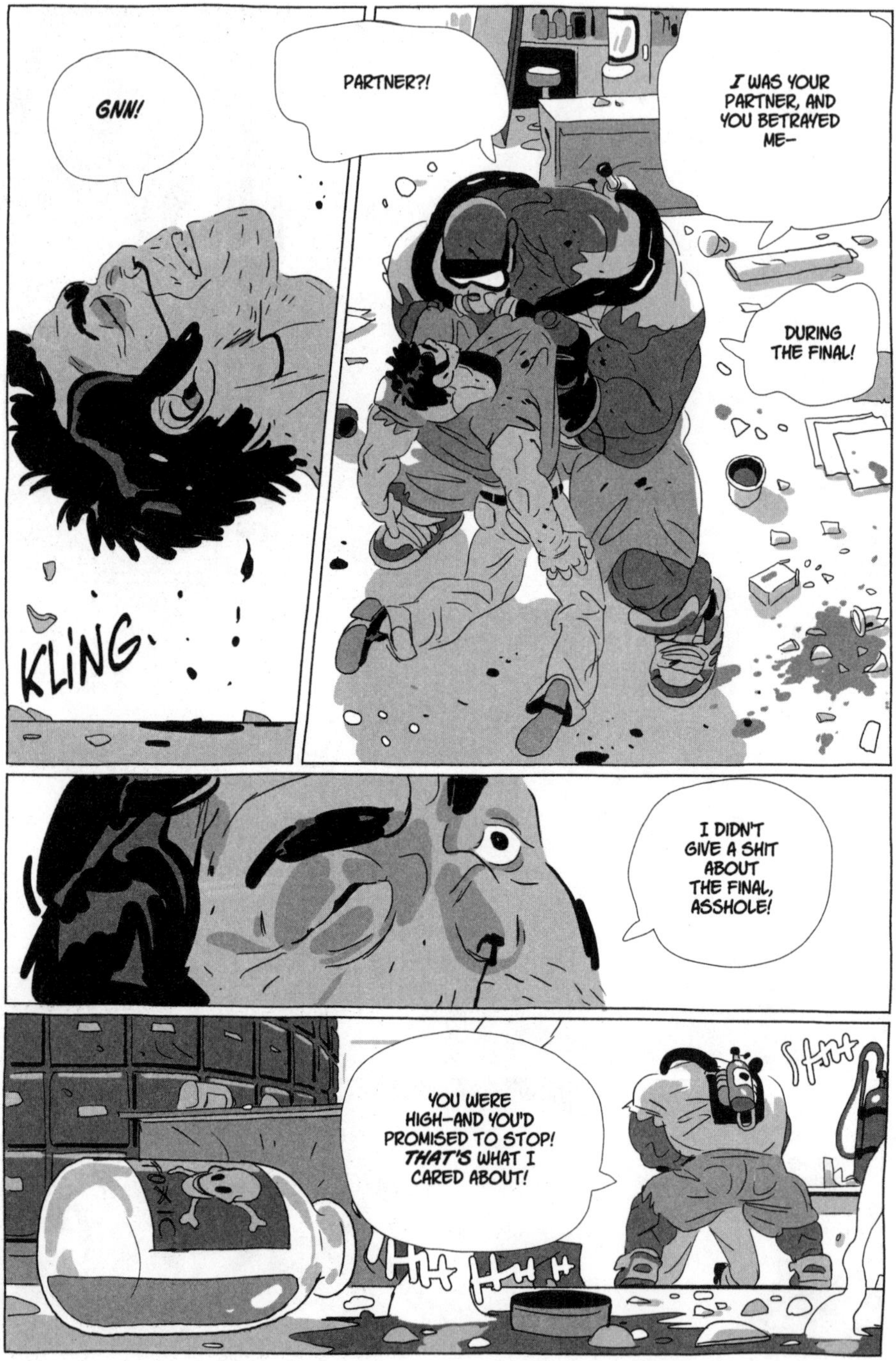
GNN!
PARTNER?!
I WAS YOUR PARTNER, AND YOU BETRAYED ME–
DURING THE FINAL!
KLING
I DIDN'T GIVE A SHIT ABOUT THE FINAL, ASSHOLE!
YOU WERE HIGH–AND YOU'D PROMISED TO STOP! THAT'S WHAT I CARED ABOUT!
TOXIC
SFRR

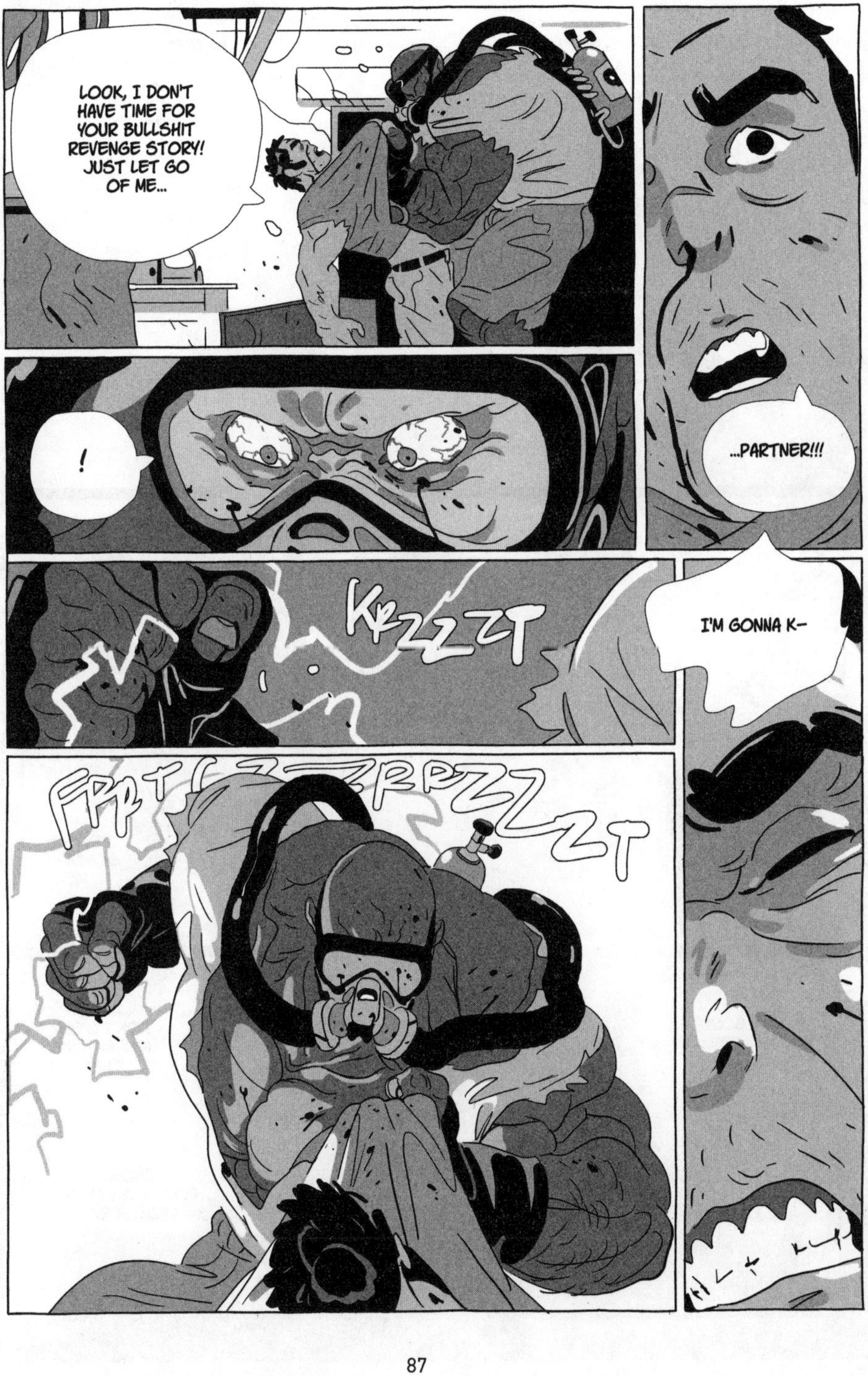
LOOK, I DON'T HAVE TIME FOR YOUR BULLSHIT REVENGE STORY! JUST LET GO OF ME...
...PARTNER!!!
!
KRZZZT
I'M GONNA K-
FPPT(ZZZRPZZZZT

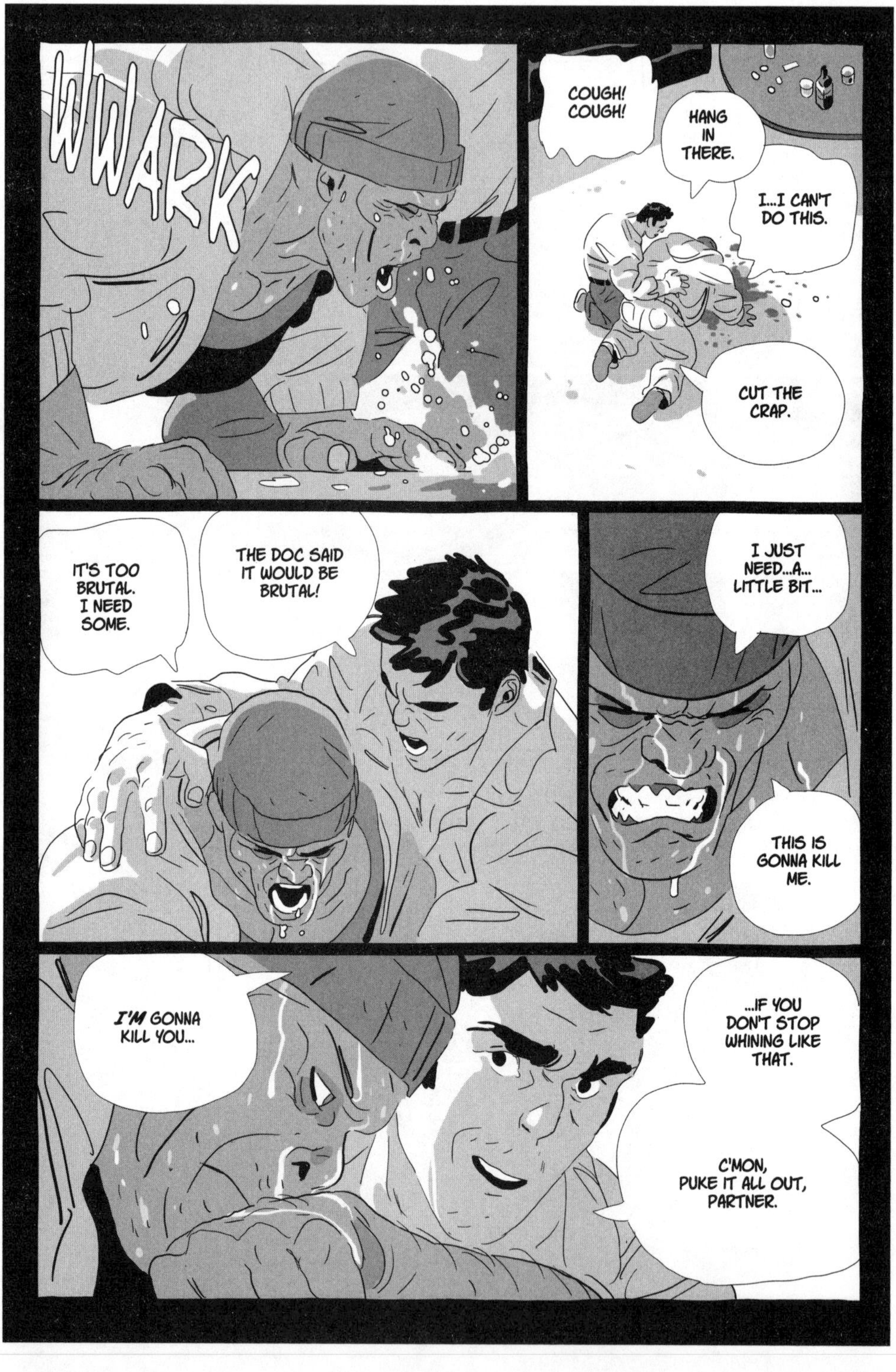
WWARK
COUGH! COUGH!
HANG IN THERE.
I...I CAN'T DO THIS.
CUT THE CRAP.
IT'S TOO BRUTAL. I NEED SOME.
THE DOC SAID IT WOULD BE BRUTAL!
I JUST NEED...A... LITTLE BIT...
THIS IS GONNA KILL ME.
I'M GONNA KILL YOU...
...IF YOU DON'T STOP WHINING LIKE THAT.
C'MON, PUKE IT ALL OUT, PARTNER.

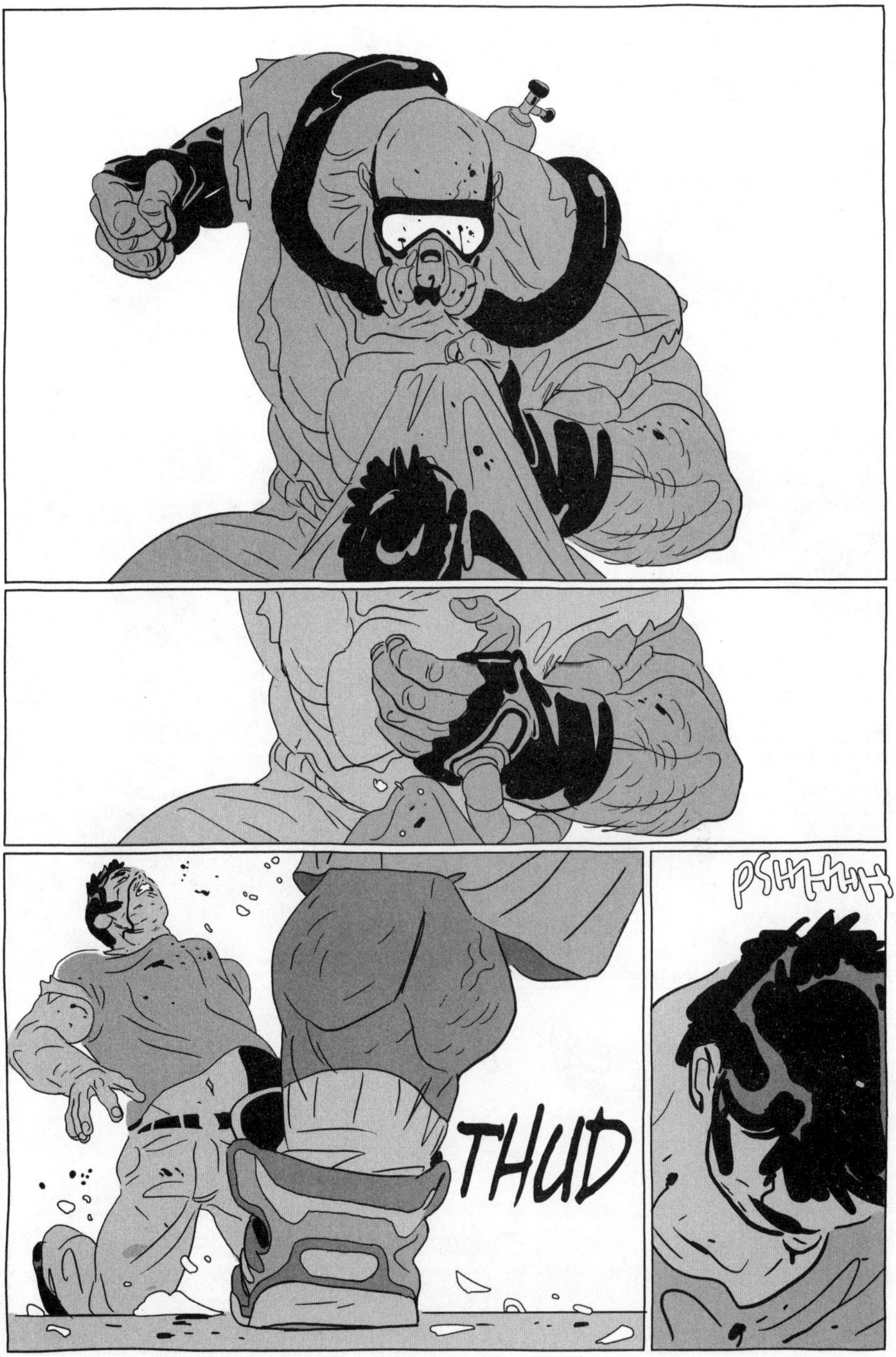
THUD
PSHHHHH

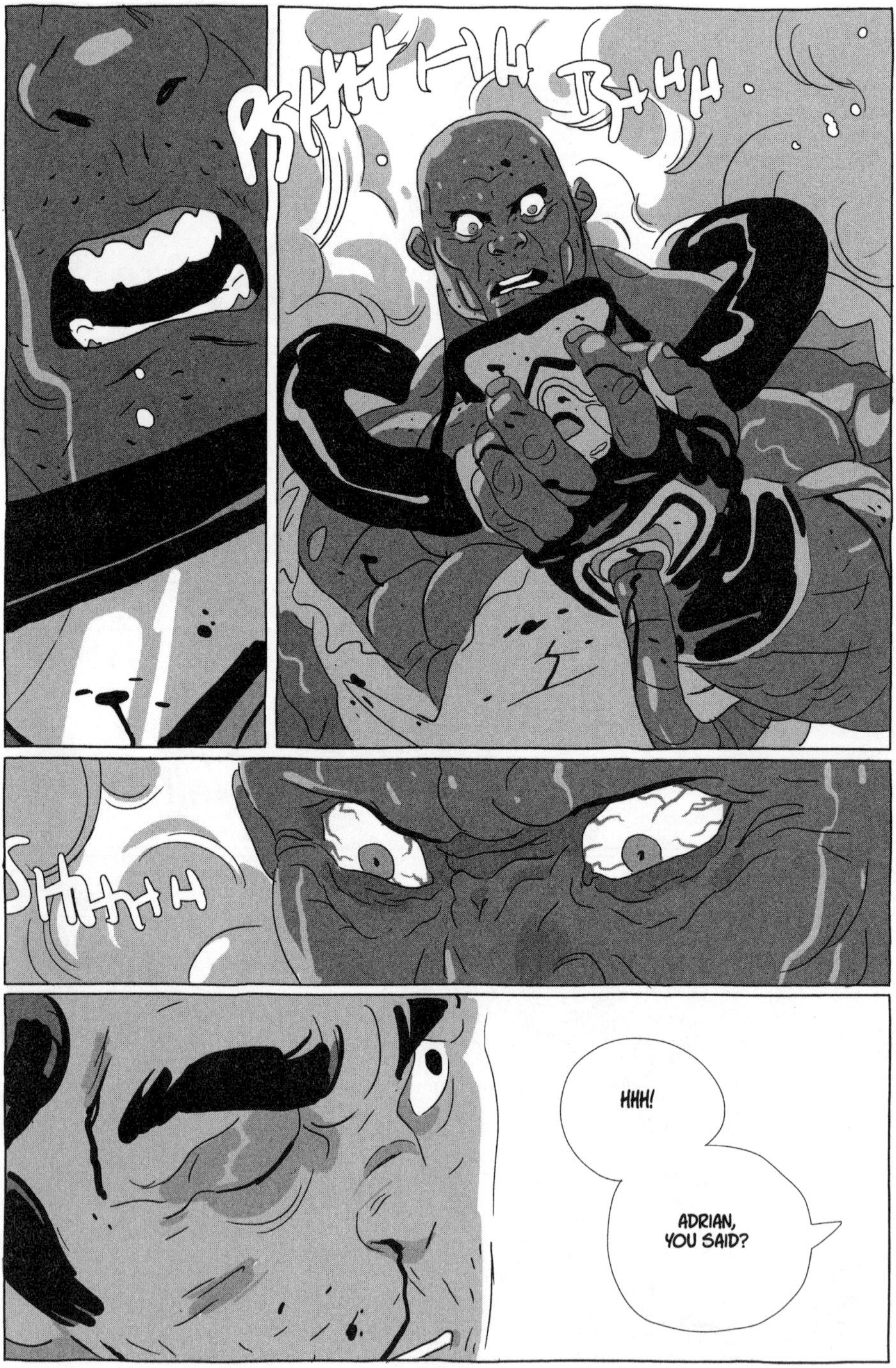
PSHHHHHH
SHHHHH
HHH!
ADRIAN,
YOU SAID?

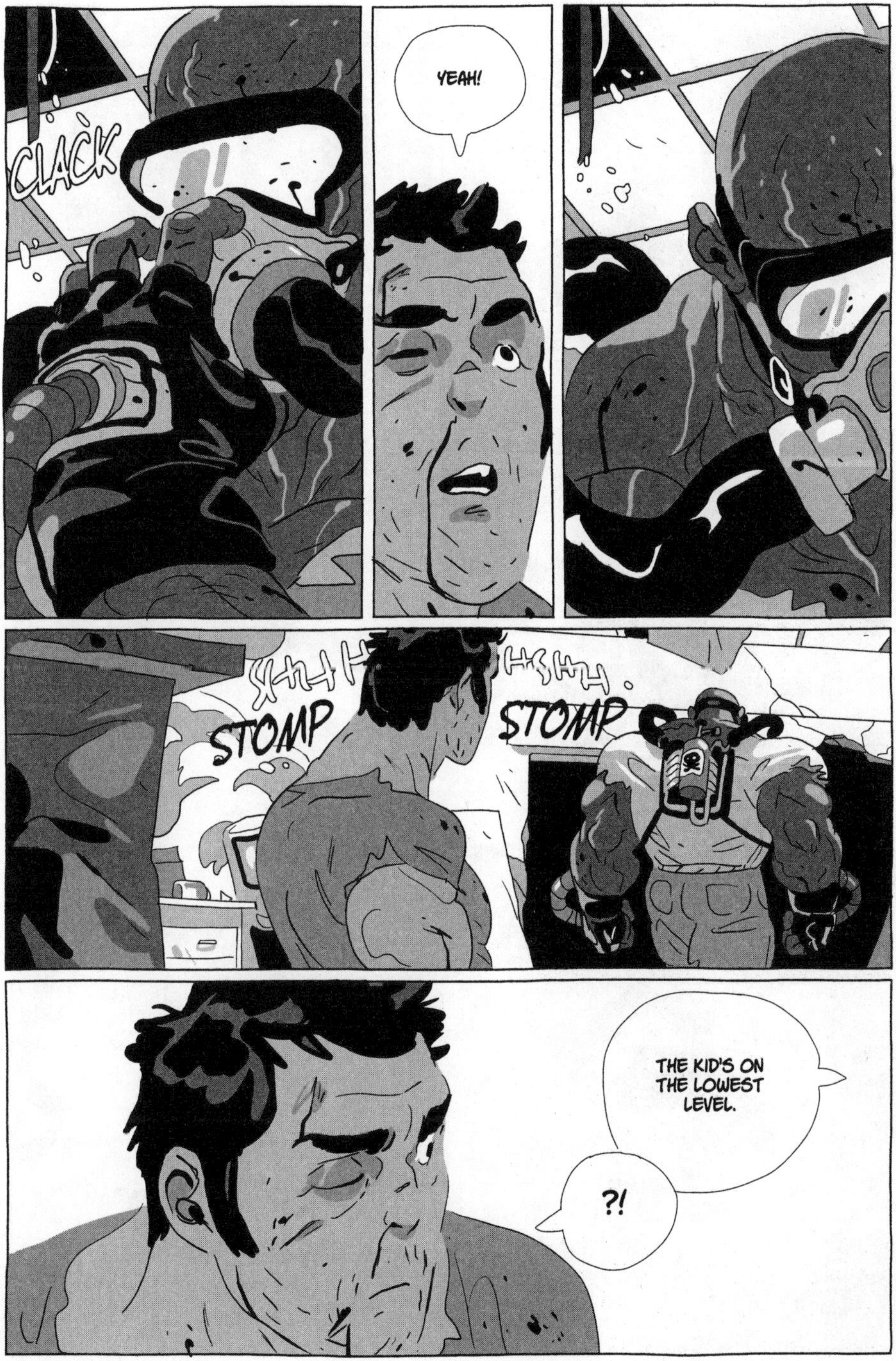
CLACK
YEAH!
STOMP
STOMP
THE KID'S ON THE LOWEST LEVEL.
?!

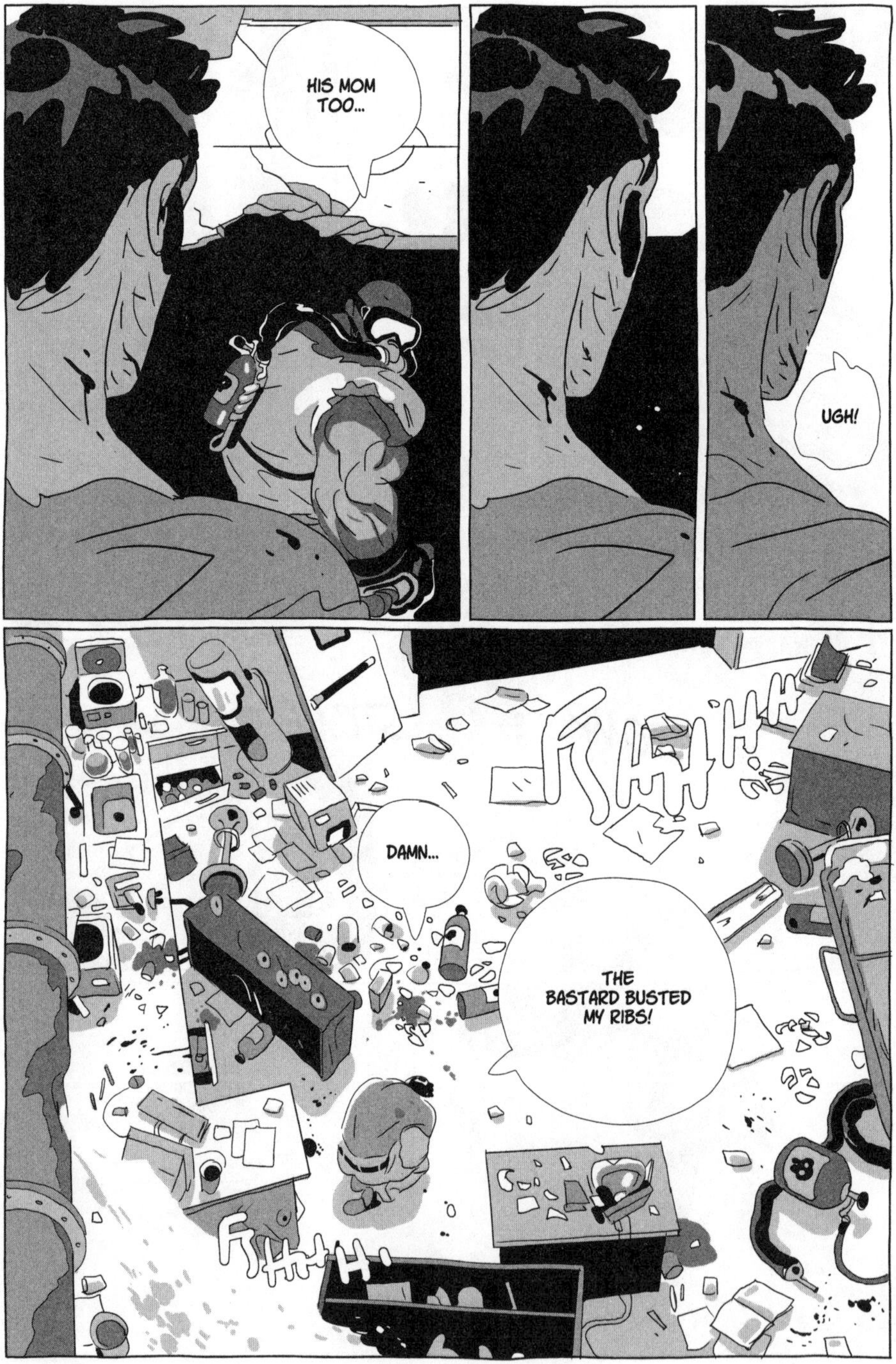
HIS MOM TOO...
UGH!
FSHHH
DAMN...
THE BASTARD BUSTED MY RIBS!
FSHHH

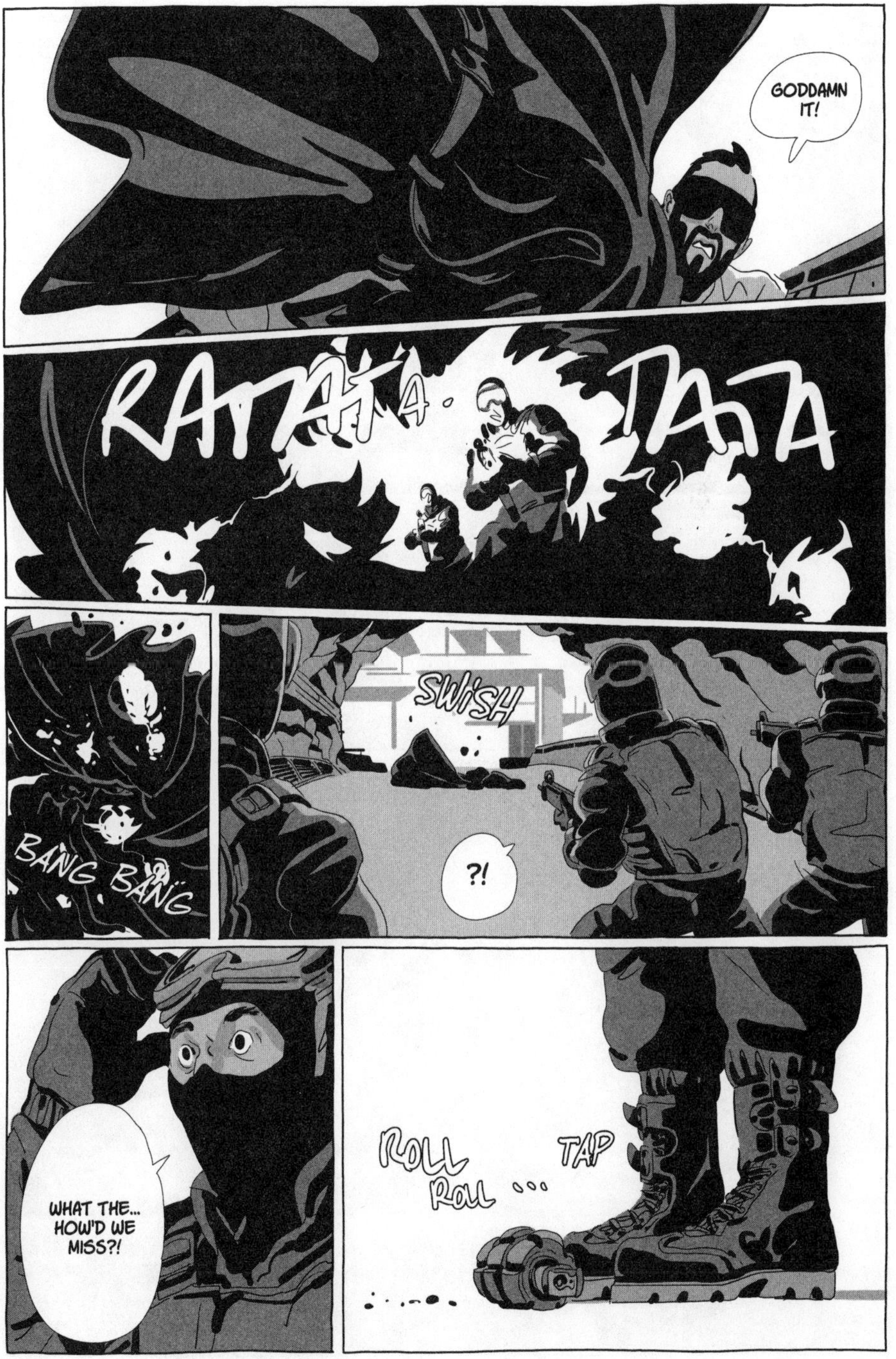
GODDAMN IT!
RATATTA-TATA
BANG BANG
SWISH
?!
WHAT THE... HOW'D WE MISS?!
ROLL ROLL...
TAP

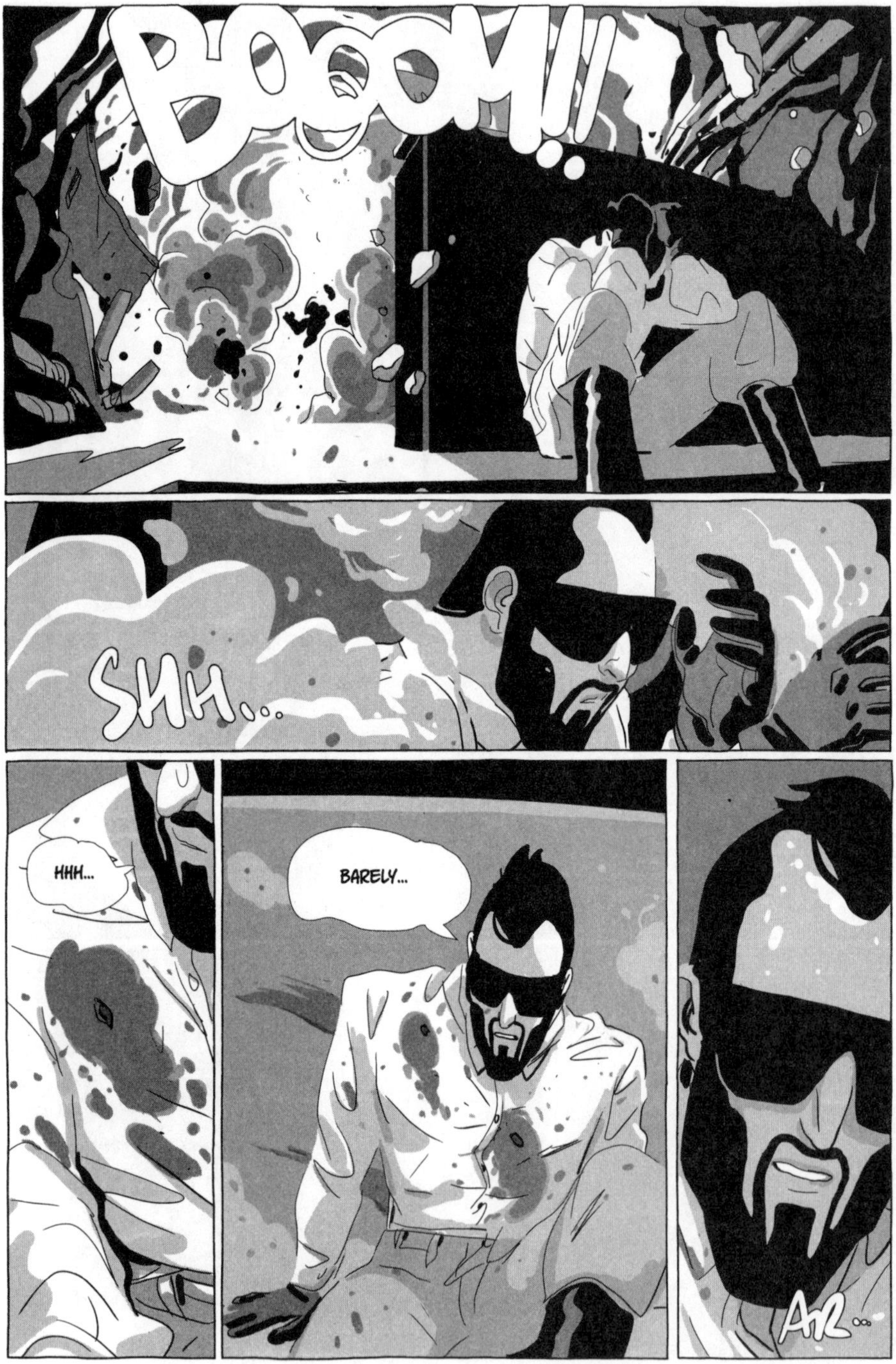
BOOOM!!
SHH...
HHH...
BARELY...
AR...

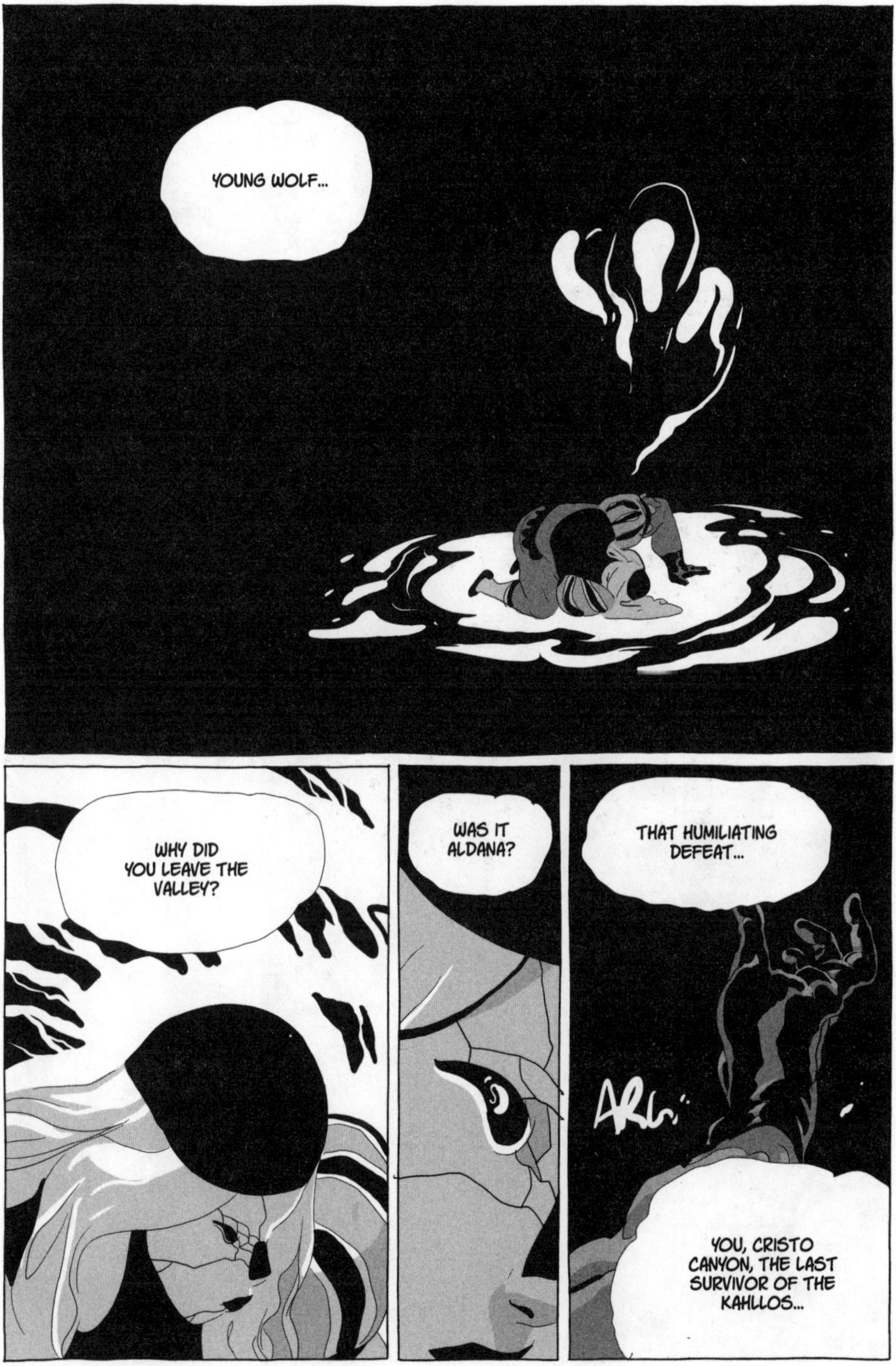
YOUNG WOLF...
WHY DID YOU LEAVE THE VALLEY?
WAS IT ALDANA?
THAT HUMILIATING DEFEAT...
YOU, CRISTO CANYON, THE LAST SURVIVOR OF THE KAHLLOS...

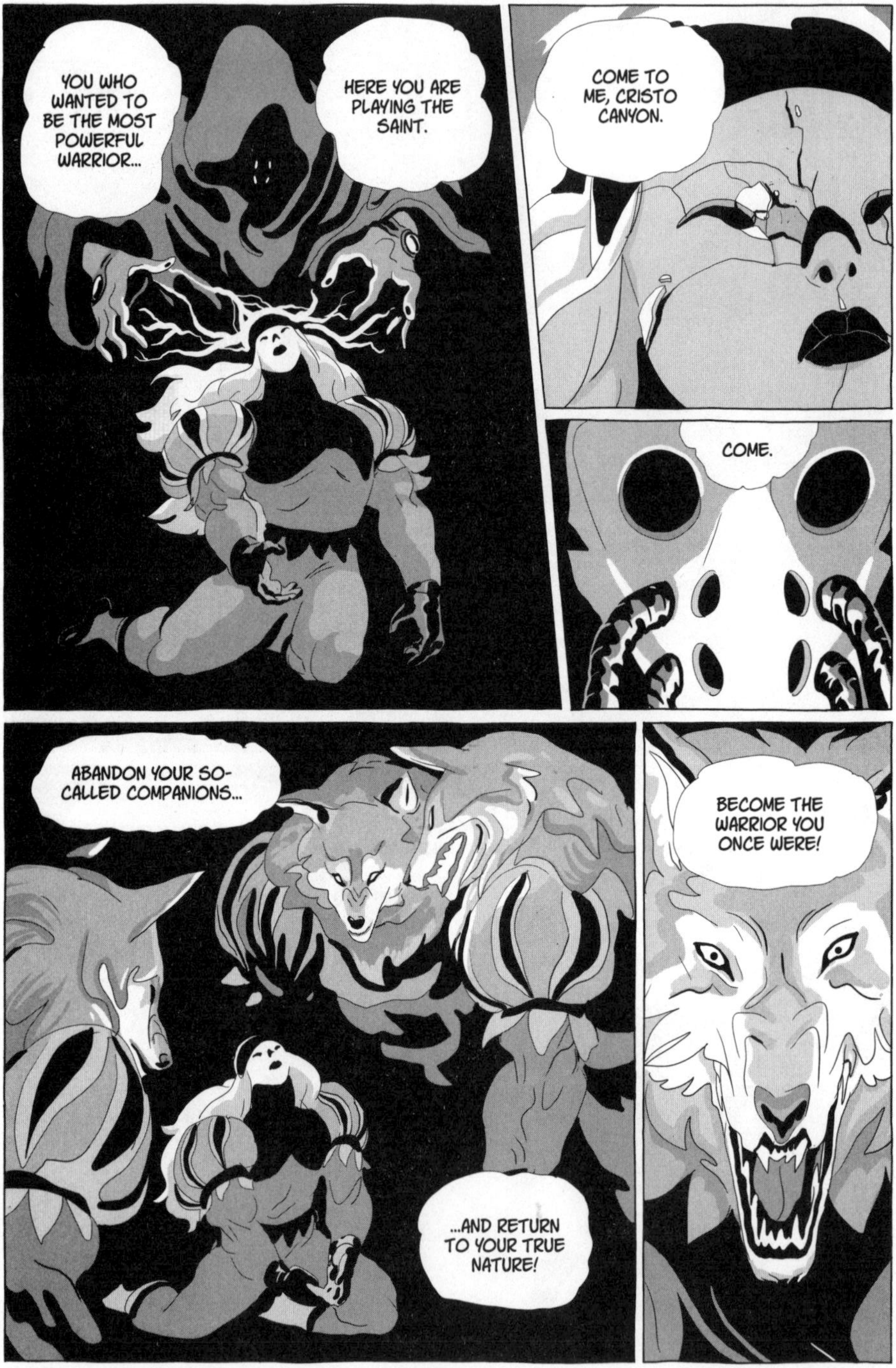
YOU WHO WANTED TO BE THE MOST POWERFUL WARRIOR...
HERE YOU ARE PLAYING THE SAINT.
COME TO ME, CRISTO CANYON.
COME.
ABANDON YOUR SO-CALLED COMPANIONS...
...AND RETURN TO YOUR TRUE NATURE!
BECOME THE WARRIOR YOU ONCE WERE!

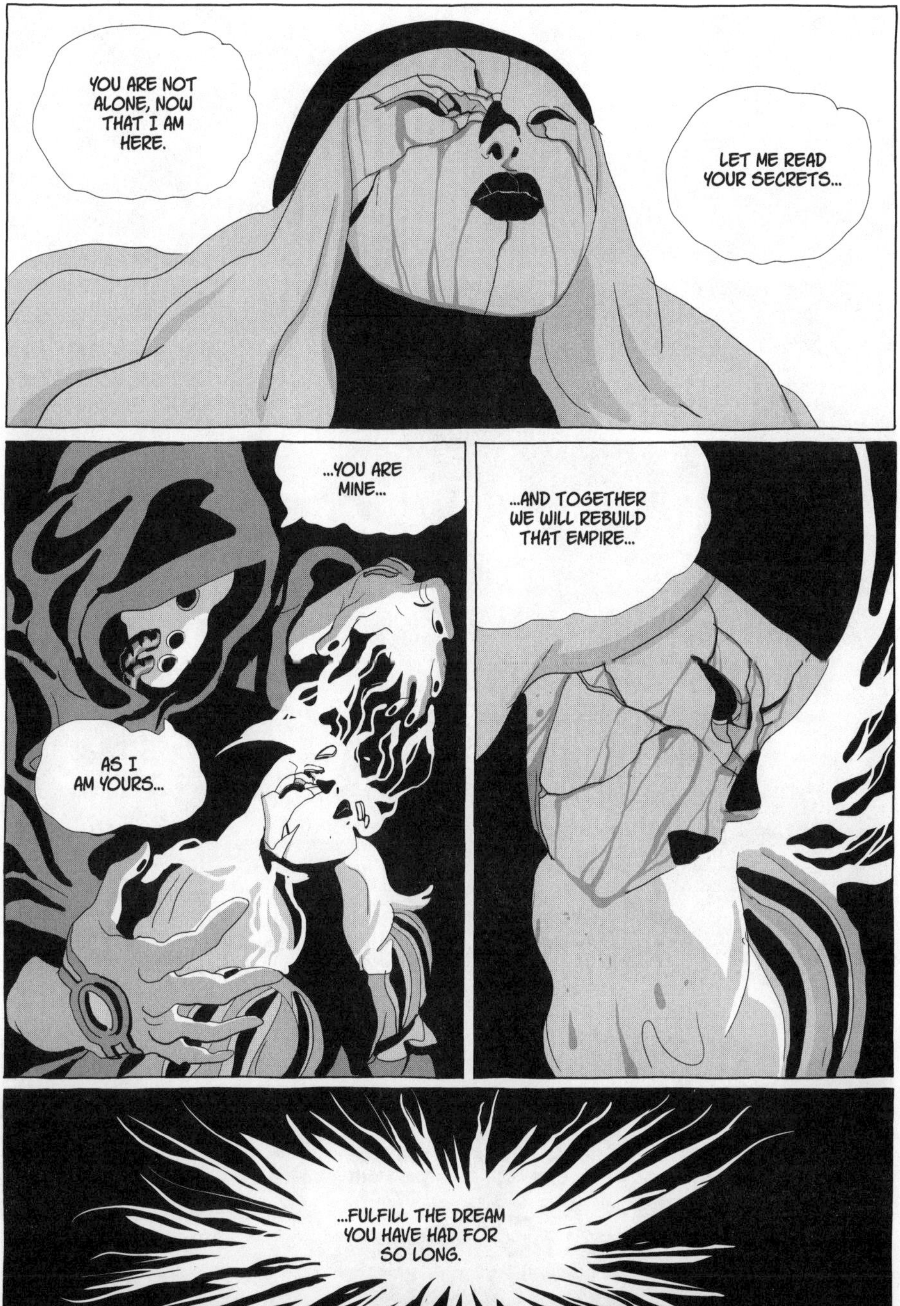
YOU ARE NOT ALONE, NOW THAT I AM HERE.
LET ME READ YOUR SECRETS...
...YOU ARE MINE...
AS I AM YOURS...
...AND TOGETHER WE WILL REBUILD THAT EMPIRE...
...FULFILL THE DREAM YOU HAVE HAD FOR SO LONG.

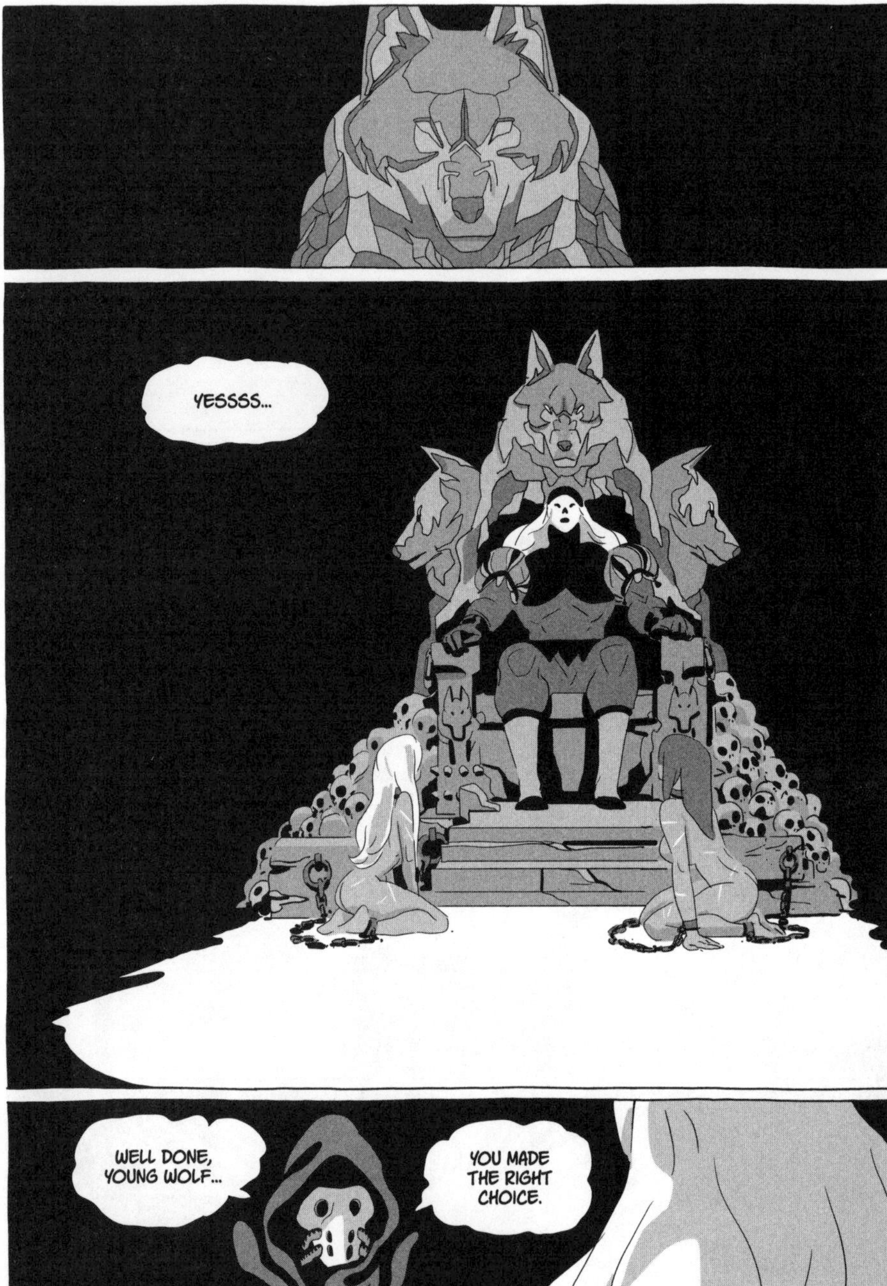
YESSSS...
WELL DONE, YOUNG WOLF...
YOU MADE THE RIGHT CHOICE.

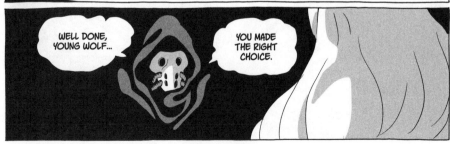

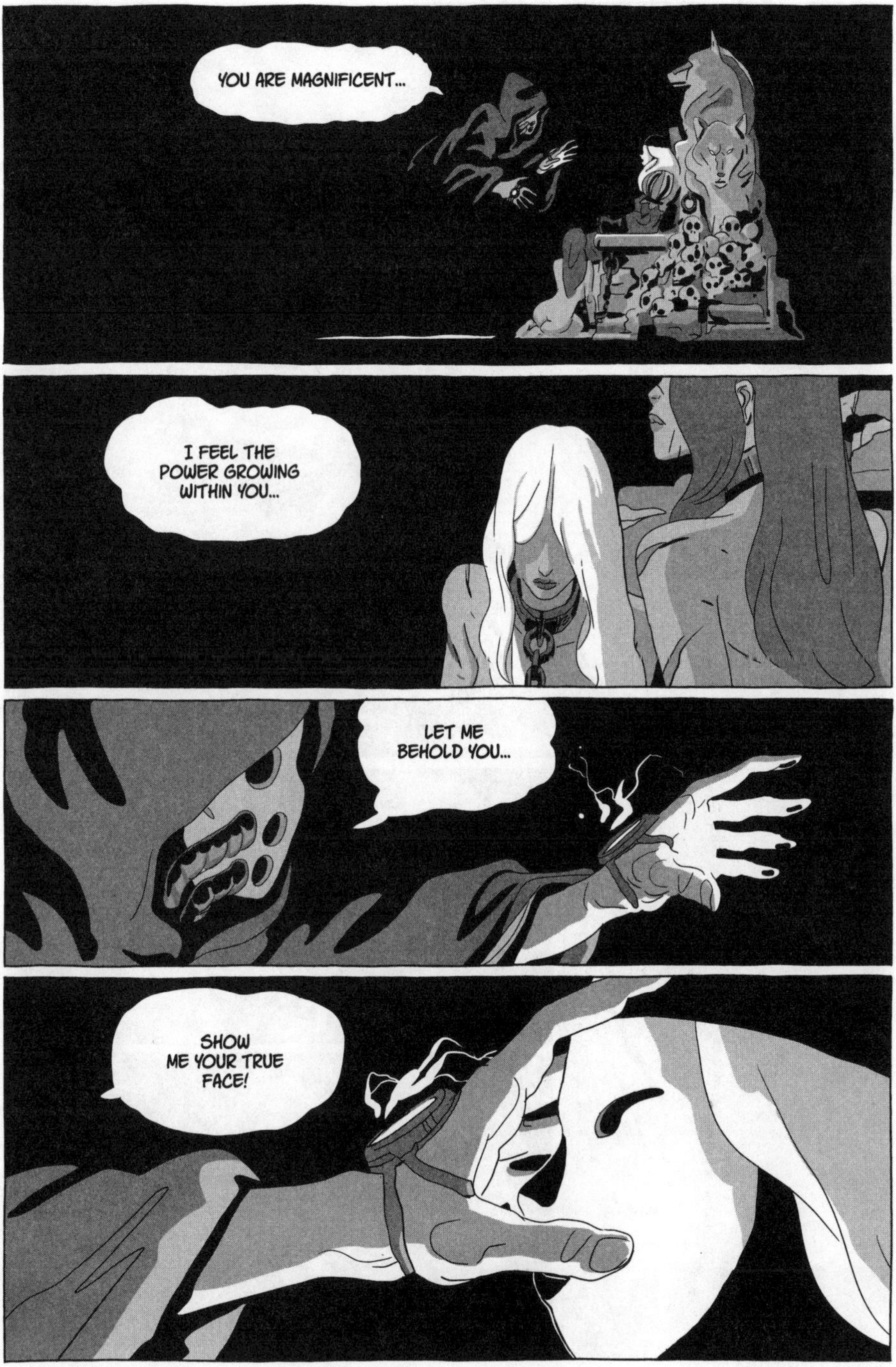
YOU ARE MAGNIFICENT...
I FEEL THE POWER GROWING WITHIN YOU...
LET ME BEHOLD YOU...
SHOW ME YOUR TRUE FACE!

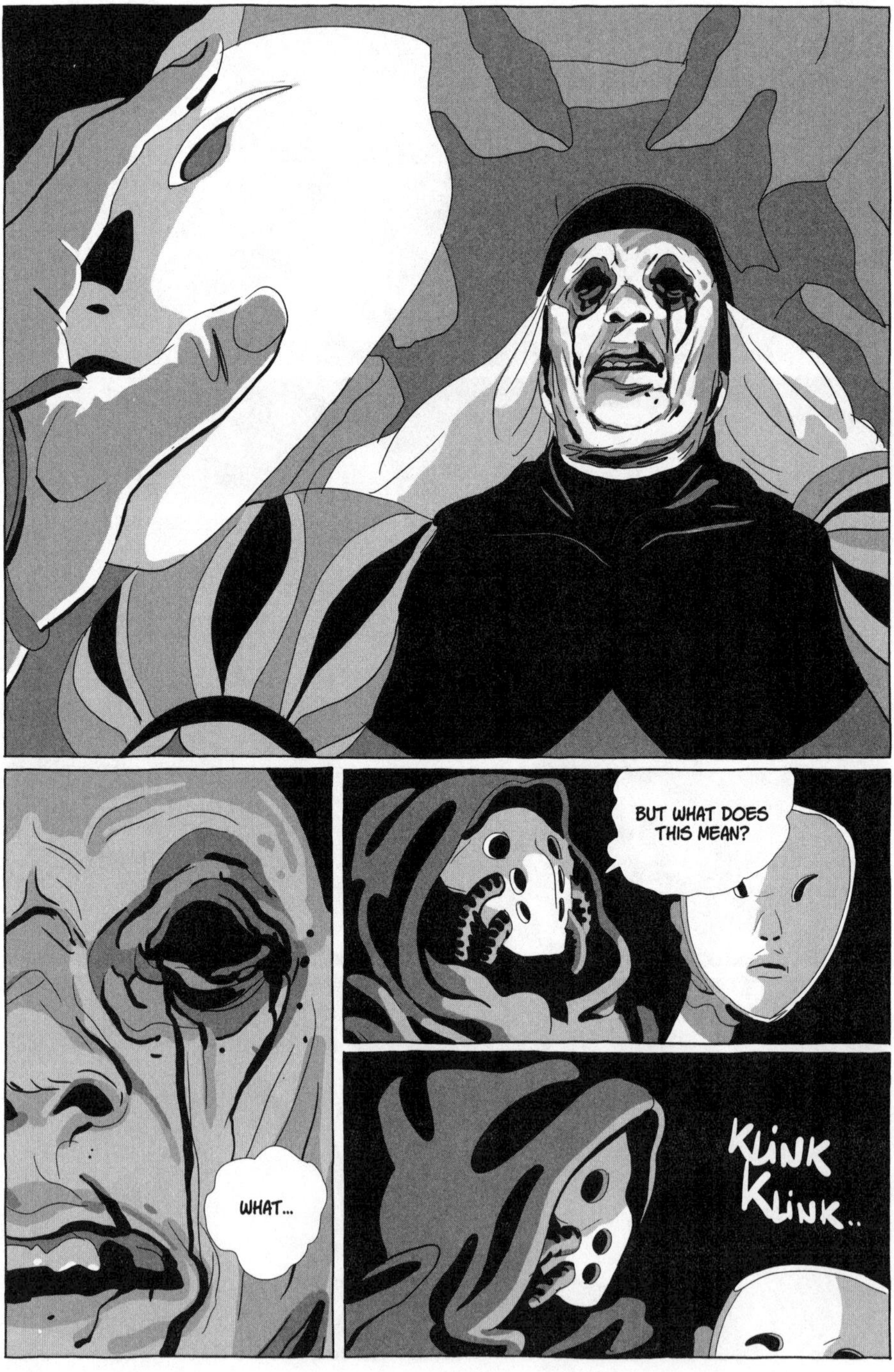
WHAT...
BUT WHAT DOES THIS MEAN?
KLINK KLINK..

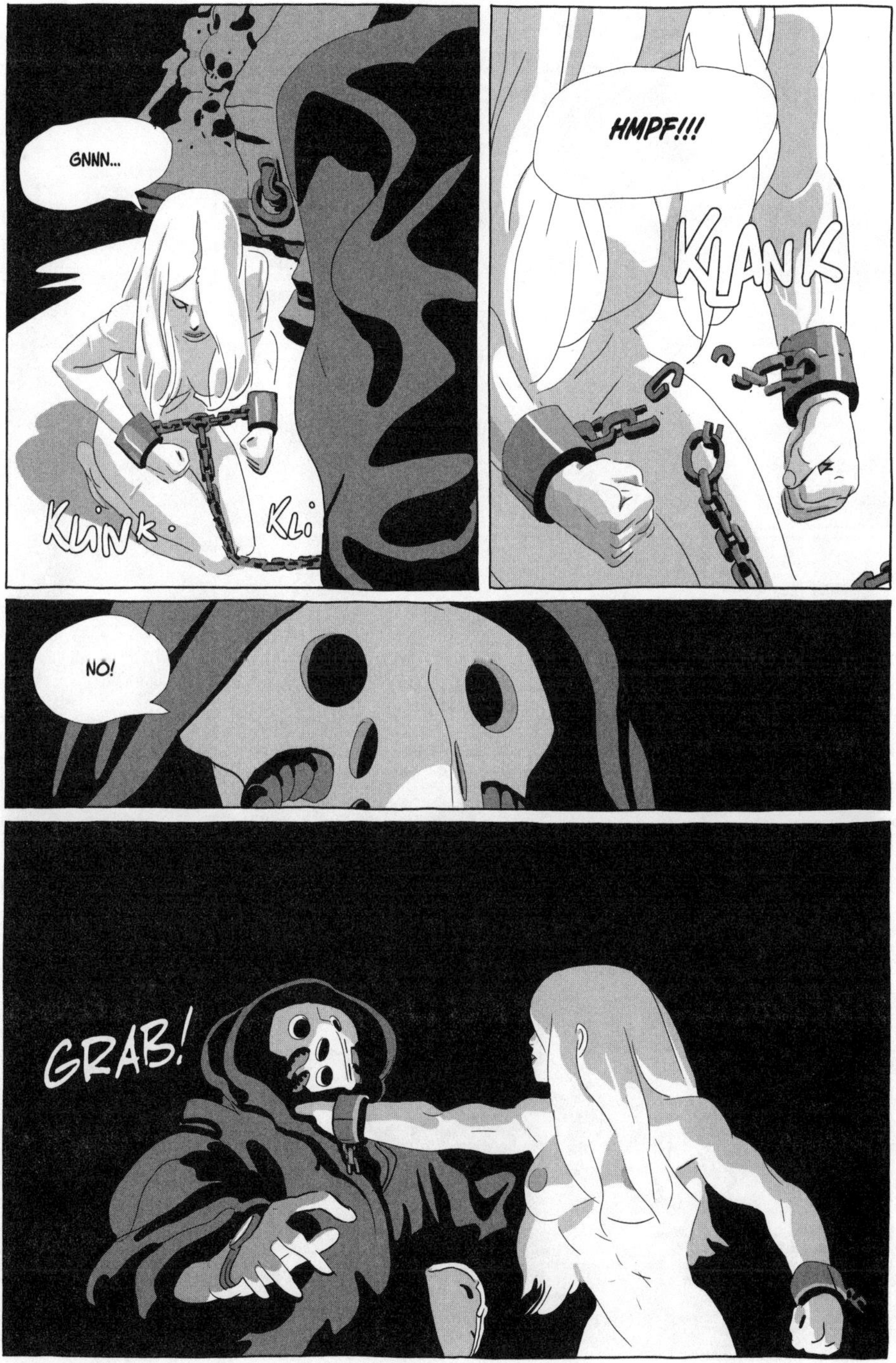
GNNN...
KLINK
KLI
HMPF!!!
KLANK
NO!
GRAB!

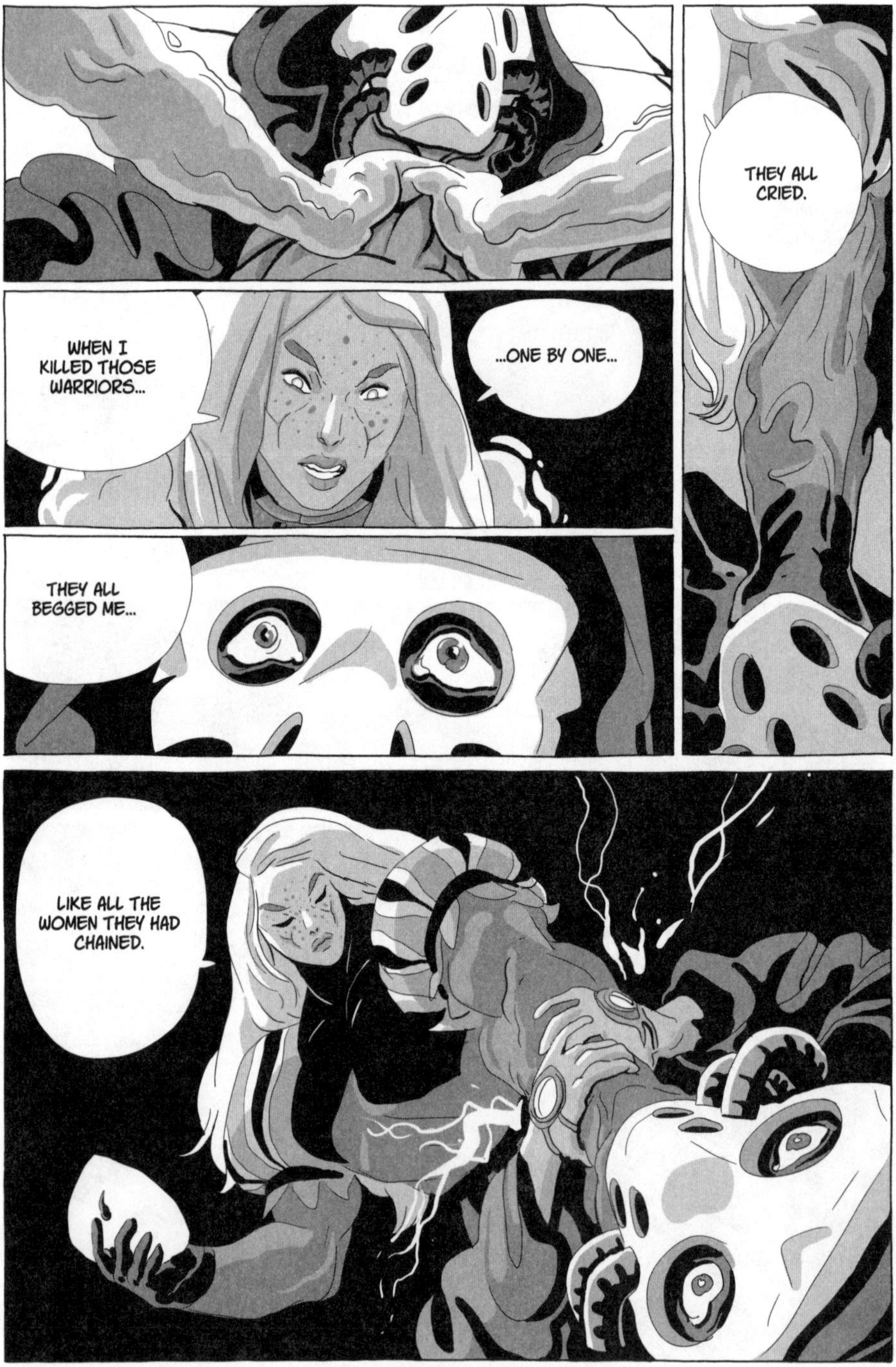

WHEN I KILLED THOSE WARRIORS...
...ONE BY ONE...
THEY ALL BEGGED ME...
THEY ALL CRIED.
LIKE ALL THE WOMEN THEY HAD CHAINED.

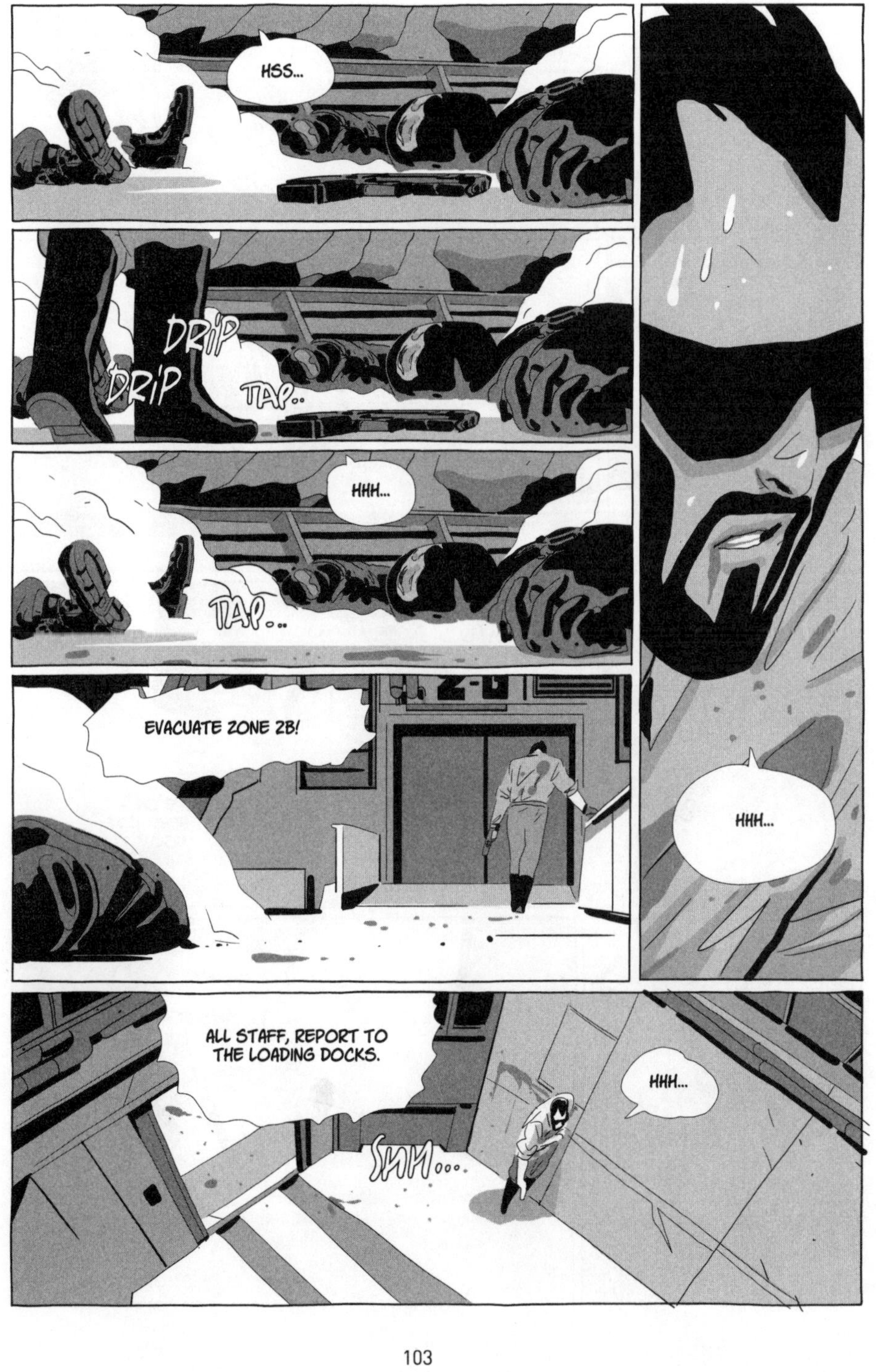

HSS...
DRIP
DRIP
TAP..
HHH...
TAP...
EVACUATE ZONE 2B!
HHH...
ALL STAFF, REPORT TO THE LOADING DOCKS.
HHH...
SHH...

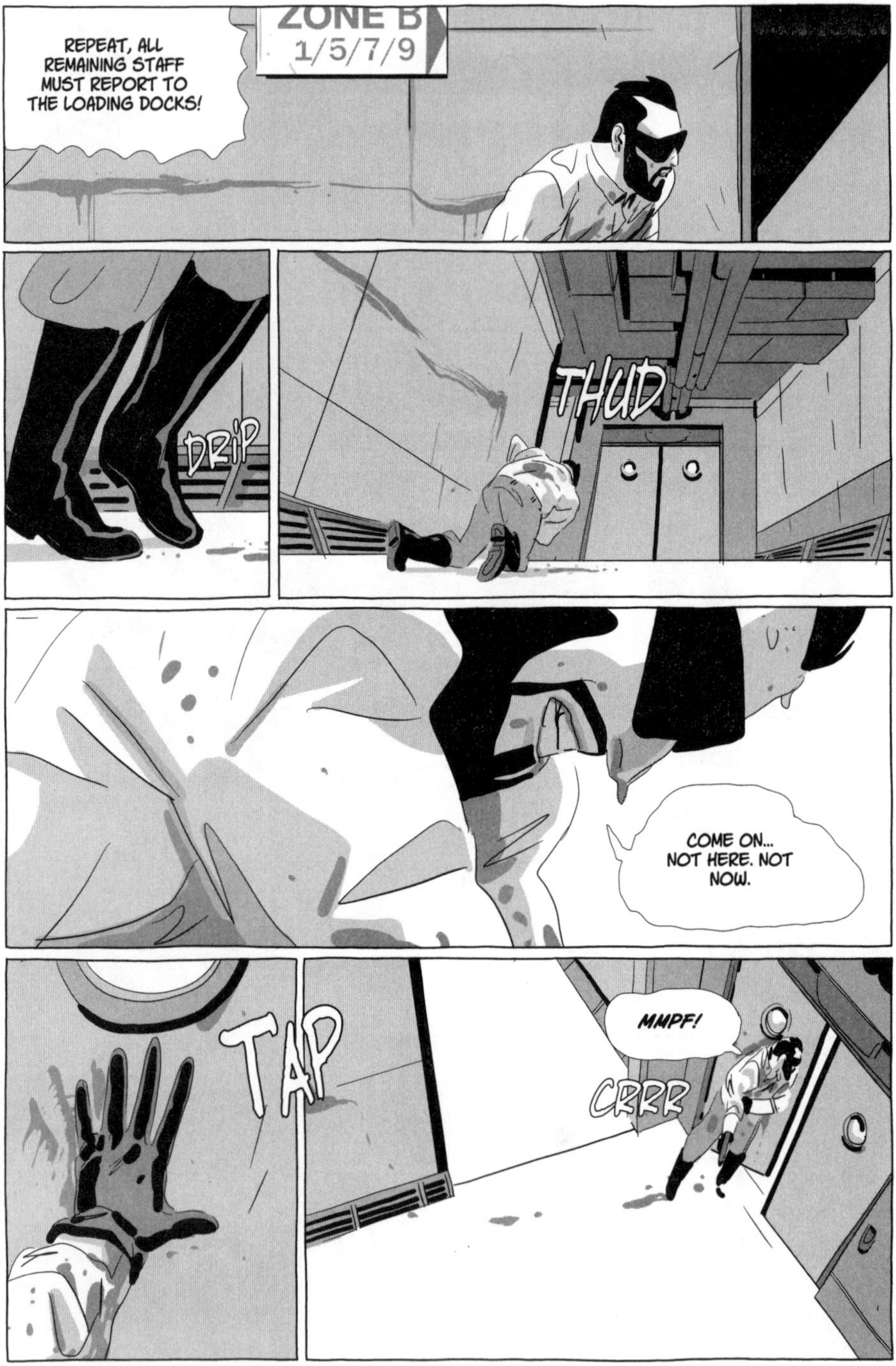

ZONE B
1/5/7/9
REPEAT, ALL REMAINING STAFF MUST REPORT TO THE LOADING DOCKS!
DRIP
THUD
COME ON... NOT HERE. NOT NOW.
TAP
MMPF!
CRRR

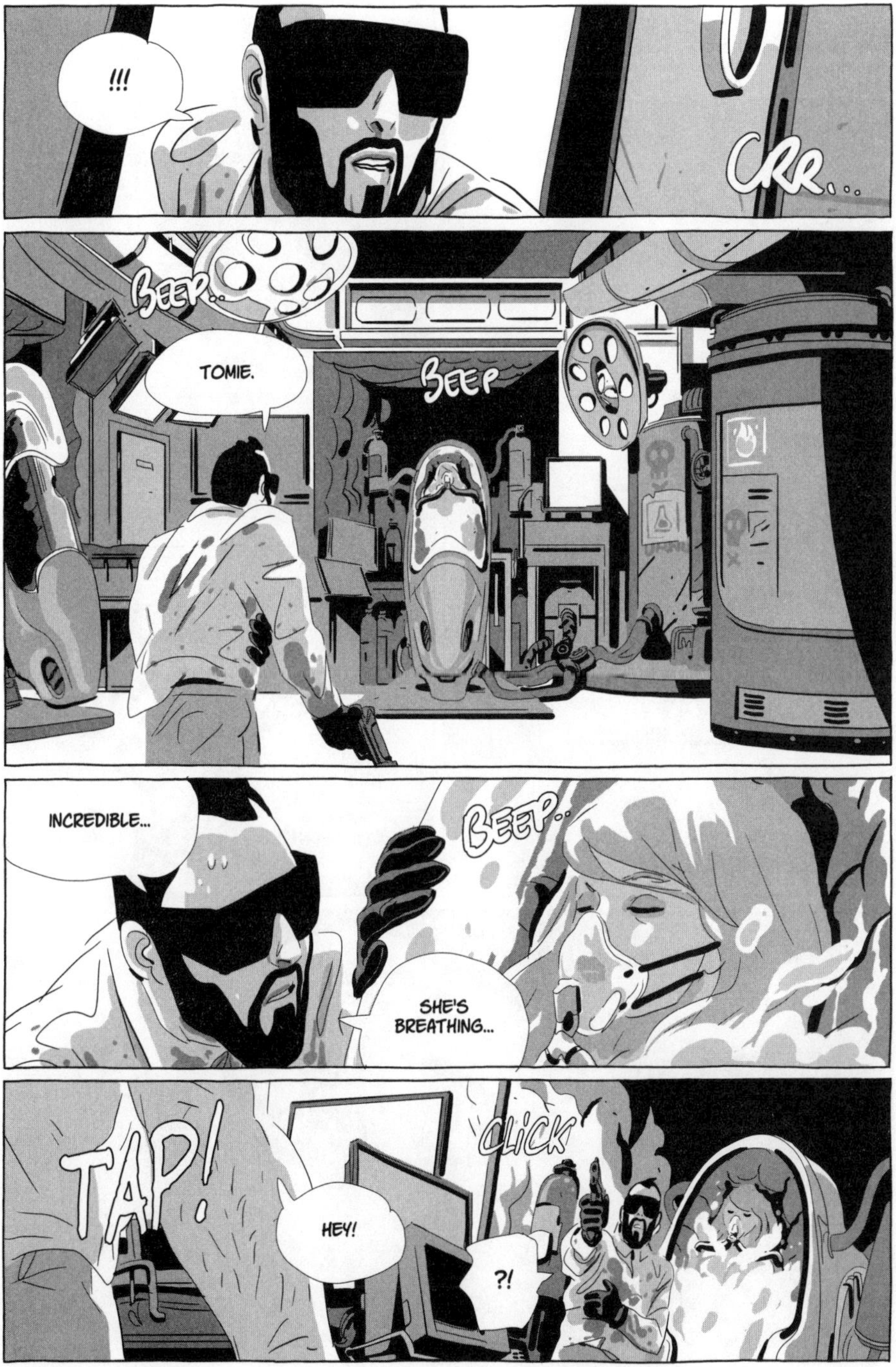
!!!
CRR...
BEEP..
TOMIE.
BEEP
INCREDIBLE...
BEEP..
SHE'S BREATHING...
TAP!
CLICK
HEY!
?!

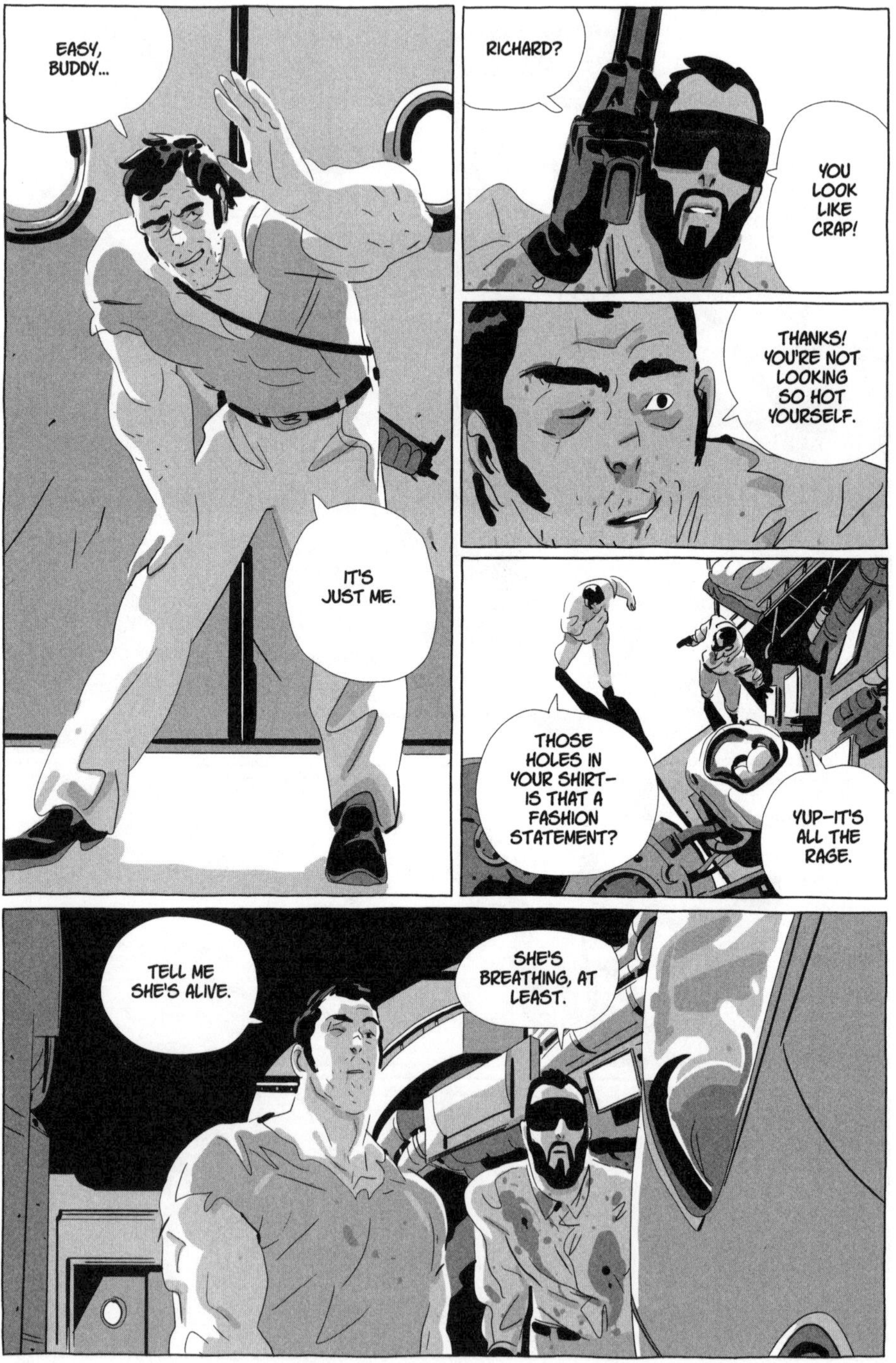
EASY, BUDDY...
IT'S JUST ME.
RICHARD?
YOU LOOK LIKE CRAP!
THANKS! YOU'RE NOT LOOKING SO HOT YOURSELF.
THOSE HOLES IN YOUR SHIRT— IS THAT A FASHION STATEMENT?
YUP—IT'S ALL THE RAGE.
TELL ME SHE'S ALIVE.
SHE'S BREATHING, AT LEAST.

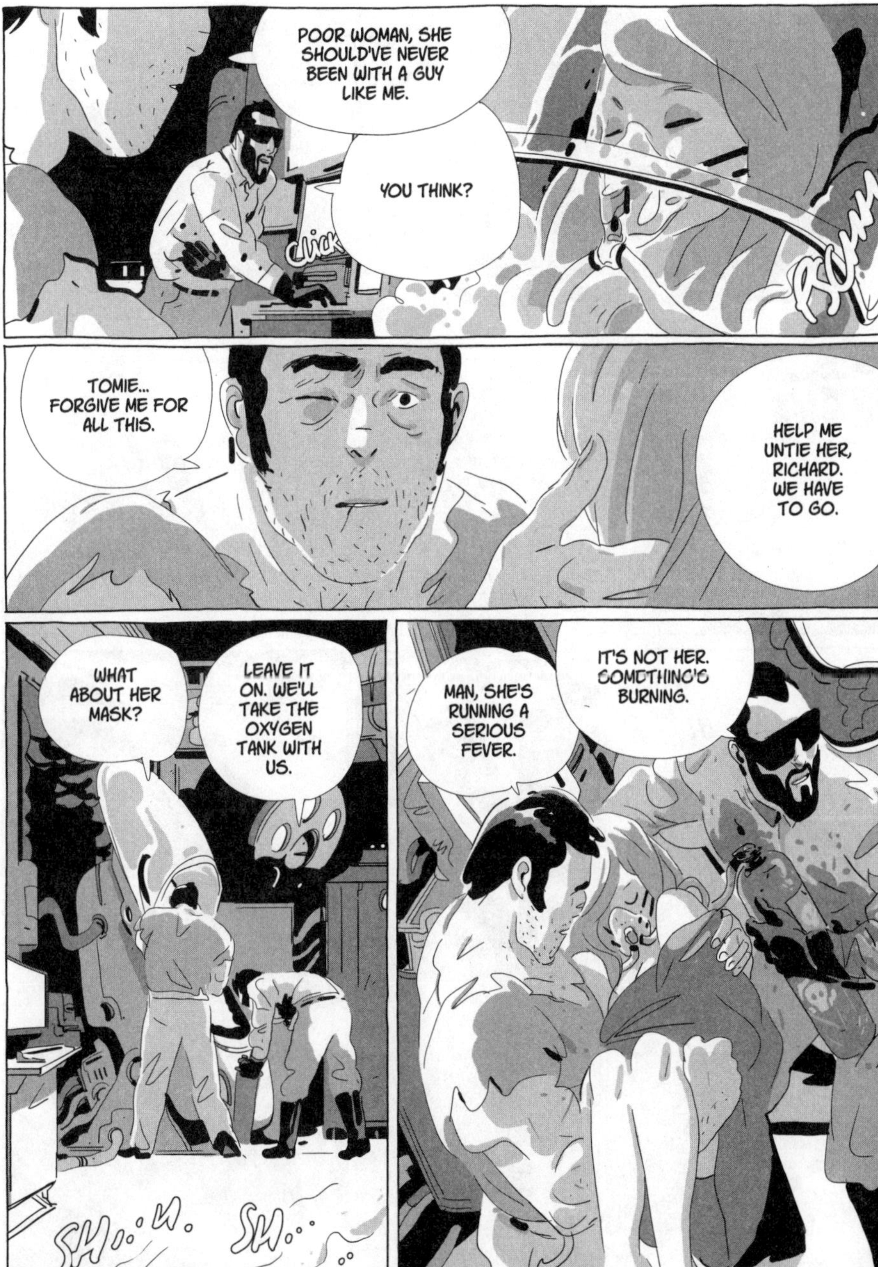
POOR WOMAN, SHE SHOULD'VE NEVER BEEN WITH A GUY LIKE ME.
CLICK
YOU THINK?
TOMIE... FORGIVE ME FOR ALL THIS.
HELP ME UNTIE HER, RICHARD. WE HAVE TO GO.
WHAT ABOUT HER MASK?
LEAVE IT ON. WE'LL TAKE THE OXYGEN TANK WITH US.
SH..U. SH...
MAN, SHE'S RUNNING A SERIOUS FEVER.
IT'S NOT HER. SOMETHING'S BURNING.

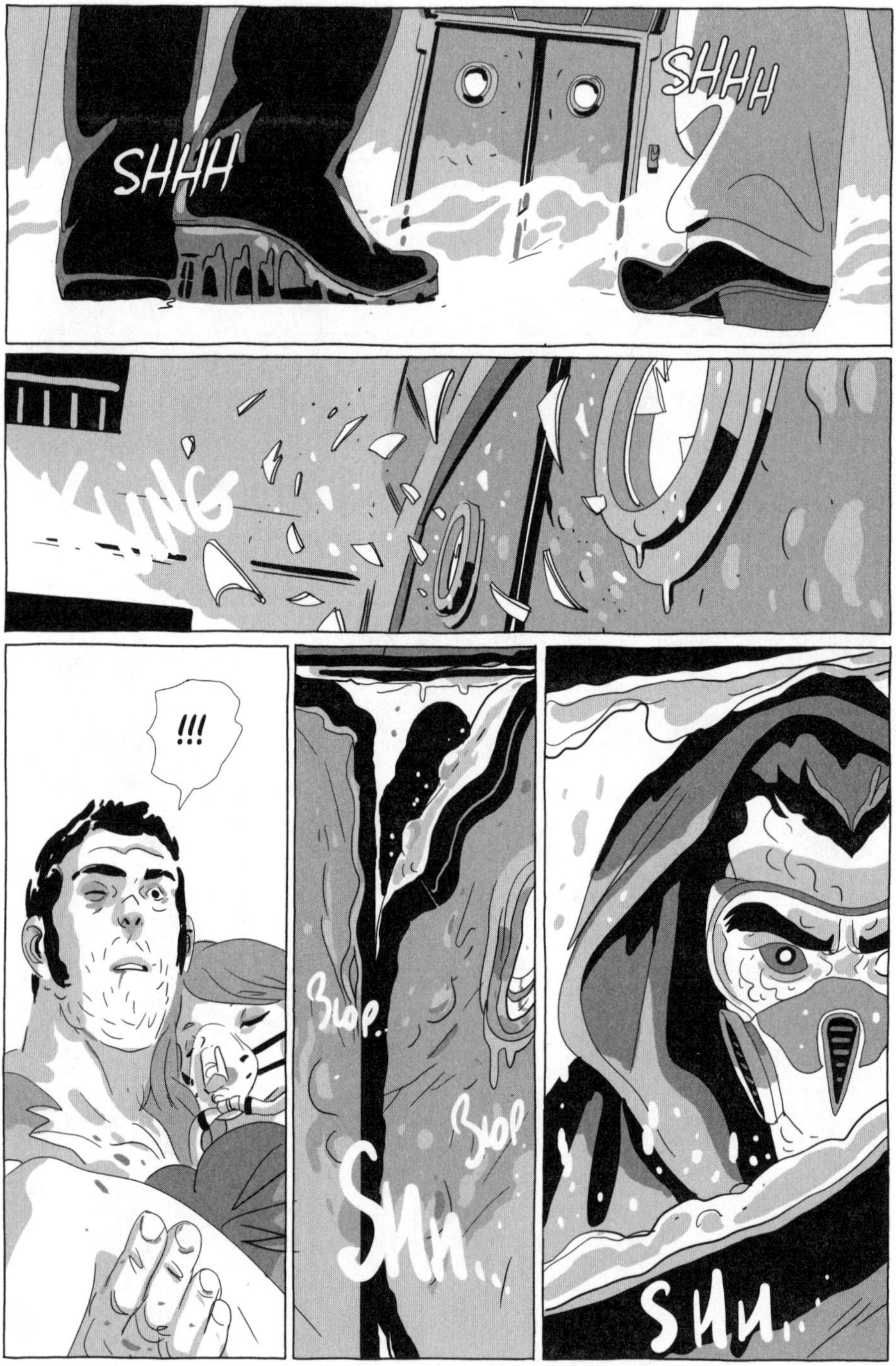
SHHH
SHHH
!!!
Blop..
Blop
SHH..
SHH..

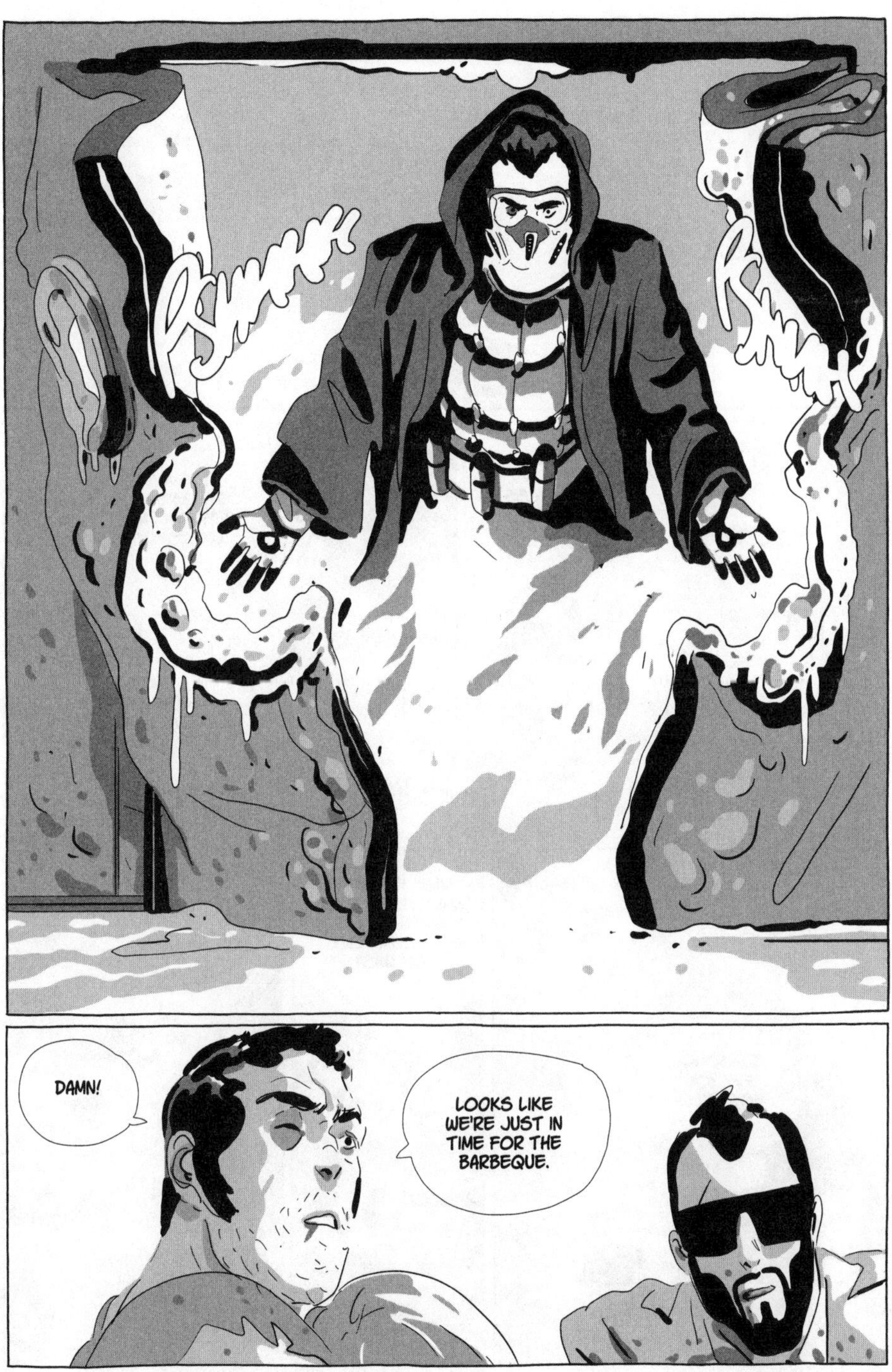
DAMN!
LOOKS LIKE WE'RE JUST IN TIME FOR THE BARBEQUE.

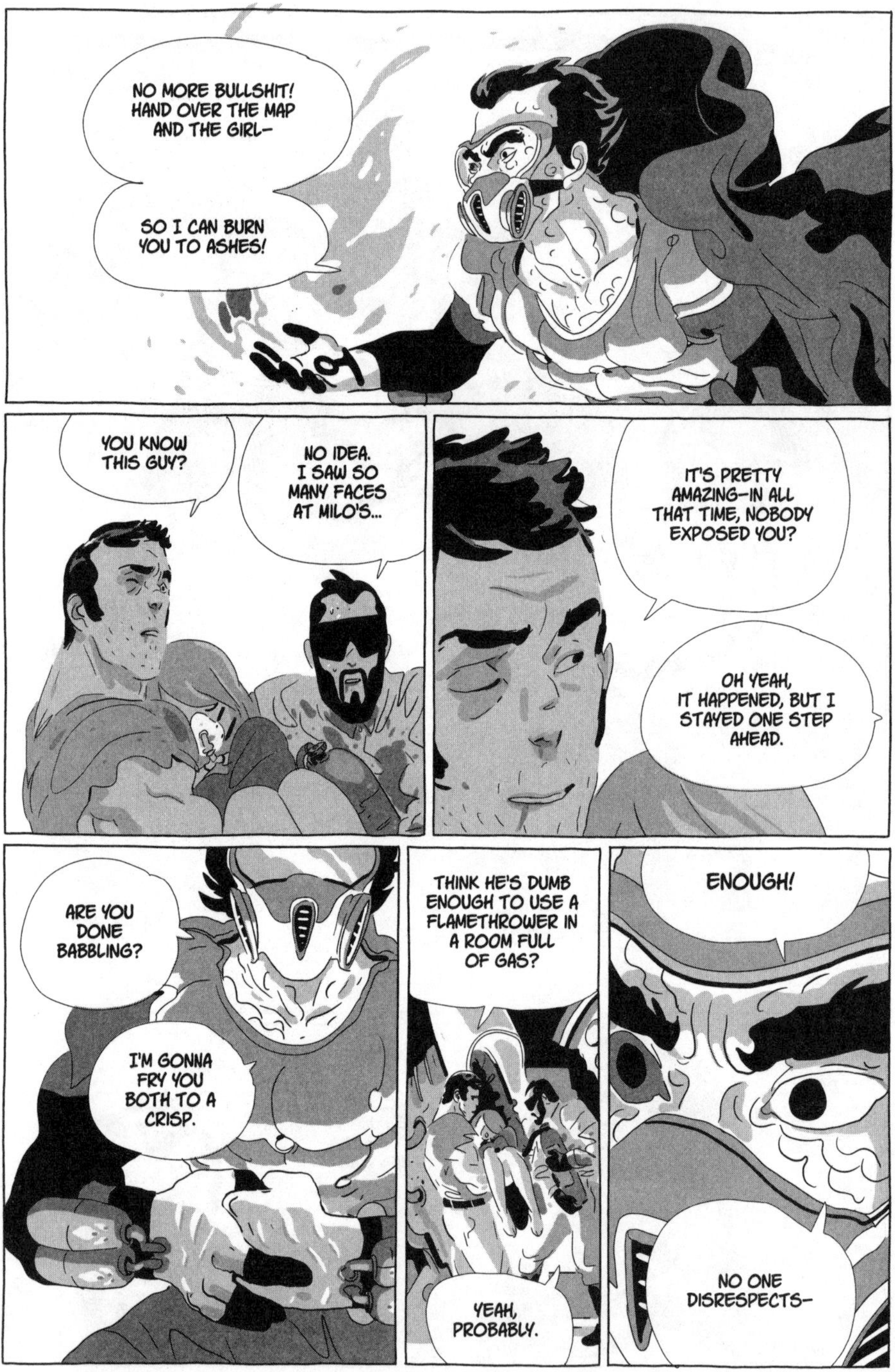
NO MORE BULLSHIT! HAND OVER THE MAP AND THE GIRL-
SO I CAN BURN YOU TO ASHES!
YOU KNOW THIS GUY?
NO IDEA. I SAW SO MANY FACES AT MILO'S...
IT'S PRETTY AMAZING—IN ALL THAT TIME, NOBODY EXPOSED YOU?
OH YEAH, IT HAPPENED, BUT I STAYED ONE STEP AHEAD.
ARE YOU DONE BABBLING?
I'M GONNA FRY YOU BOTH TO A CRISP.
THINK HE'S DUMB ENOUGH TO USE A FLAMETHROWER IN A ROOM FULL OF GAS?
YEAH, PROBABLY.
ENOUGH!
NO ONE DISRESPECTS-

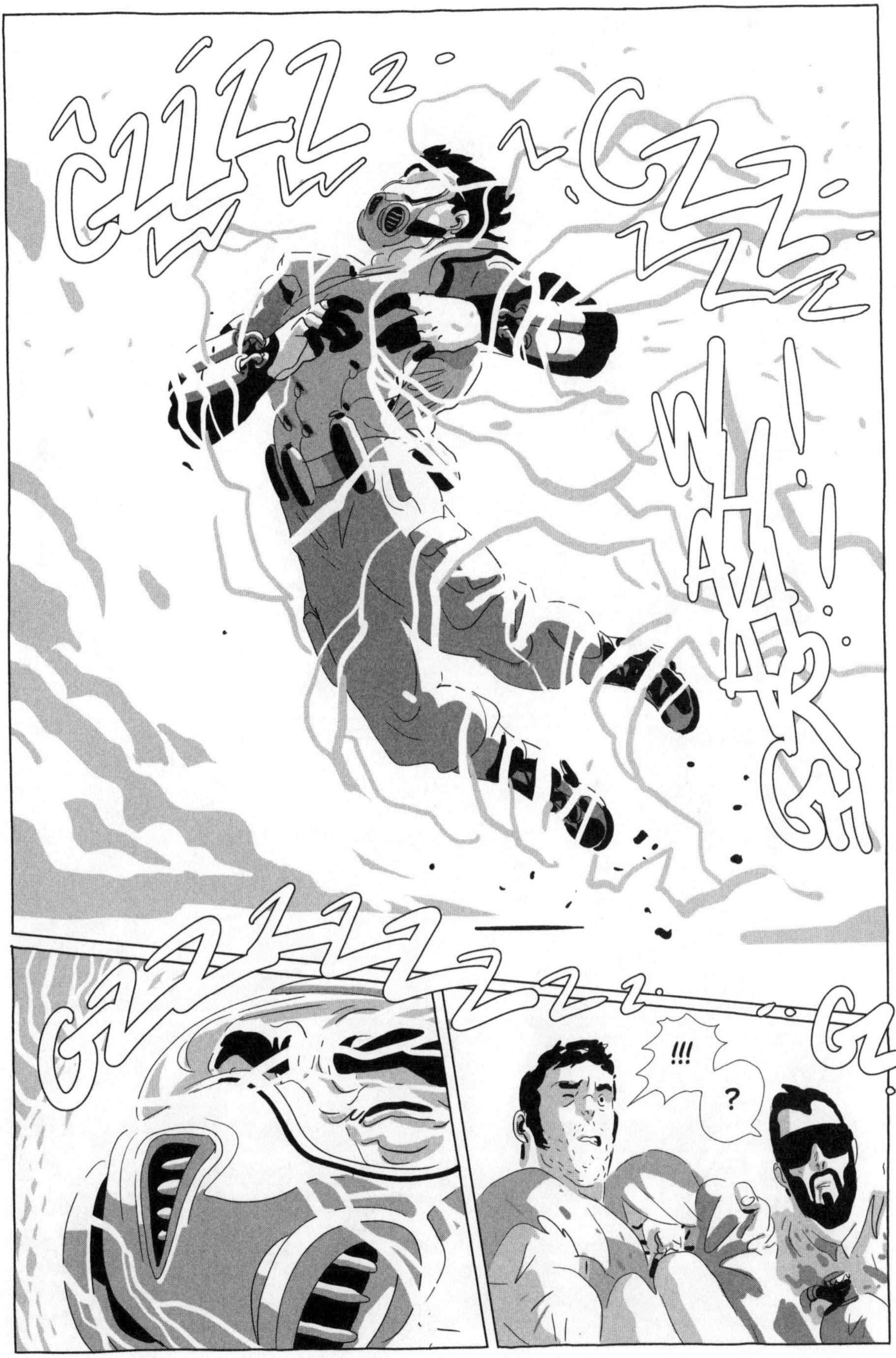
CZZZz
zCZZZZ
WHAARGH!!!
GZZZZZZzzz..GZ
!!!
?

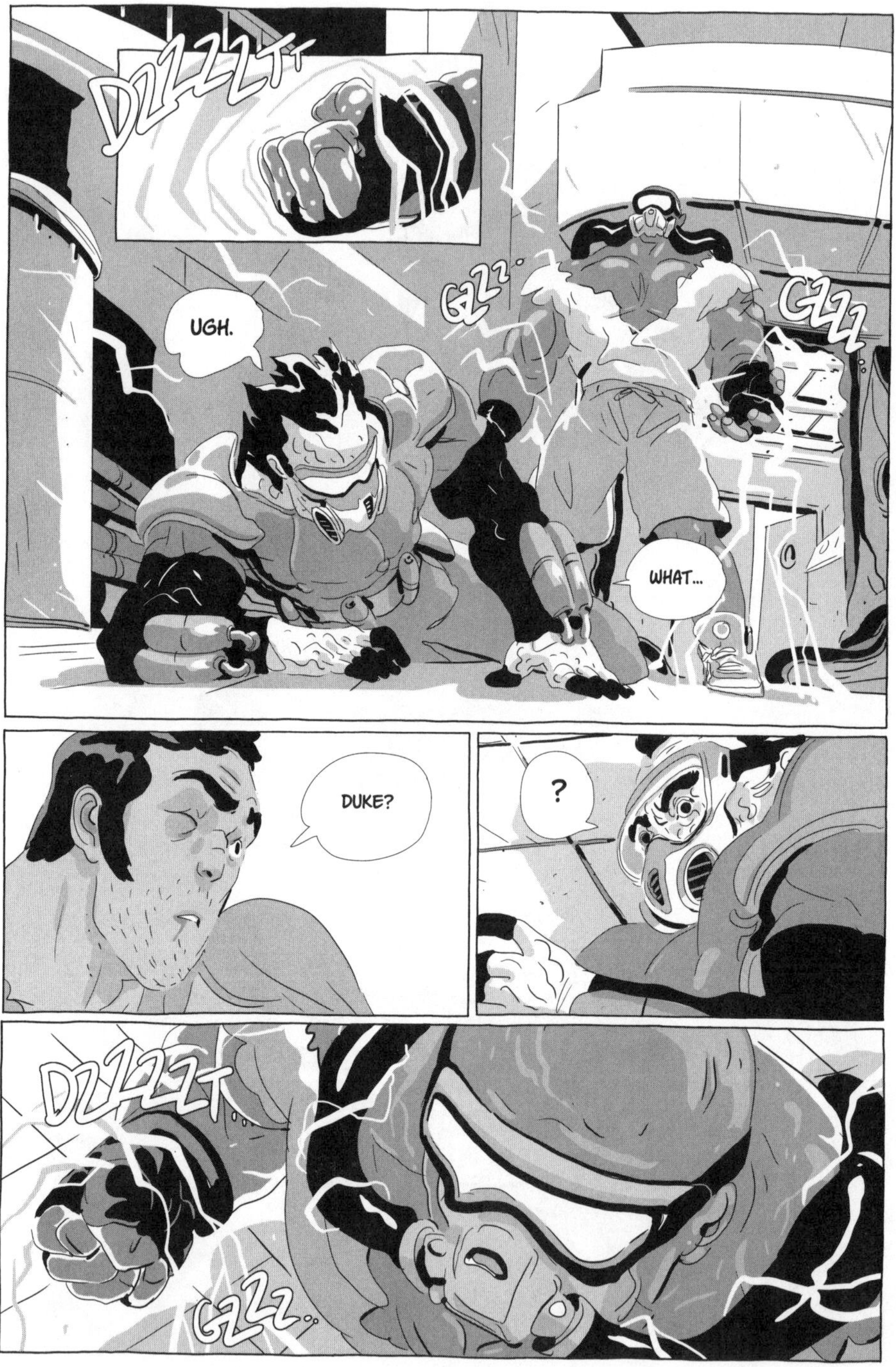
DZZZZZTT
GZZZ..
GZZZ
UGH.
WHAT...
DUKE?
?
DZZZZZT
GZZZ..

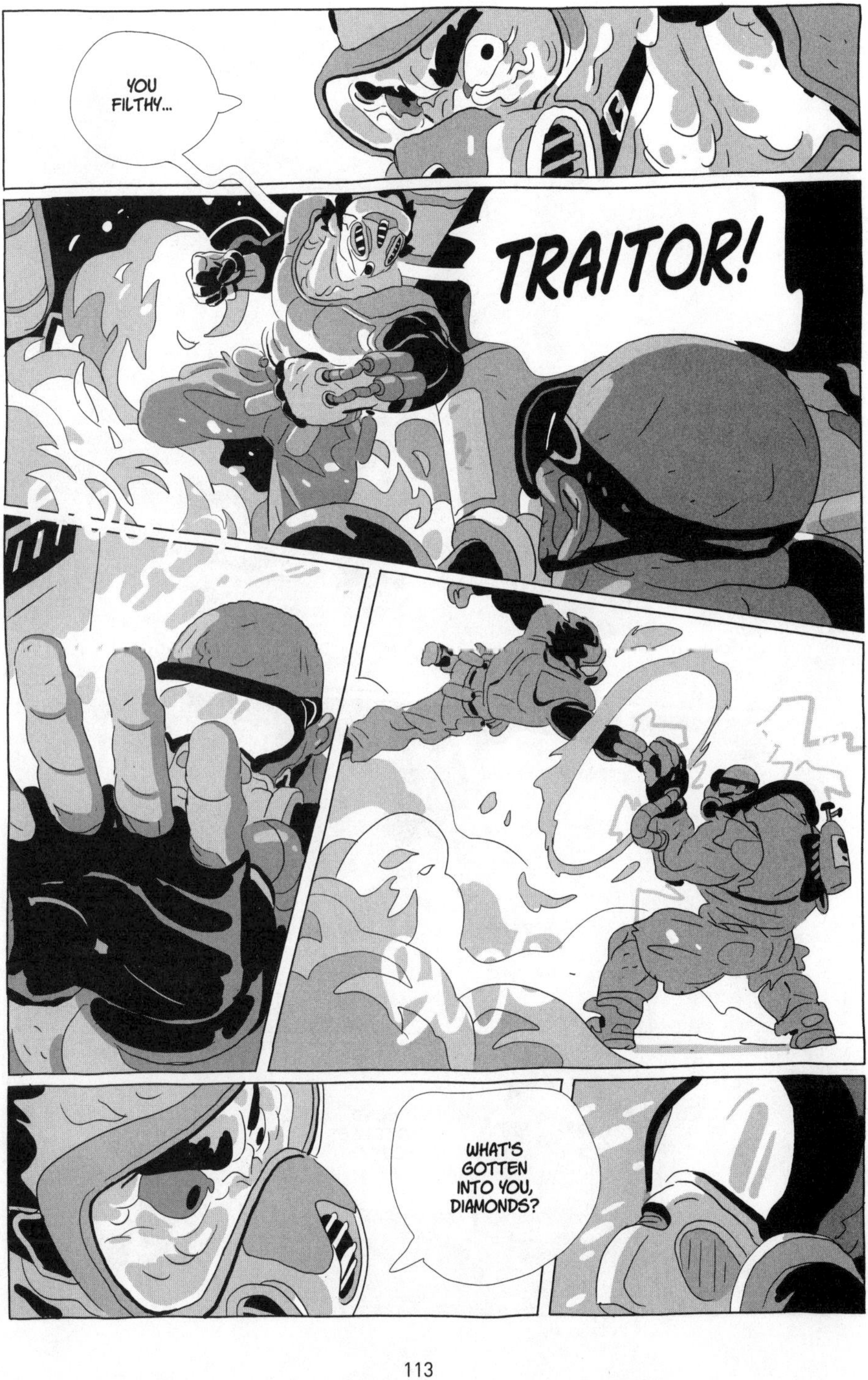

YOU FILTHY...
TRAITOR!
WHAT'S GOTTEN INTO YOU, DIAMONDS?

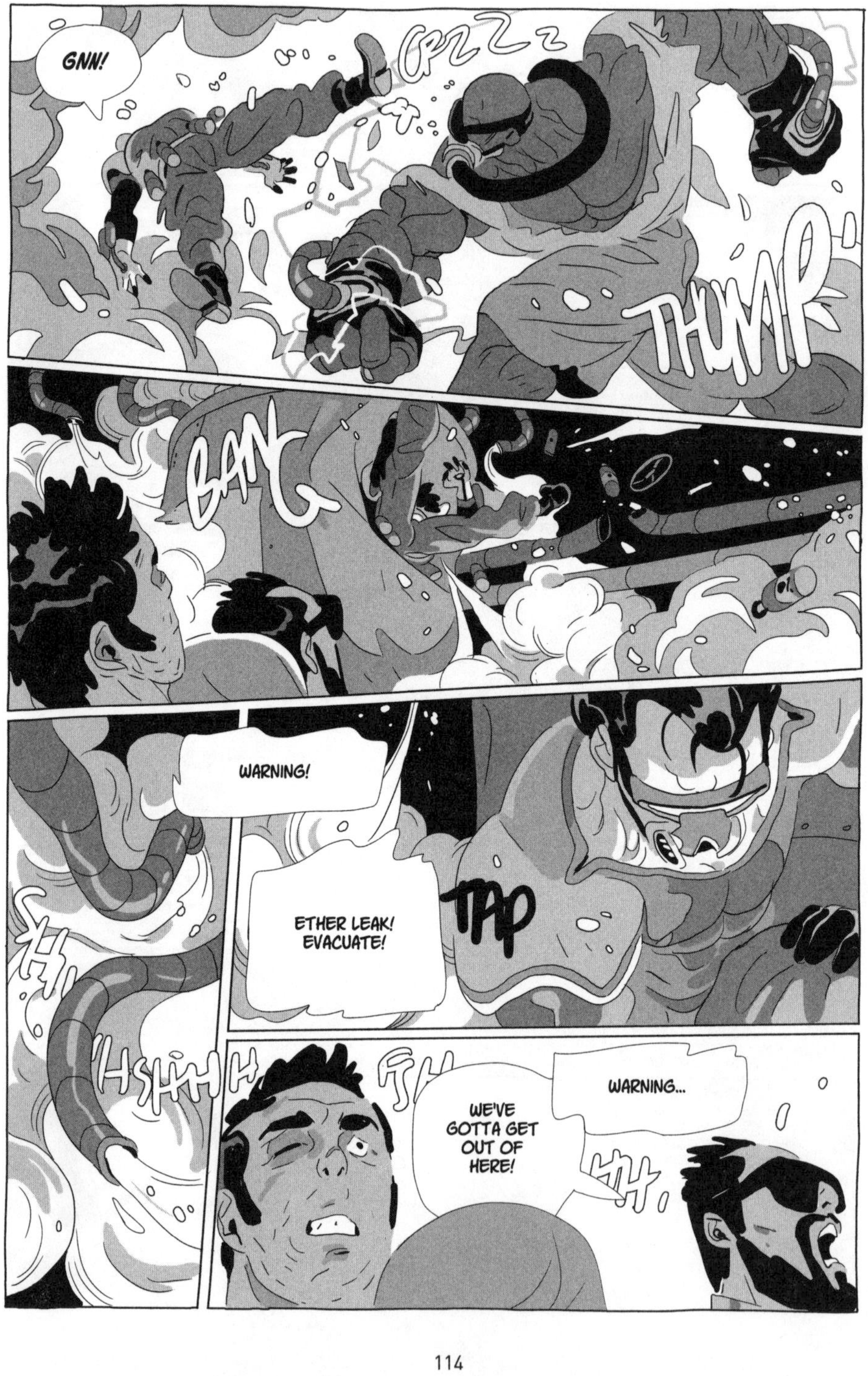
GNN!
CRZZZz
THUMP
BANG
WARNING!
ETHER LEAK! EVACUATE!
TAP
WARNING...
WE'VE GOTTA GET OUT OF HERE!

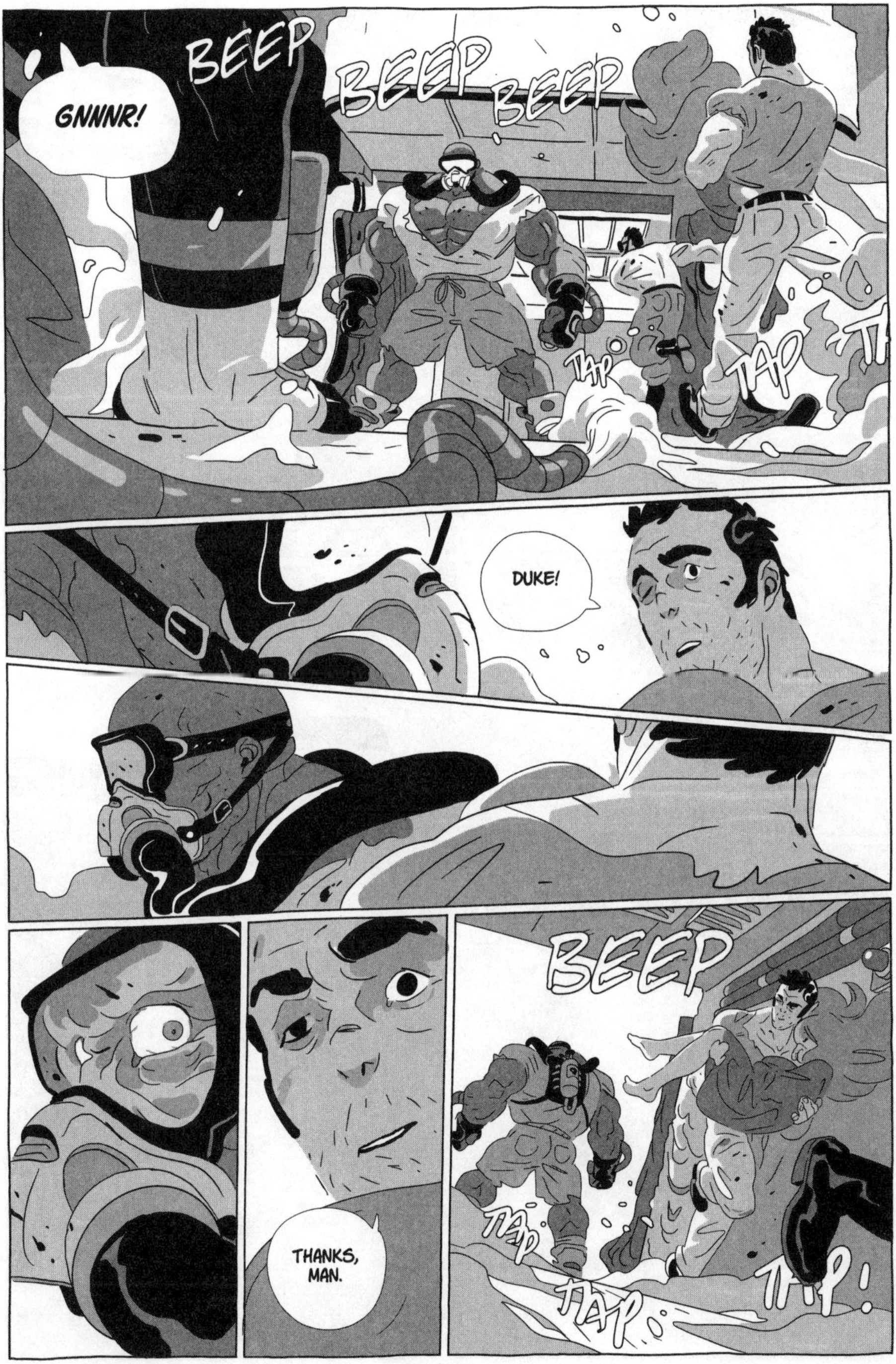
GNNNR!
BEEP
BEEP
BEEP
TAP
TAP
TA
DUKE!
BEEP
THANKS, MAN.
TAP
TAP
TAP!

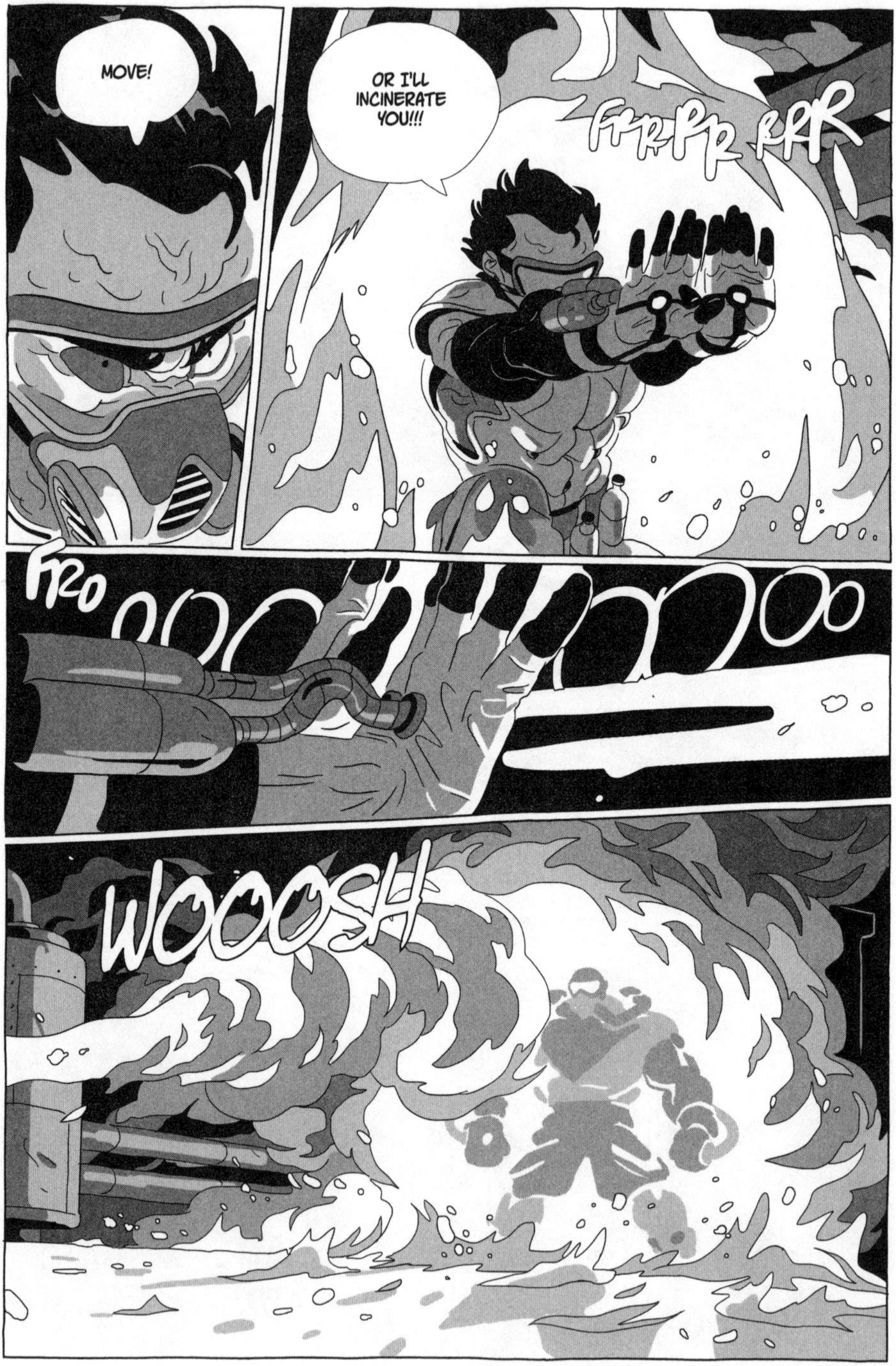
MOVE!
OR I'LL INCINERATE YOU!!!
FRRRR RRR
FROOOOOOOOOOO
WOOOSH

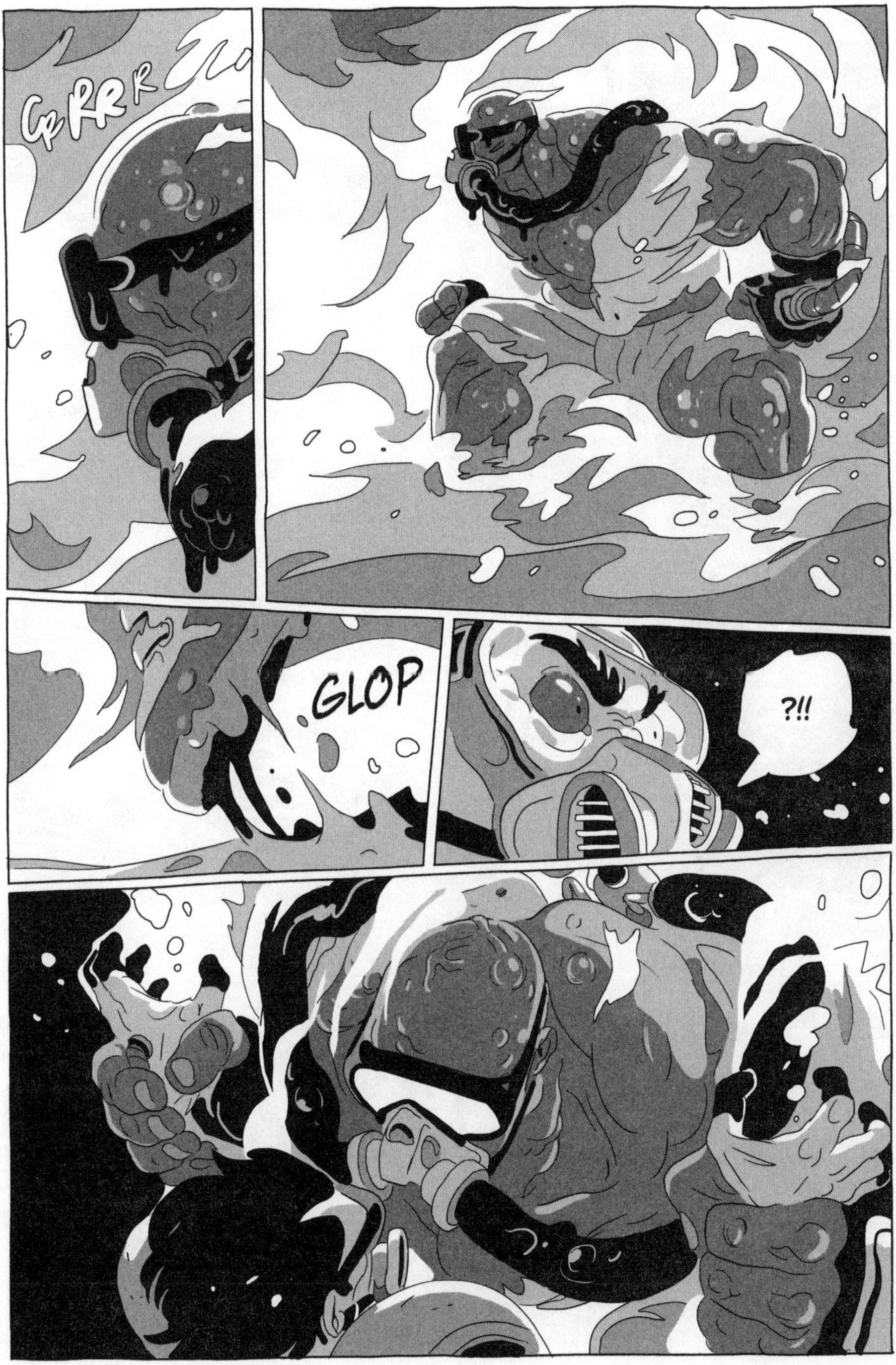
GRRR
GLOP
?!!

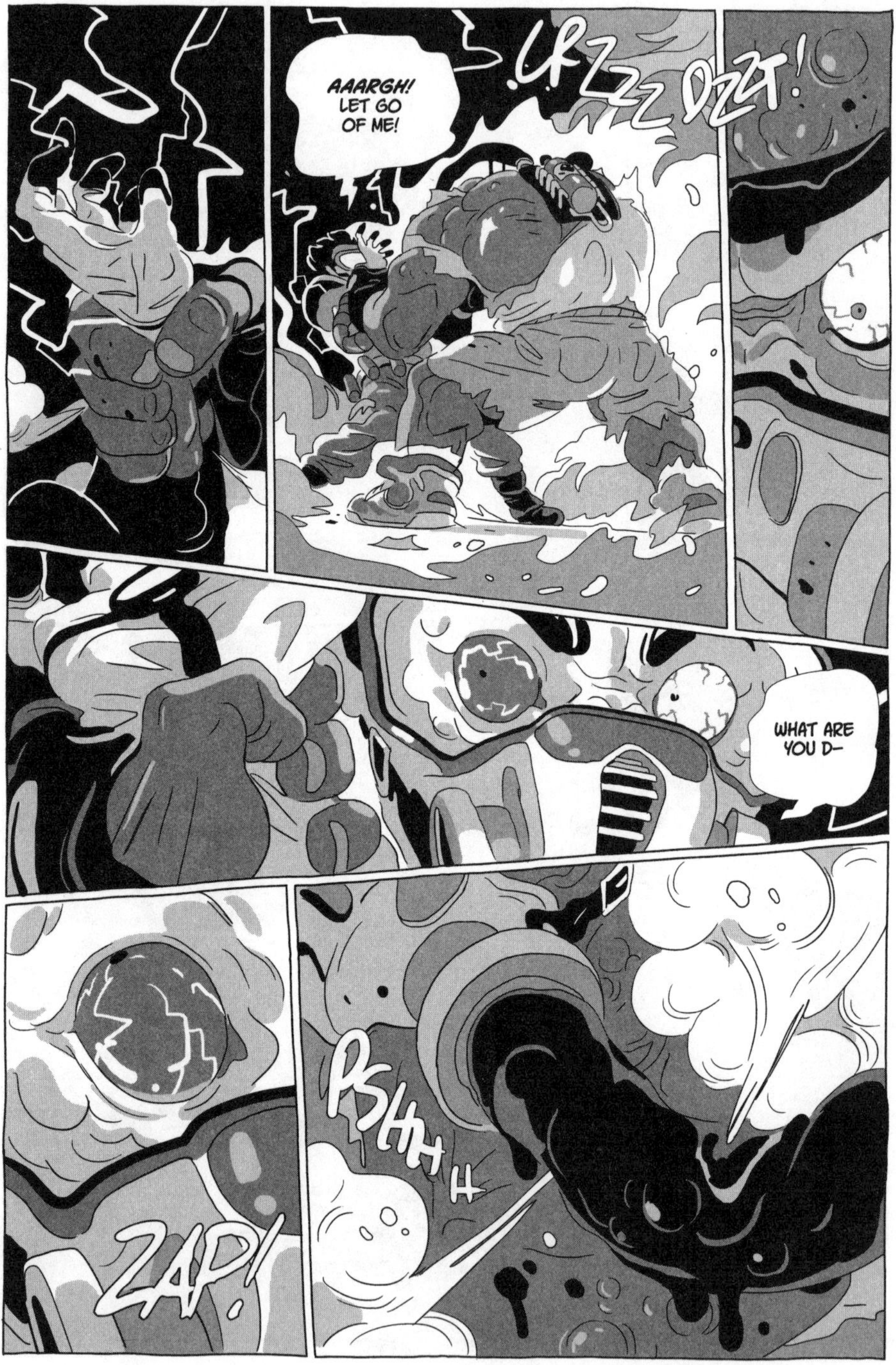
AAARGH! LET GO OF ME!
CRZZZ DZZT!
WHAT ARE YOU D–
ZAP!
PSHHHH

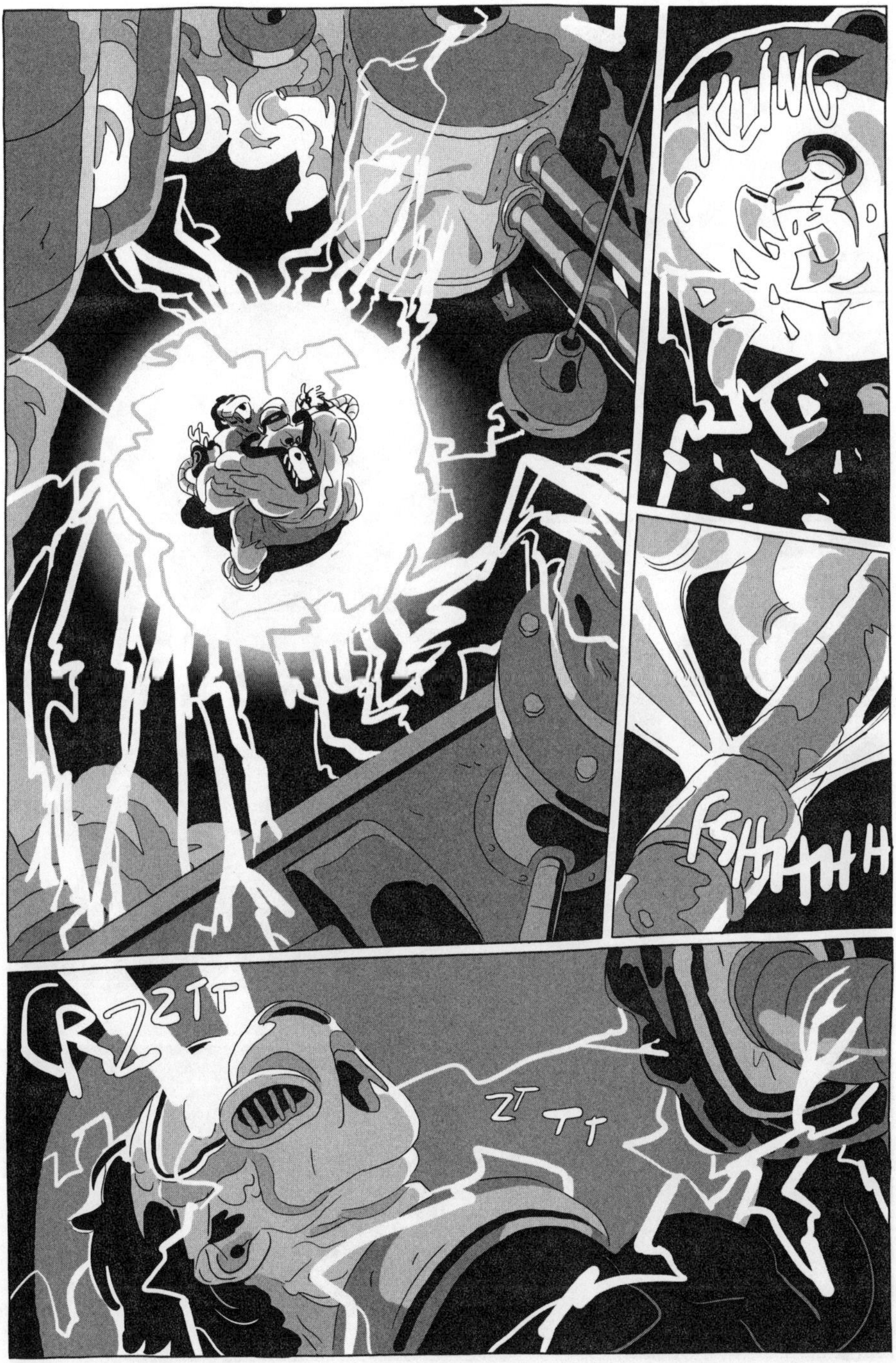
KLING
FSHHHHHH
CRZZTT
ZTTT

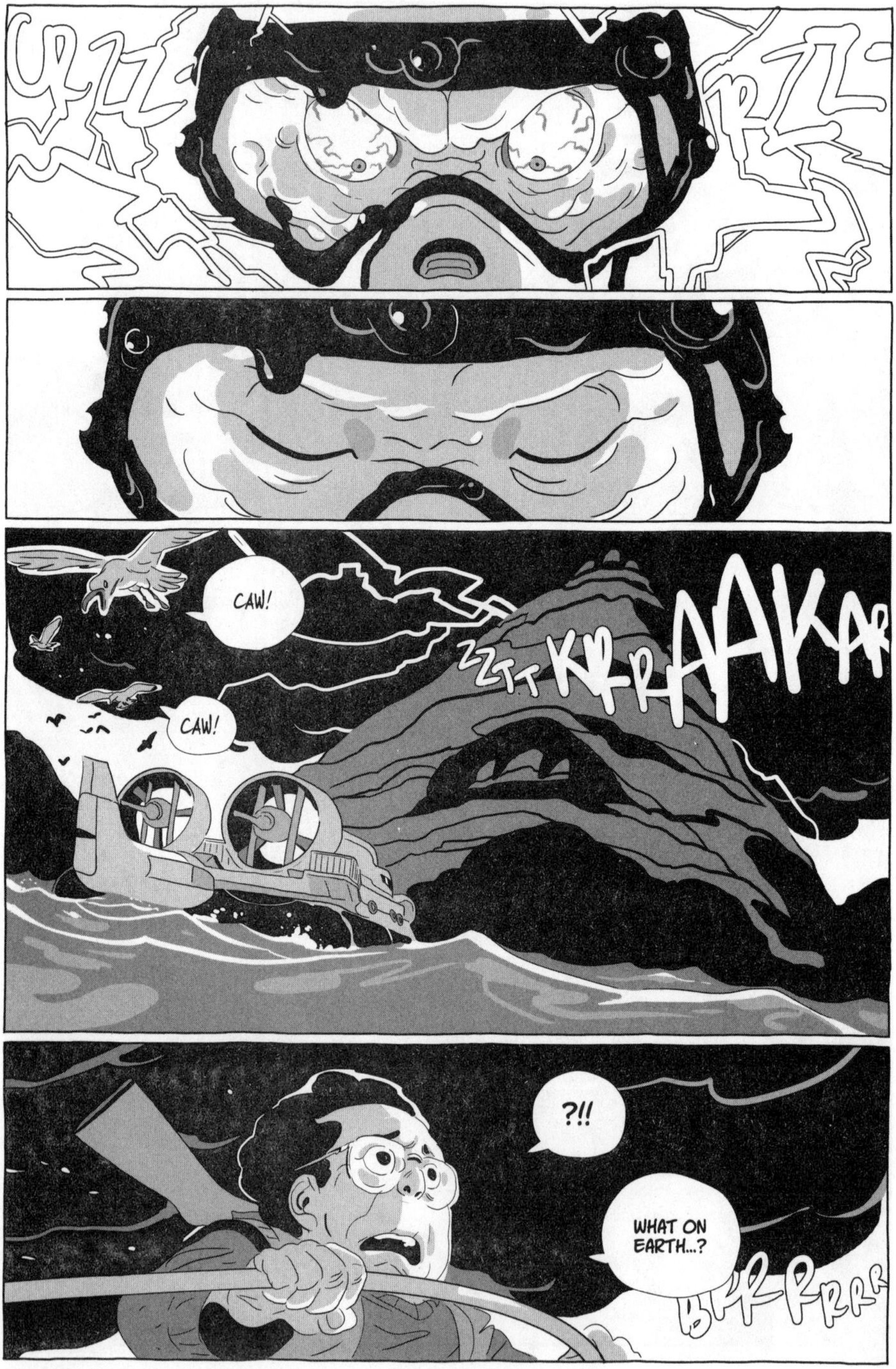
CAW!
CAW!
?!!
WHAT ON EARTH...?

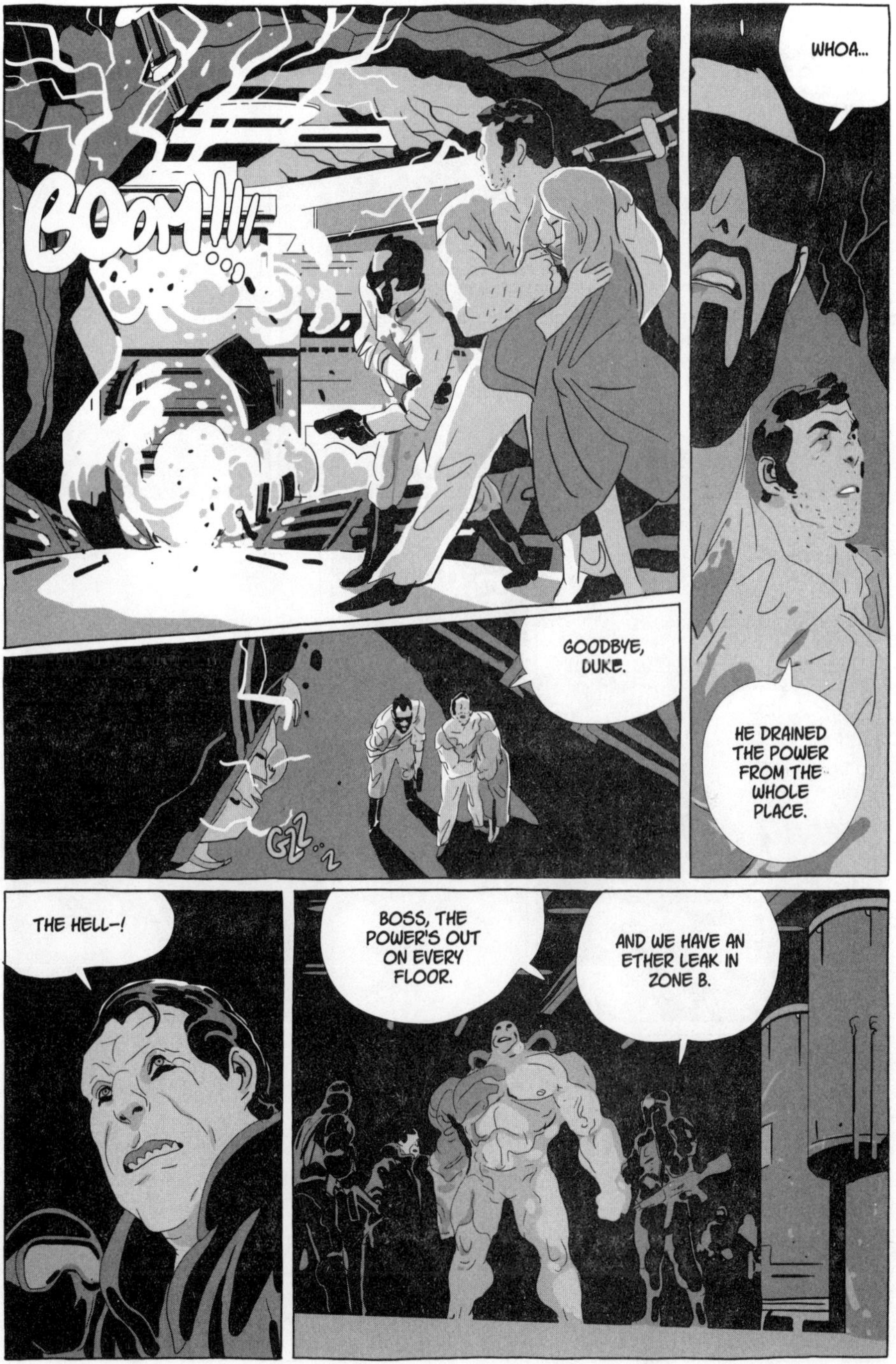
BOOM!!!!
GOODBYE, DUKE.
GZZ..Z
WHOA...
HE DRAINED THE POWER FROM THE WHOLE PLACE.
THE HELL-!
BOSS, THE POWER'S OUT ON EVERY FLOOR.
AND WE HAVE AN ETHER LEAK IN ZONE B.

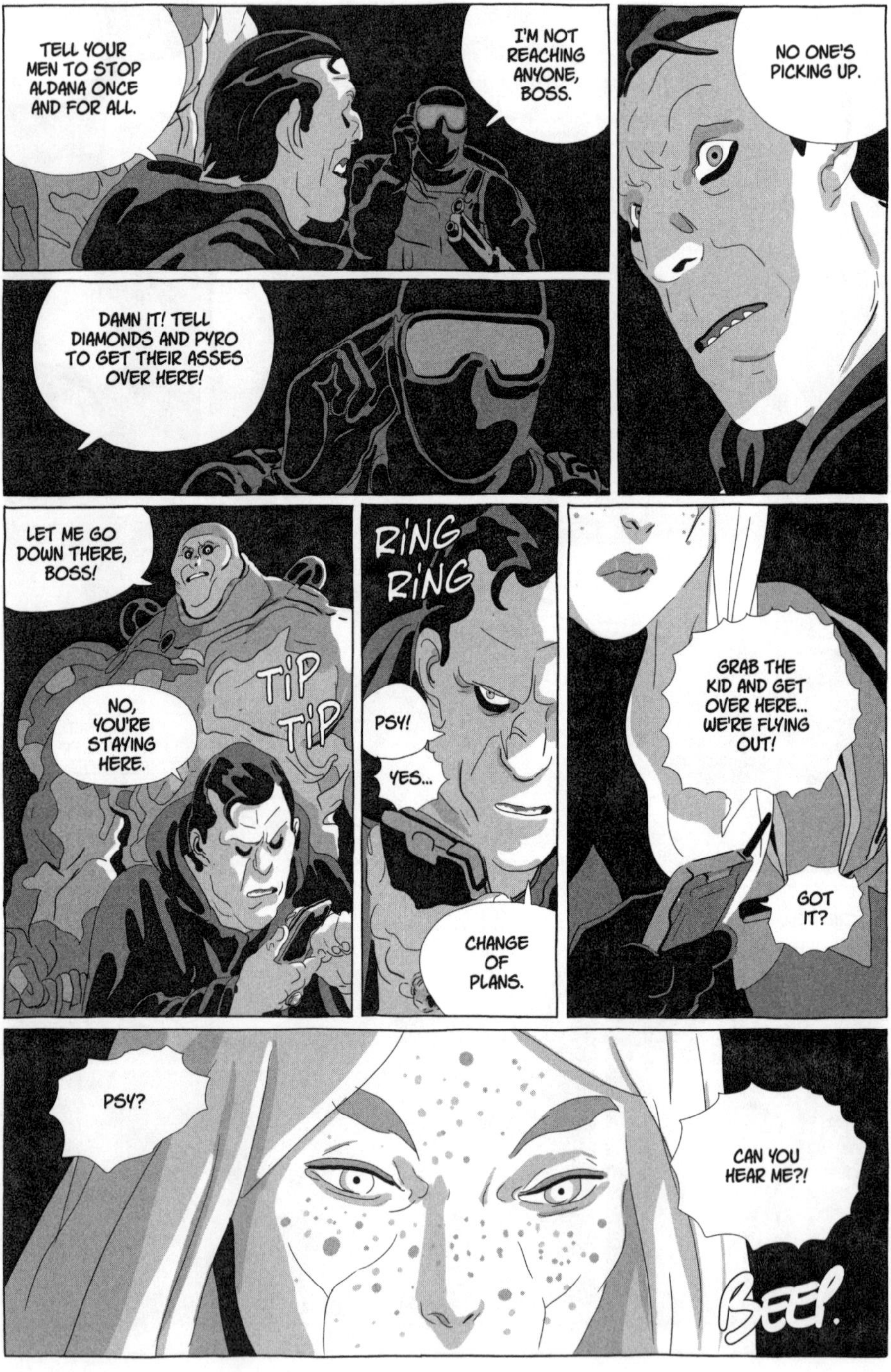
TELL YOUR MEN TO STOP ALDANA ONCE AND FOR ALL.
I'M NOT REACHING ANYONE, BOSS.
NO ONE'S PICKING UP.
DAMN IT! TELL DIAMONDS AND PYRO TO GET THEIR ASSES OVER HERE!
LET ME GO DOWN THERE, BOSS!
TIP TIP
NO, YOU'RE STAYING HERE.
RING RING
PSY!
YES...
CHANGE OF PLANS.
GRAB THE KID AND GET OVER HERE... WE'RE FLYING OUT!
GOT IT?
PSY?
CAN YOU HEAR ME?!
BEEP.

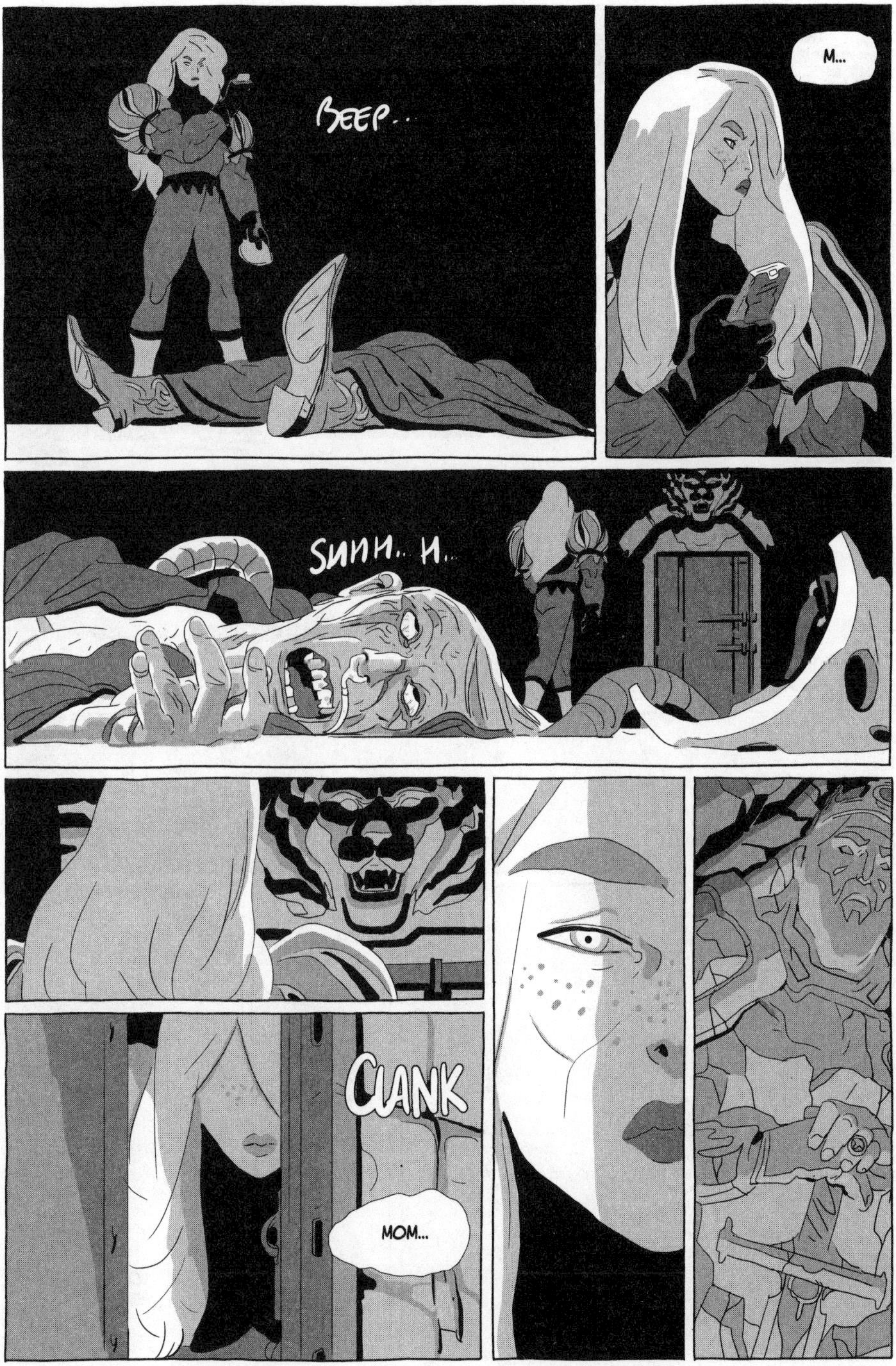
BEEP...
M...
SUHH... H...
CLANK
MOM...

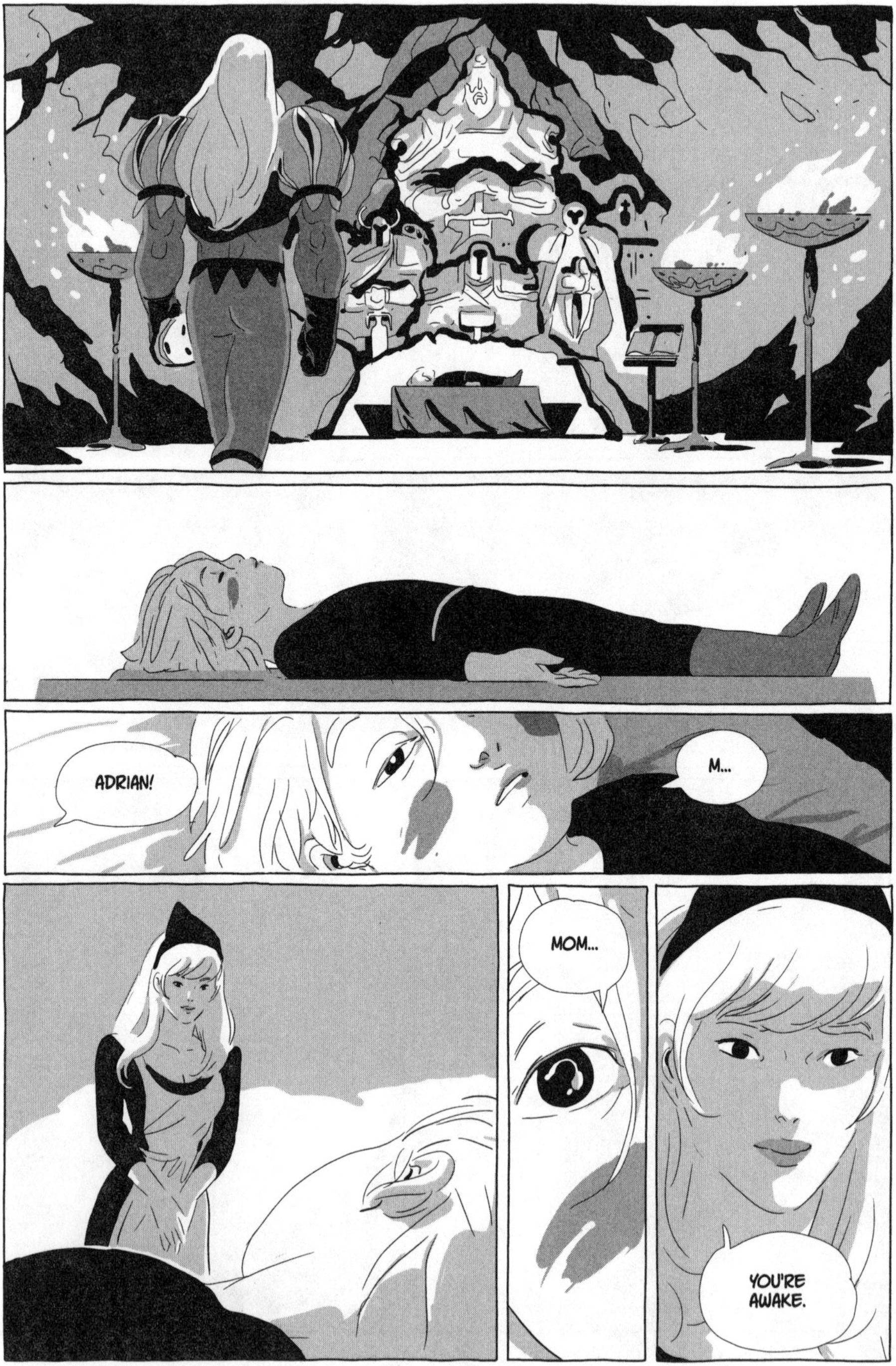
ADRIAN!
M...
MOM...
YOU'RE AWAKE.

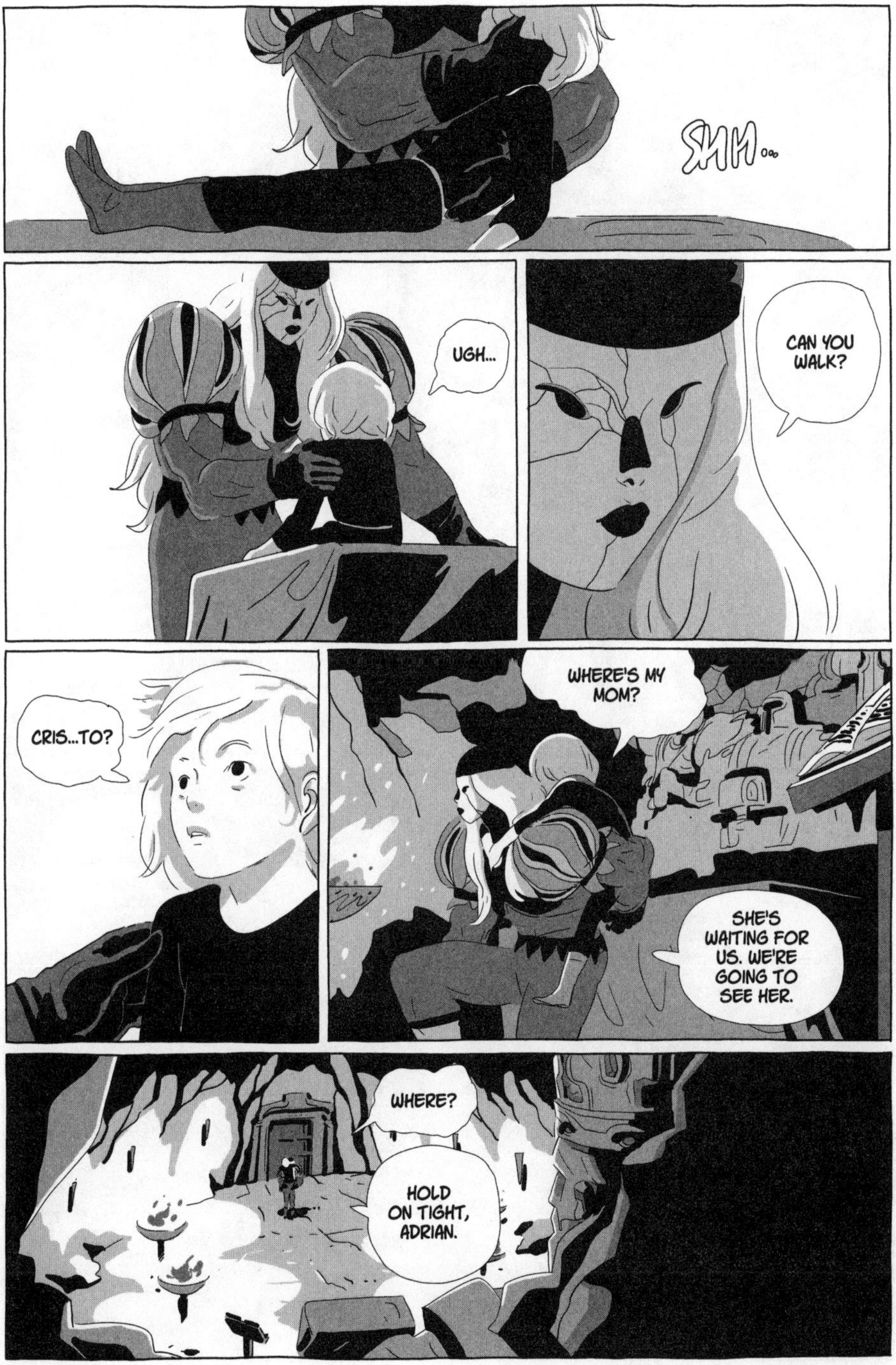
SHH...
UGH...
CAN YOU WALK?
CRIS...TO?
WHERE'S MY MOM?
SHE'S WAITING FOR US. WE'RE GOING TO SEE HER.
WHERE?
HOLD ON TIGHT, ADRIAN.

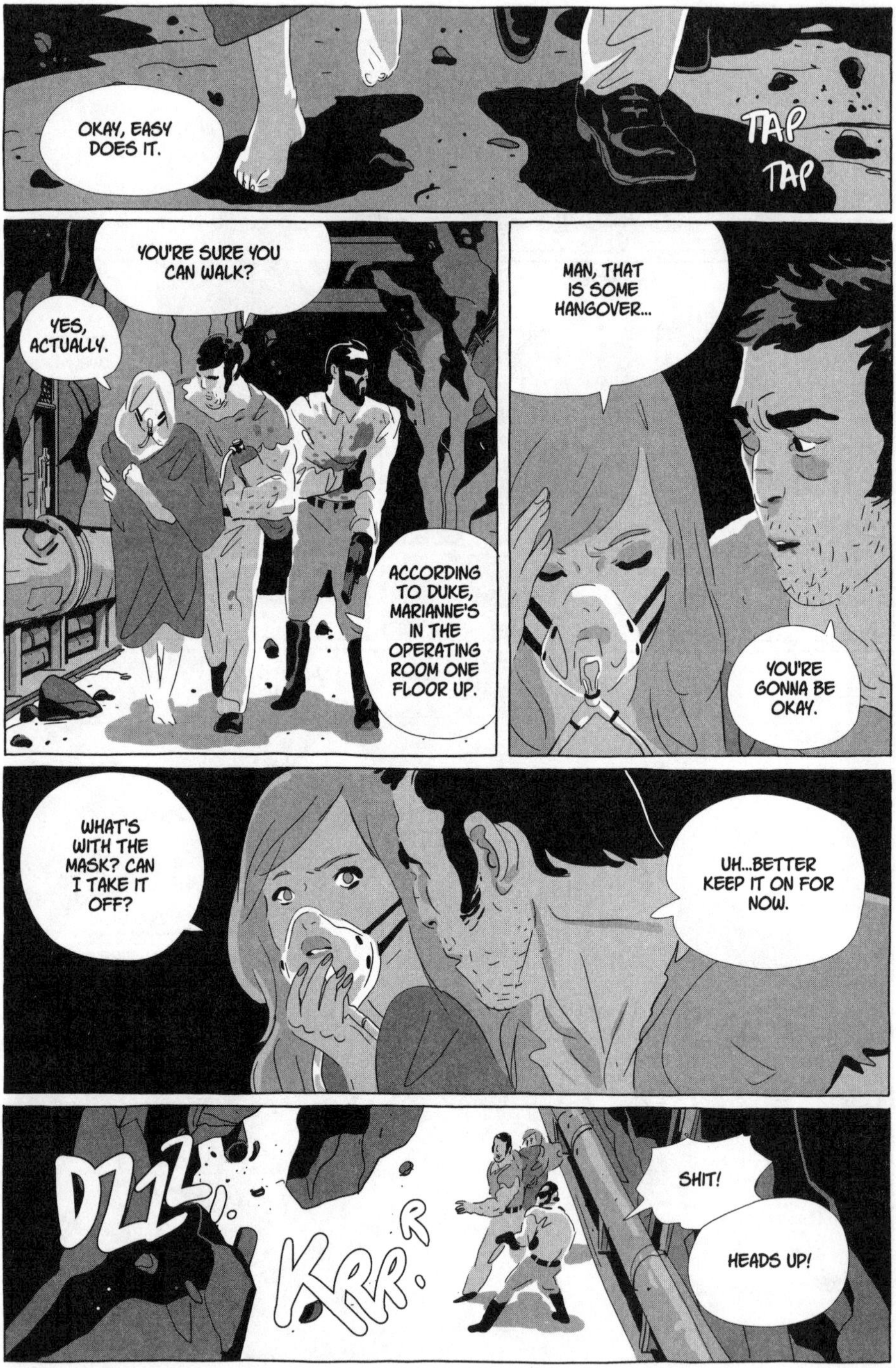
OKAY, EASY DOES IT.
TAP TAP
YOU'RE SURE YOU CAN WALK?
YES, ACTUALLY.
ACCORDING TO DUKE, MARIANNE'S IN THE OPERATING ROOM ONE FLOOR UP.
MAN, THAT IS SOME HANGOVER...
YOU'RE GONNA BE OKAY.
WHAT'S WITH THE MASK? CAN I TAKE IT OFF?
UH...BETTER KEEP IT ON FOR NOW.
DZZZ
KRRR
SHIT!
HEADS UP!

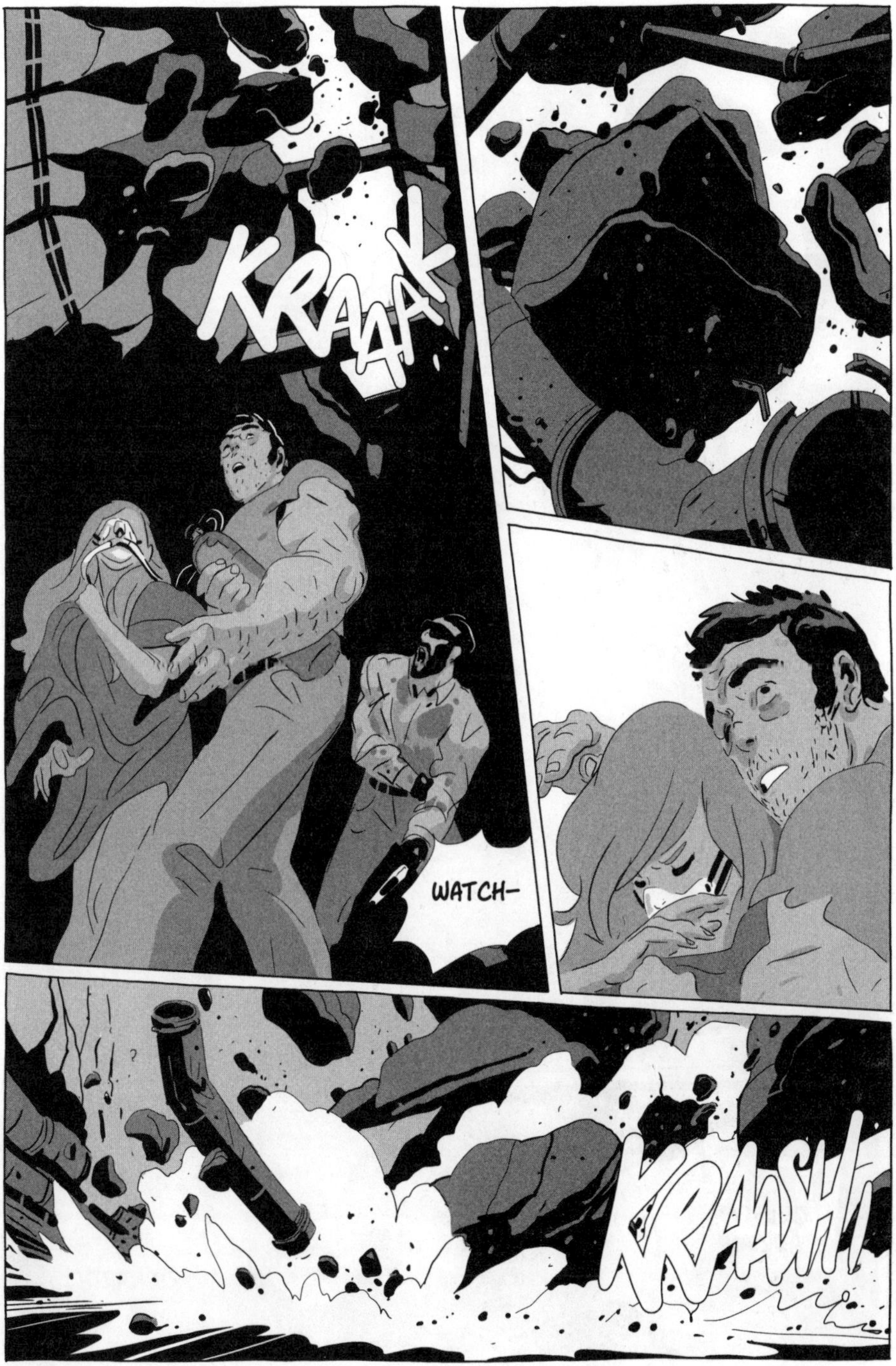
KRAAAK
WATCH-
KRAASH!

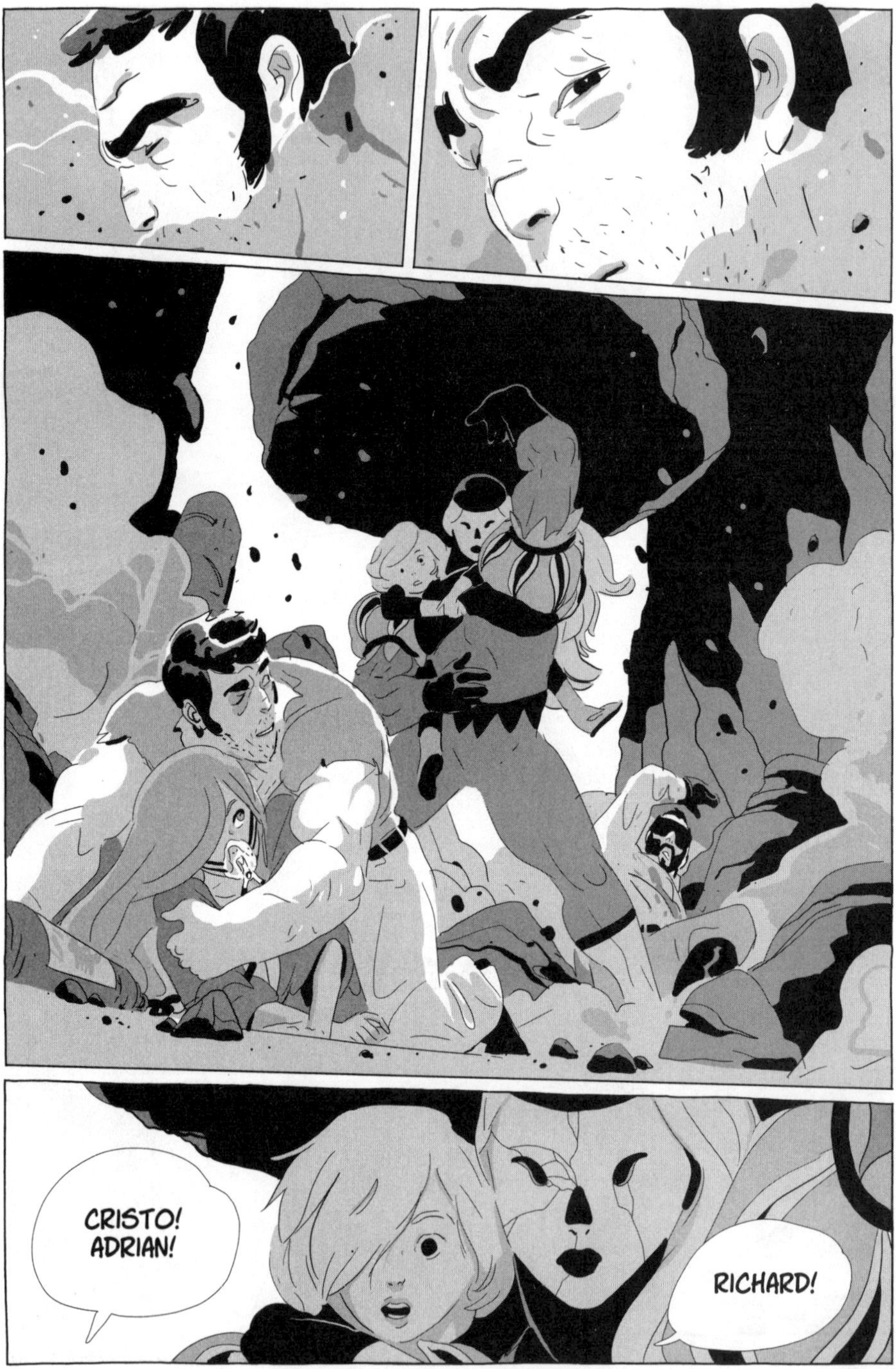
CRISTO!
ADRIAN!
RICHARD!

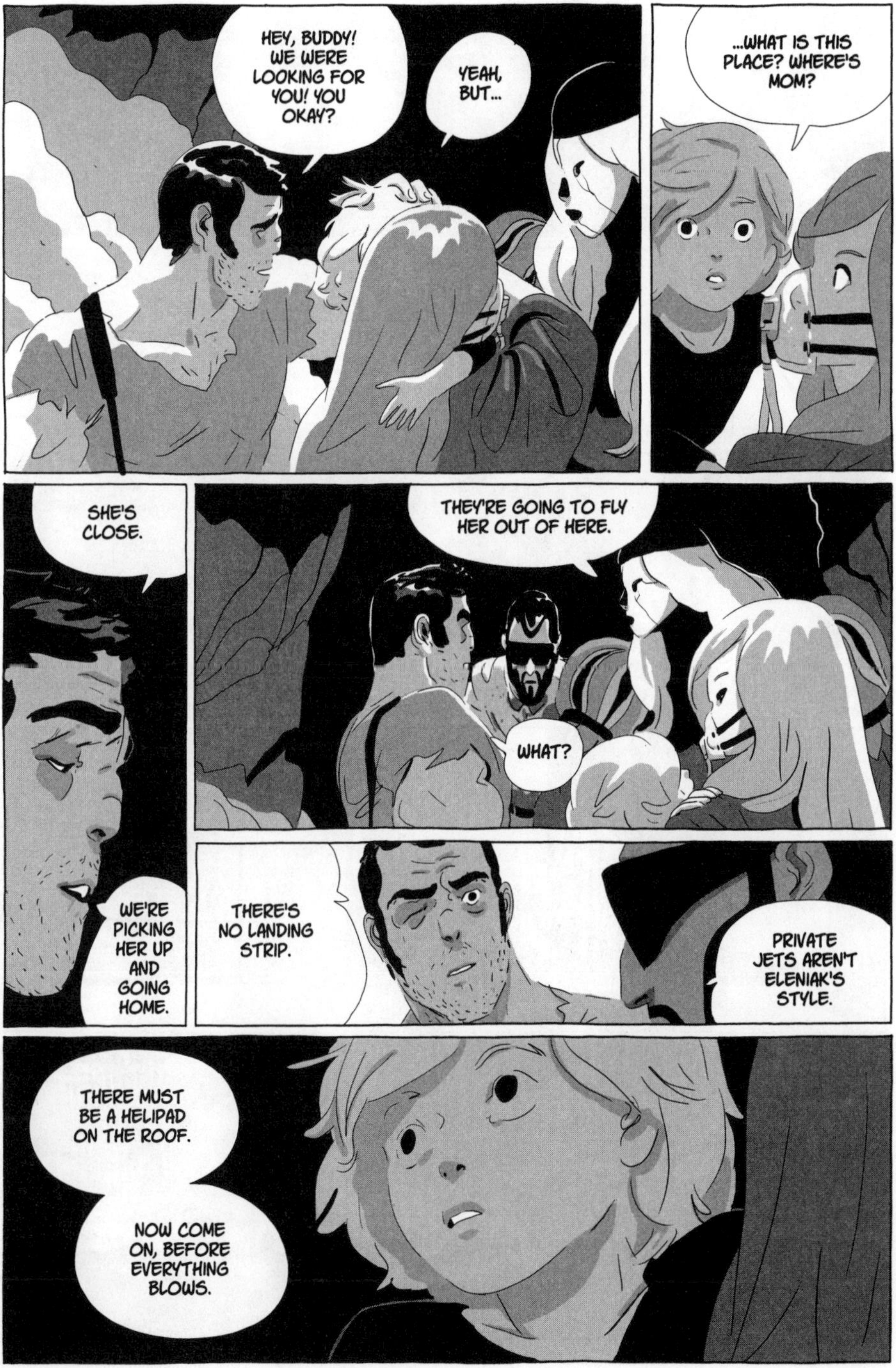
HEY, BUDDY! WE WERE LOOKING FOR YOU! YOU OKAY?
YEAH, BUT...
...WHAT IS THIS PLACE? WHERE'S MOM?
SHE'S CLOSE.
WE'RE PICKING HER UP AND GOING HOME.
THEY'RE GOING TO FLY HER OUT OF HERE.
WHAT?
THERE'S NO LANDING STRIP.
PRIVATE JETS AREN'T ELENIAK'S STYLE.
THERE MUST BE A HELIPAD ON THE ROOF.
NOW COME ON, BEFORE EVERYTHING BLOWS.

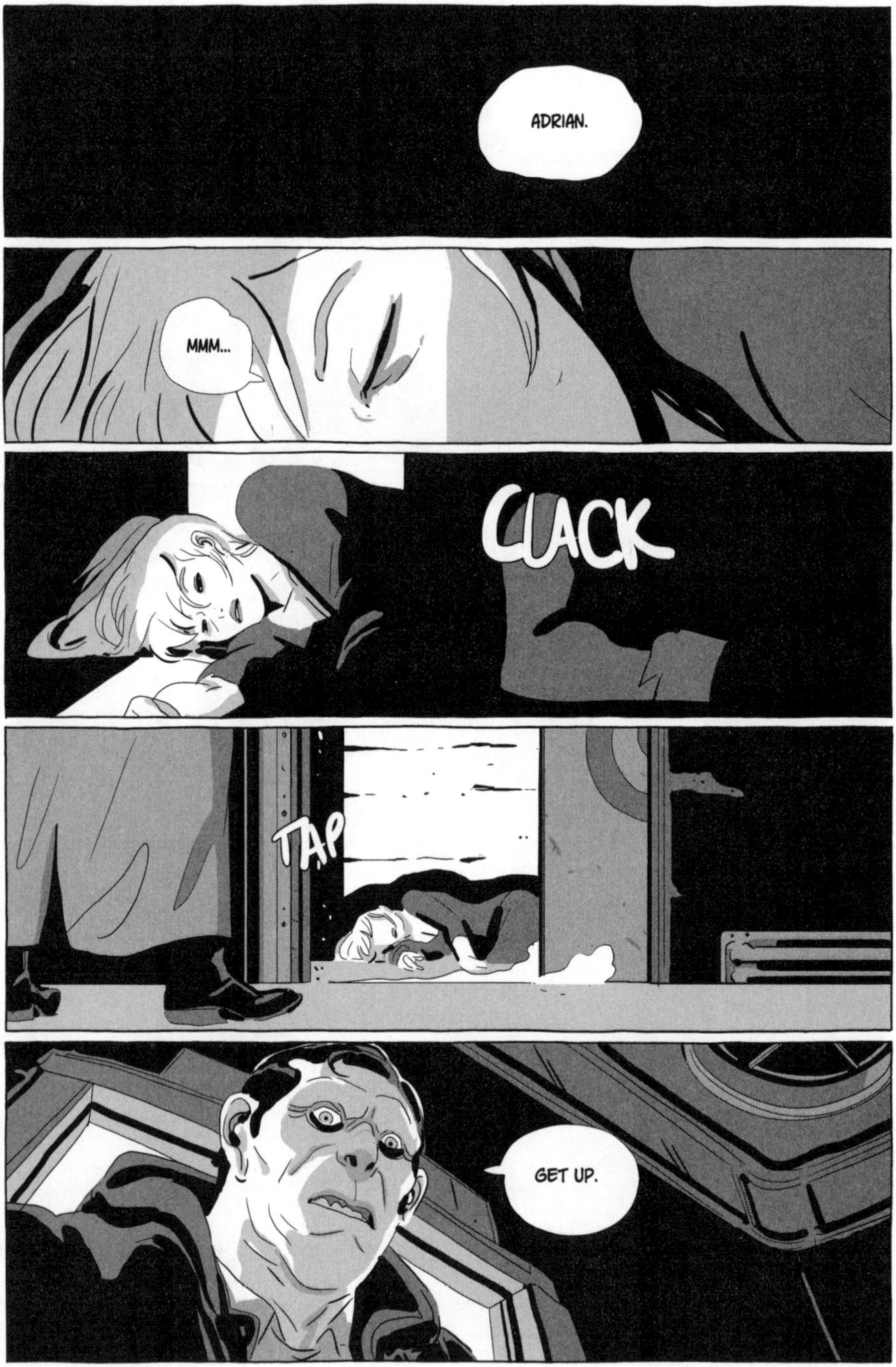
ADRIAN.
MMM...
CLACK
TAP
GET UP.

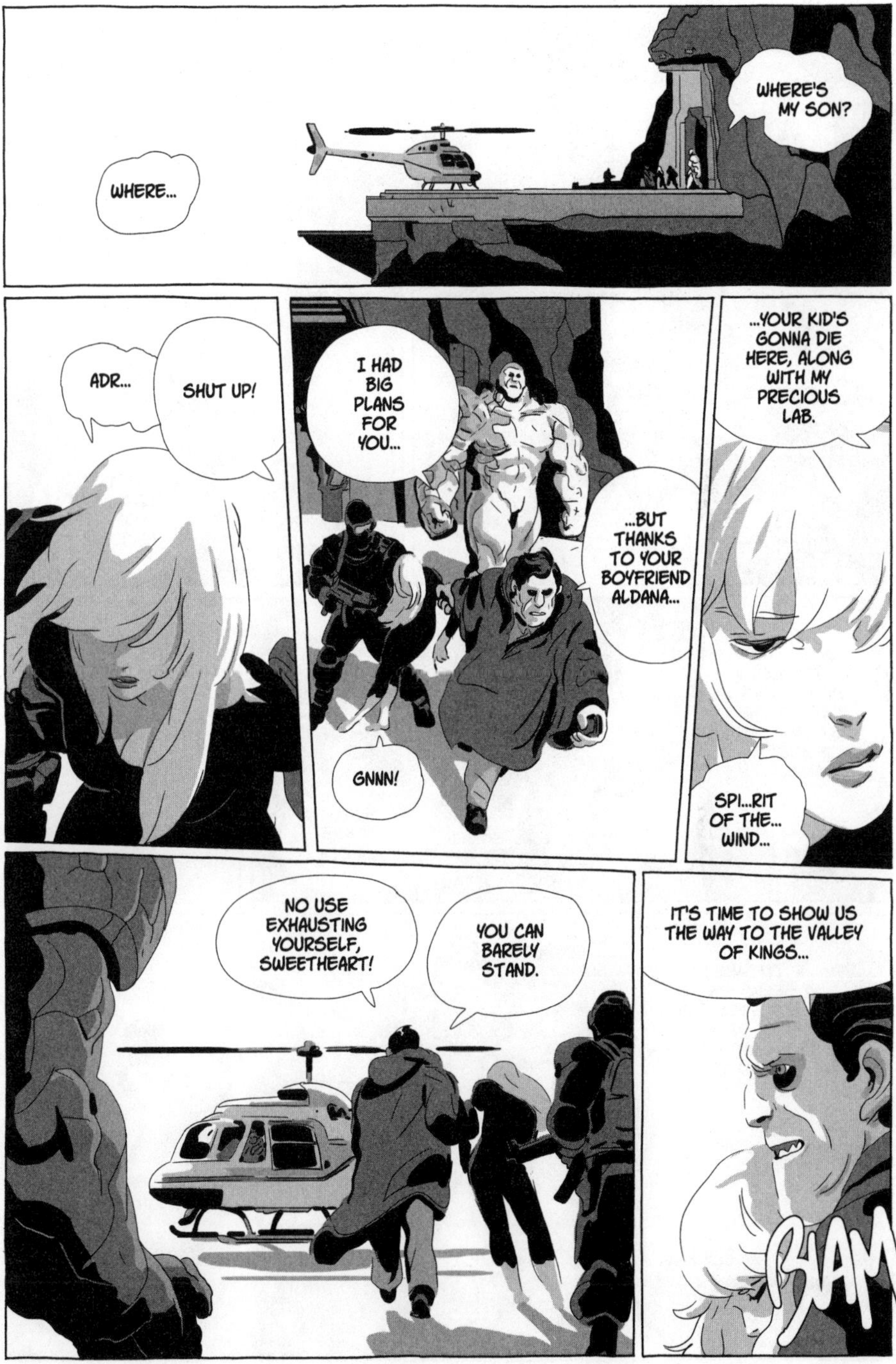
WHERE...
WHERE'S MY SON?
ADR...
SHUT UP!
I HAD BIG PLANS FOR YOU...
...BUT THANKS TO YOUR BOYFRIEND ALDANA...
GNNN!
...YOUR KID'S GONNA DIE HERE, ALONG WITH MY PRECIOUS LAB.
SPI...RIT OF THE... WIND...
NO USE EXHAUSTING YOURSELF, SWEETHEART!
YOU CAN BARELY STAND.
IT'S TIME TO SHOW US THE WAY TO THE VALLEY OF KINGS...
BLAM

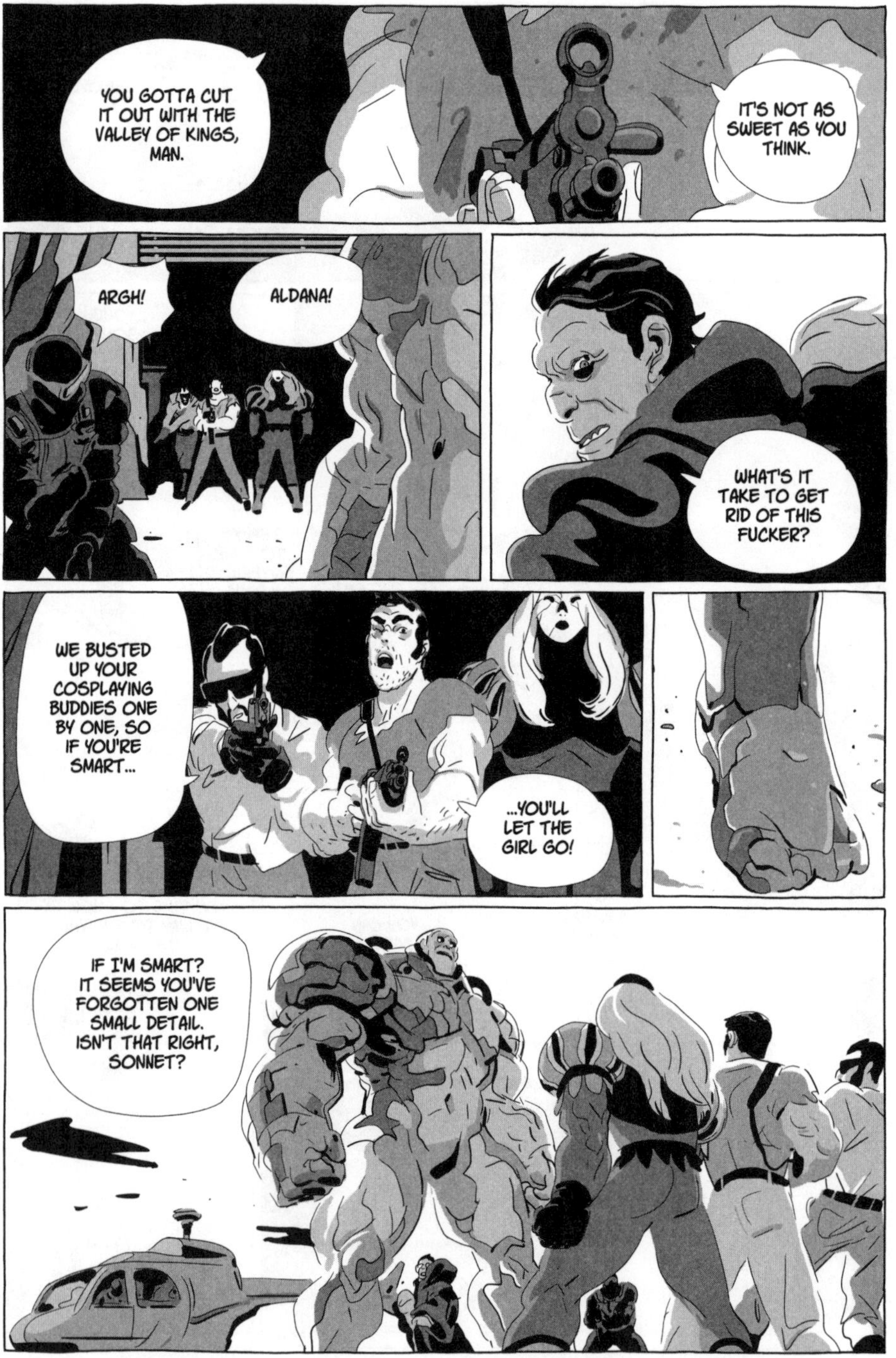
YOU GOTTA CUT IT OUT WITH THE VALLEY OF KINGS, MAN.
IT'S NOT AS SWEET AS YOU THINK.
ARGH!
ALDANA!
WHAT'S IT TAKE TO GET RID OF THIS FUCKER?
WE BUSTED UP YOUR COSPLAYING BUDDIES ONE BY ONE, SO IF YOU'RE SMART...
...YOU'LL LET THE GIRL GO!
IF I'M SMART? IT SEEMS YOU'VE FORGOTTEN ONE SMALL DETAIL. ISN'T THAT RIGHT, SONNET?

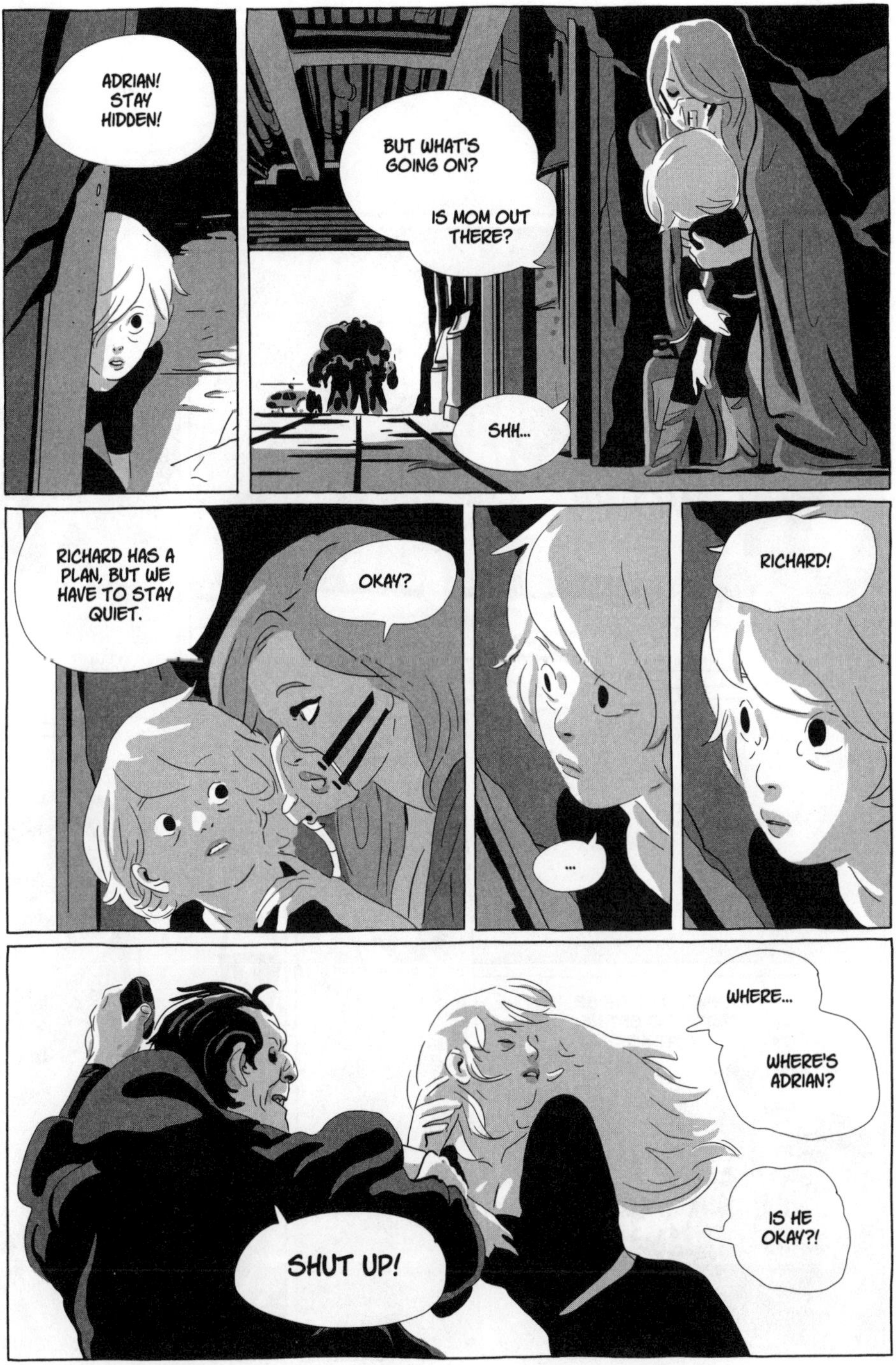
ADRIAN! STAY HIDDEN!
BUT WHAT'S GOING ON?
IS MOM OUT THERE?
SHH...
RICHARD HAS A PLAN, BUT WE HAVE TO STAY QUIET.
OKAY?
...
RICHARD!
WHERE...
WHERE'S ADRIAN?
IS HE OKAY?!
SHUT UP!

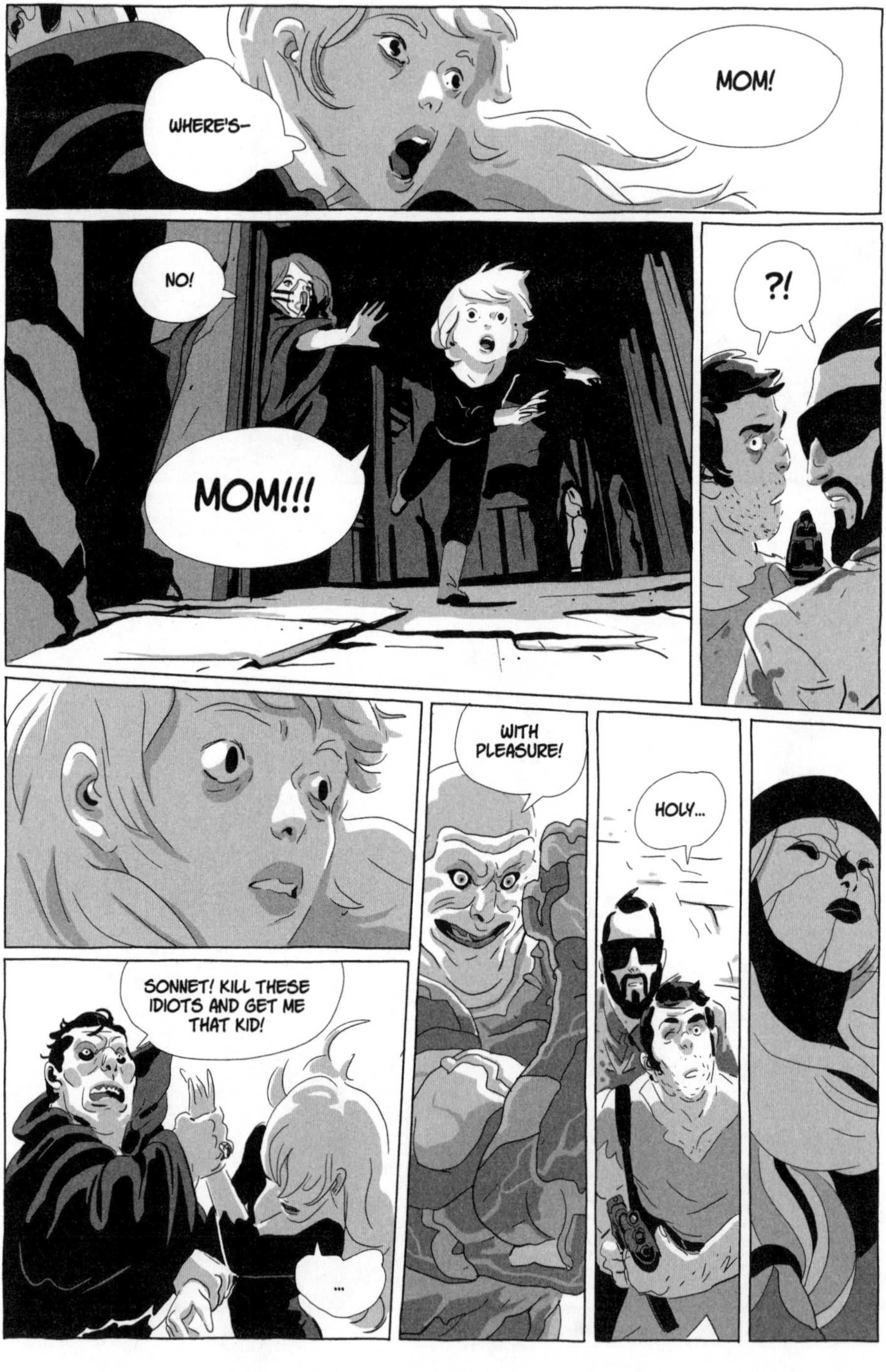
WHERE'S-
MOM!
NO!
MOM!!!
?!
SONNET! KILL THESE IDIOTS AND GET ME THAT KID!
...
WITH PLEASURE!
HOLY...

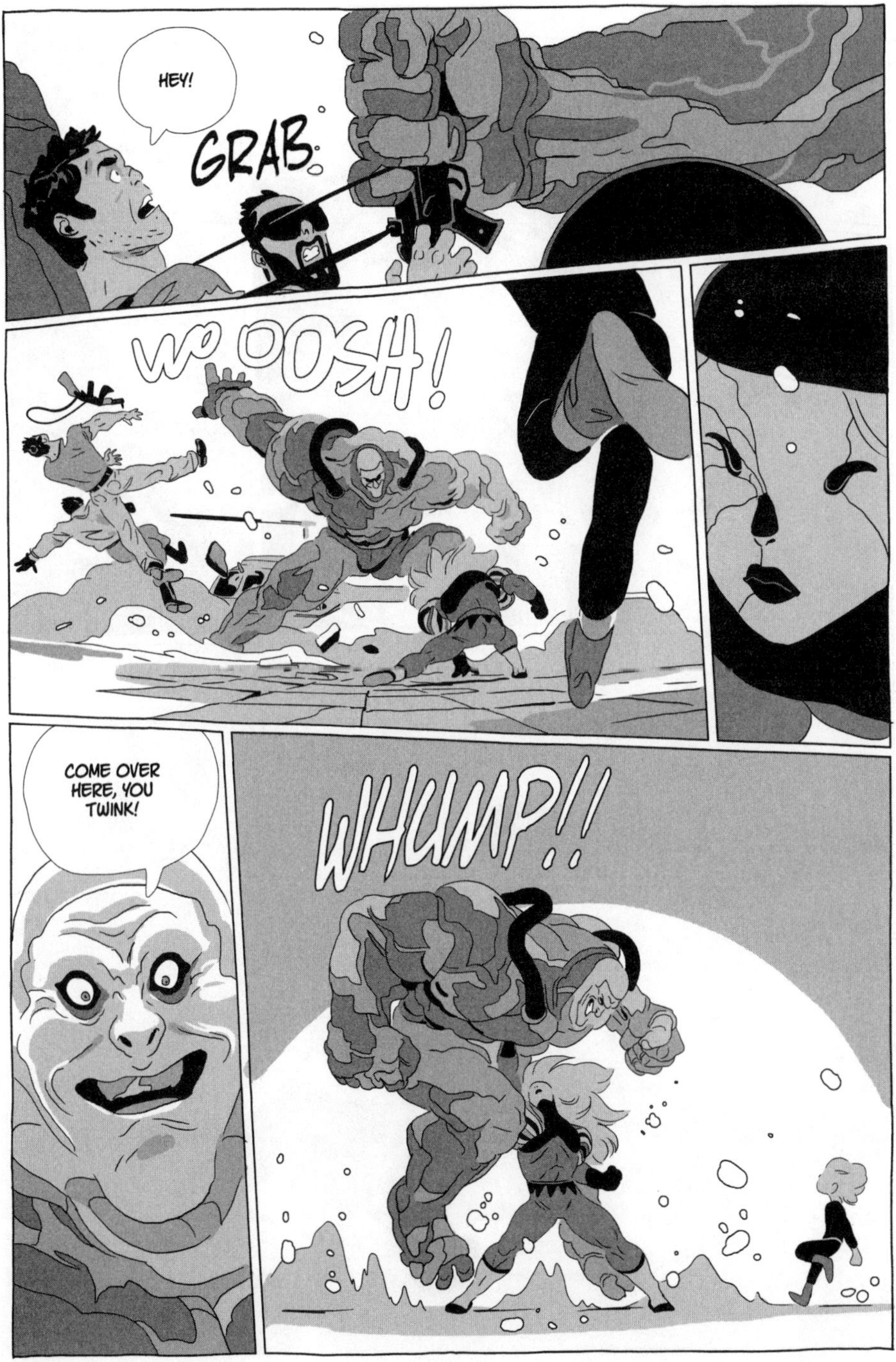
HEY!
GRAB
WOOOSH!
COME OVER HERE, YOU TWINK!
WHUMP!!

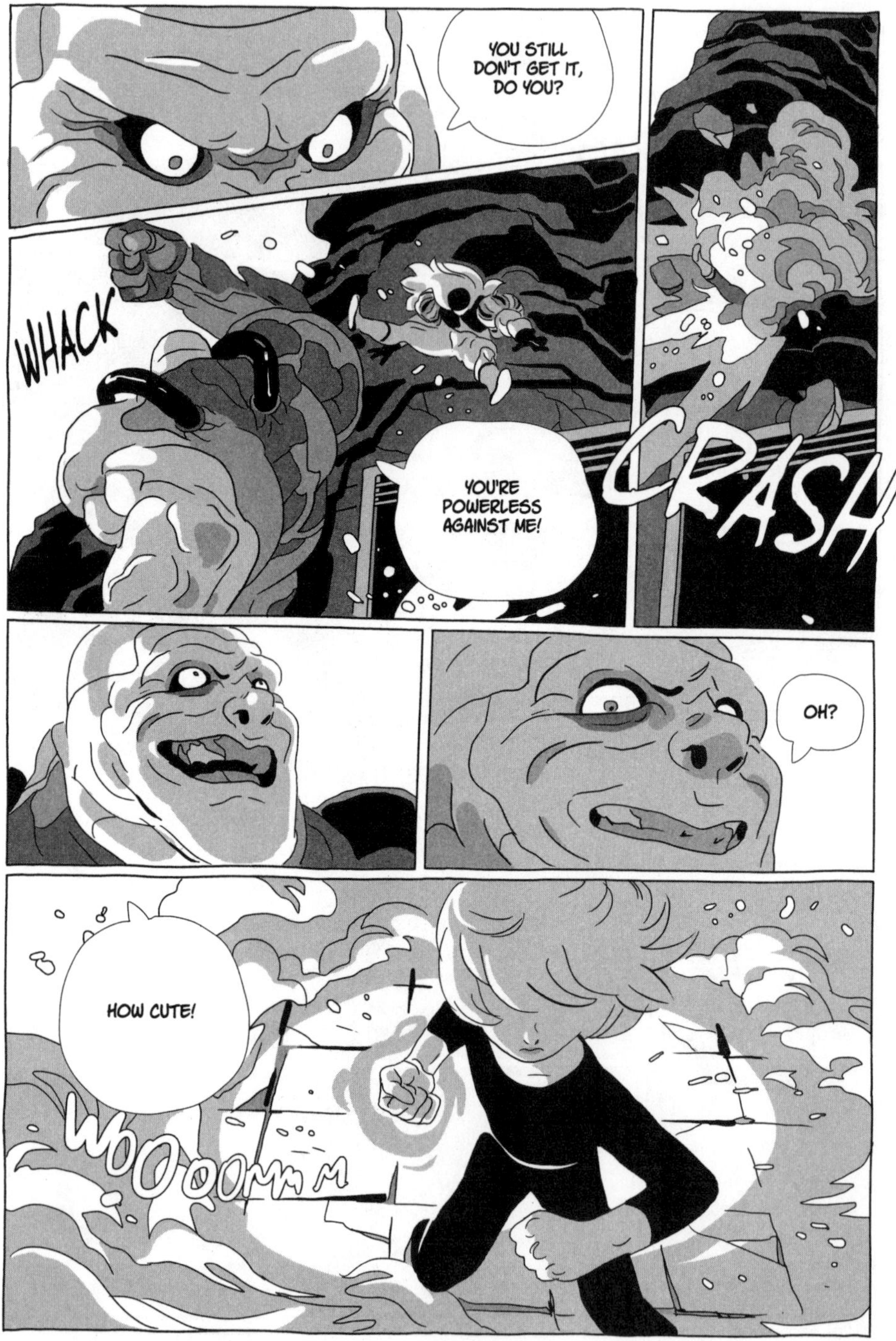
YOU STILL DON'T GET IT, DO YOU?
WHACK
YOU'RE POWERLESS AGAINST ME!
CRASH
OH?
HOW CUTE!
WOOOOOMM M

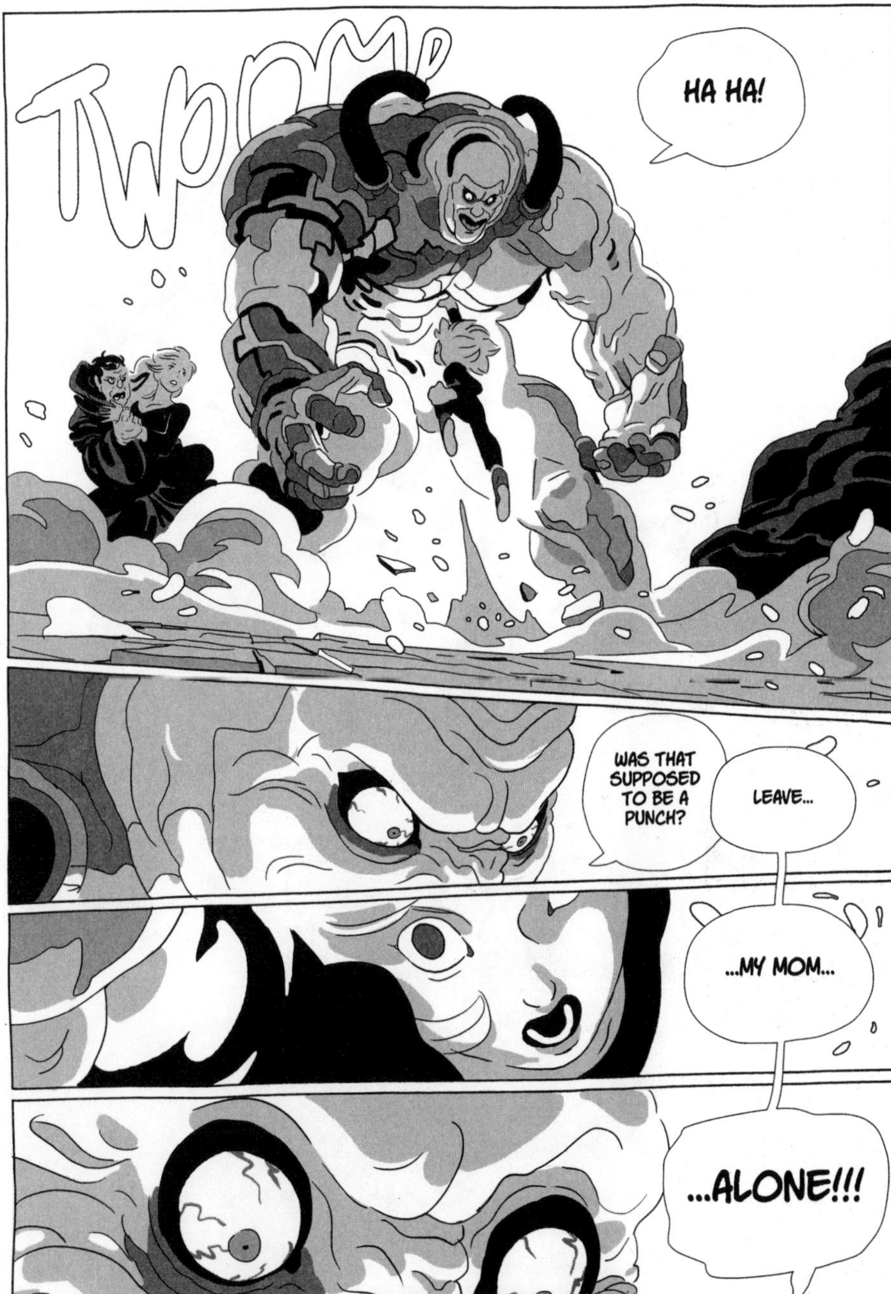
TWOOMP
HA HA!
WAS THAT SUPPOSED TO BE A PUNCH?
LEAVE...
...MY MOM...
...ALONE!!!

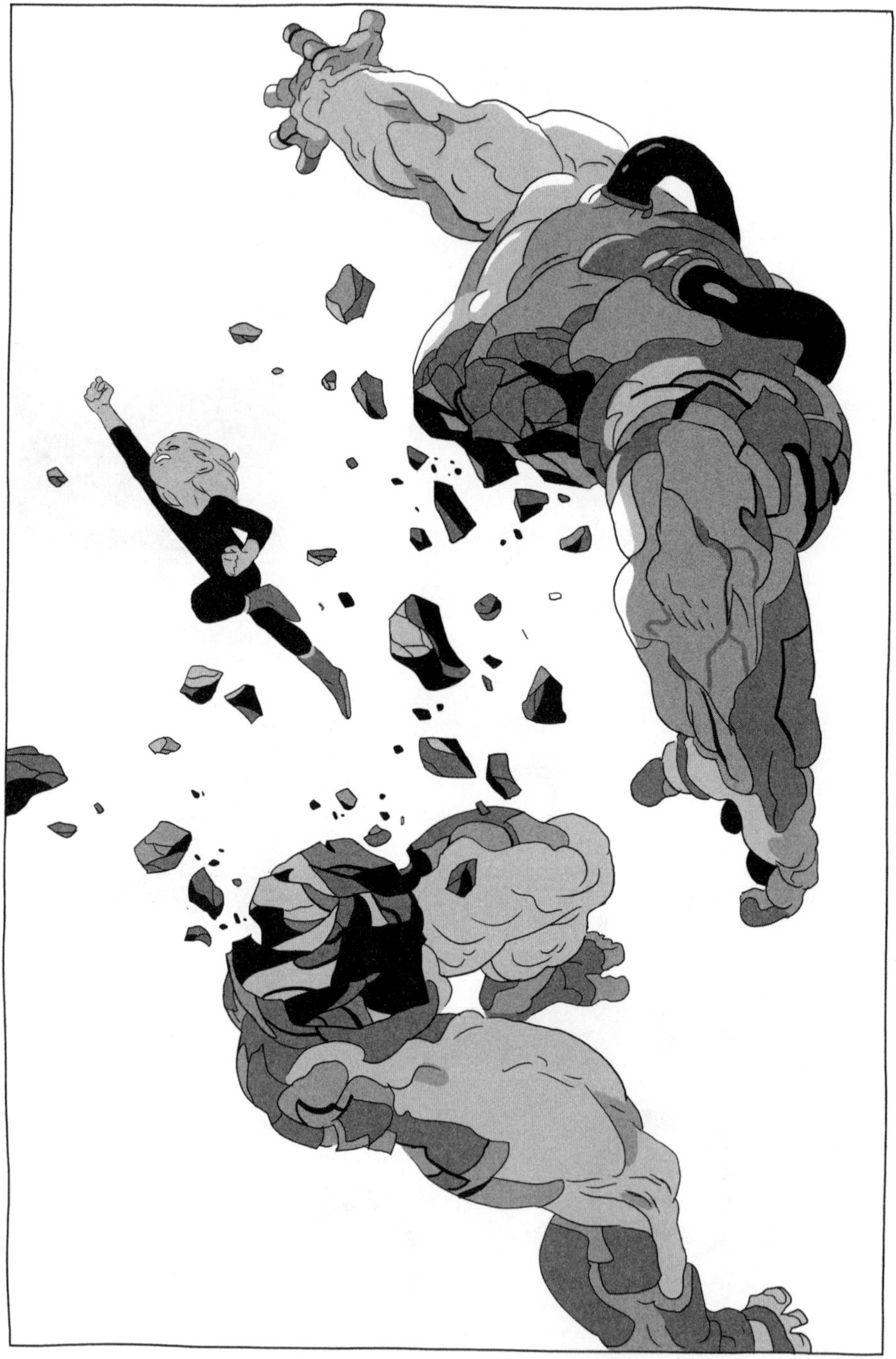

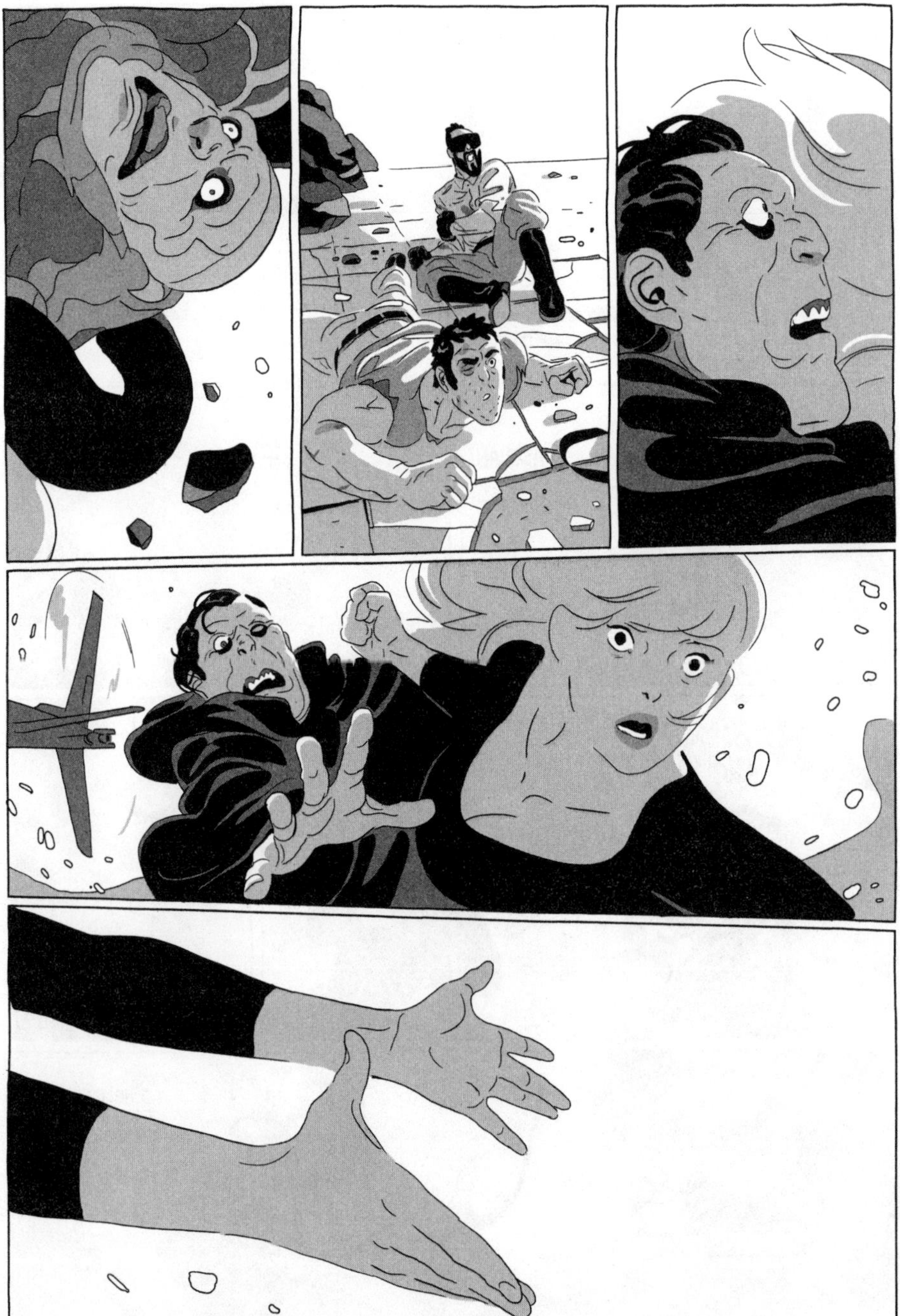

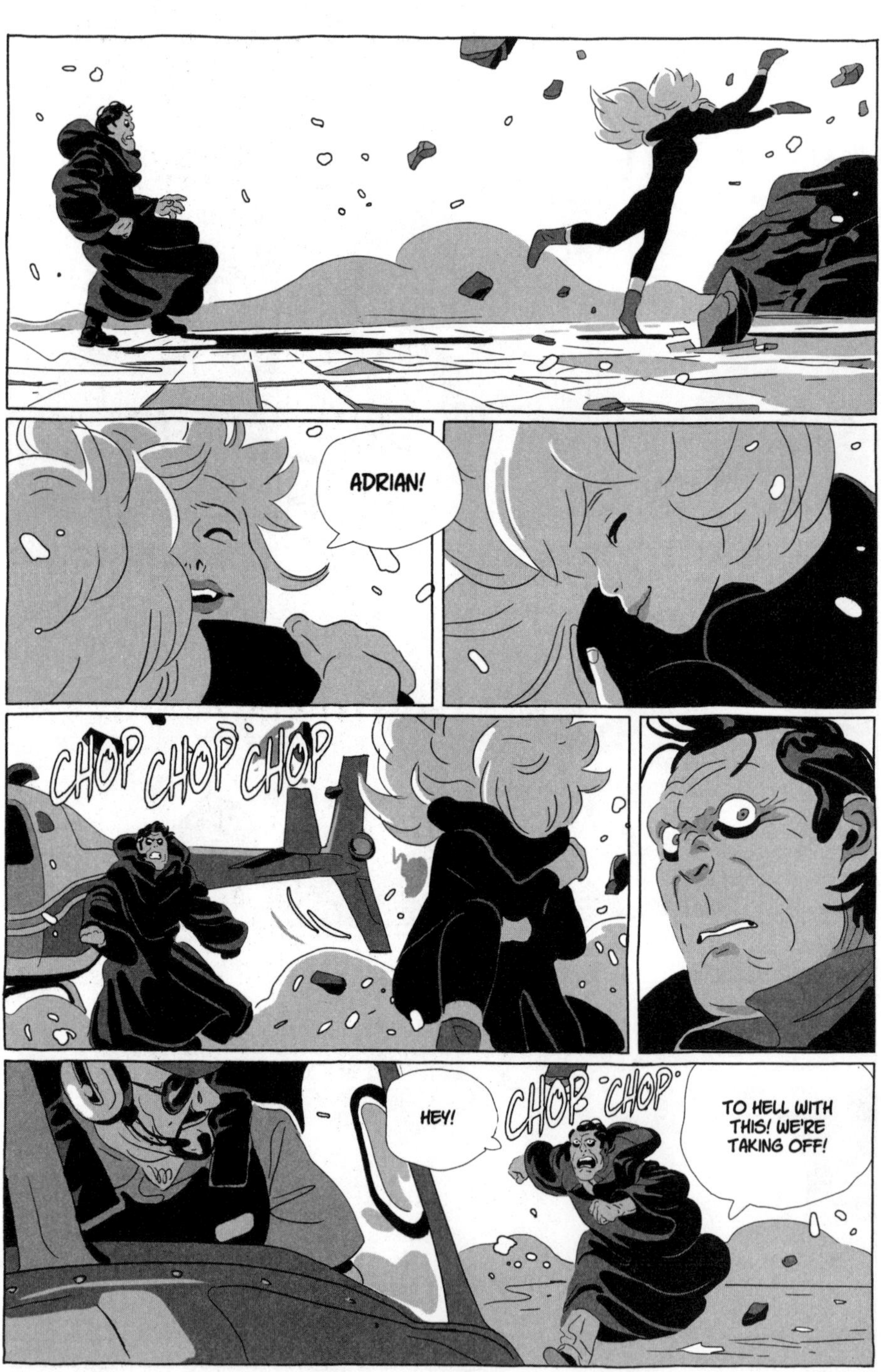
ADRIAN!
CHOP CHOP CHOP
HEY!
CHOP CHOP
TO HELL WITH THIS! WE'RE TAKING OFF!

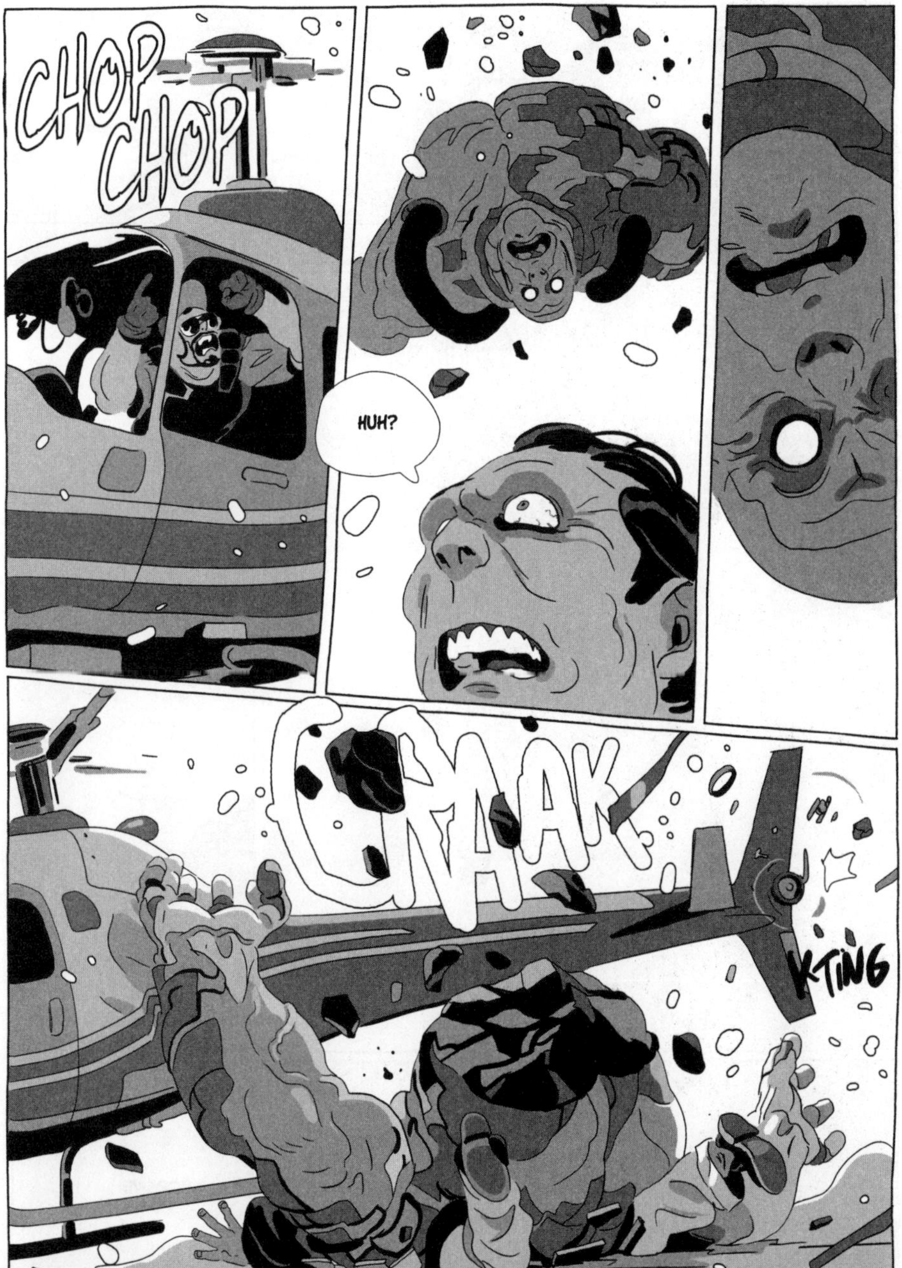
CHOP CHOP
HUH?
CRAAK
K-TING

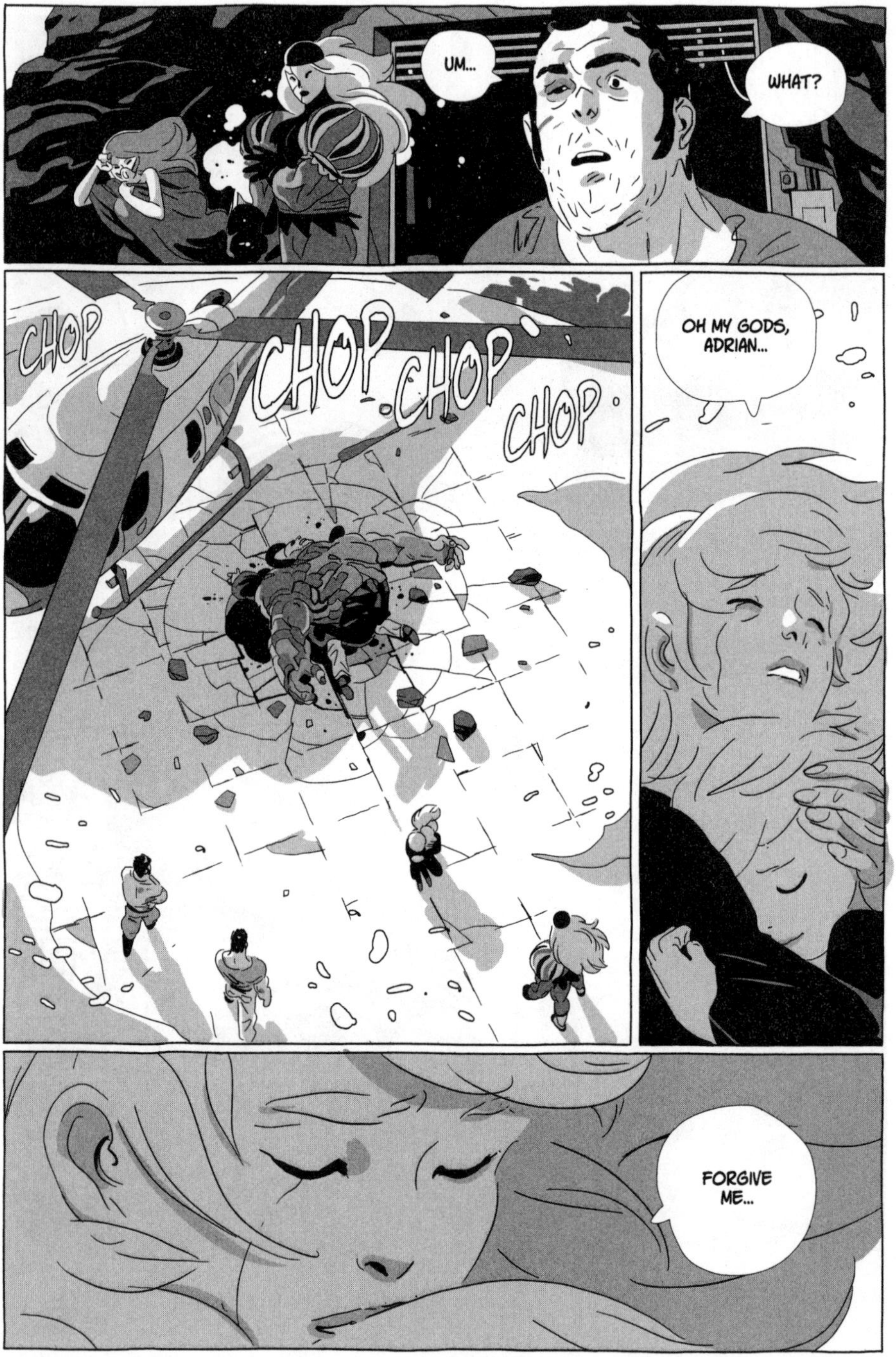
UM...
WHAT?
CHOP
CHOP
CHOP
CHOP
OH MY GODS, ADRIAN...
FORGIVE ME...

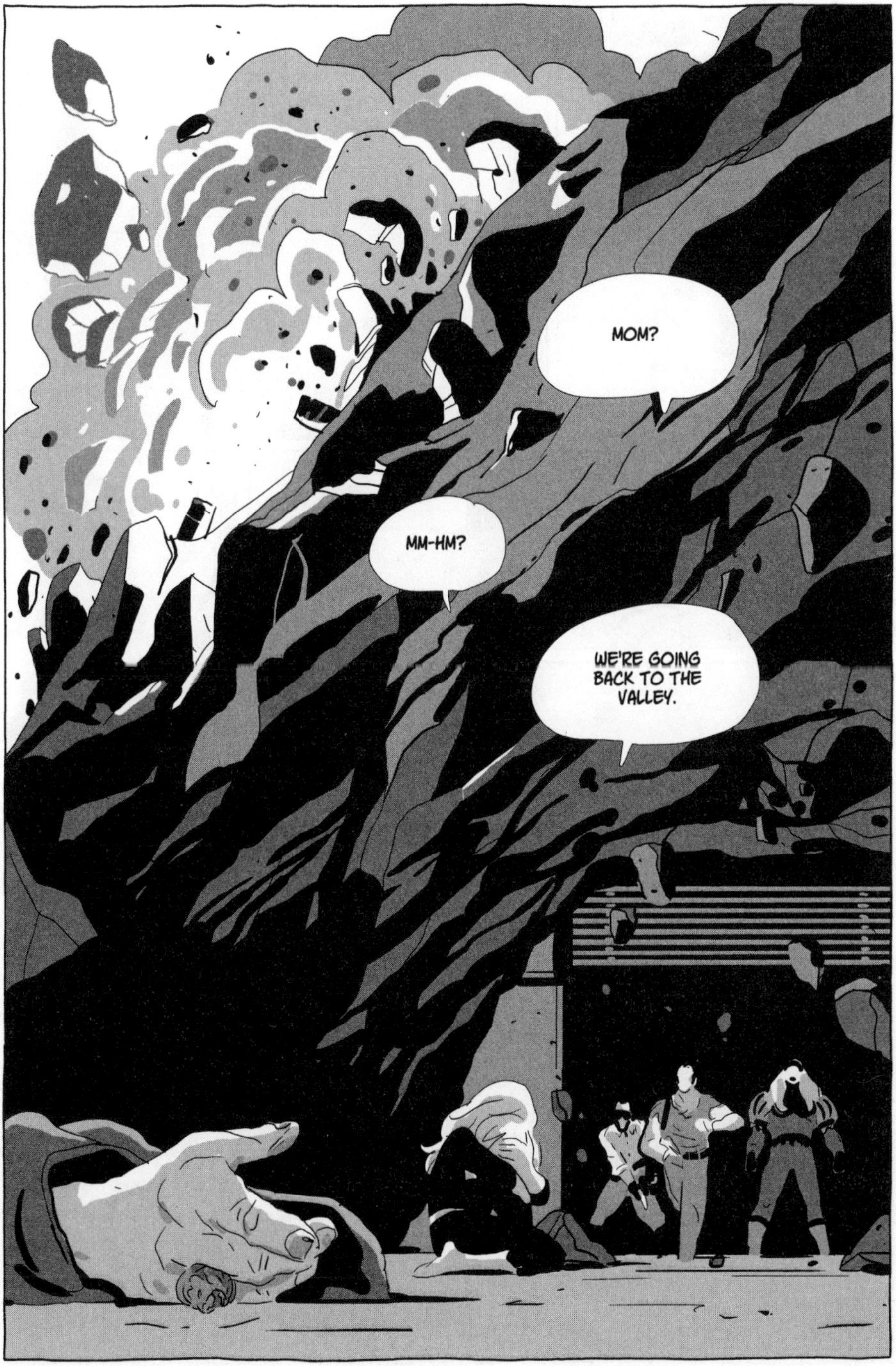
MOM?
MM-HM?
WE'RE GOING BACK TO THE VALLEY.

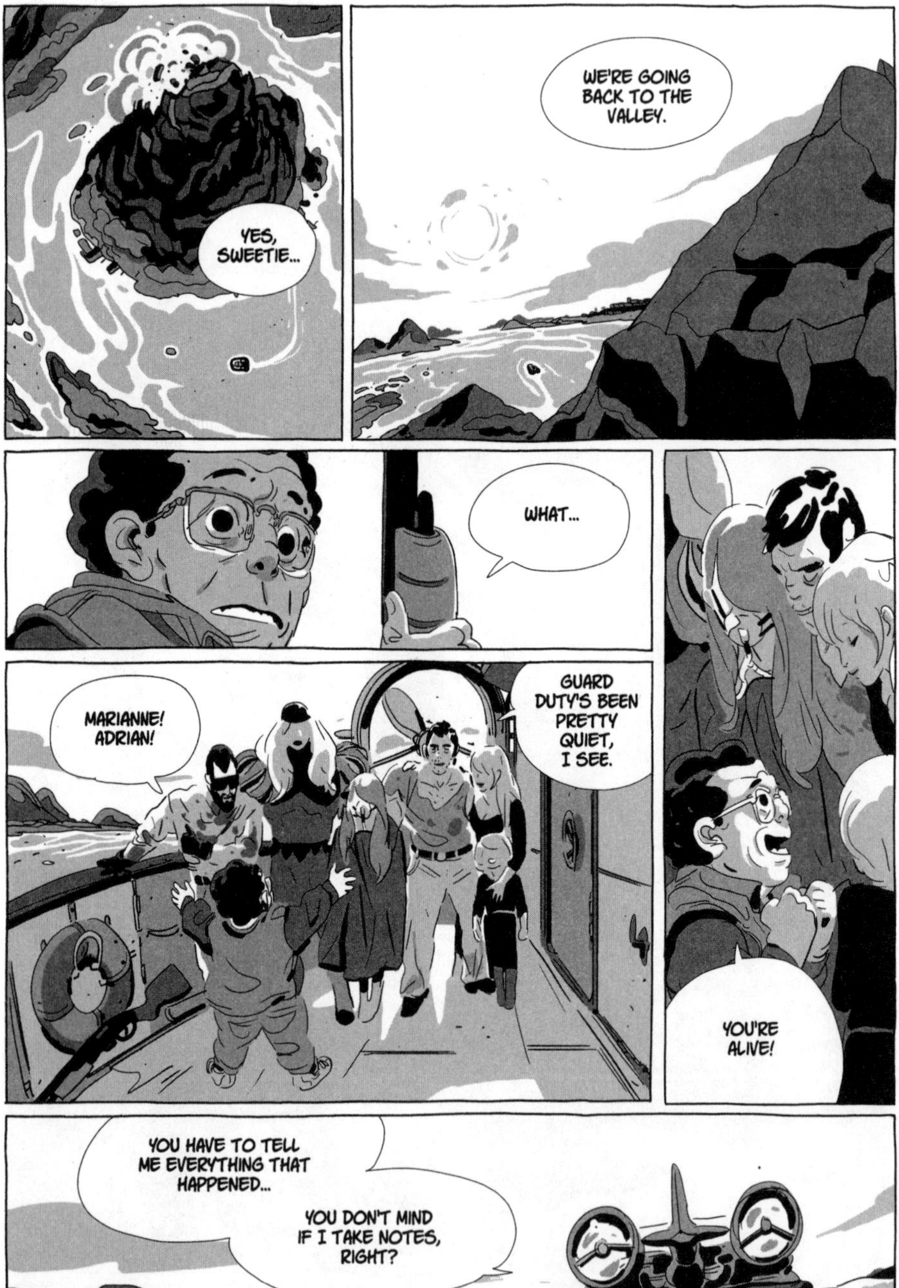
YES, SWEETIE...
WE'RE GOING BACK TO THE VALLEY.
WHAT...
MARIANNE! ADRIAN!
GUARD DUTY'S BEEN PRETTY QUIET, I SEE.
YOU'RE ALIVE!
YOU HAVE TO TELL ME EVERYTHING THAT HAPPENED...
YOU DON'T MIND IF I TAKE NOTES, RIGHT?

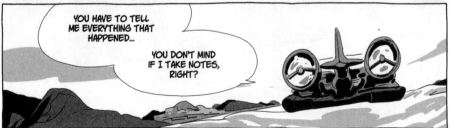

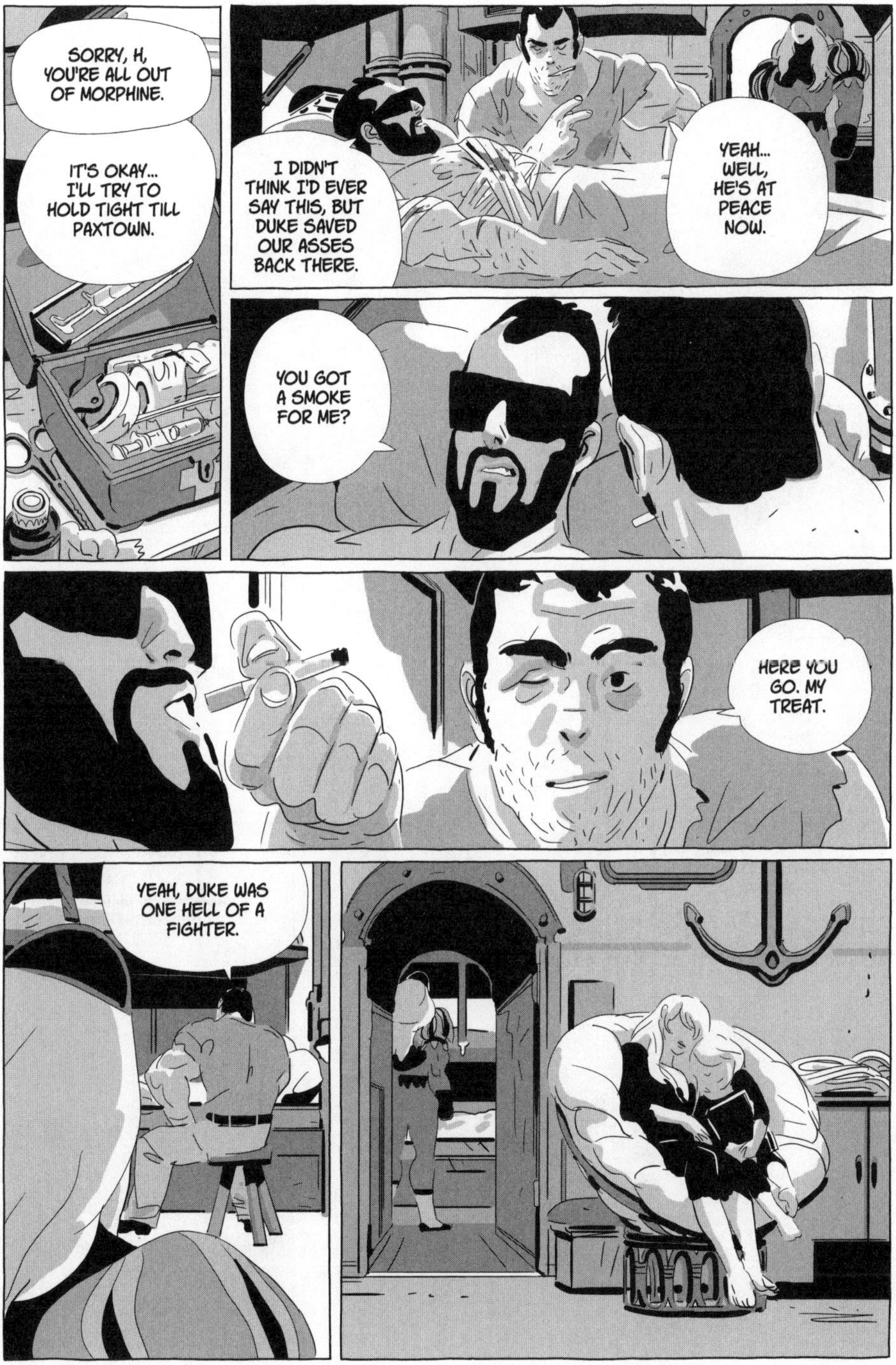
SORRY, H, YOU'RE ALL OUT OF MORPHINE.
IT'S OKAY... I'LL TRY TO HOLD TIGHT TILL PAXTOWN.
I DIDN'T THINK I'D EVER SAY THIS, BUT DUKE SAVED OUR ASSES BACK THERE.
YEAH... WELL, HE'S AT PEACE NOW.
YOU GOT A SMOKE FOR ME?
HERE YOU GO. MY TREAT.
YEAH, DUKE WAS ONE HELL OF A FIGHTER.

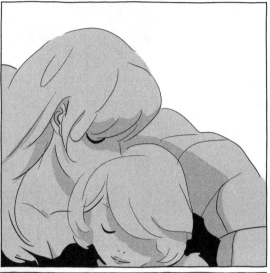

HEY, MOM? HOW'LL WE GET HOME WITHOUT THE MOTORCYCLE?

WE'LL TAKE RICHARD'S.

RICHARD'S COMING TO THE VALLEY TOO?

YES.

DOES THAT MEAN HE'LL LIVE WITH US FOR REAL?

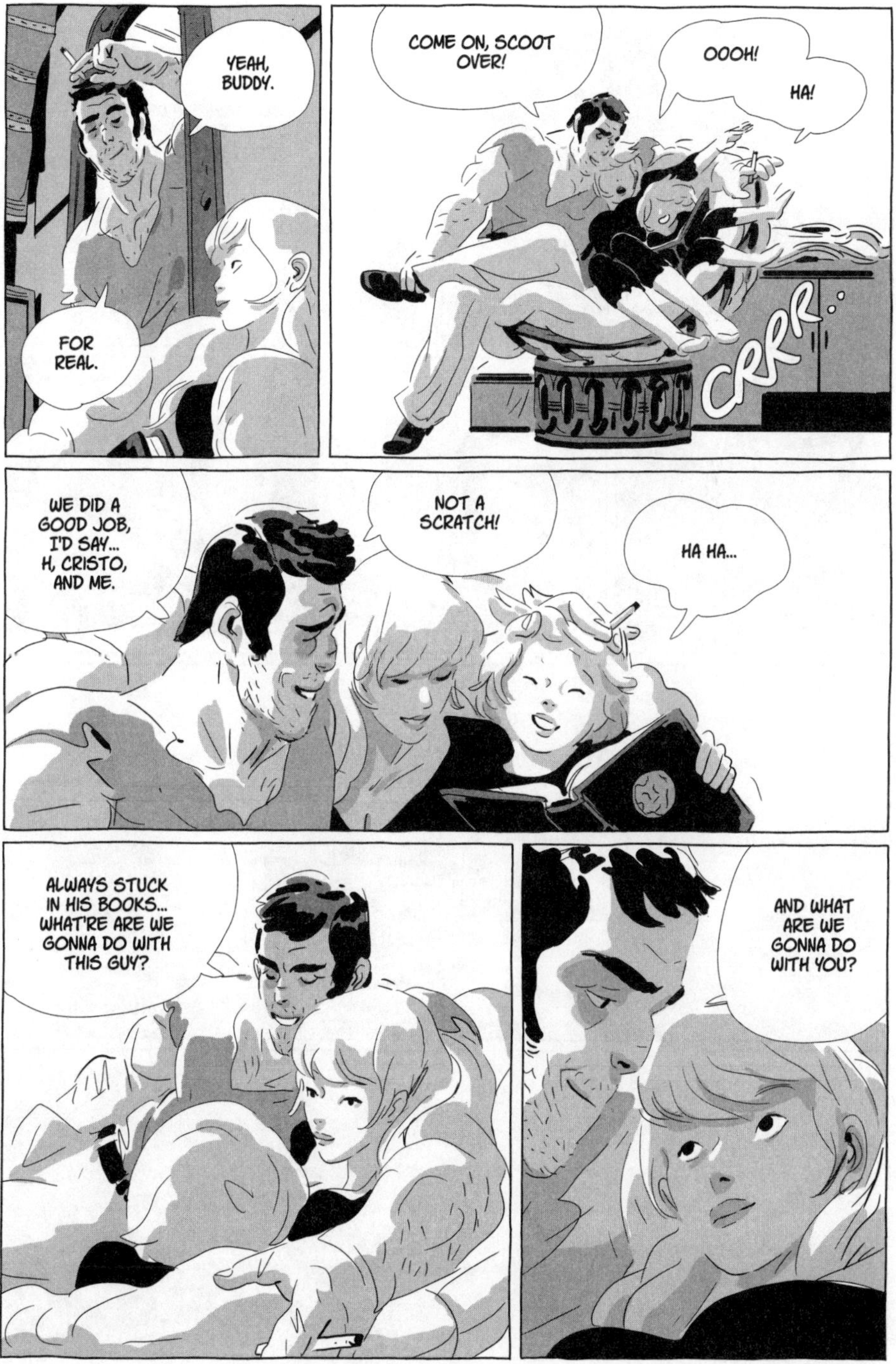
YEAH, BUDDY.
FOR REAL.
COME ON, SCOOT OVER!
OOOH!
HA!
CRRR
WE DID A GOOD JOB, I'D SAY... H, CRISTO, AND ME.
NOT A SCRATCH!
HA HA...
ALWAYS STUCK IN HIS BOOKS... WHAT'RE ARE WE GONNA DO WITH THIS GUY?
AND WHAT ARE WE GONNA DO WITH YOU?

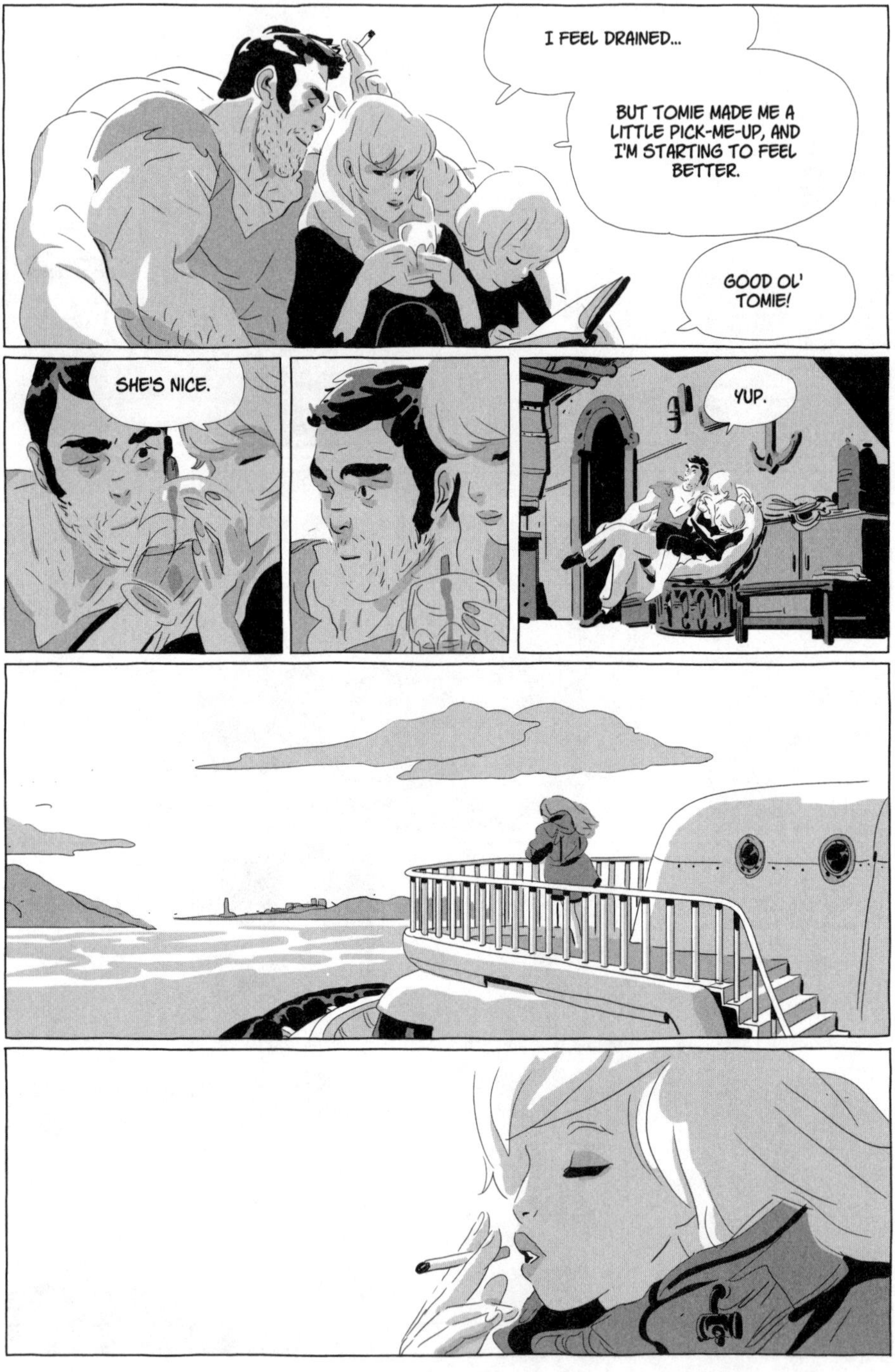
I FEEL DRAINED...
BUT TOMIE MADE ME A LITTLE PICK-ME-UP, AND I'M STARTING TO FEEL BETTER.
GOOD OL' TOMIE!
SHE'S NICE.
YUP.

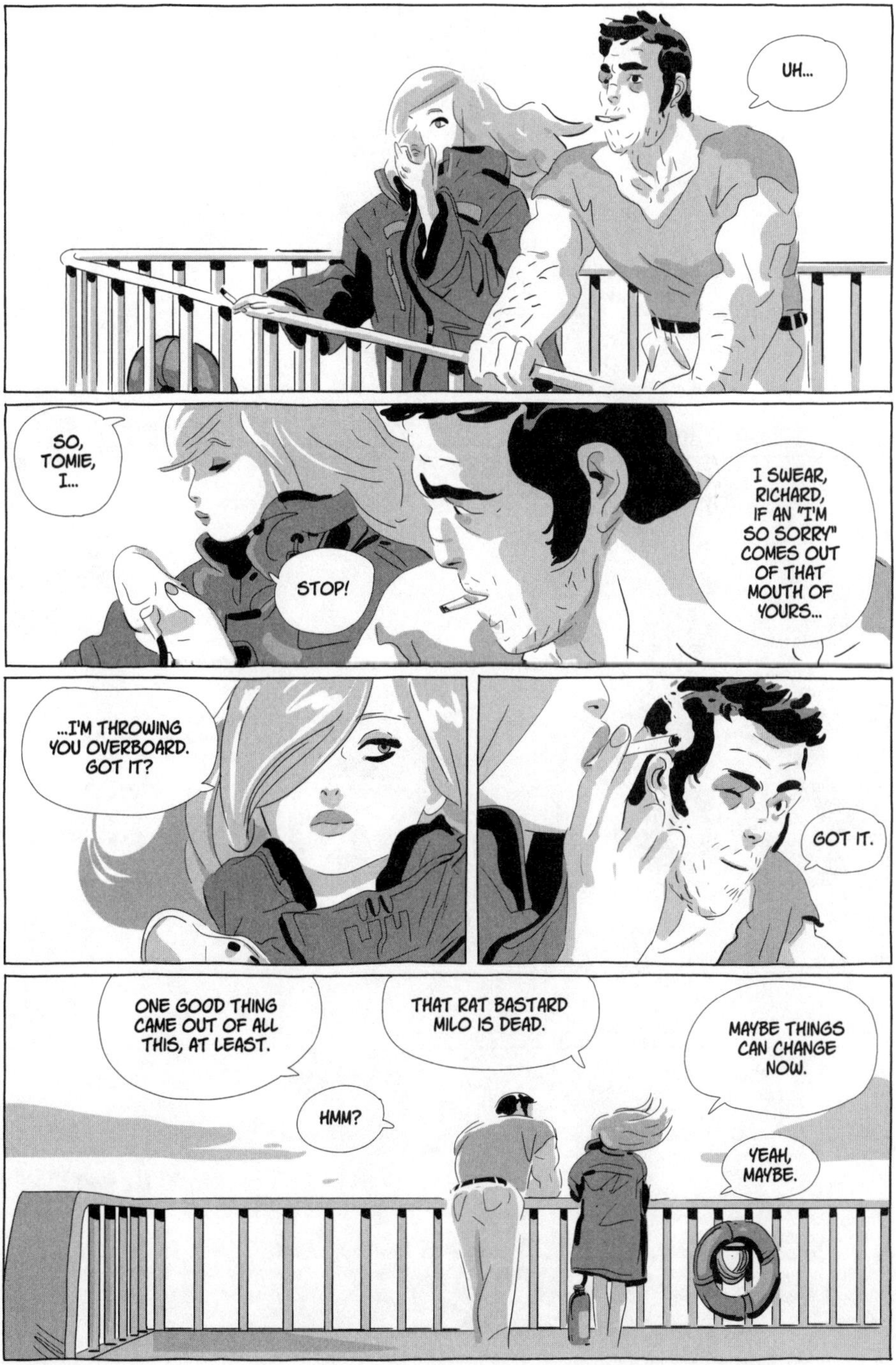
UH...
SO, TOMIE, I...
STOP!
I SWEAR, RICHARD, IF AN "I'M SO SORRY" COMES OUT OF THAT MOUTH OF YOURS...
...I'M THROWING YOU OVERBOARD. GOT IT?
GOT IT.
ONE GOOD THING CAME OUT OF ALL THIS, AT LEAST.
HMM?
THAT RAT BASTARD MILO IS DEAD.
MAYBE THINGS CAN CHANGE NOW.
YEAH, MAYBE.

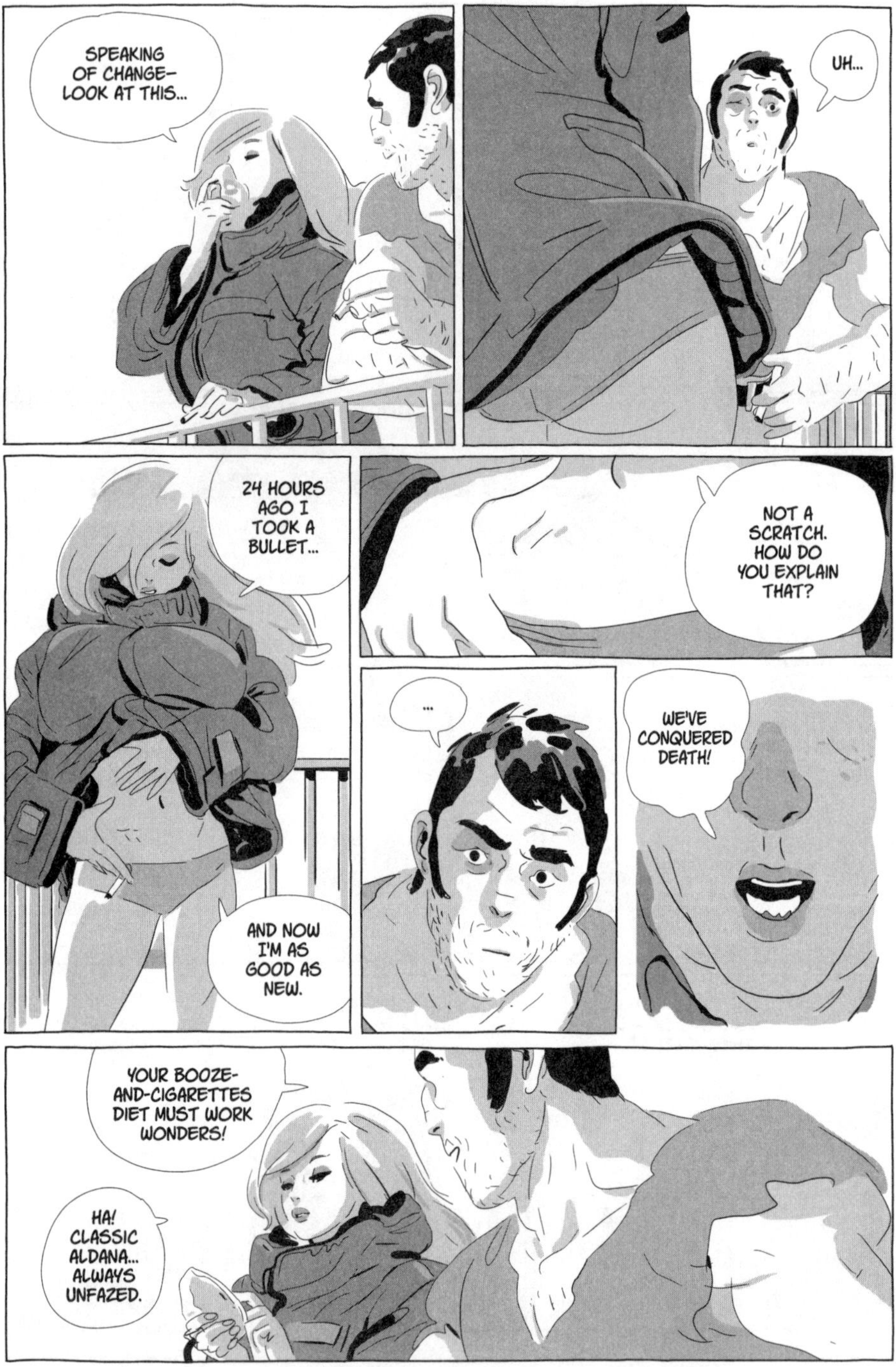
SPEAKING OF CHANGE– LOOK AT THIS...
UH...
24 HOURS AGO I TOOK A BULLET...
AND NOW I'M AS GOOD AS NEW.
NOT A SCRATCH. HOW DO YOU EXPLAIN THAT?
...
WE'VE CONQUERED DEATH!
YOUR BOOZE-AND-CIGARETTES DIET MUST WORK WONDERS!
HA! CLASSIC ALDANA... ALWAYS UNFAZED.

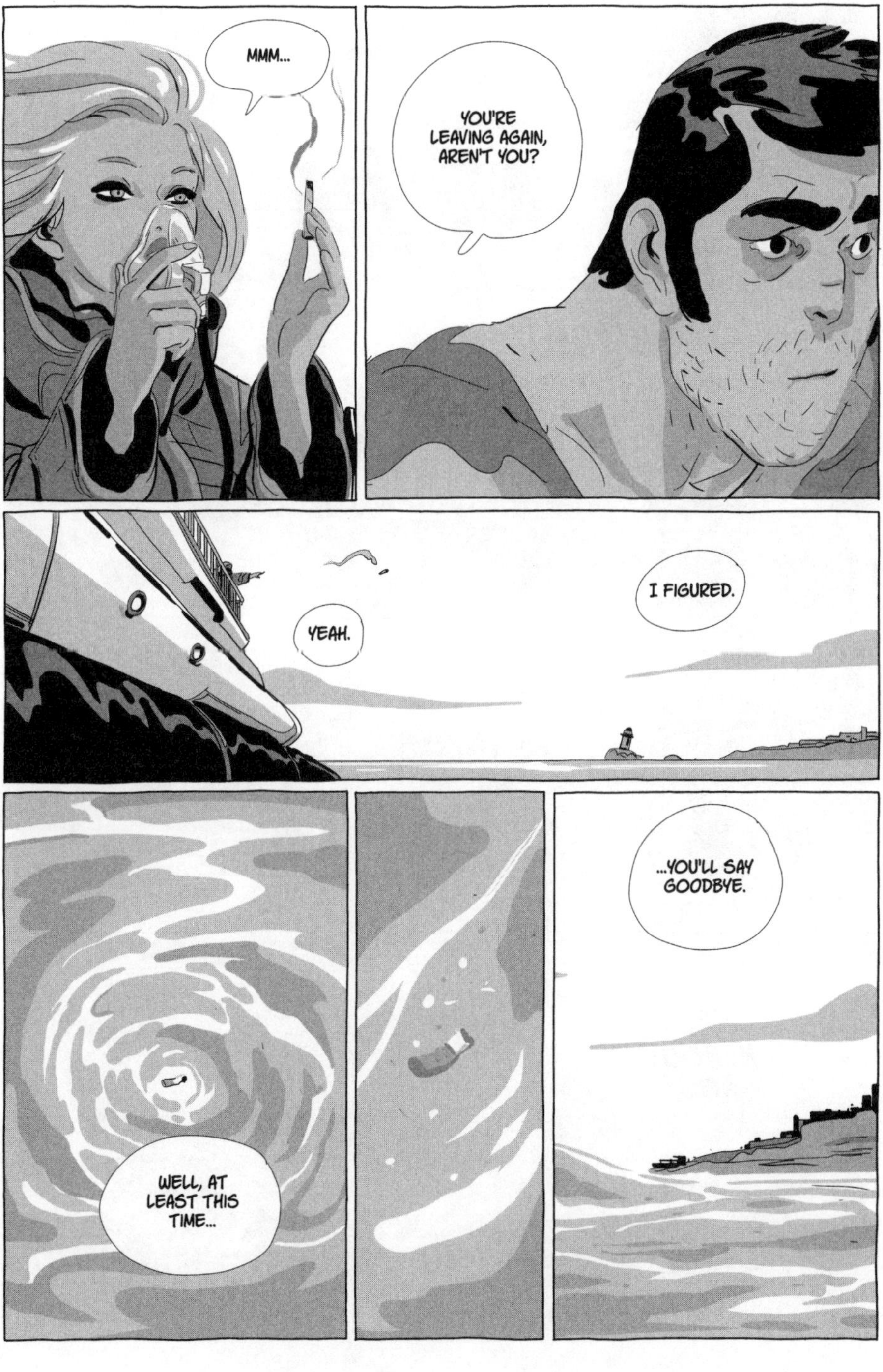
MMM...
YOU'RE LEAVING AGAIN, AREN'T YOU?
YEAH.
I FIGURED.
WELL, AT LEAST THIS TIME...
...YOU'LL SAY GOODBYE.

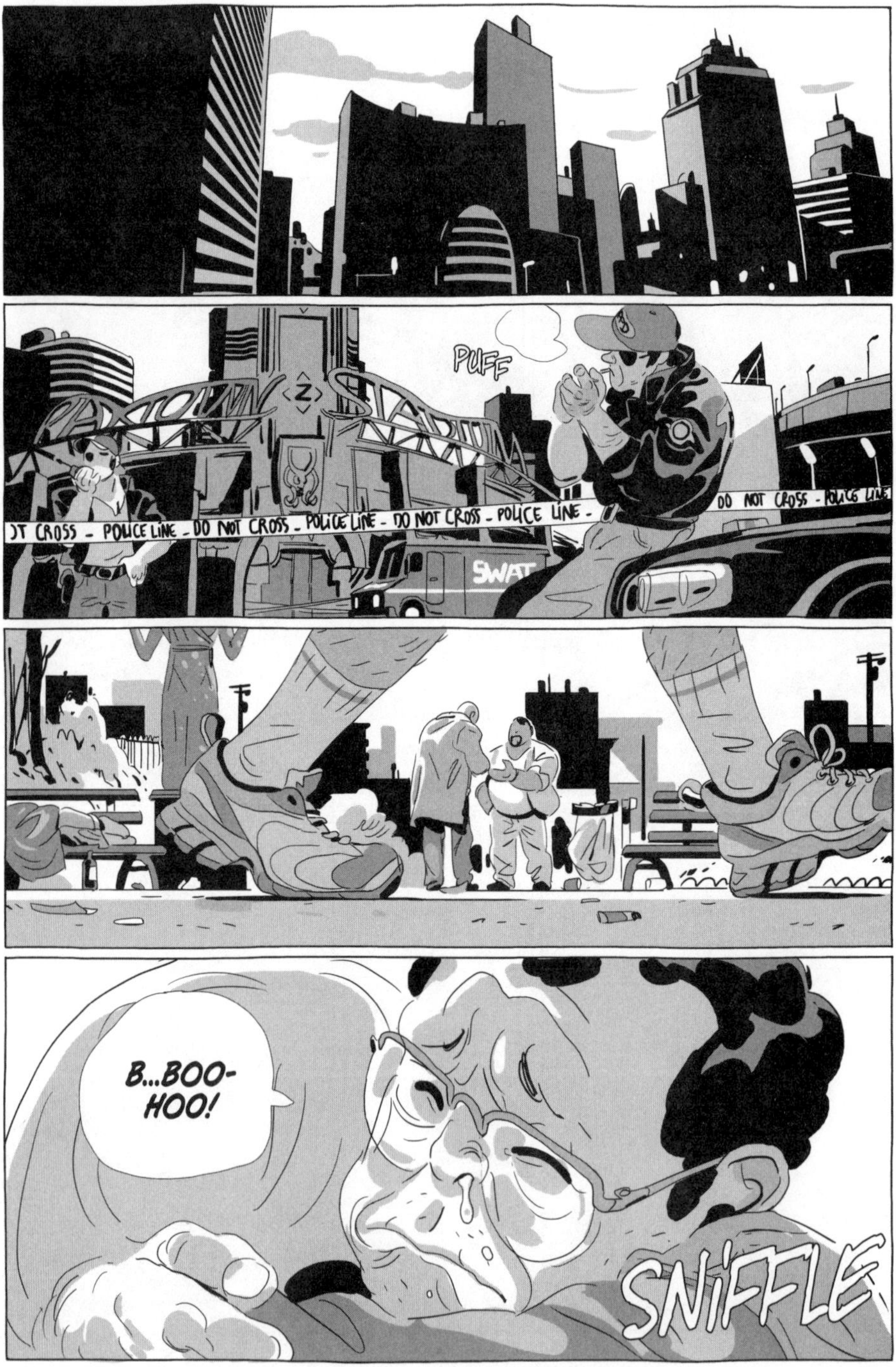
PUFF
CROSS - POLICE LINE - DO NOT CROSS - POLICE LINE - DO NOT CROSS - POLICE LINE -
DO NOT CROSS - POLICE LINE
SWAT
B...BOO-HOO!
SNIFFLE

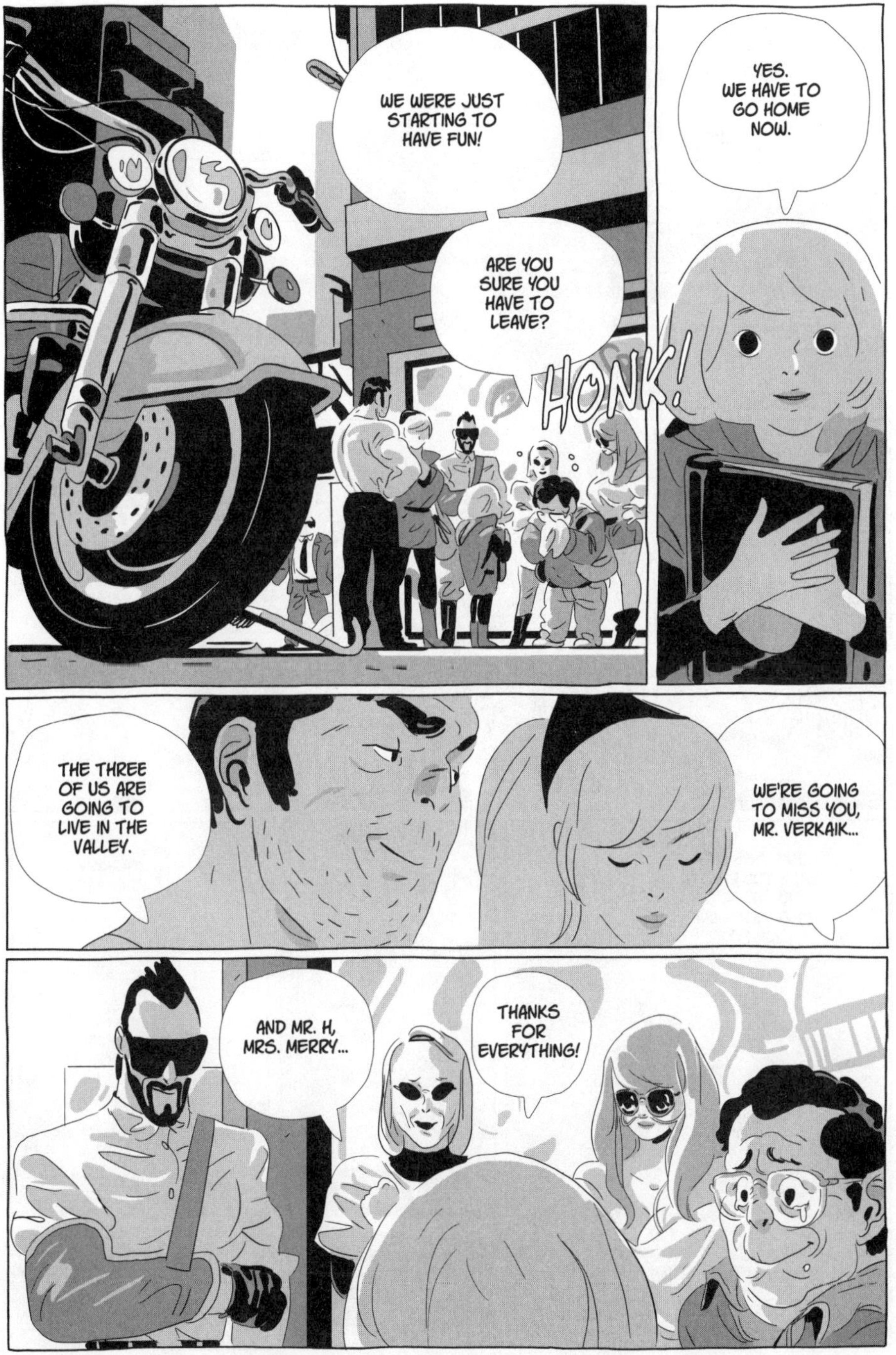
WE WERE JUST STARTING TO HAVE FUN!
ARE YOU SURE YOU HAVE TO LEAVE?
HONK!
YES. WE HAVE TO GO HOME NOW.
THE THREE OF US ARE GOING TO LIVE IN THE VALLEY.
WE'RE GOING TO MISS YOU, MR. VERKAIK...
AND MR. H, MRS. MERRY...
THANKS FOR EVERYTHING!

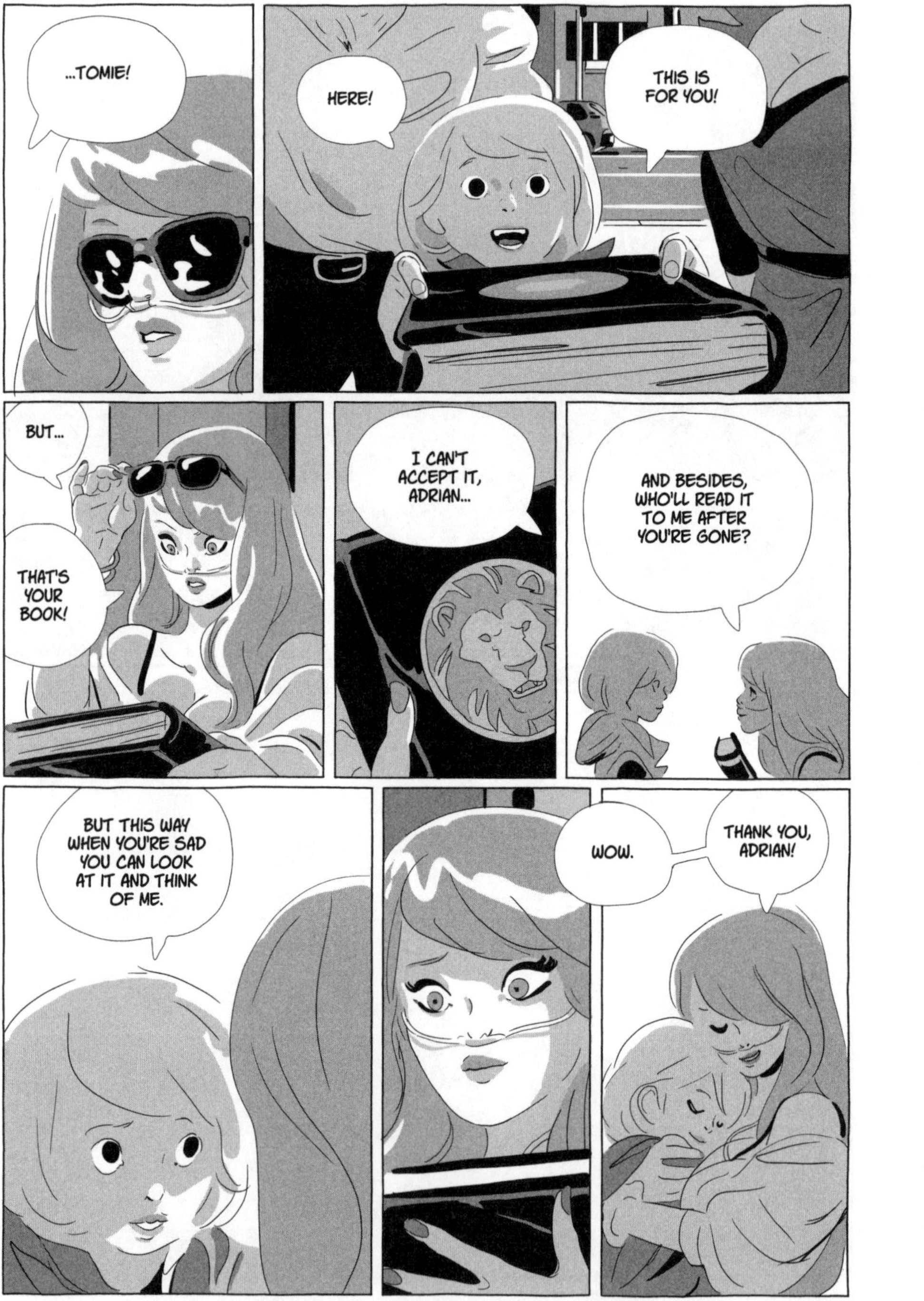
...TOMIE!
HERE!
THIS IS FOR YOU!
BUT...
THAT'S YOUR BOOK!
I CAN'T ACCEPT IT, ADRIAN...
AND BESIDES, WHO'LL READ IT TO ME AFTER YOU'RE GONE?
BUT THIS WAY WHEN YOU'RE SAD YOU CAN LOOK AT IT AND THINK OF ME.
WOW.
THANK YOU, ADRIAN!

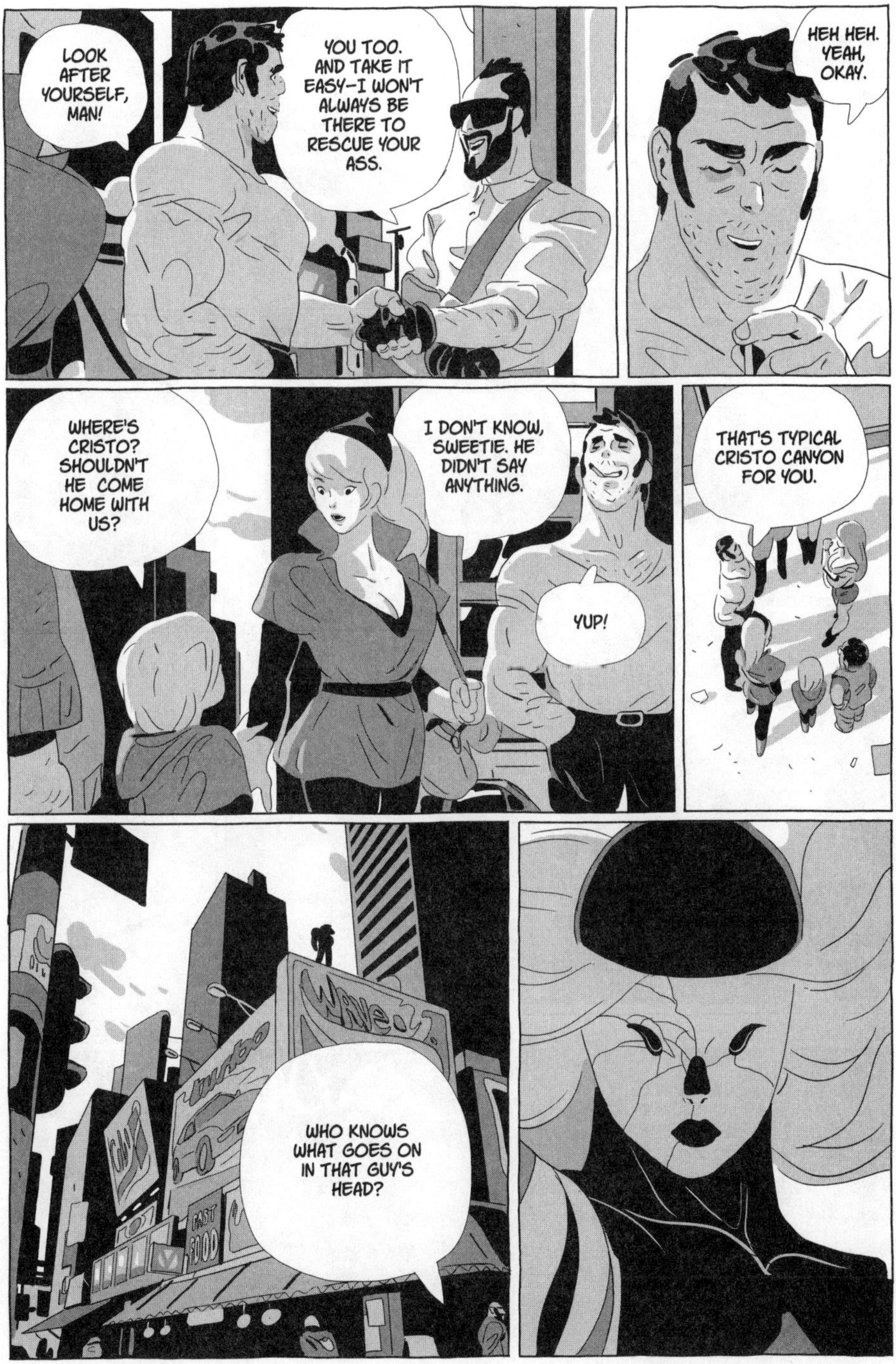
LOOK AFTER YOURSELF, MAN!
YOU TOO. AND TAKE IT EASY—I WON'T ALWAYS BE THERE TO RESCUE YOUR ASS.
HEH HEH. YEAH, OKAY.
WHERE'S CRISTO? SHOULDN'T HE COME HOME WITH US?
I DON'T KNOW, SWEETIE. HE DIDN'T SAY ANYTHING.
YUP!
THAT'S TYPICAL CRISTO CANYON FOR YOU.
WHO KNOWS WHAT GOES ON IN THAT GUY'S HEAD?

CLACK
VROOOOOOO
CLACK
VROOO
OOM

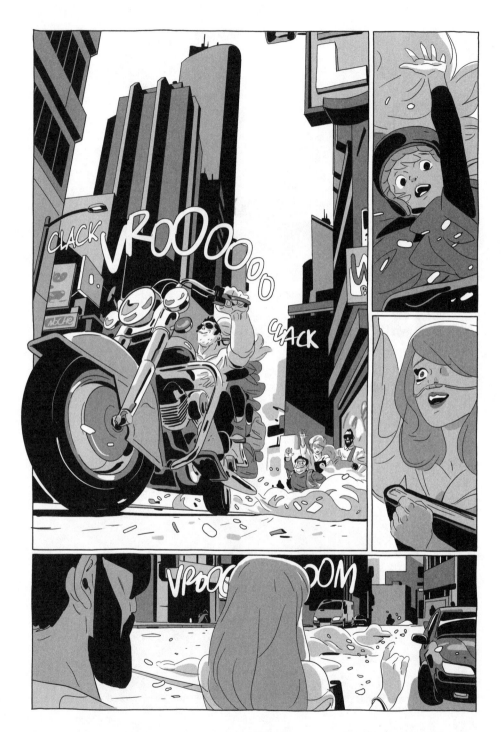

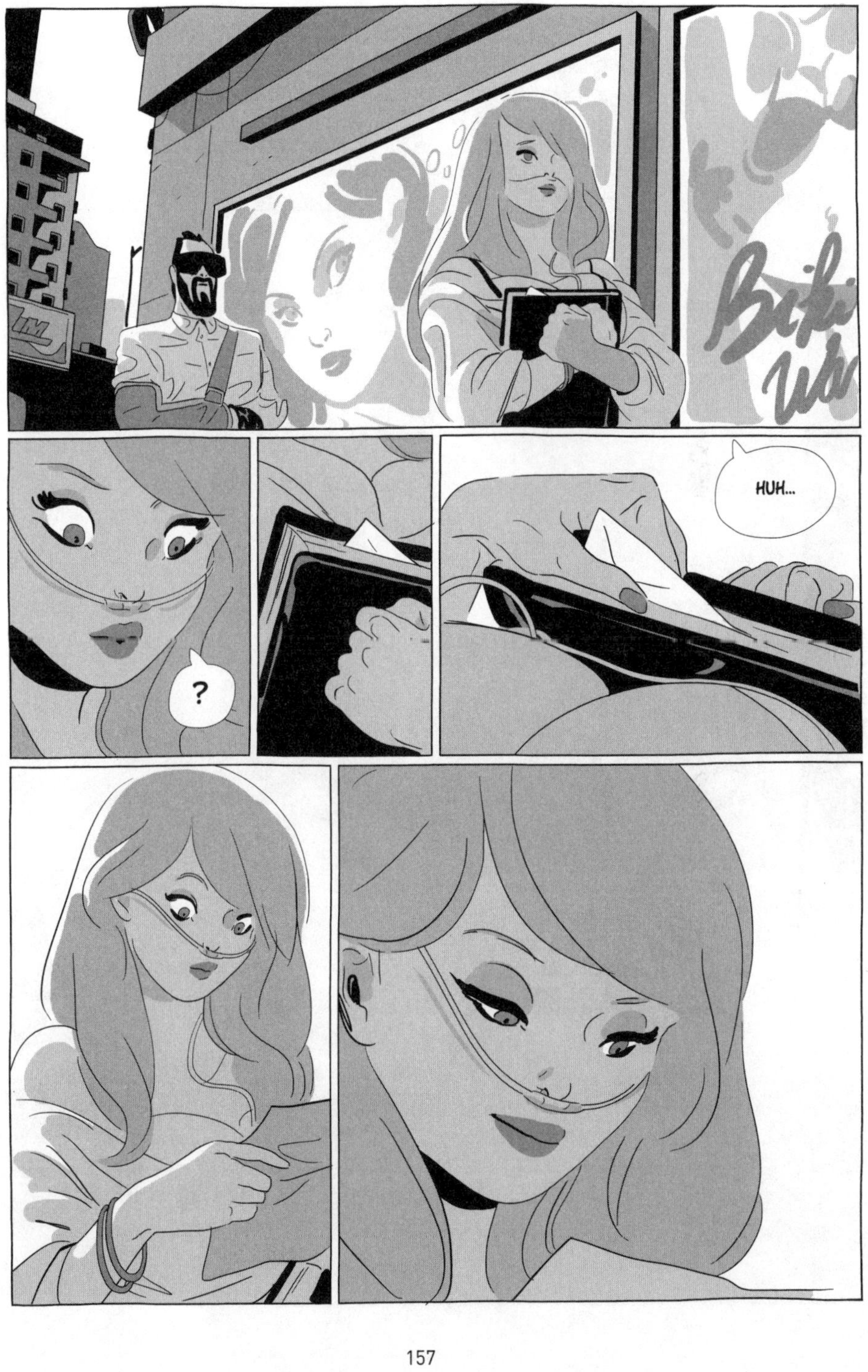
?
HUH...

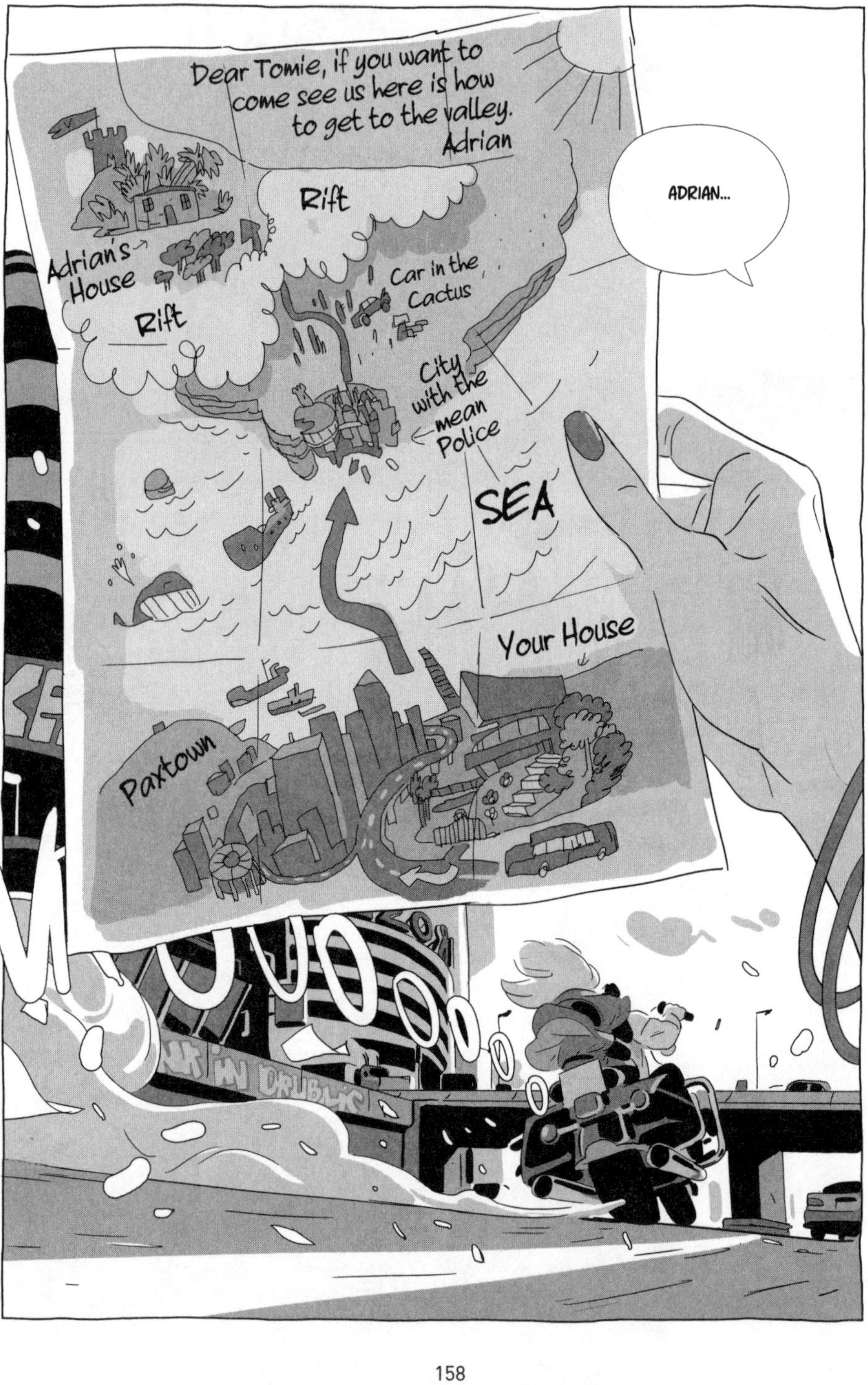
Dear Tomie, if you want to come see us here is how to get to the valley. Adrian
Rift
Adrian's House
Rift
Car in the Cactus
City with the mean Police
SEA
Your House
Paxtown
ADRIAN...

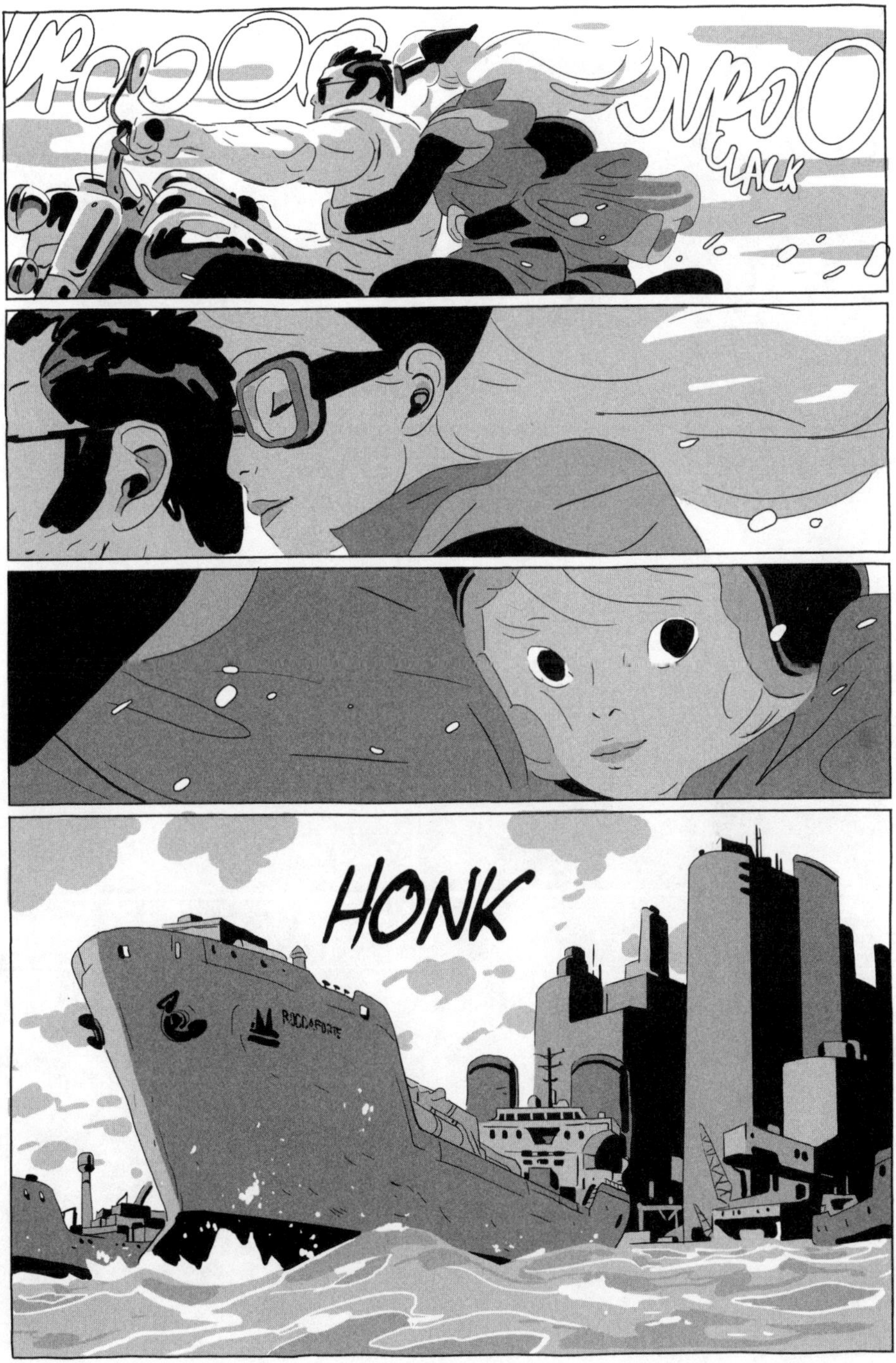
CLACK
HONK
ROCCAFORTE

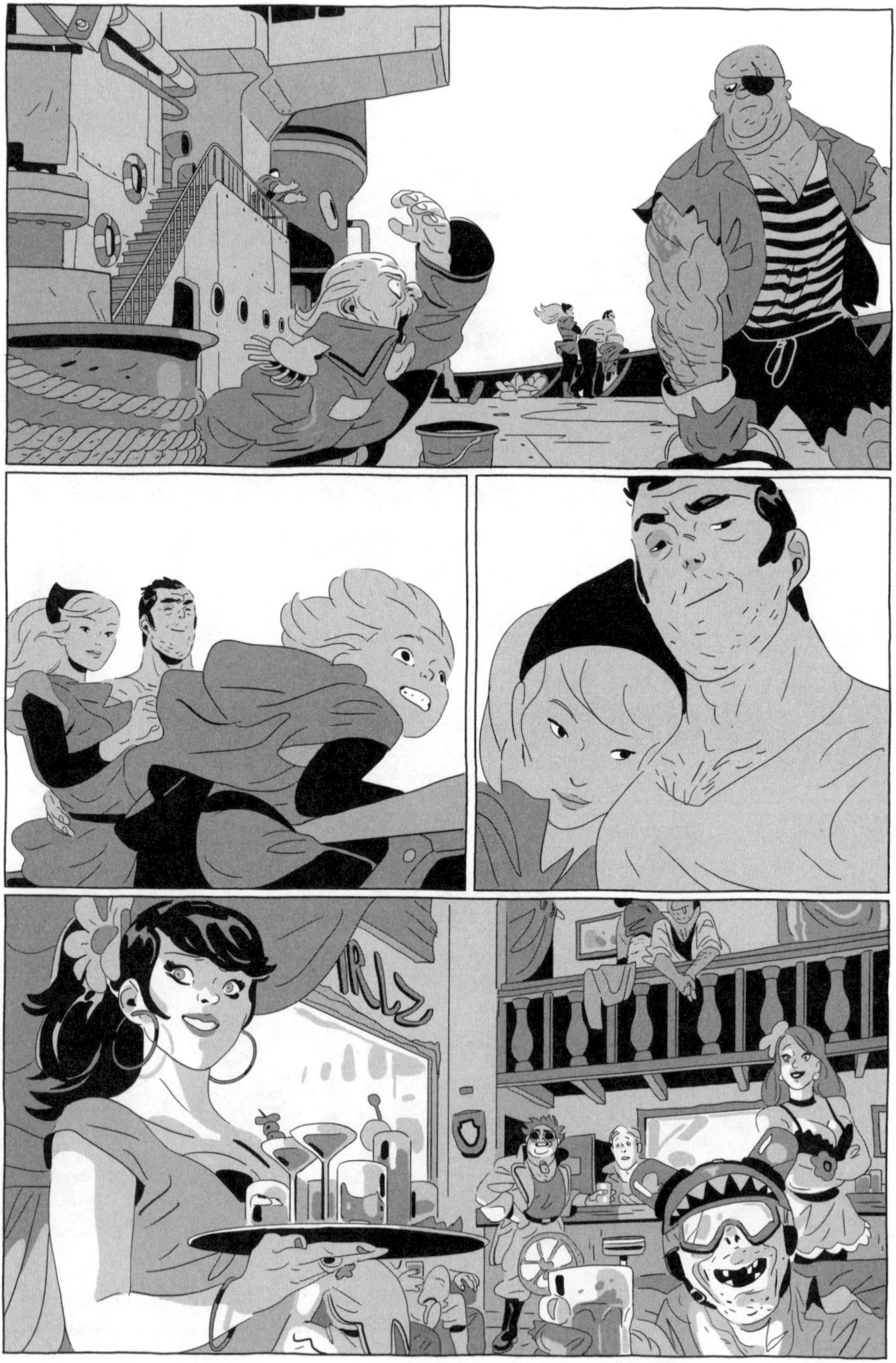

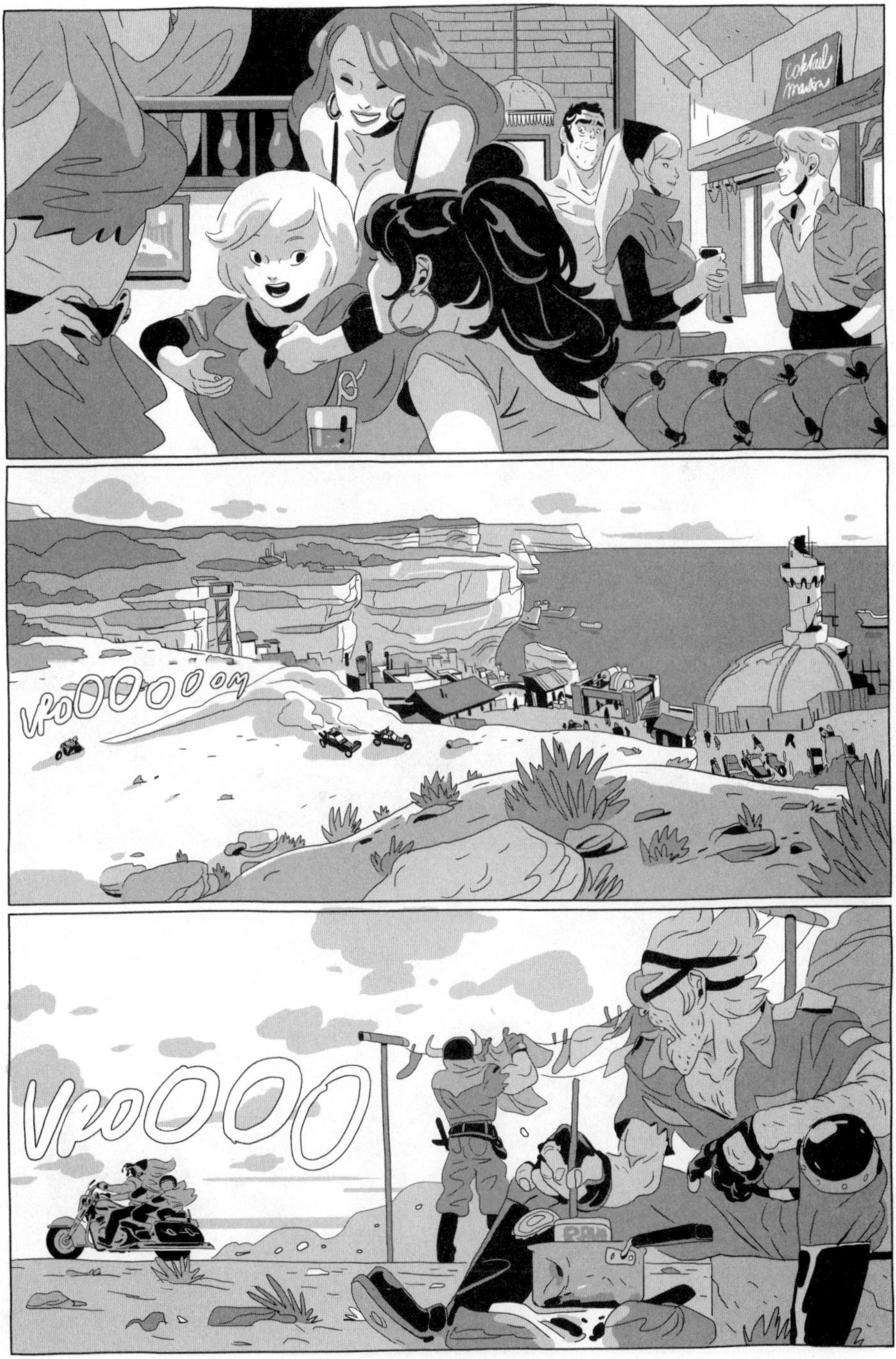
VROOOOOOM
VROOOO

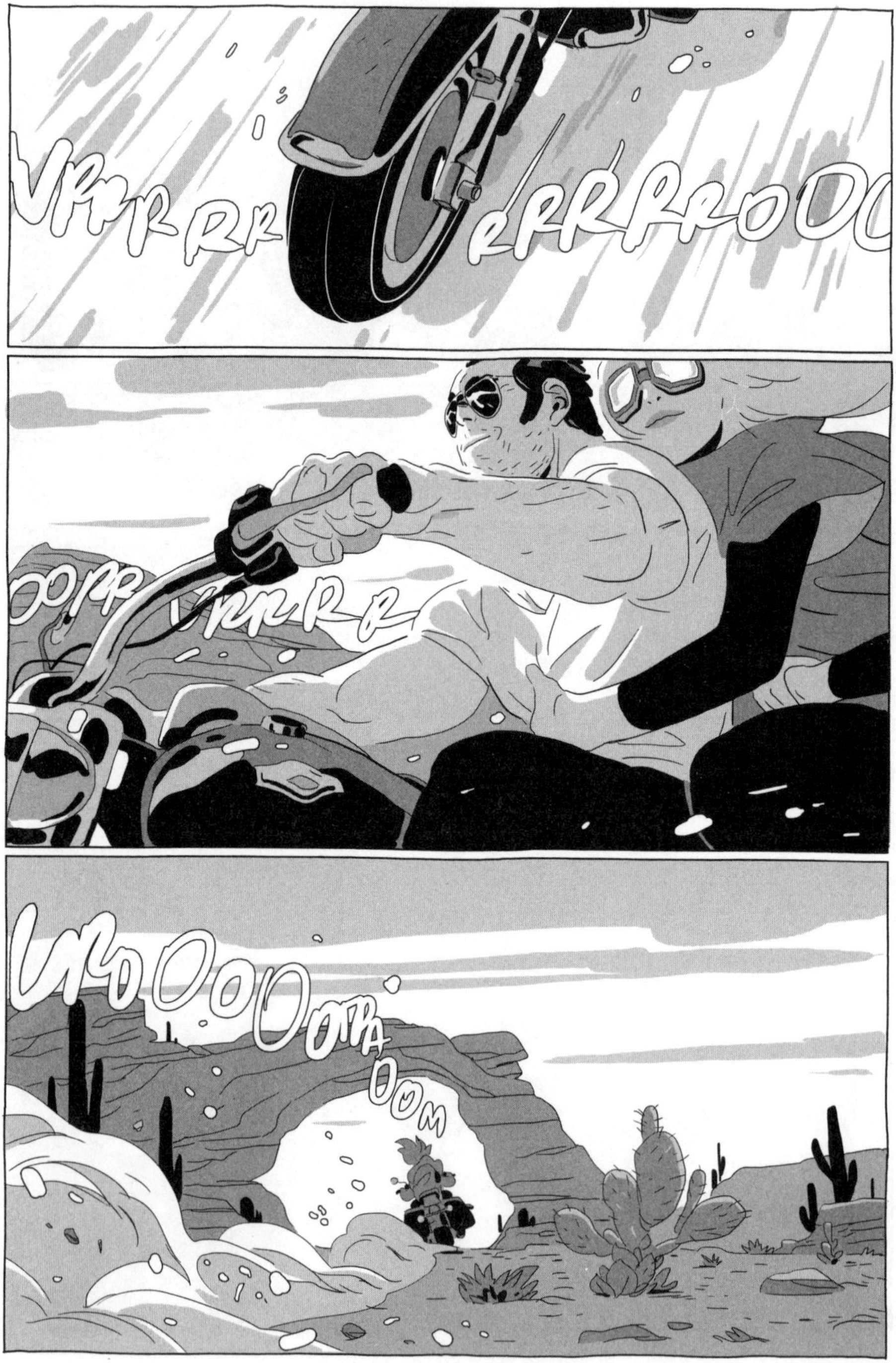
VRRRRR
RRRRRROOO
OORR
RRRRR
VROOOOOO
OTPA
OOM

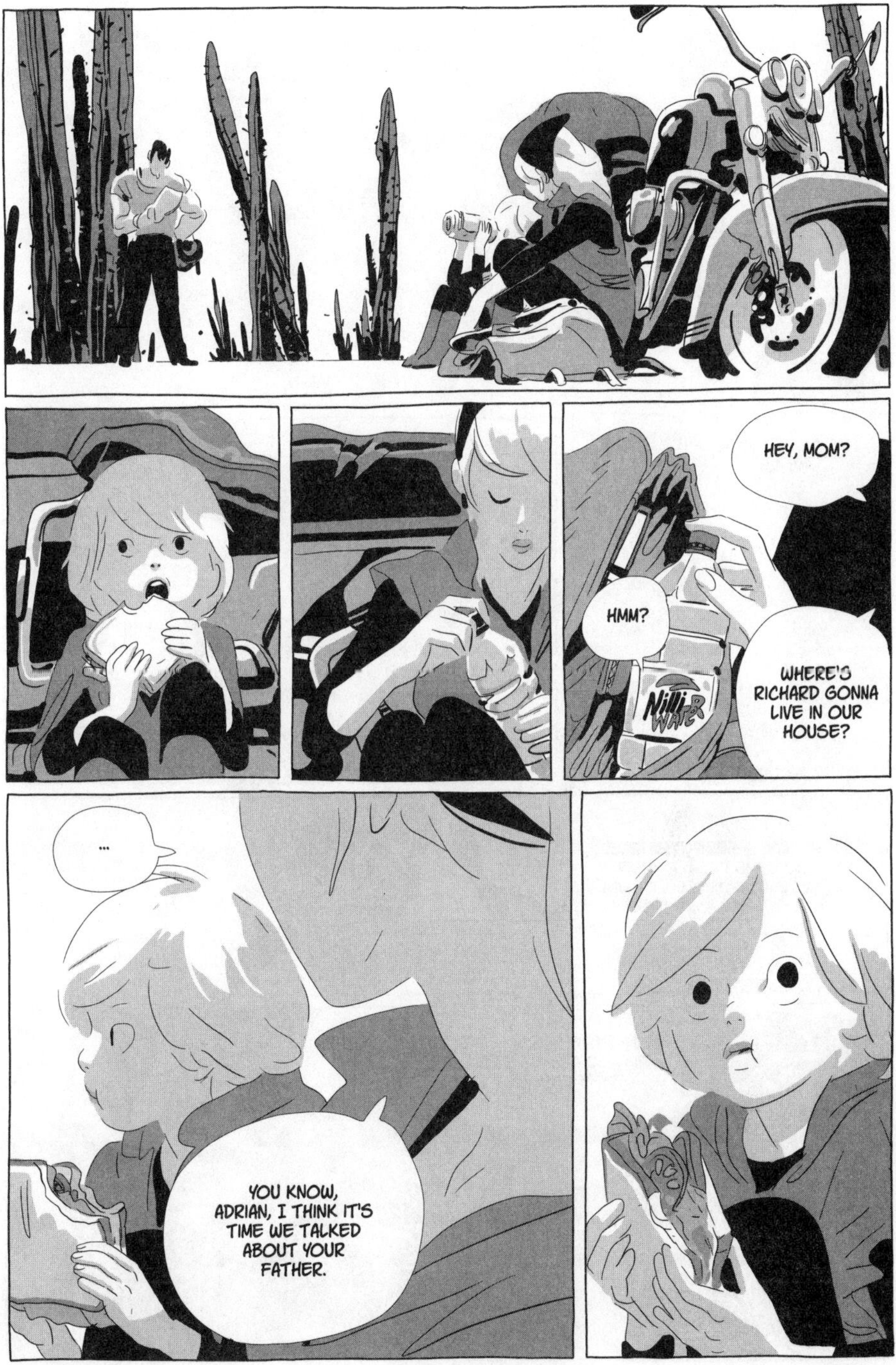
HEY, MOM?
HMM?
WHERE'S RICHARD GONNA LIVE IN OUR HOUSE?
...
YOU KNOW, ADRIAN, I THINK IT'S TIME WE TALKED ABOUT YOUR FATHER.

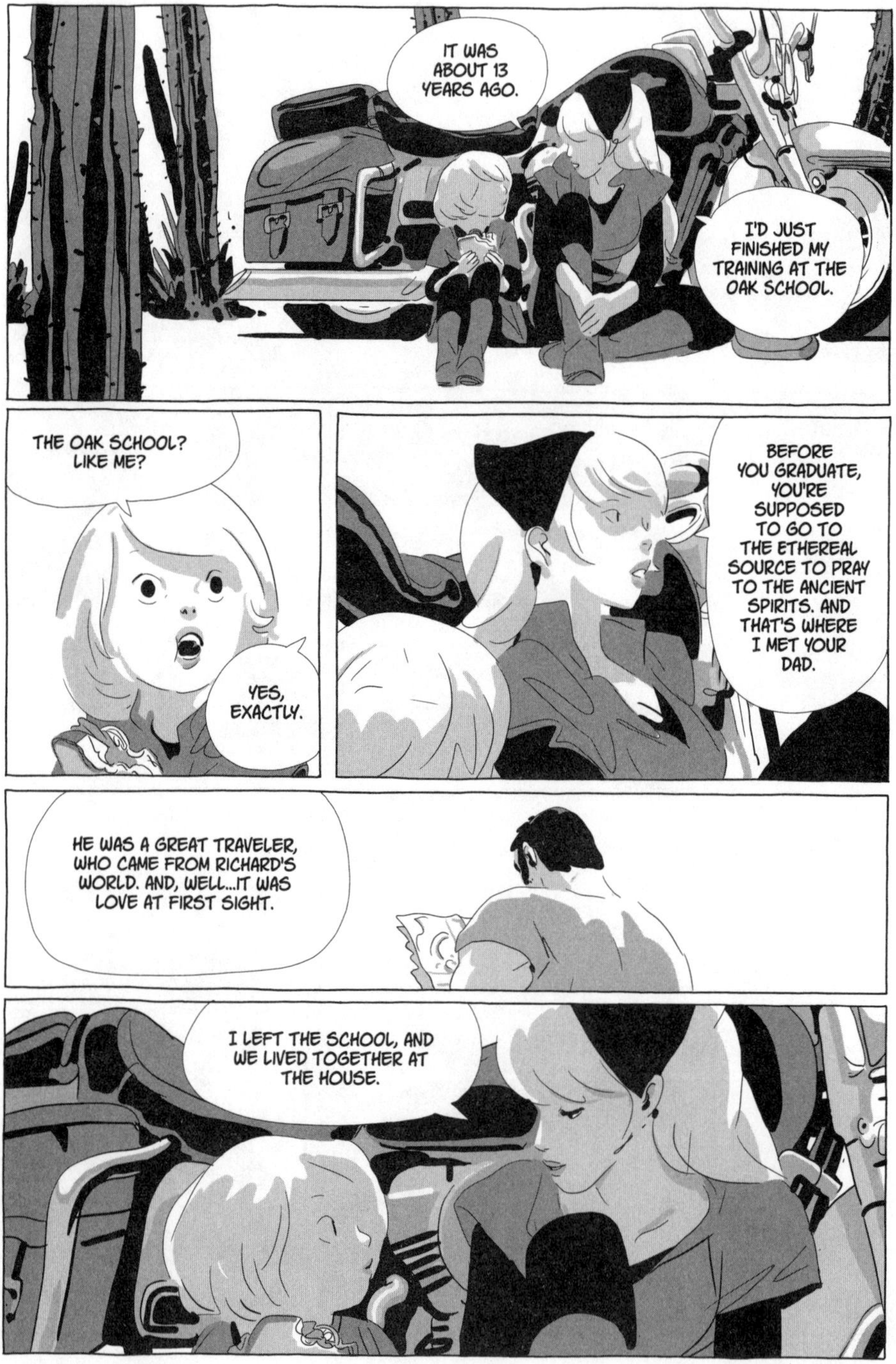
IT WAS ABOUT 13 YEARS AGO.
I'D JUST FINISHED MY TRAINING AT THE OAK SCHOOL.
THE OAK SCHOOL? LIKE ME?
YES, EXACTLY.
BEFORE YOU GRADUATE, YOU'RE SUPPOSED TO GO TO THE ETHEREAL SOURCE TO PRAY TO THE ANCIENT SPIRITS. AND THAT'S WHERE I MET YOUR DAD.
HE WAS A GREAT TRAVELER, WHO CAME FROM RICHARD'S WORLD. AND, WELL...IT WAS LOVE AT FIRST SIGHT.
I LEFT THE SCHOOL, AND WE LIVED TOGETHER AT THE HOUSE.

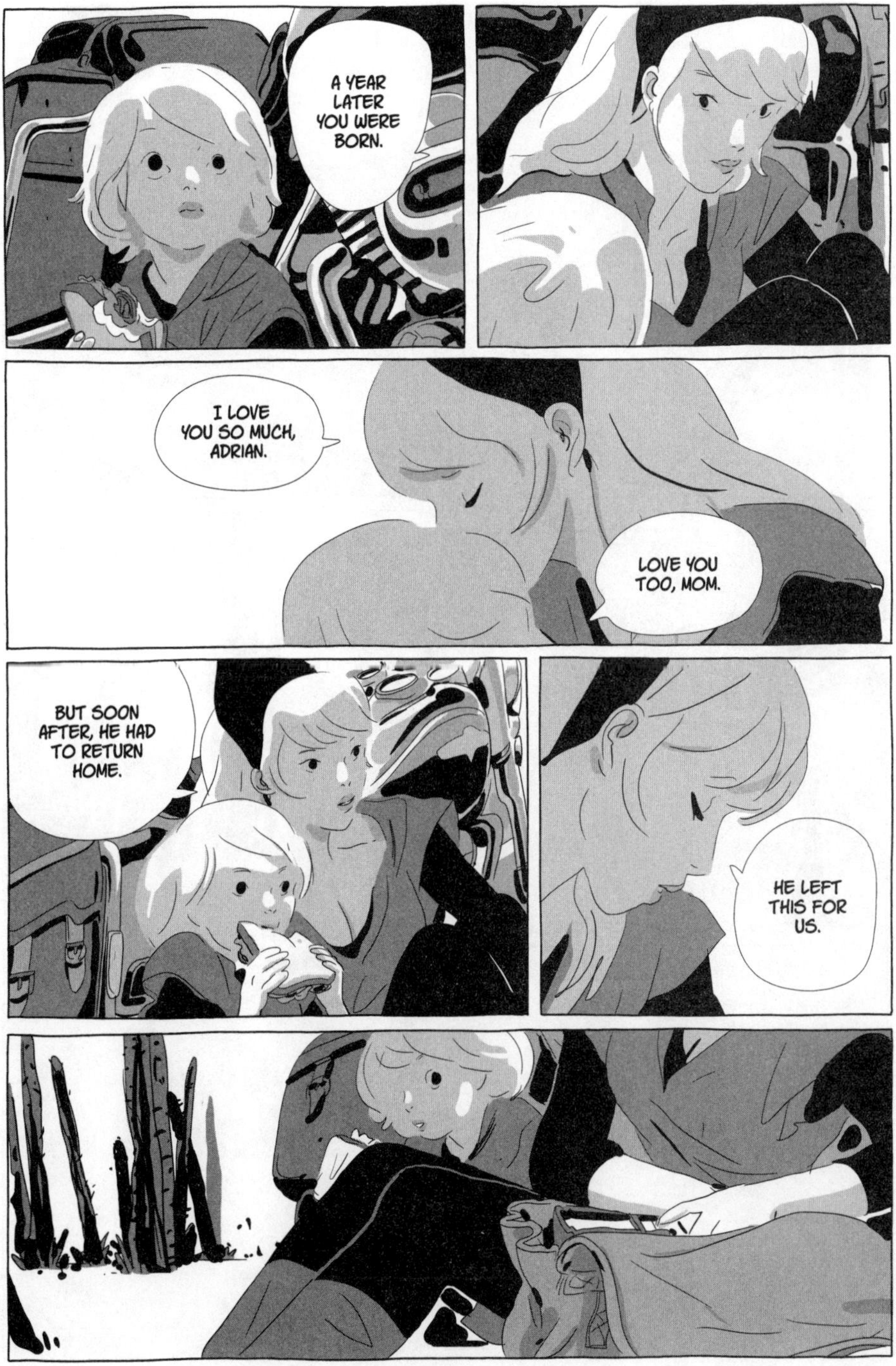
A YEAR LATER YOU WERE BORN.
I LOVE YOU SO MUCH, ADRIAN.
LOVE YOU TOO, MOM.
BUT SOON AFTER, HE HAD TO RETURN HOME.
HE LEFT THIS FOR US.

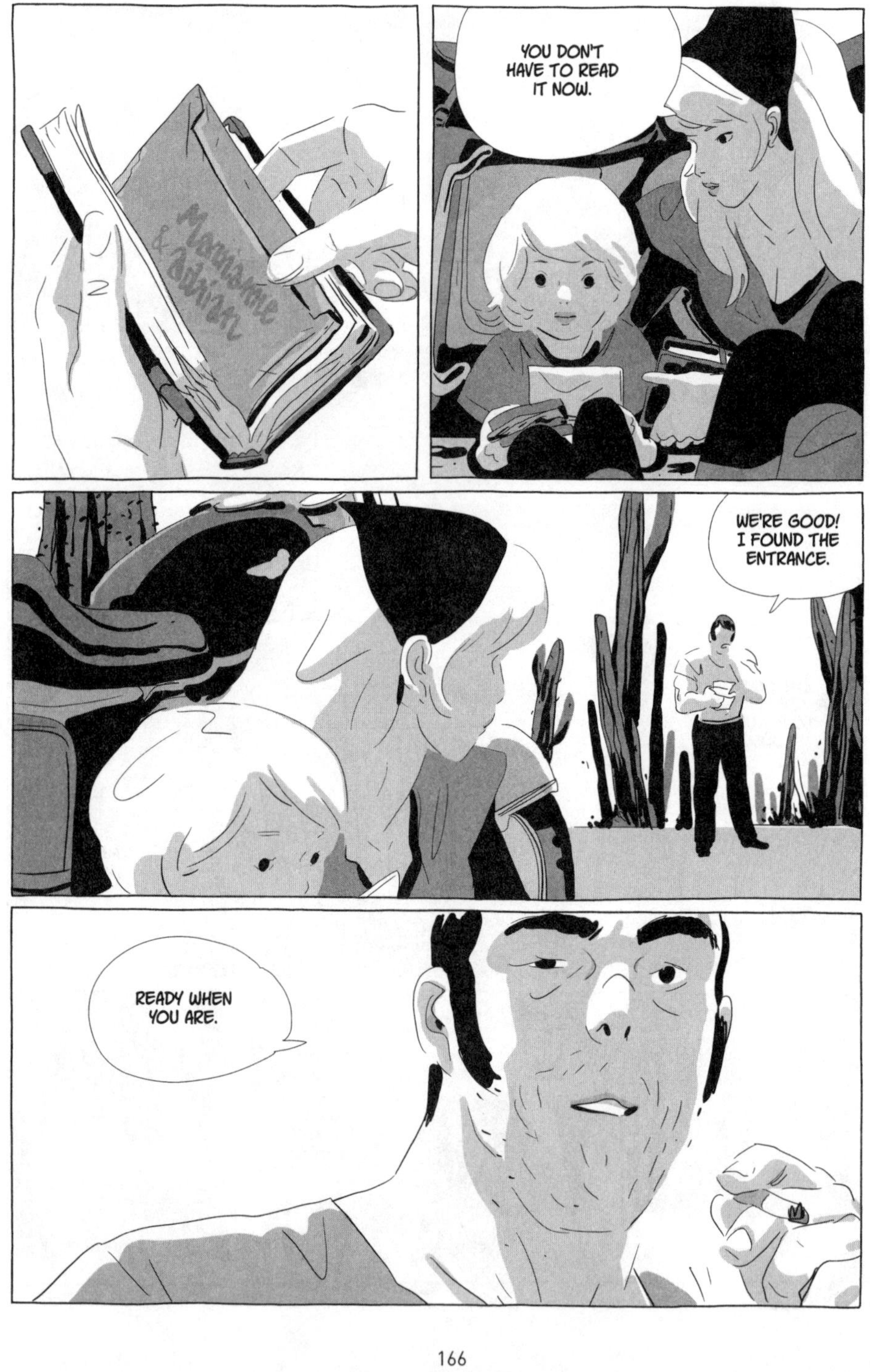
YOU DON'T HAVE TO READ IT NOW.
WE'RE GOOD! I FOUND THE ENTRANCE.
READY WHEN YOU ARE.

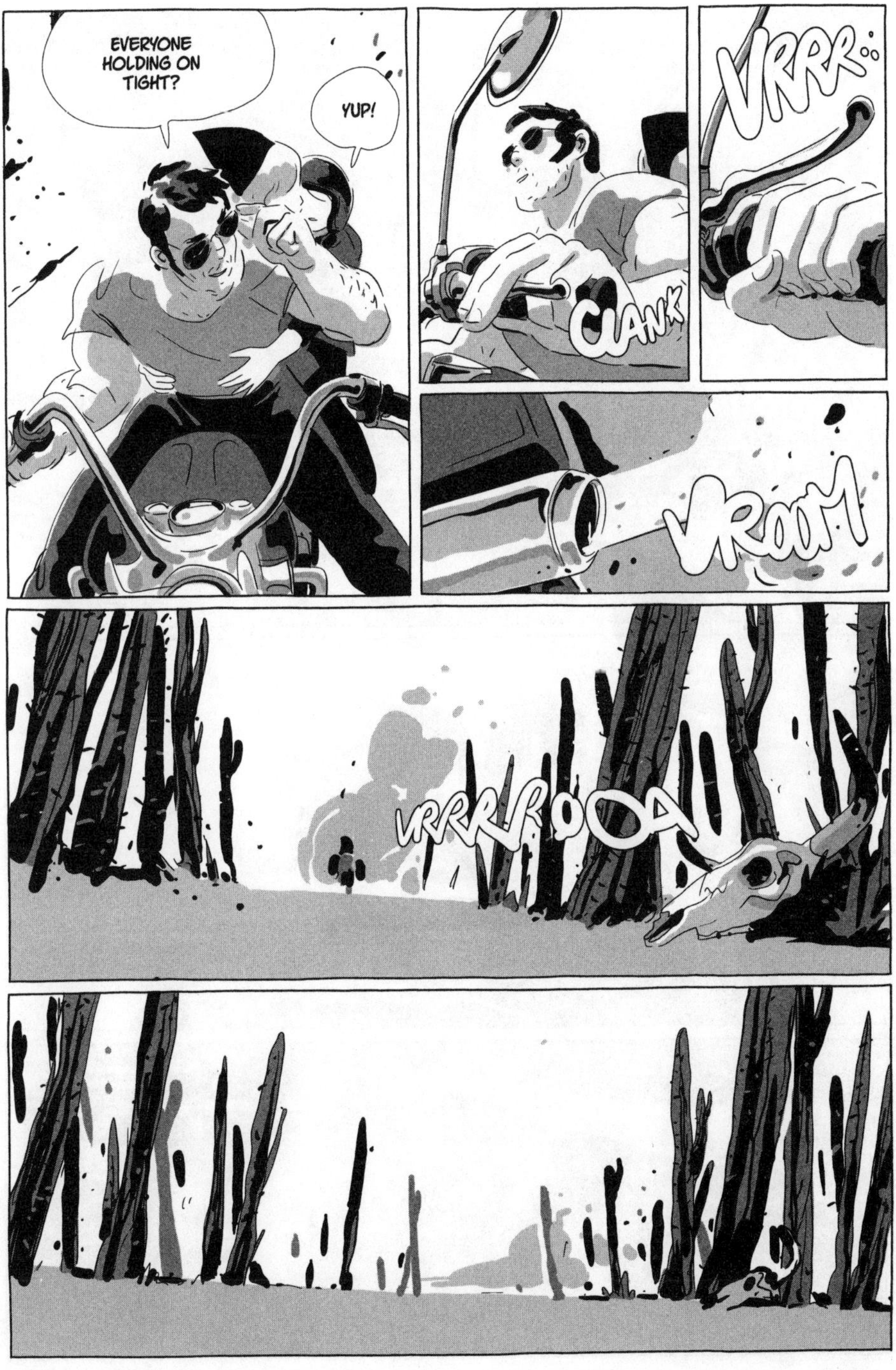

EVERYONE HOLDING ON TIGHT?
YUP!
CLANK
VRRR
VROOM
VRRRROOA

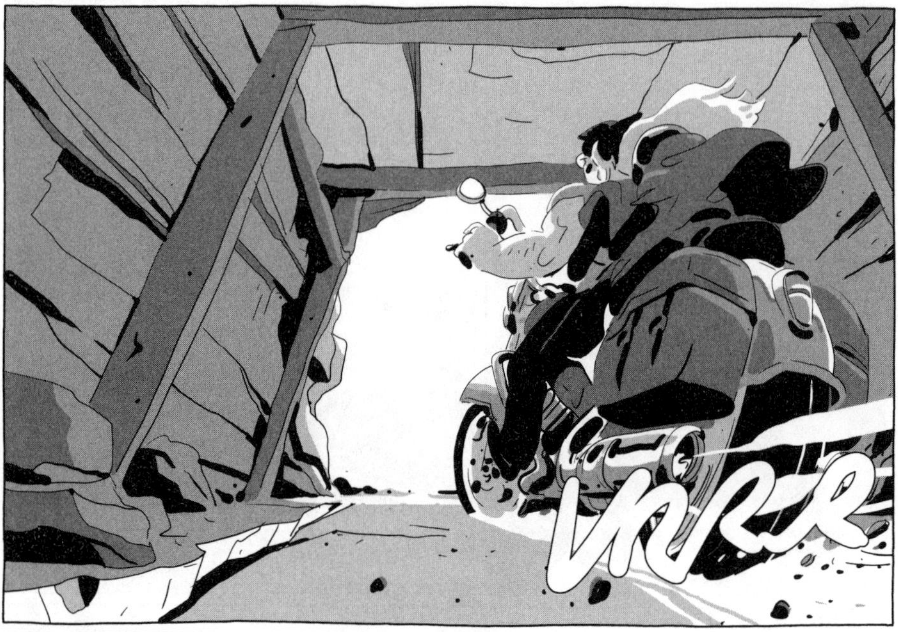
VRRR

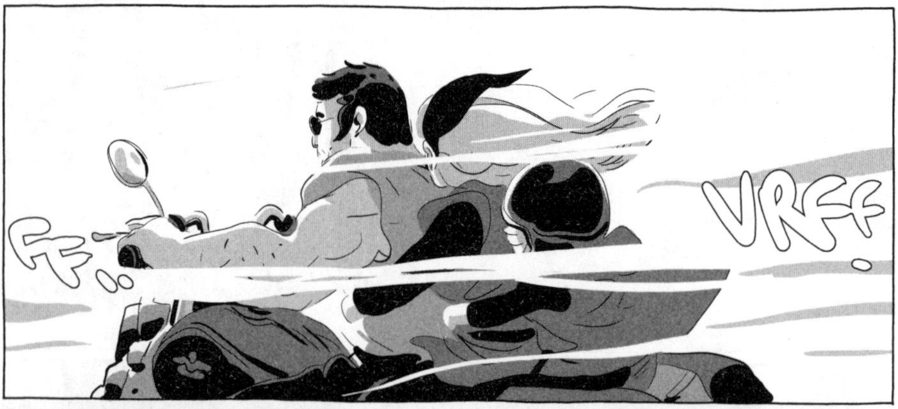
FF..
VRFF

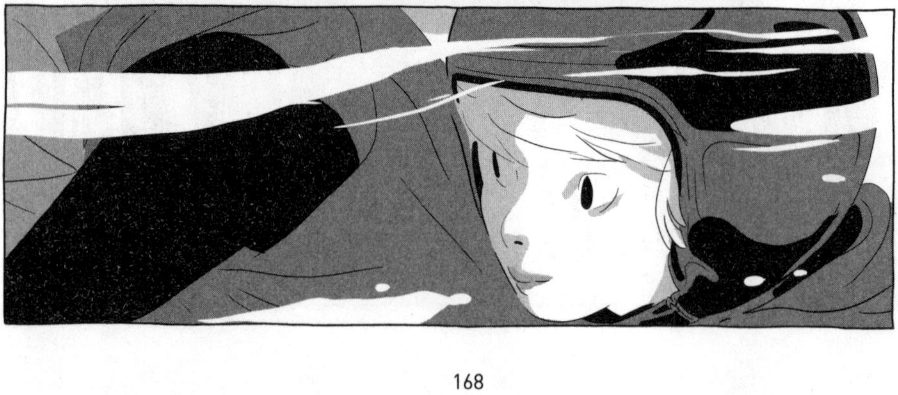

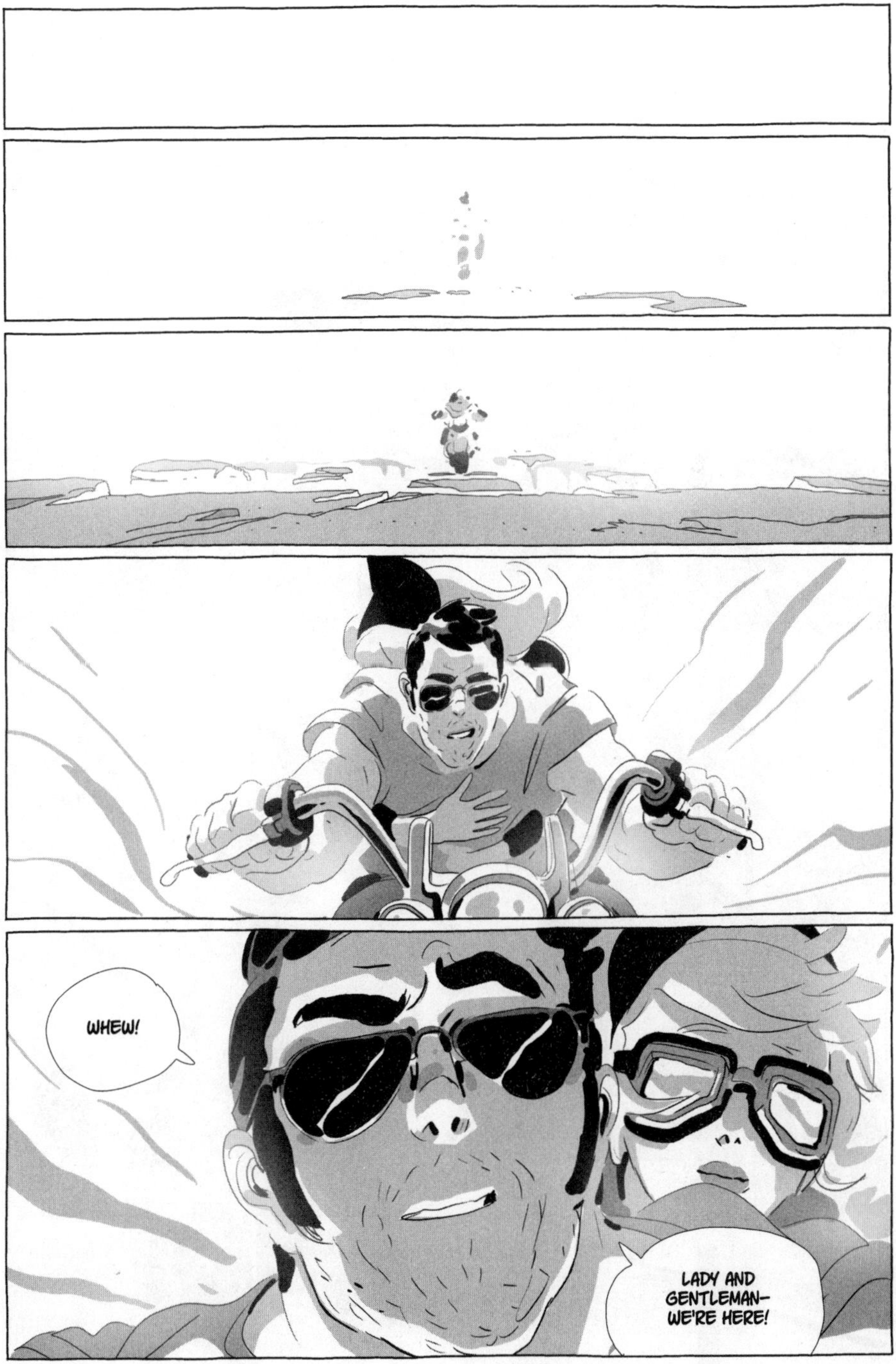
WHEW!
LADY AND GENTLEMAN-WE'RE HERE!

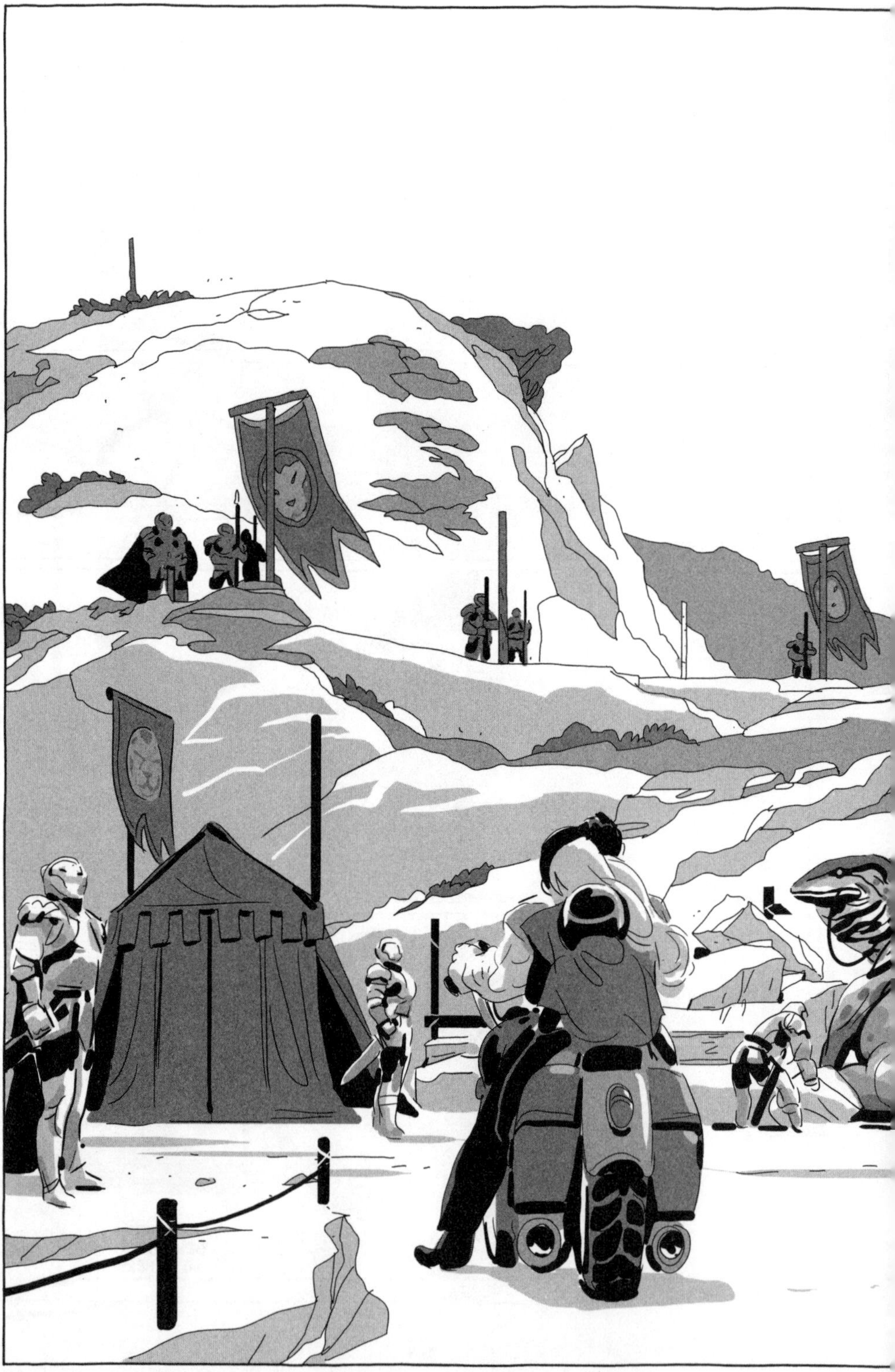

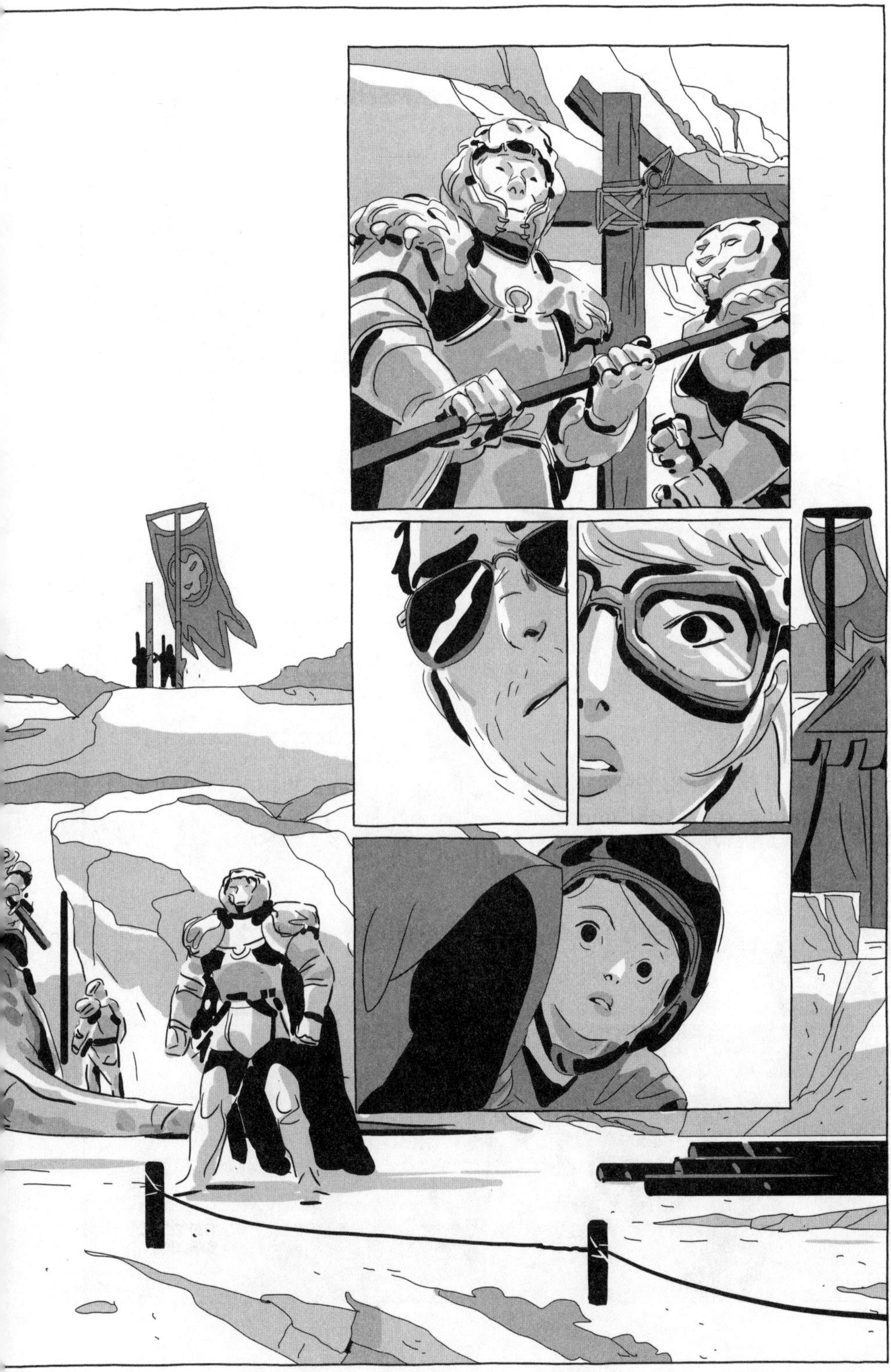

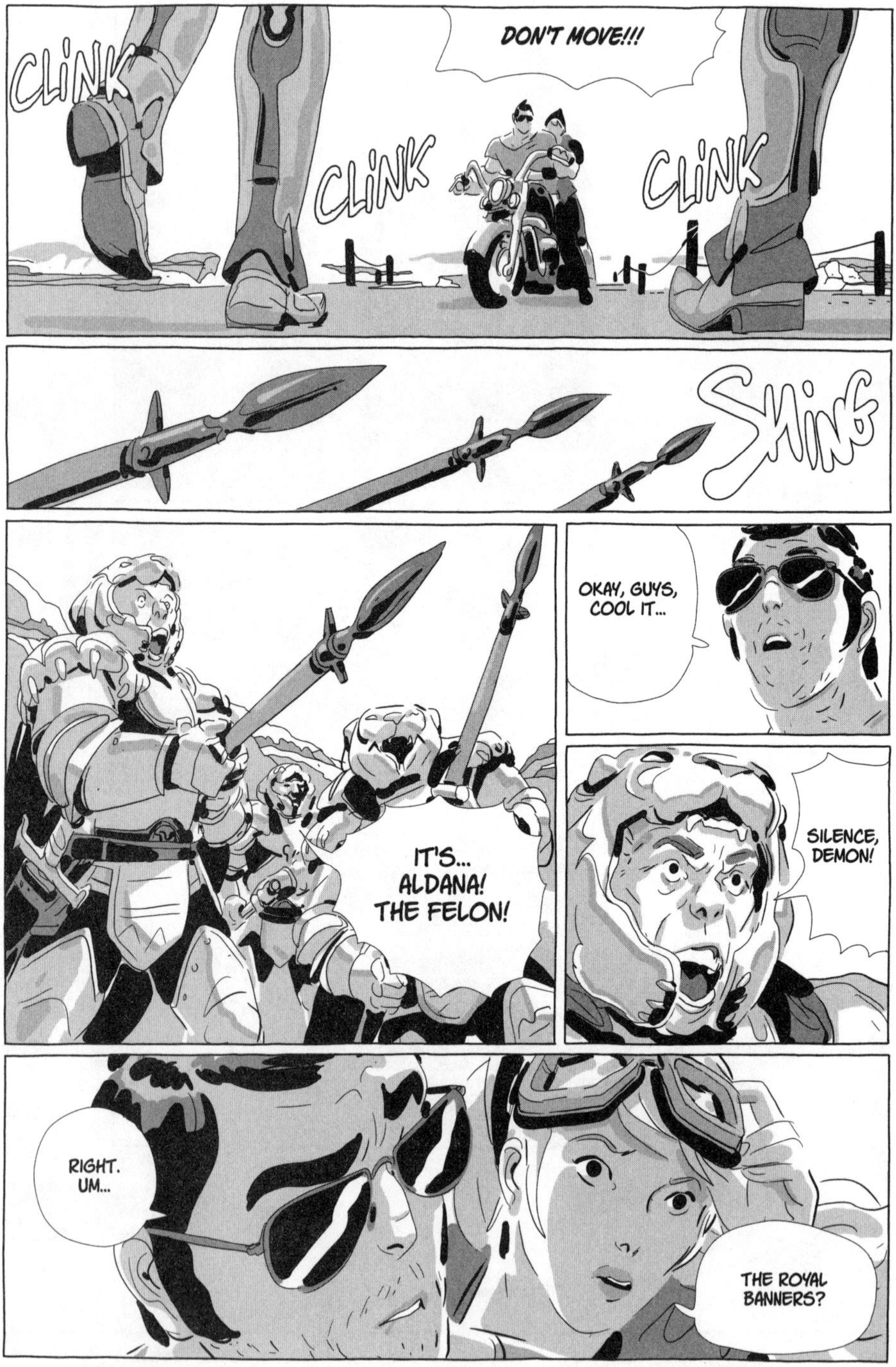

CLINK
DON'T MOVE!!!
CLINK
CLINK
SHING
IT'S... ALDANA! THE FELON!
OKAY, GUYS, COOL IT...
SILENCE, DEMON!
RIGHT. UM...
THE ROYAL BANNERS?

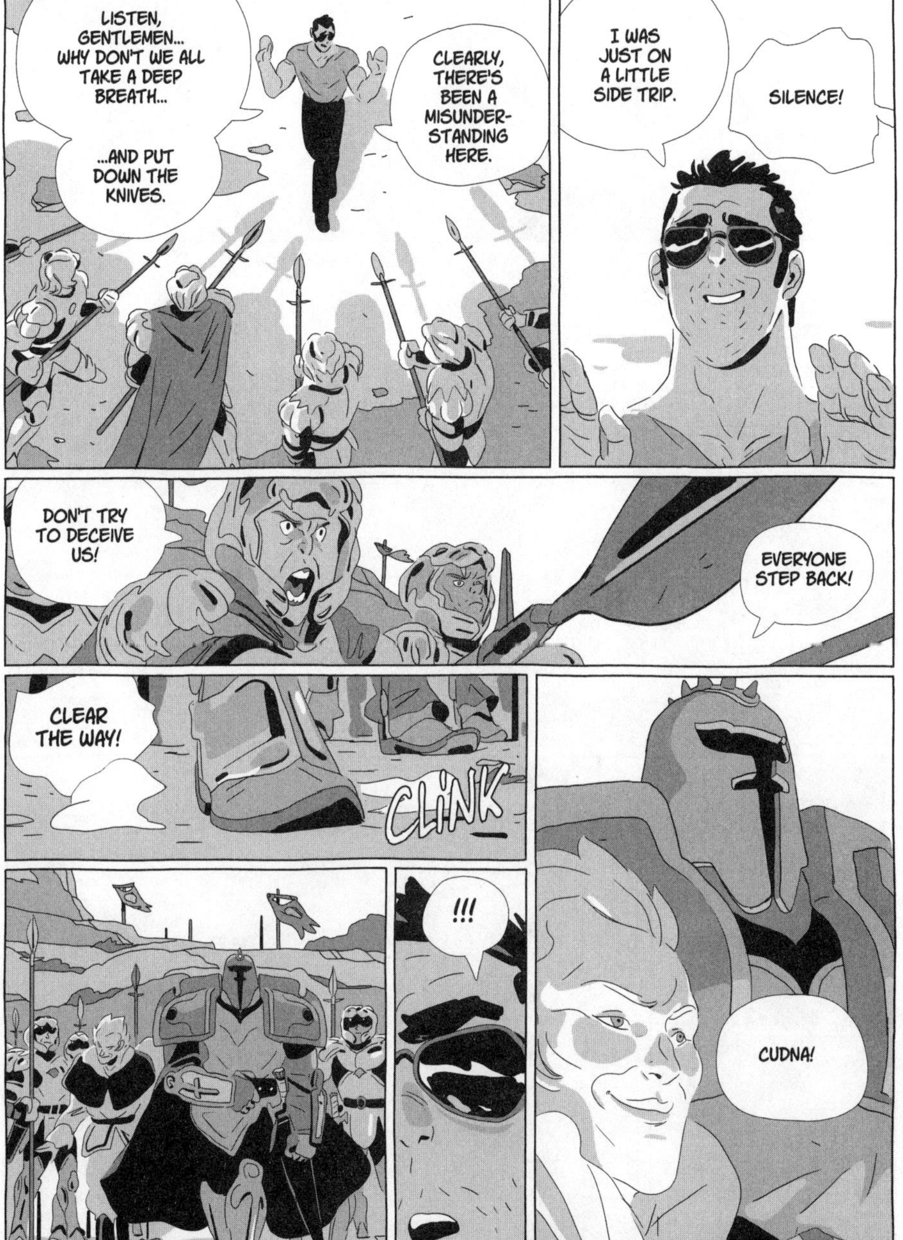
LISTEN, GENTLEMEN... WHY DON'T WE ALL TAKE A DEEP BREATH...
...AND PUT DOWN THE KNIVES.
CLEARLY, THERE'S BEEN A MISUNDER-STANDING HERE.
I WAS JUST ON A LITTLE SIDE TRIP.
SILENCE!
DON'T TRY TO DECEIVE US!
EVERYONE STEP BACK!
CLEAR THE WAY!
CLINK
!!!
CUDNA!

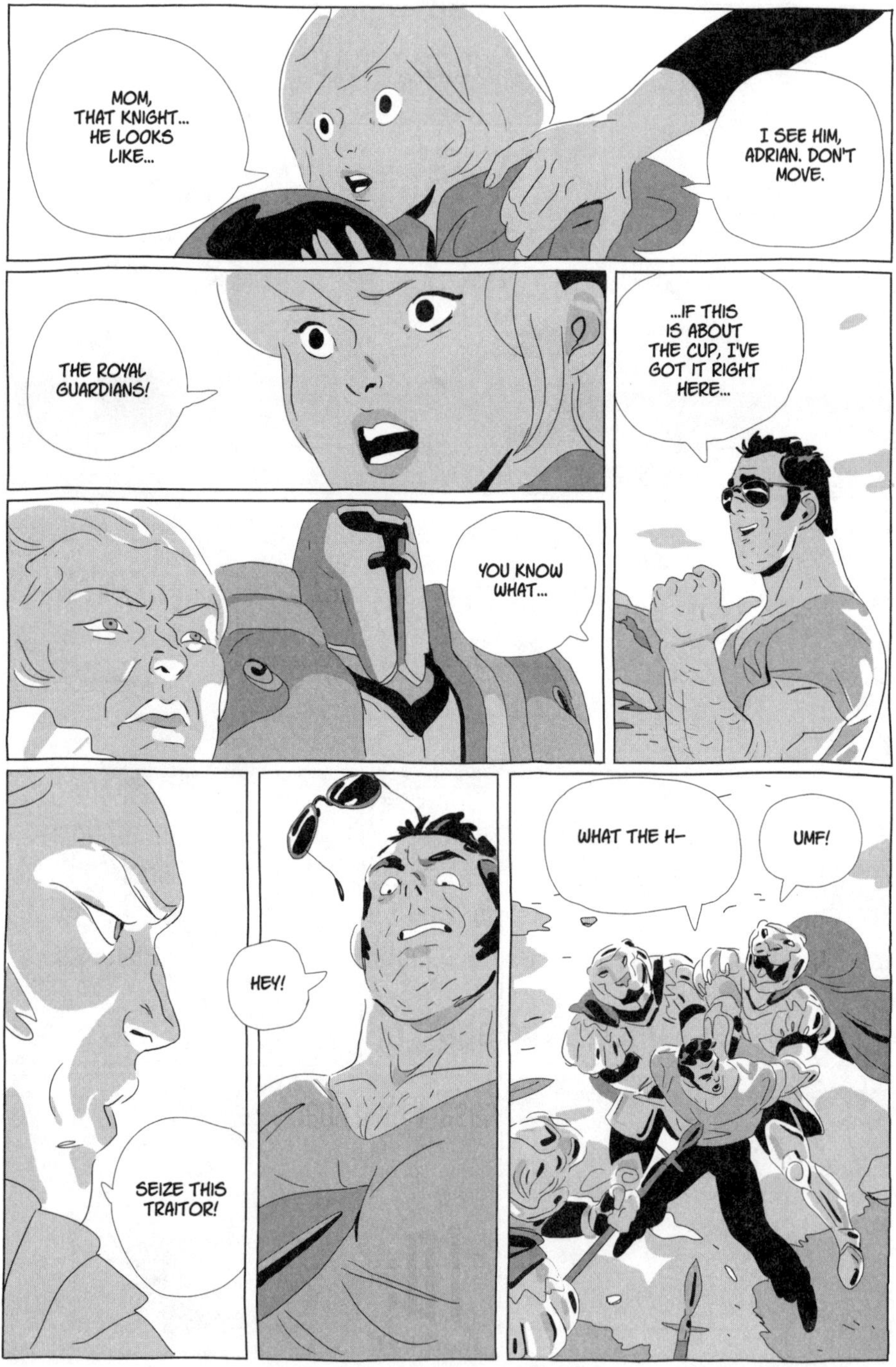
MOM, THAT KNIGHT... HE LOOKS LIKE...
I SEE HIM, ADRIAN. DON'T MOVE.
THE ROYAL GUARDIANS!
...IF THIS IS ABOUT THE CUP, I'VE GOT IT RIGHT HERE...
YOU KNOW WHAT...
SEIZE THIS TRAITOR!
HEY!
WHAT THE H—
UMF!

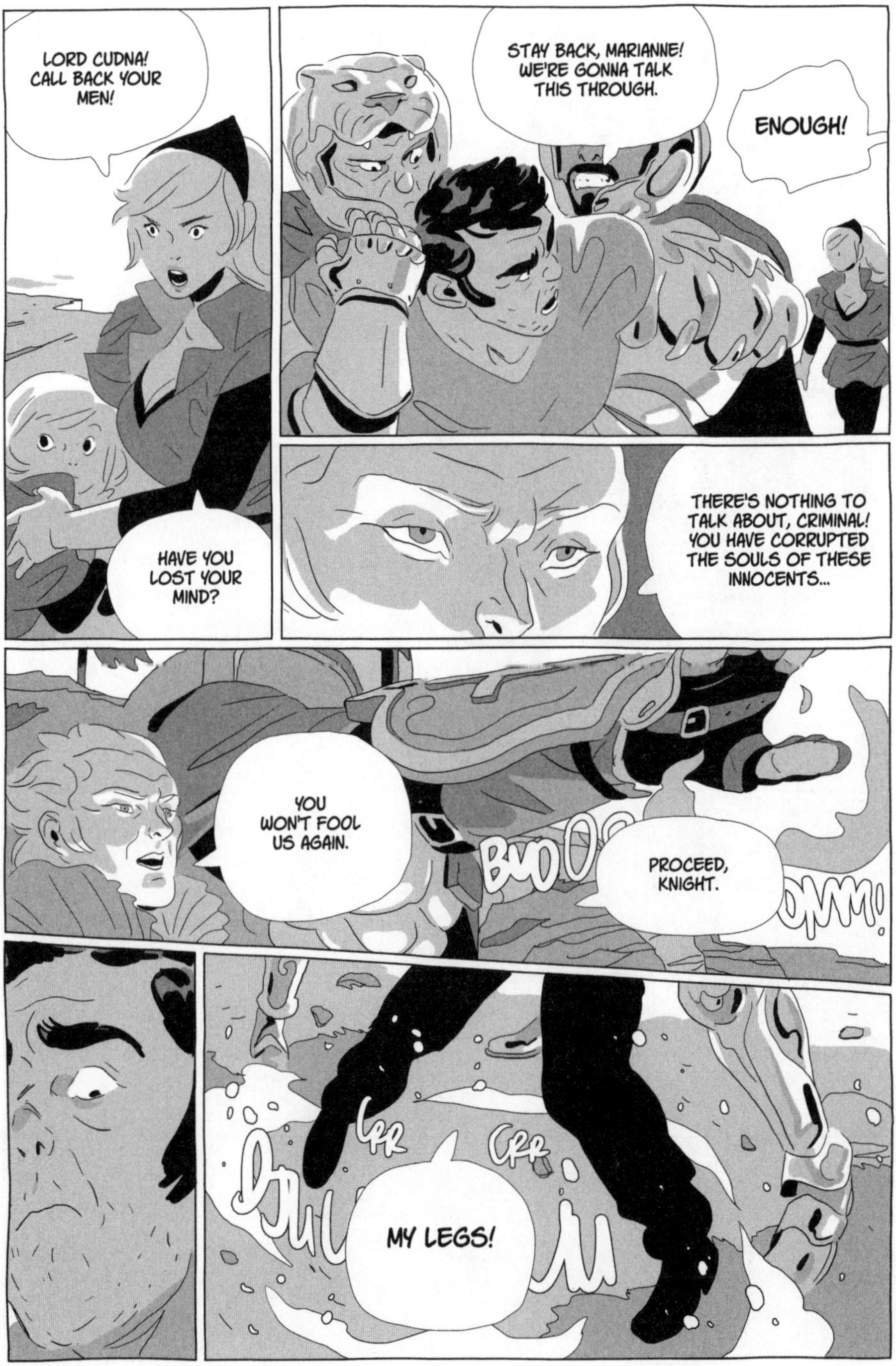
LORD CUDNA! CALL BACK YOUR MEN!
HAVE YOU LOST YOUR MIND?
STAY BACK, MARIANNE! WE'RE GONNA TALK THIS THROUGH.
ENOUGH!
THERE'S NOTHING TO TALK ABOUT, CRIMINAL! YOU HAVE CORRUPTED THE SOULS OF THESE INNOCENTS...
YOU WON'T FOOL US AGAIN.
BVOO
PROCEED, KNIGHT.
OMM!
CRR
CRR
MY LEGS!

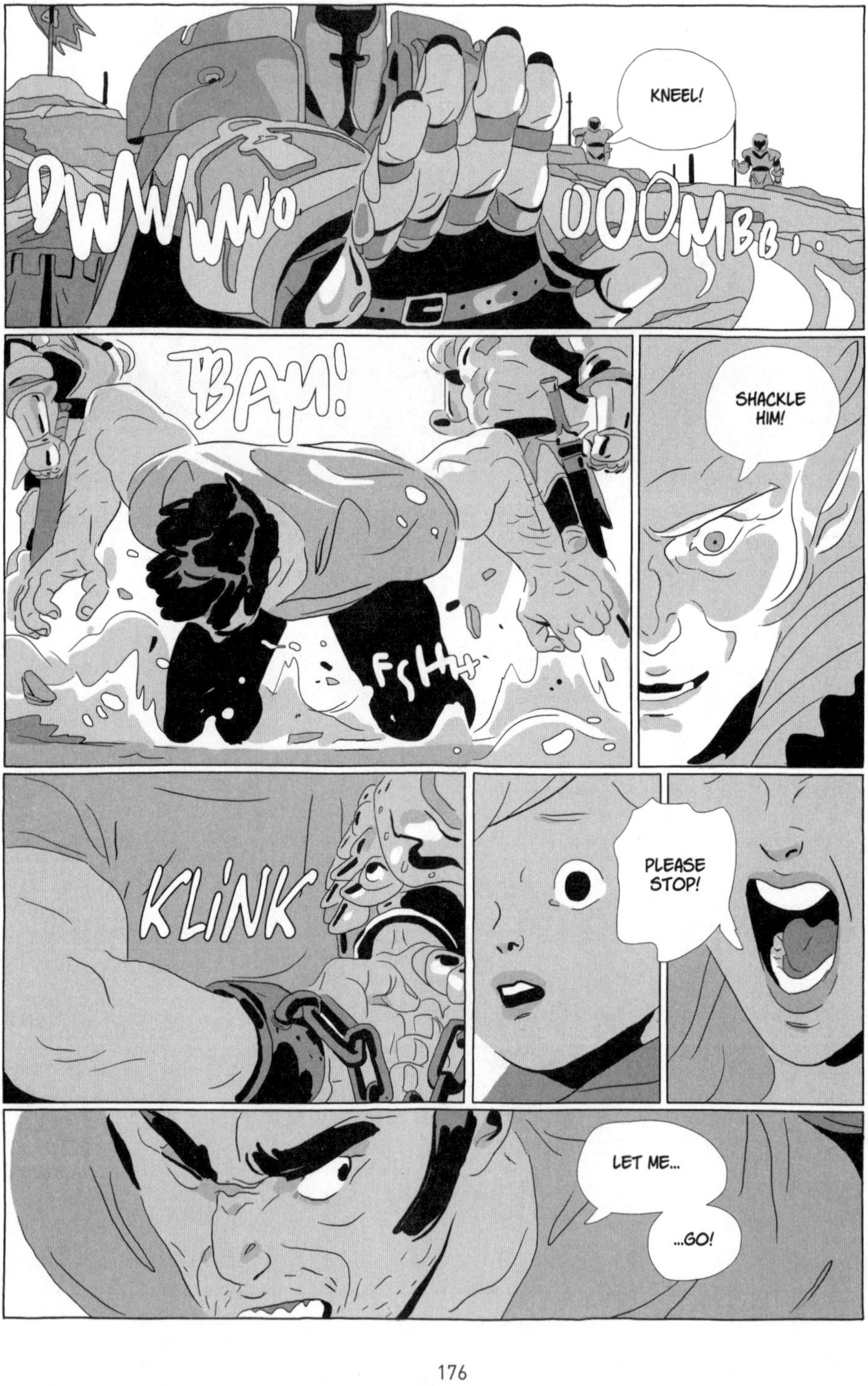
KNEEL!
DWWWWWO OOOMBB..
BAM!
FSHH
SHACKLE HIM!
KLINK
PLEASE STOP!
LET ME...
...GO!

GOOD! TAKE HIM TO THE CASTLE DUNGEON.

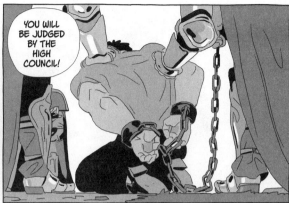

YOU WILL BE JUDGED BY THE HIGH COUNCIL!

EXPECT NO MERCY FROM KING VIRGIL!

YOUR CRIMES WARRANT CAPITAL PUNISHMENT!

CUDNA!

RELEASE HIM! HE'S DONE NOTHING WRONG!

I DEMAND AN AUDIENCE WITH THE KING! DO YOU HEAR ME?

LISTEN TO HER, MORONS!

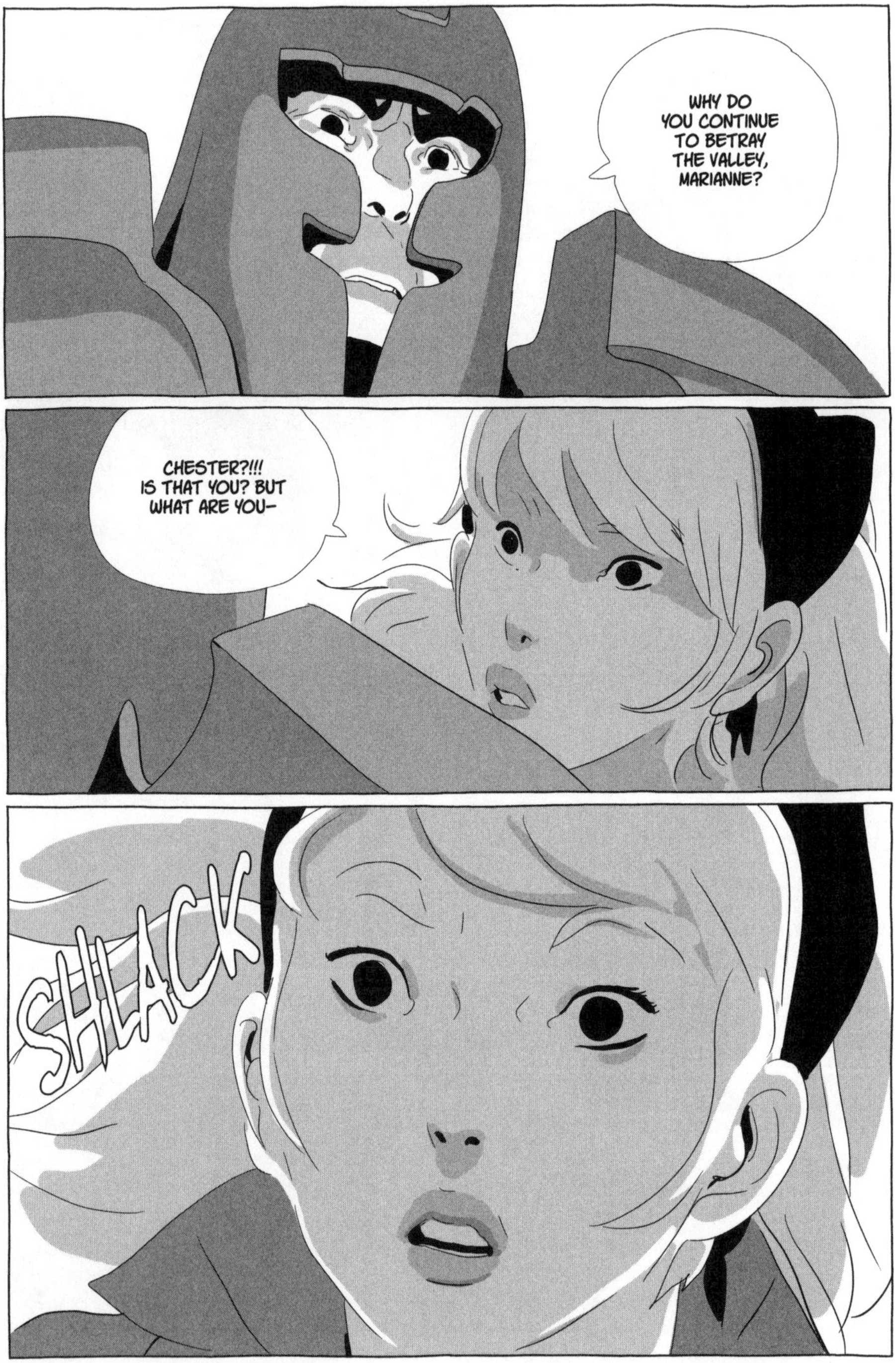
WHY DO YOU CONTINUE TO BETRAY THE VALLEY, MARIANNE?
CHESTER?!!! IS THAT YOU? BUT WHAT ARE YOU-
SHLACK

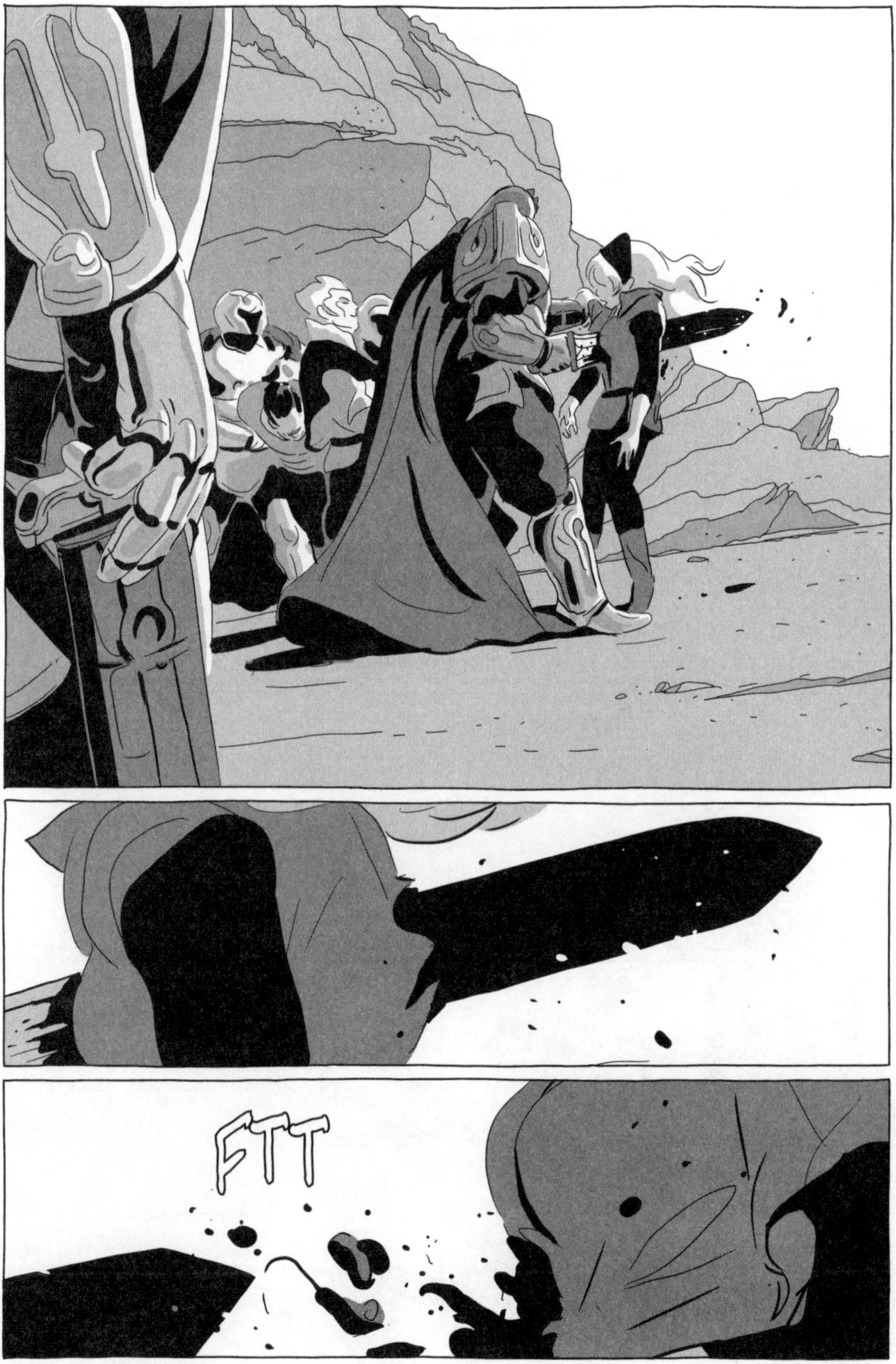
FTT

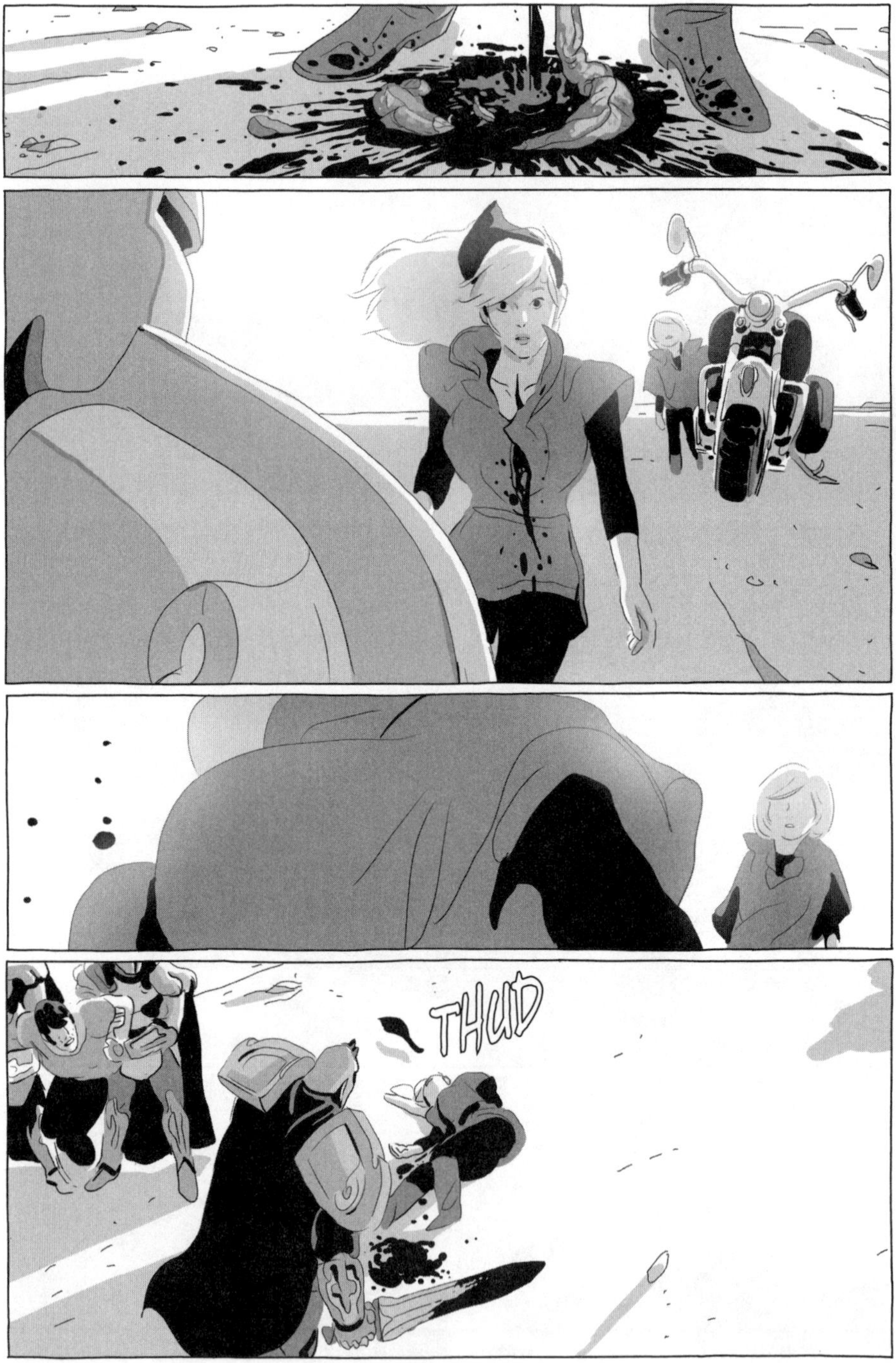
THUD

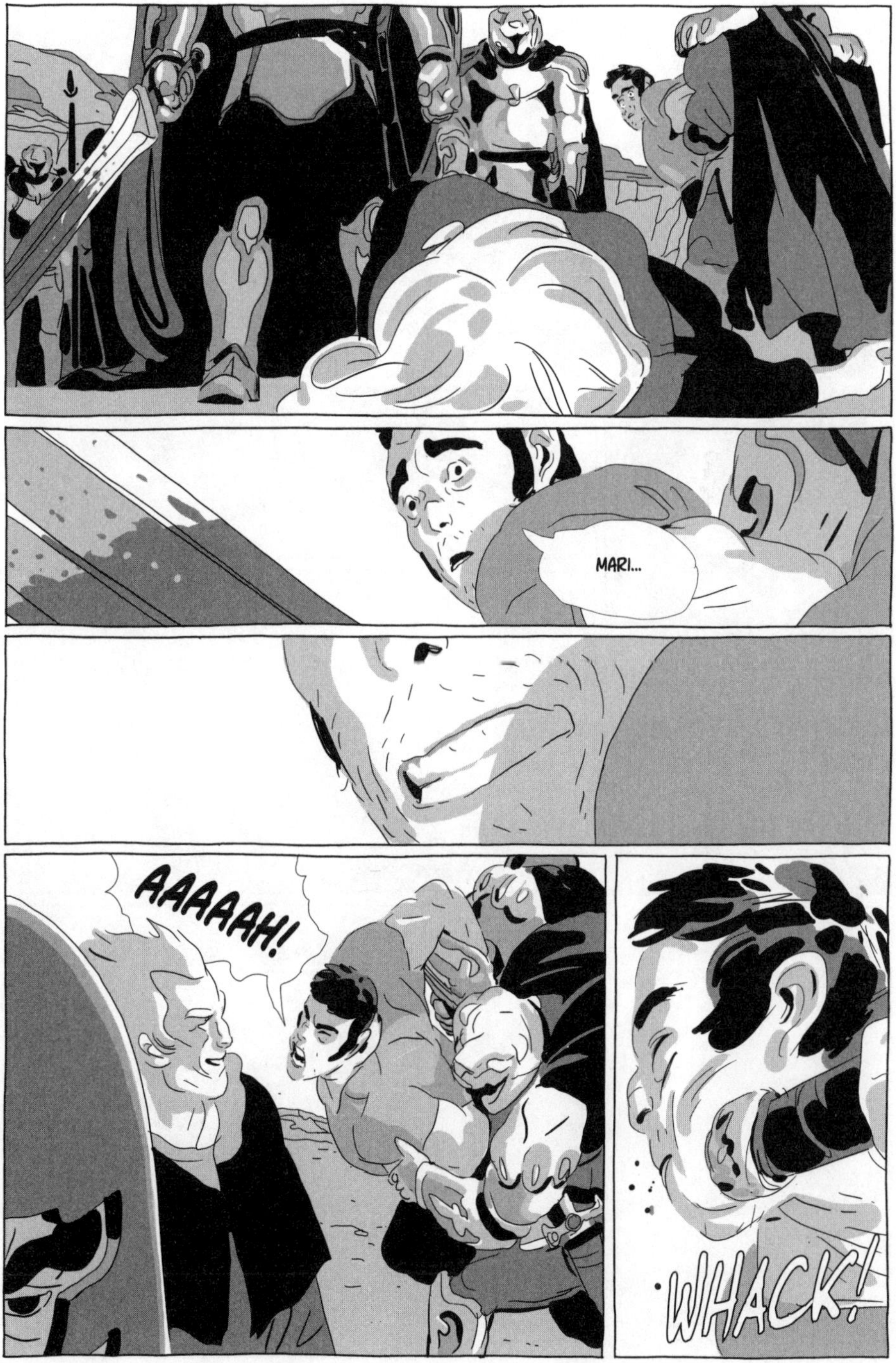
MARI...
AAAAAAH!
WHACK!

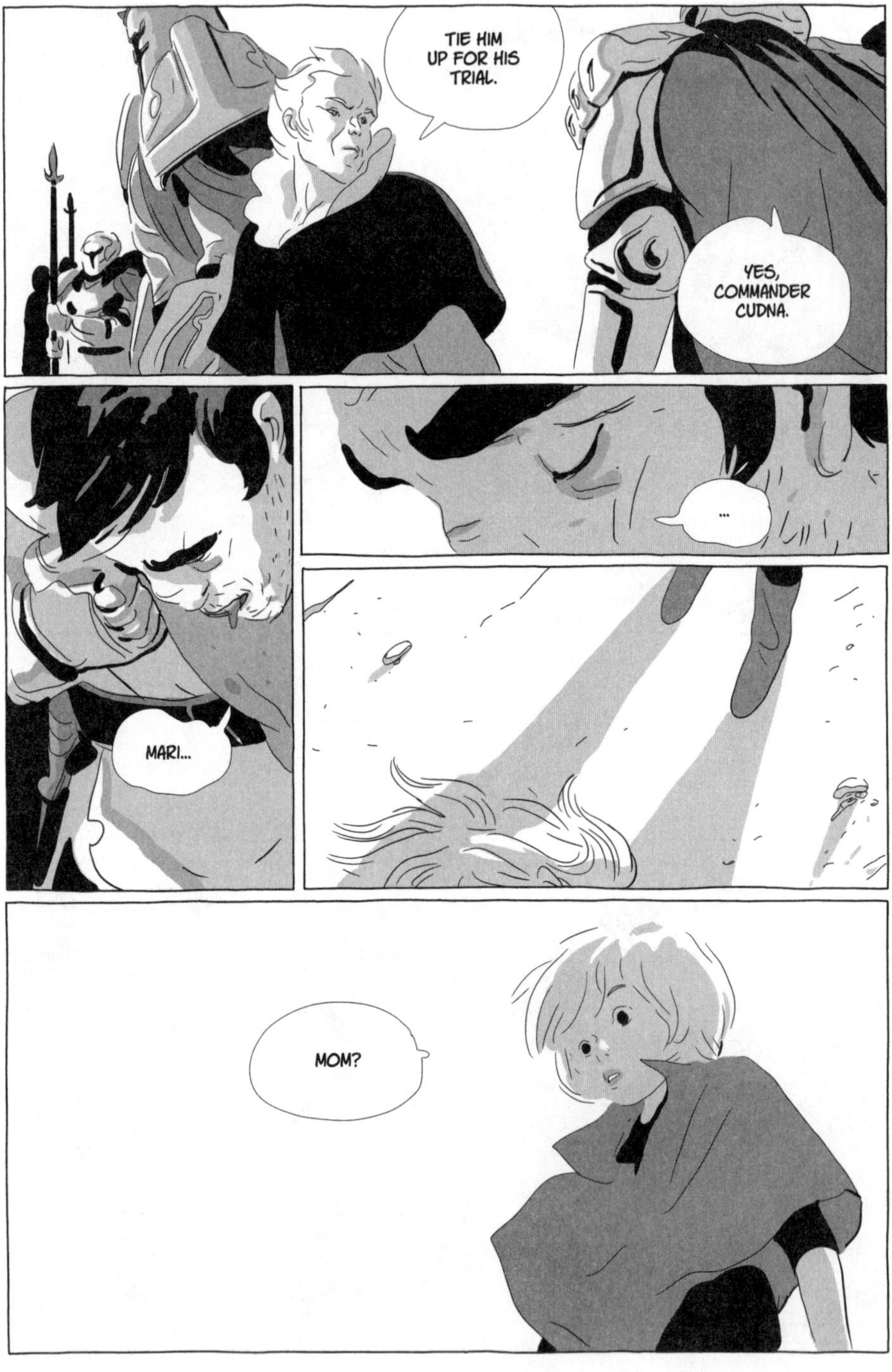
TIE HIM UP FOR HIS TRIAL.
YES, COMMANDER CUDNA.
MARI...
...
MOM?

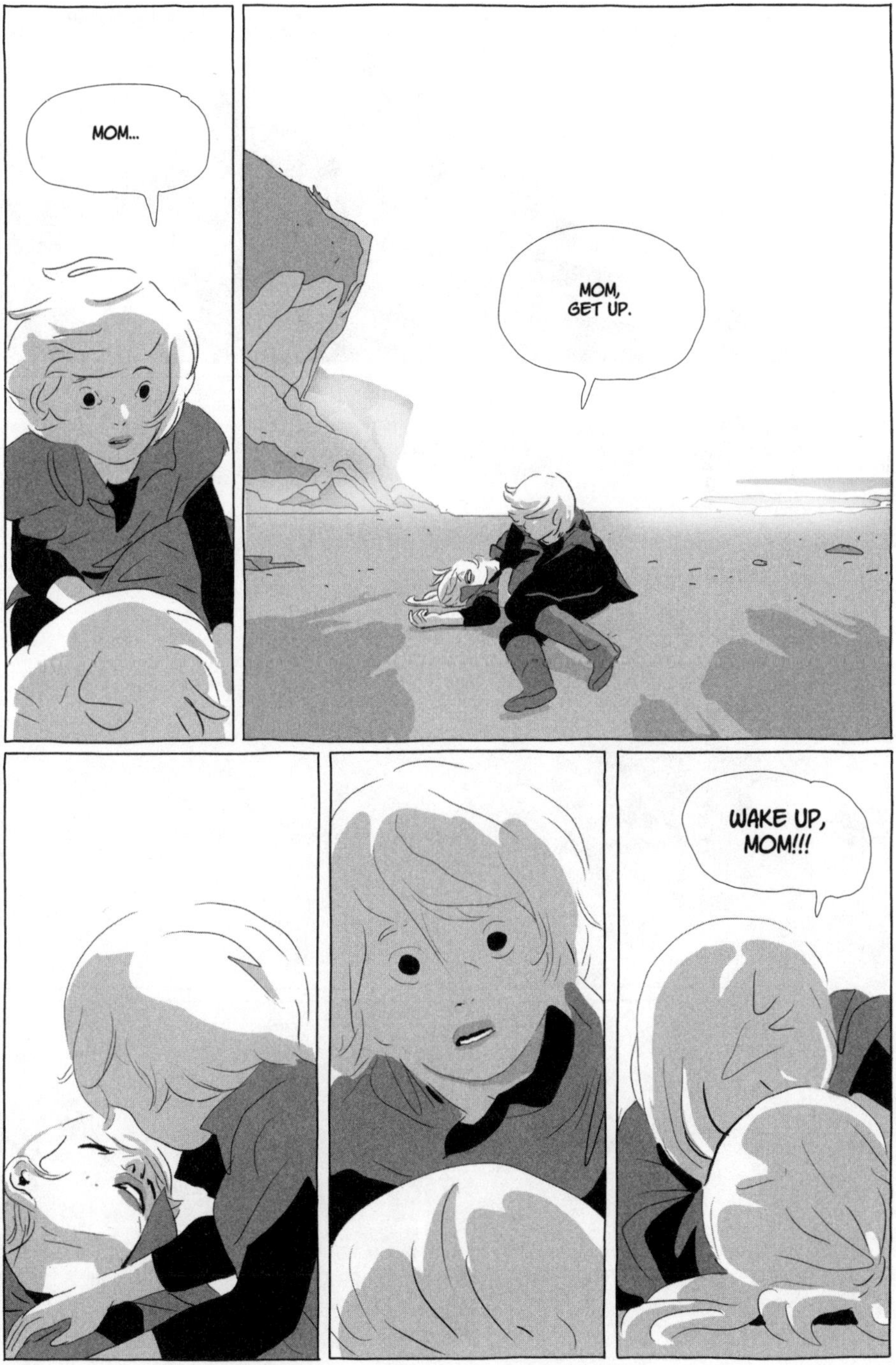
MOM...
MOM, GET UP.
WAKE UP, MOM!!!

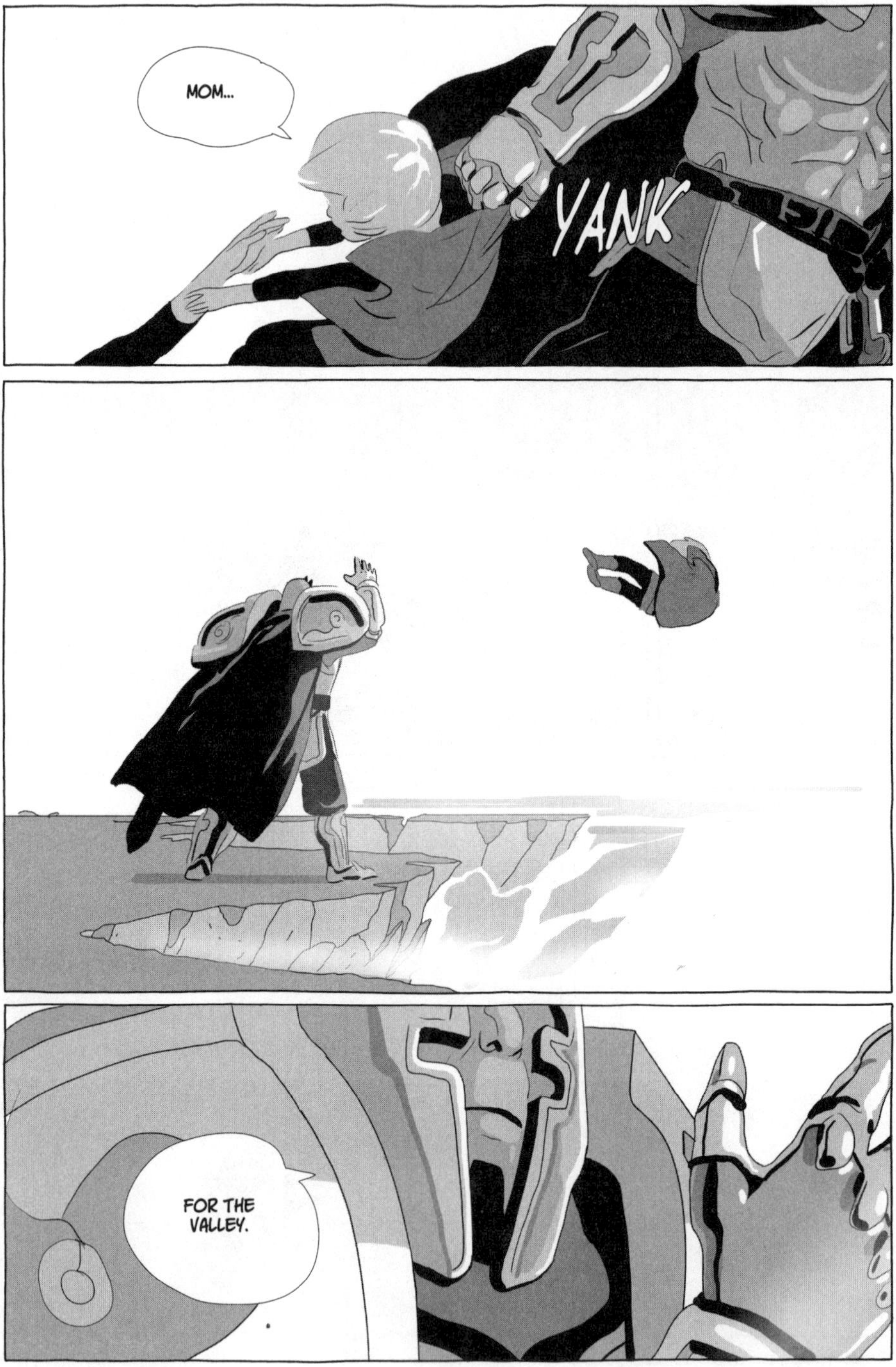
MOM...
YANK
FOR THE VALLEY.

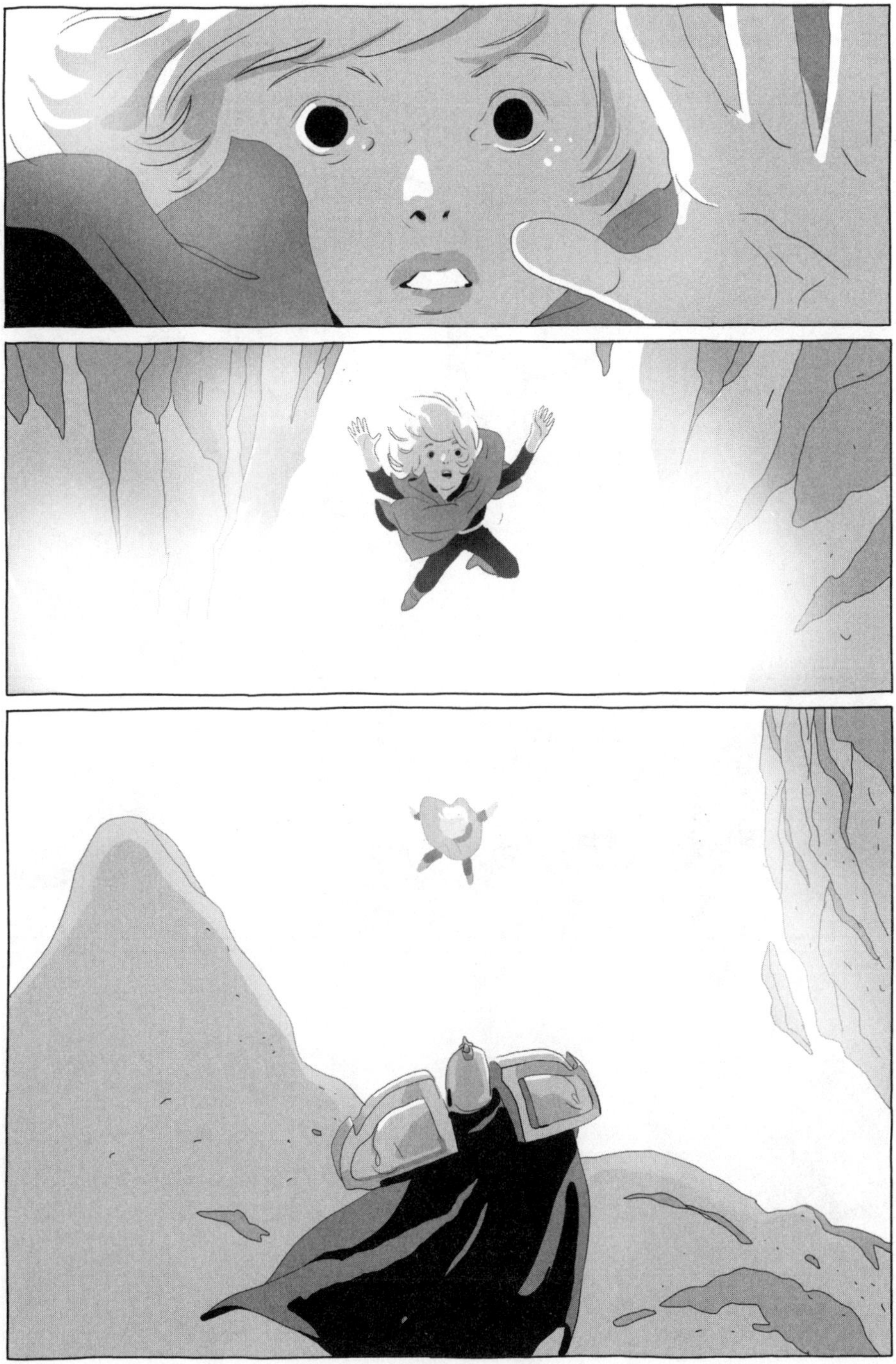

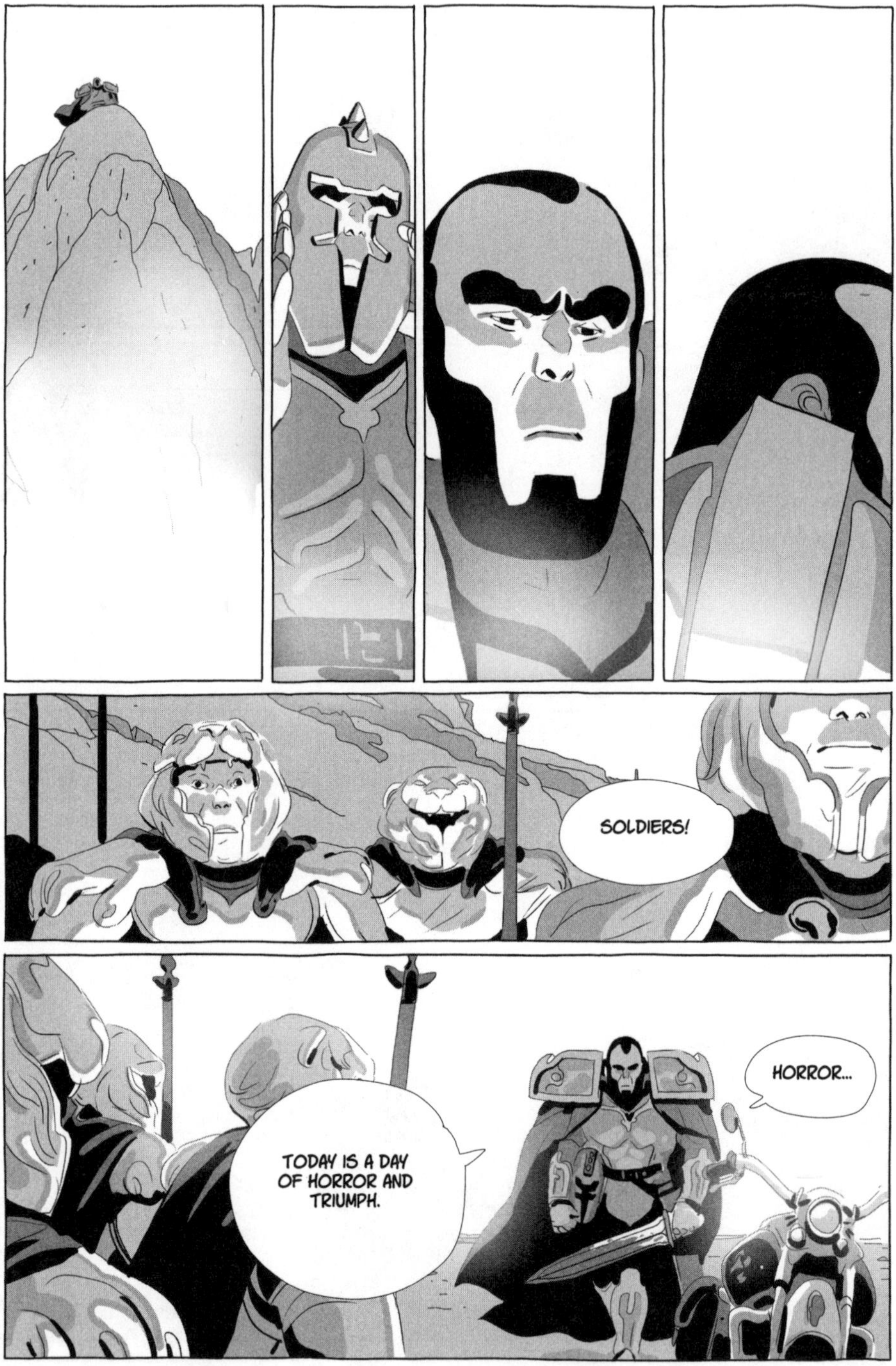
SOLDIERS!
TODAY IS A DAY OF HORROR AND TRIUMPH.
HORROR...

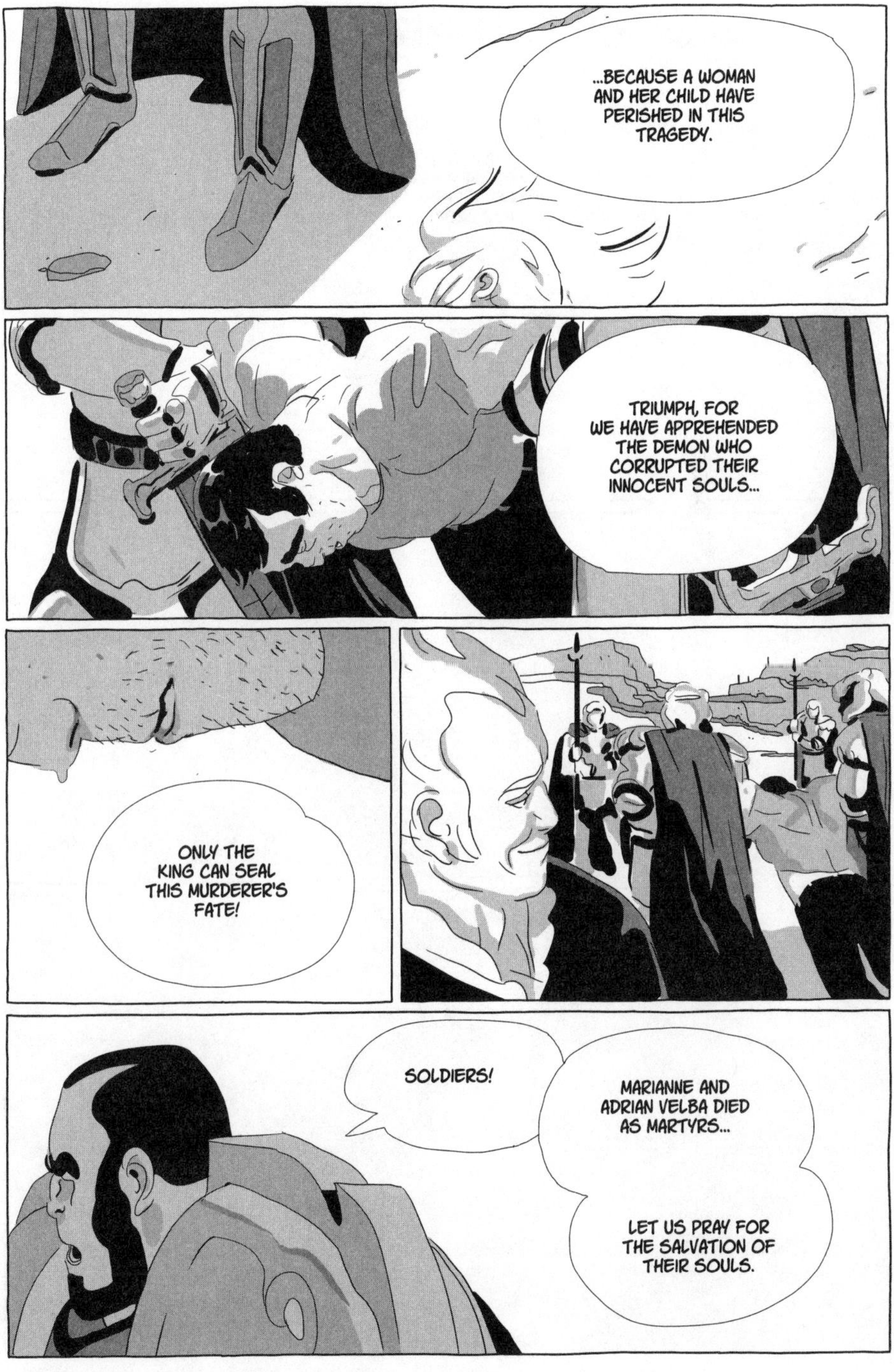
...BECAUSE A WOMAN AND HER CHILD HAVE PERISHED IN THIS TRAGEDY.
TRIUMPH, FOR WE HAVE APPREHENDED THE DEMON WHO CORRUPTED THEIR INNOCENT SOULS...
ONLY THE KING CAN SEAL THIS MURDERER'S FATE!
SOLDIERS!
MARIANNE AND ADRIAN VELBA DIED AS MARTYRS...
LET US PRAY FOR THE SALVATION OF THEIR SOULS.

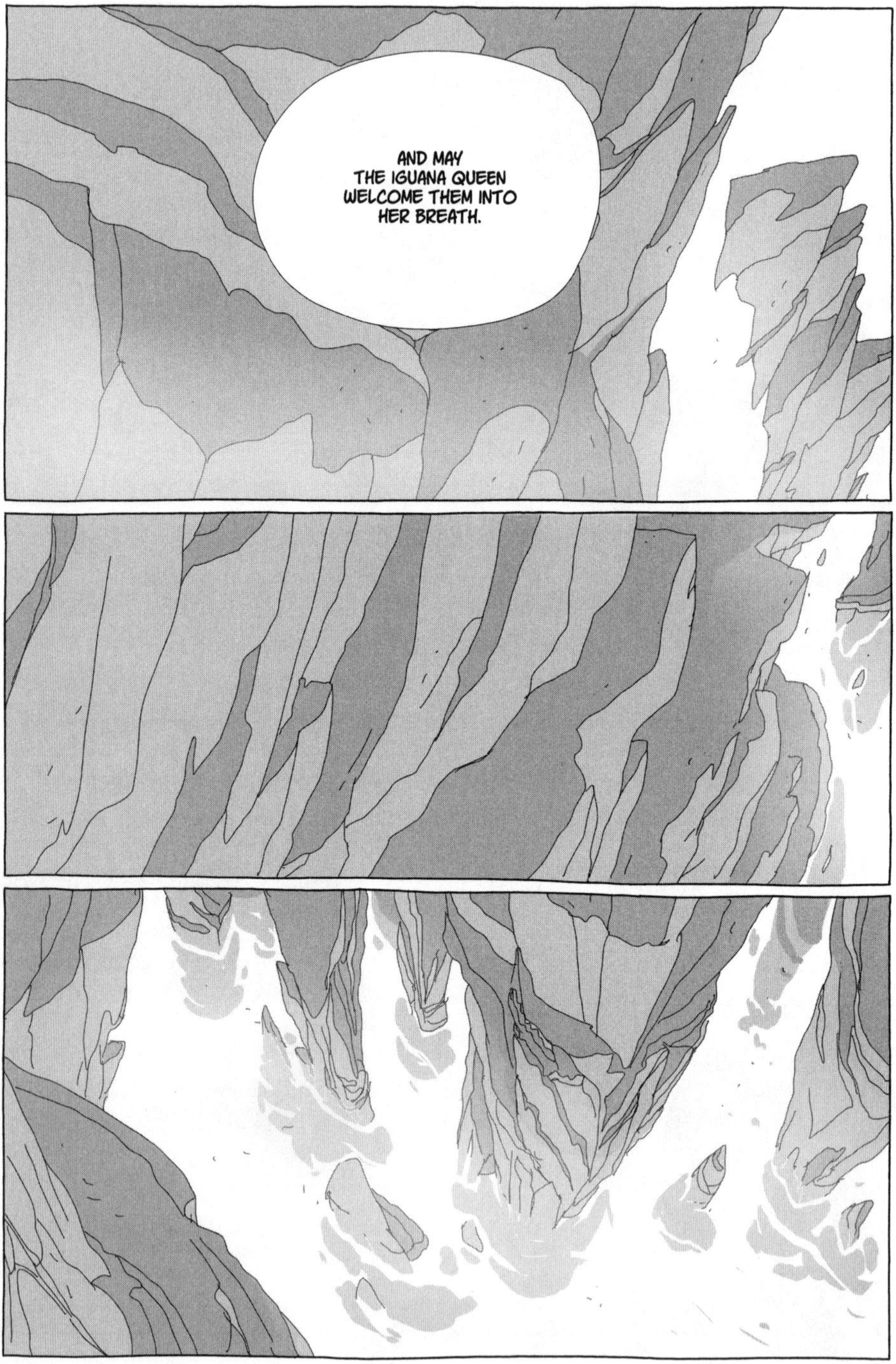
AND MAY THE IGUANA QUEEN WELCOME THEM INTO HER BREATH.

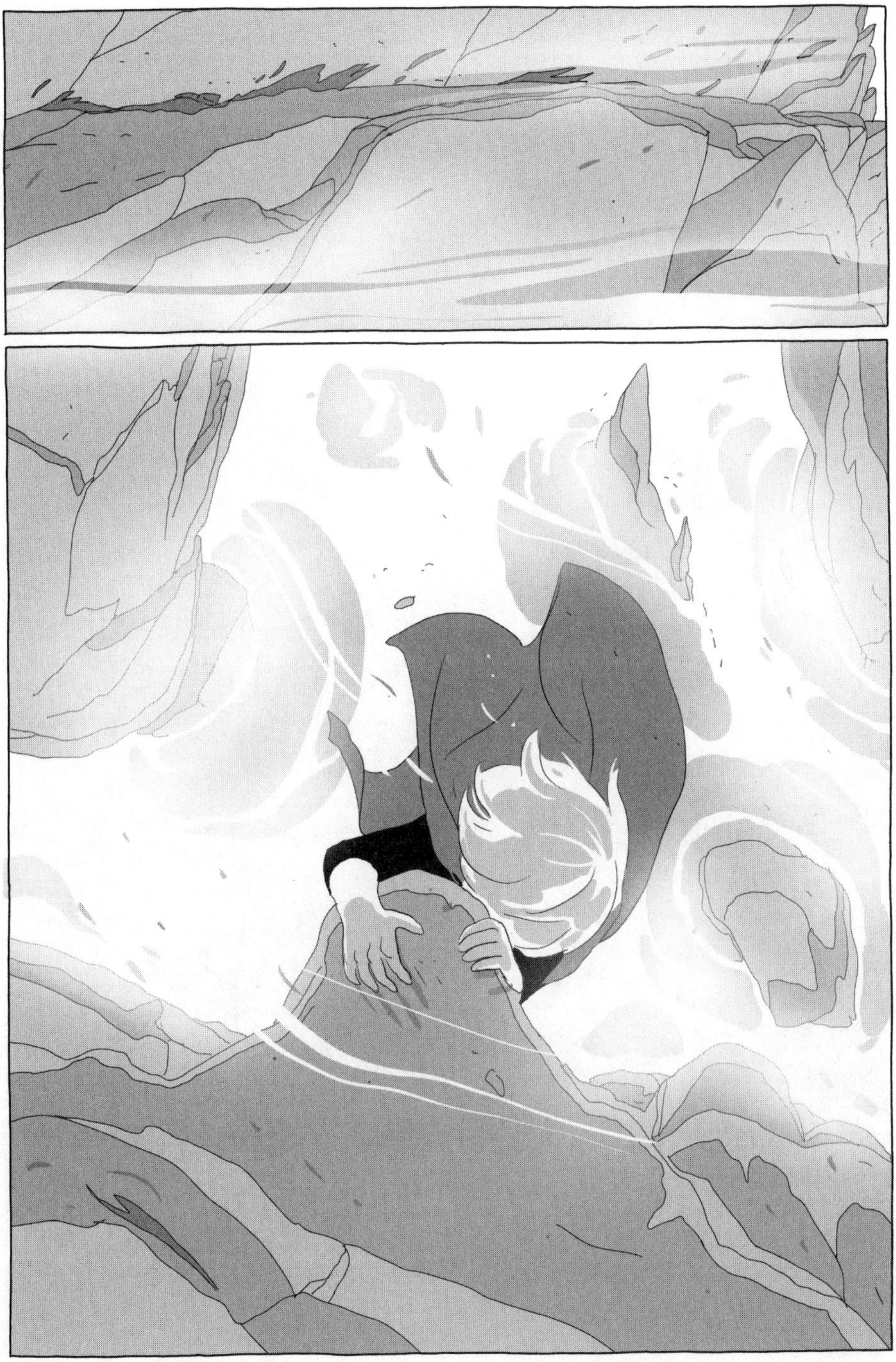

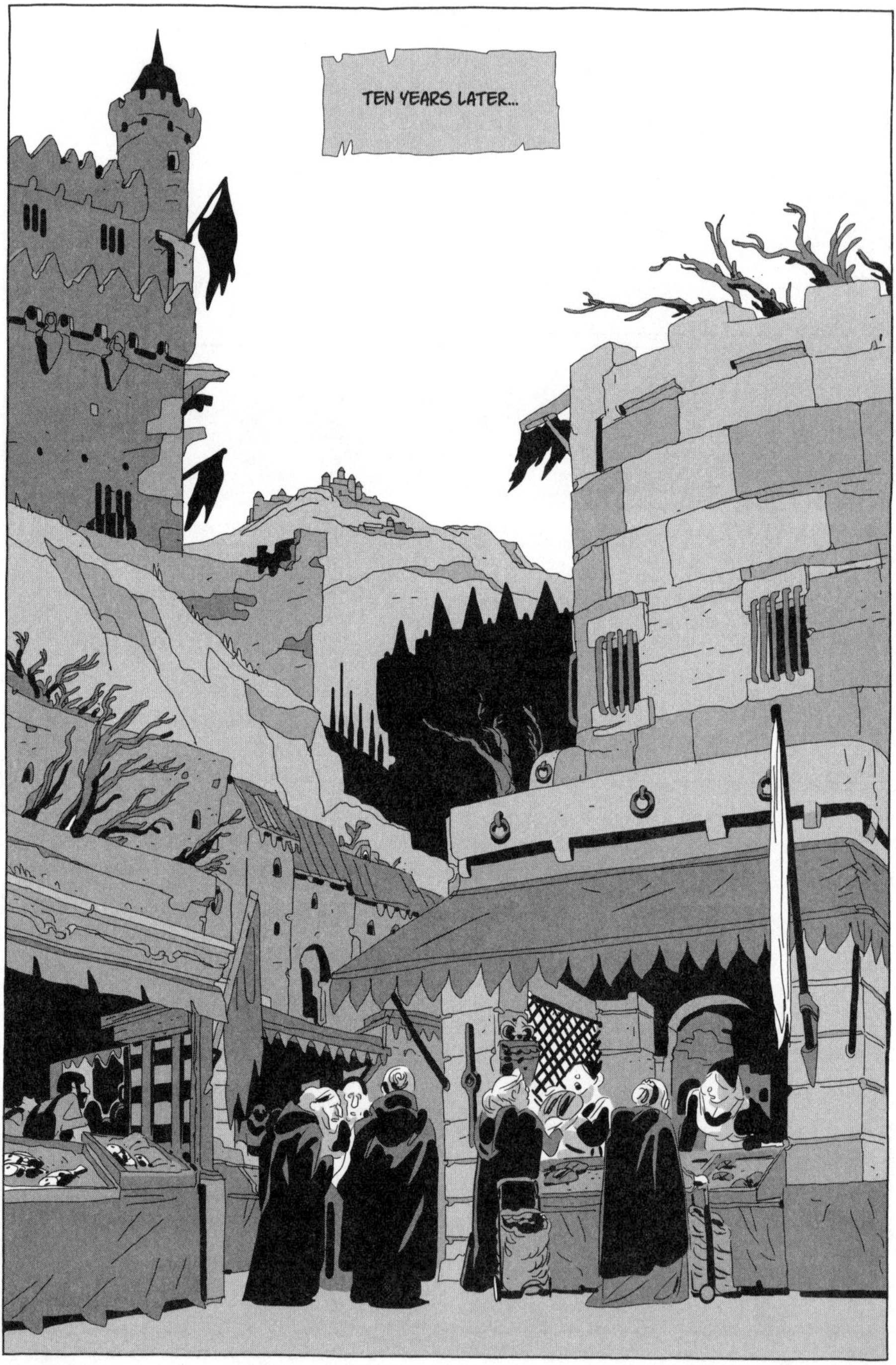
TEN YEARS LATER...

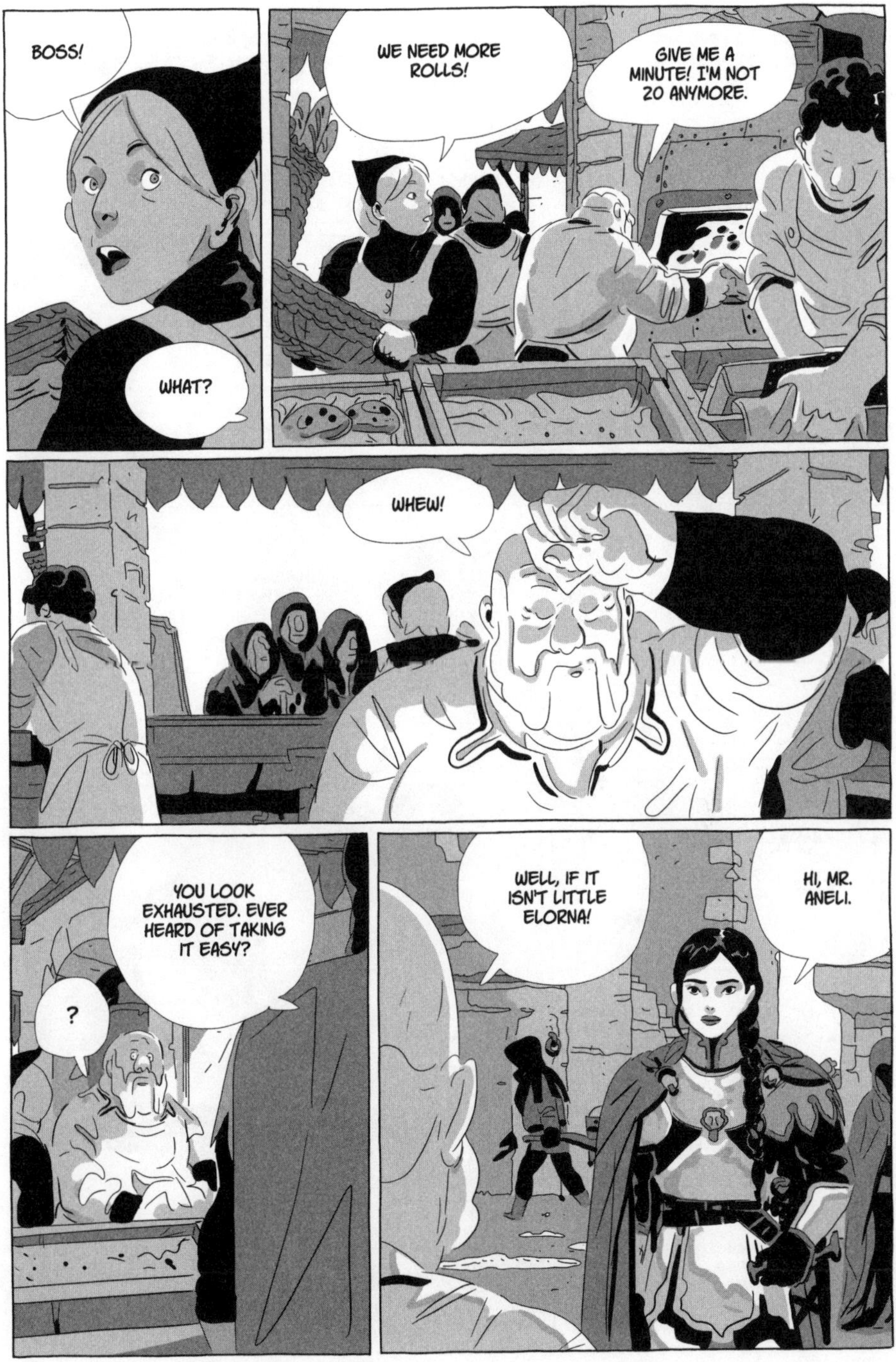
BOSS!
WHAT?
WE NEED MORE ROLLS!
GIVE ME A MINUTE! I'M NOT 20 ANYMORE.
WHEW!
YOU LOOK EXHAUSTED. EVER HEARD OF TAKING IT EASY?
?
WELL, IF IT ISN'T LITTLE ELORNA!
HI, MR. ANELI.

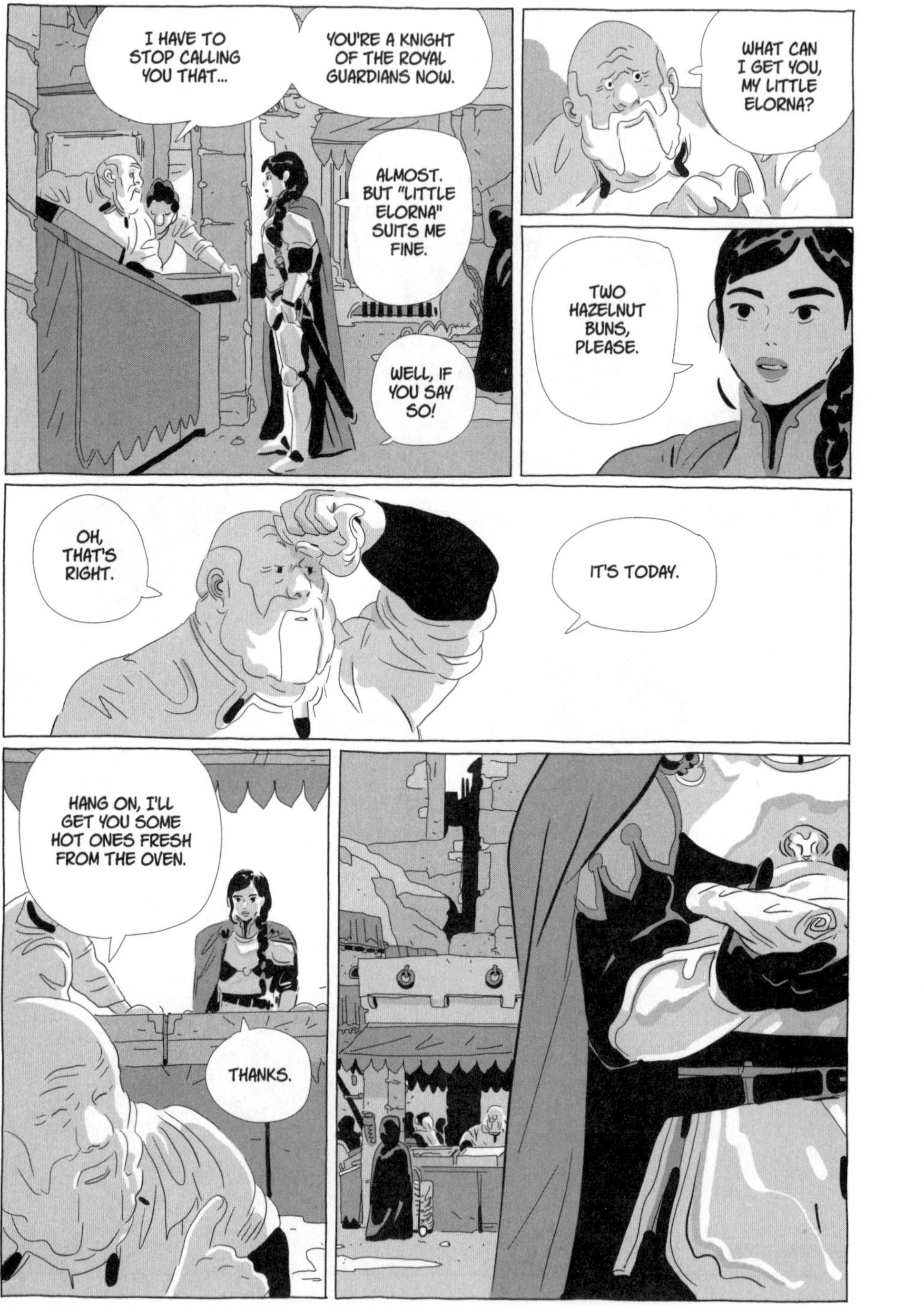
I HAVE TO STOP CALLING YOU THAT...
YOU'RE A KNIGHT OF THE ROYAL GUARDIANS NOW.
ALMOST. BUT "LITTLE ELORNA" SUITS ME FINE.
WELL, IF YOU SAY SO!
WHAT CAN I GET YOU, MY LITTLE ELORNA?
TWO HAZELNUT BUNS, PLEASE.
OH, THAT'S RIGHT.
IT'S TODAY.
HANG ON, I'LL GET YOU SOME HOT ONES FRESH FROM THE OVEN.
THANKS.

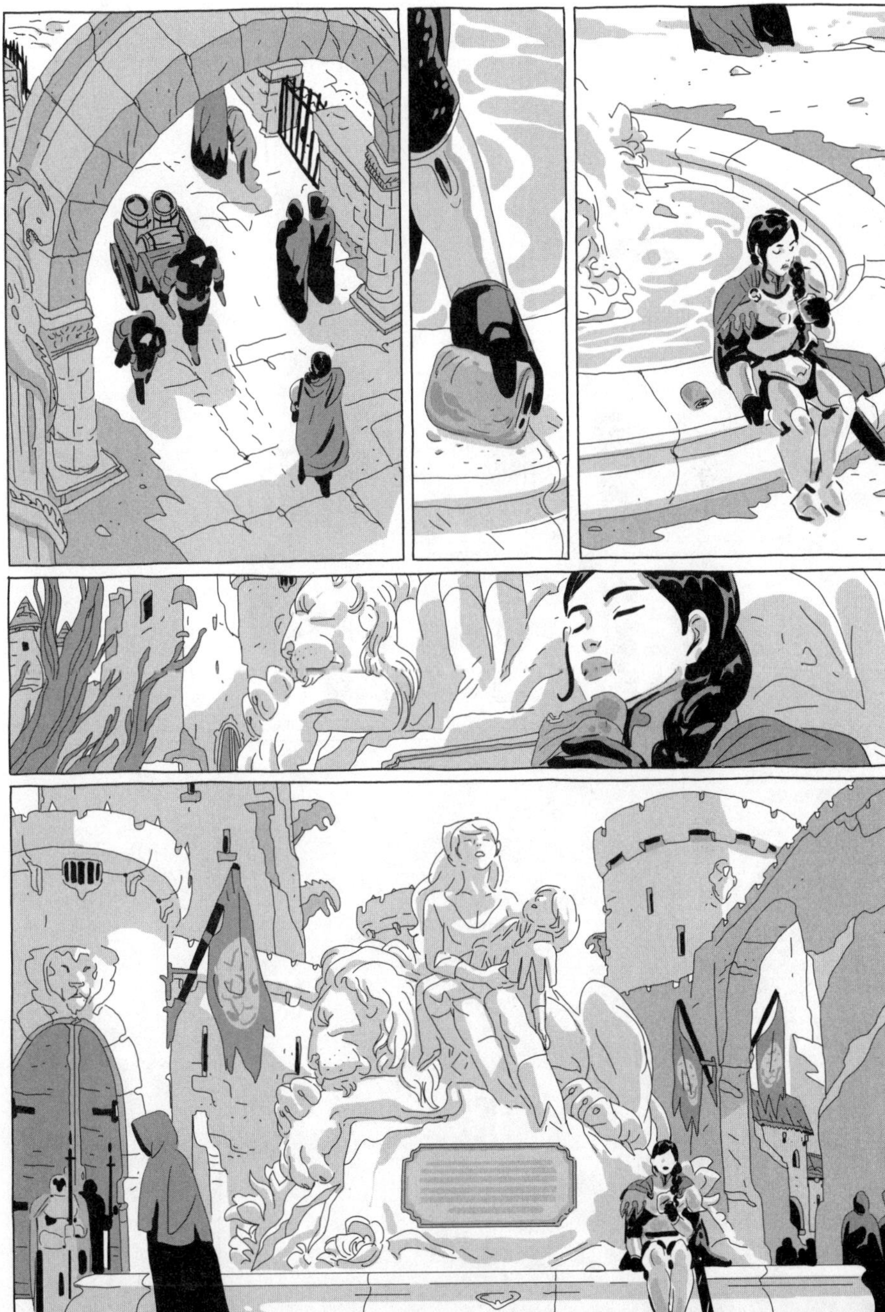

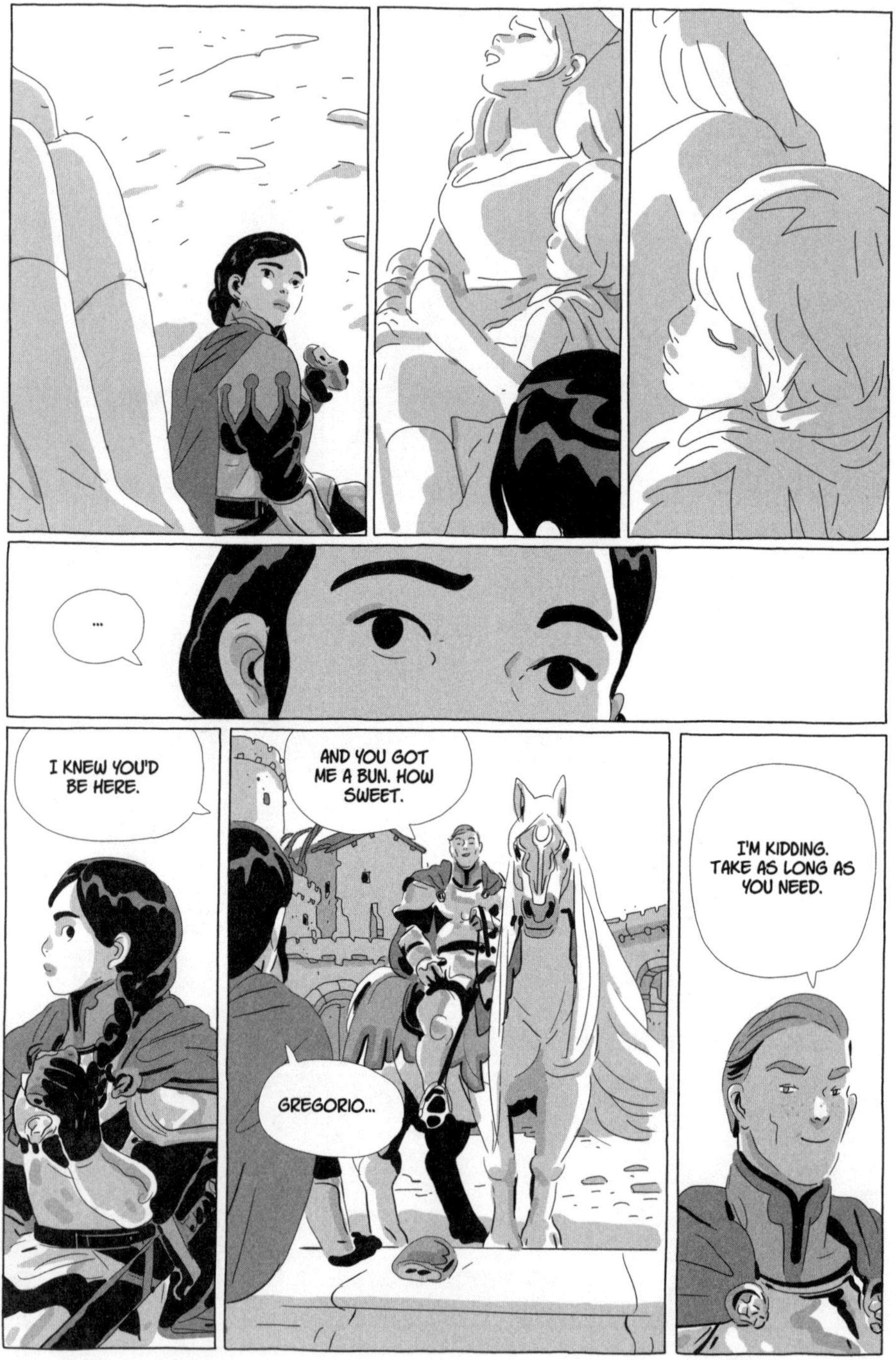
...
I KNEW YOU'D BE HERE.
AND YOU GOT ME A BUN. HOW SWEET.
GREGORIO...
I'M KIDDING. TAKE AS LONG AS YOU NEED.

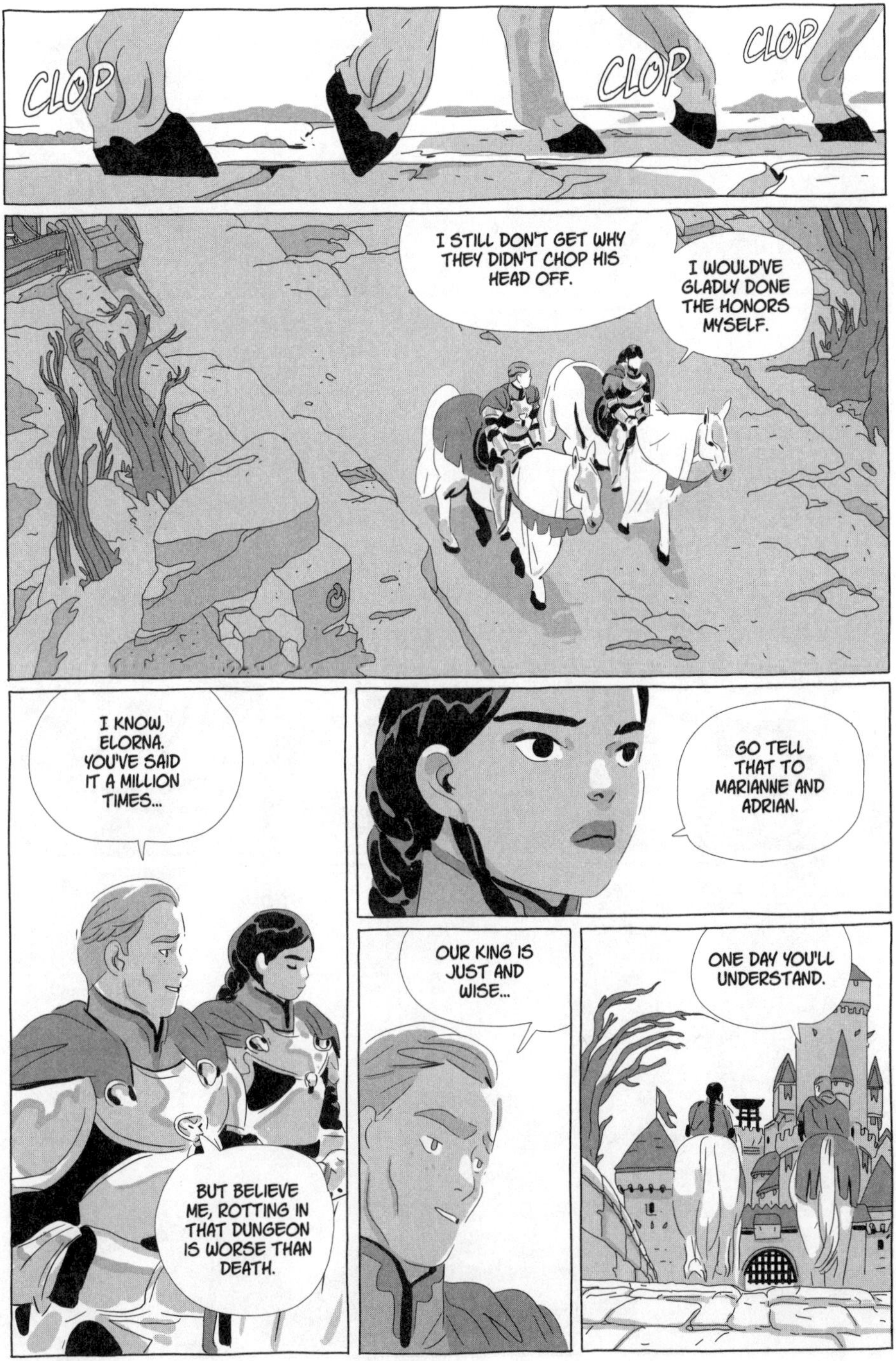
CLOP
CLOP
CLOP
I STILL DON'T GET WHY THEY DIDN'T CHOP HIS HEAD OFF.
I WOULD'VE GLADLY DONE THE HONORS MYSELF.
I KNOW, ELORNA. YOU'VE SAID IT A MILLION TIMES...
BUT BELIEVE ME, ROTTING IN THAT DUNGEON IS WORSE THAN DEATH.
GO TELL THAT TO MARIANNE AND ADRIAN.
OUR KING IS JUST AND WISE...
ONE DAY YOU'LL UNDERSTAND.

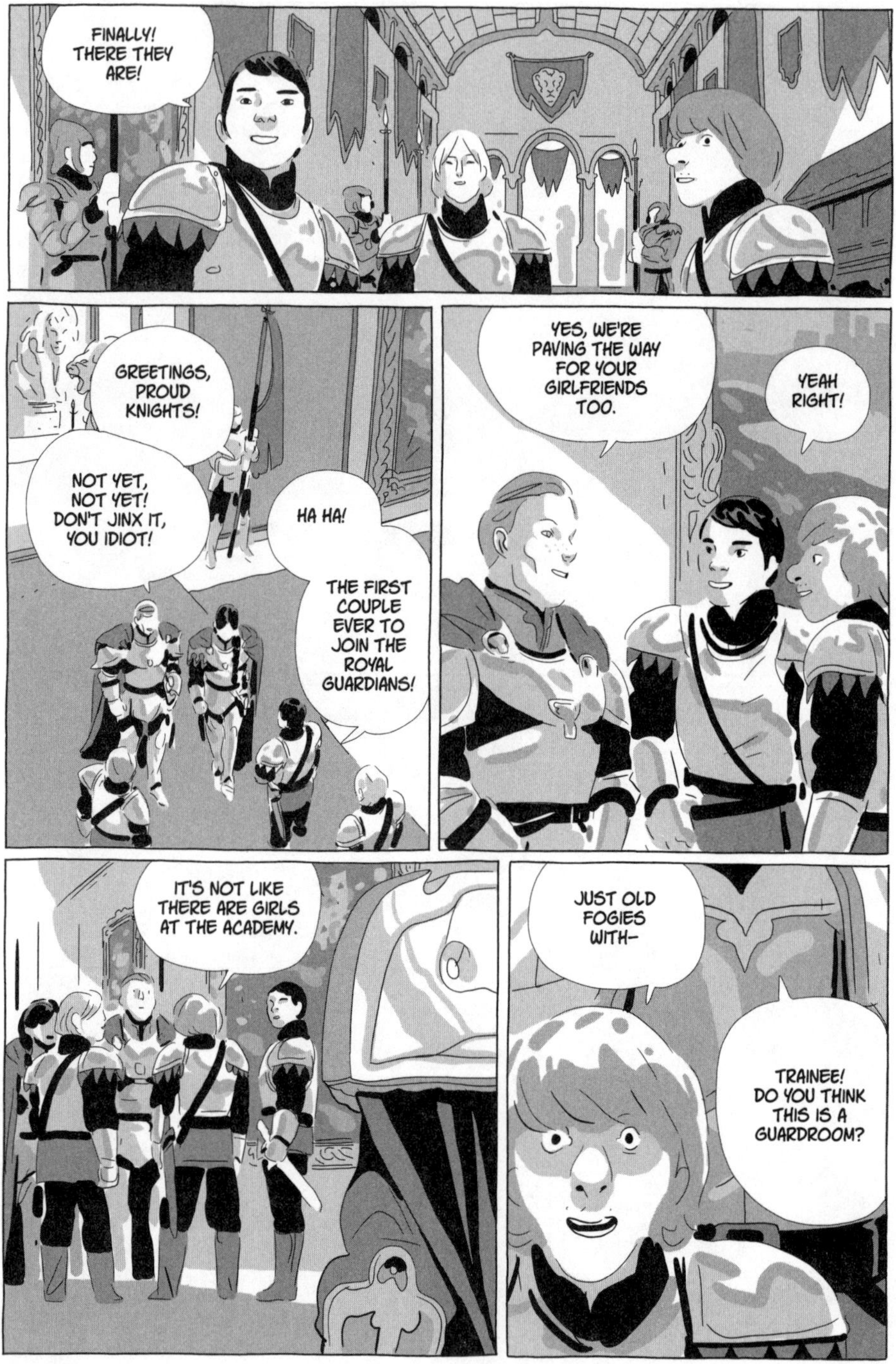
FINALLY! THERE THEY ARE!
GREETINGS, PROUD KNIGHTS!
NOT YET, NOT YET! DON'T JINX IT, YOU IDIOT!
HA HA!
THE FIRST COUPLE EVER TO JOIN THE ROYAL GUARDIANS!
YES, WE'RE PAVING THE WAY FOR YOUR GIRLFRIENDS TOO.
YEAH RIGHT!
IT'S NOT LIKE THERE ARE GIRLS AT THE ACADEMY.
JUST OLD FOGIES WITH-
TRAINEE! DO YOU THINK THIS IS A GUARDROOM?

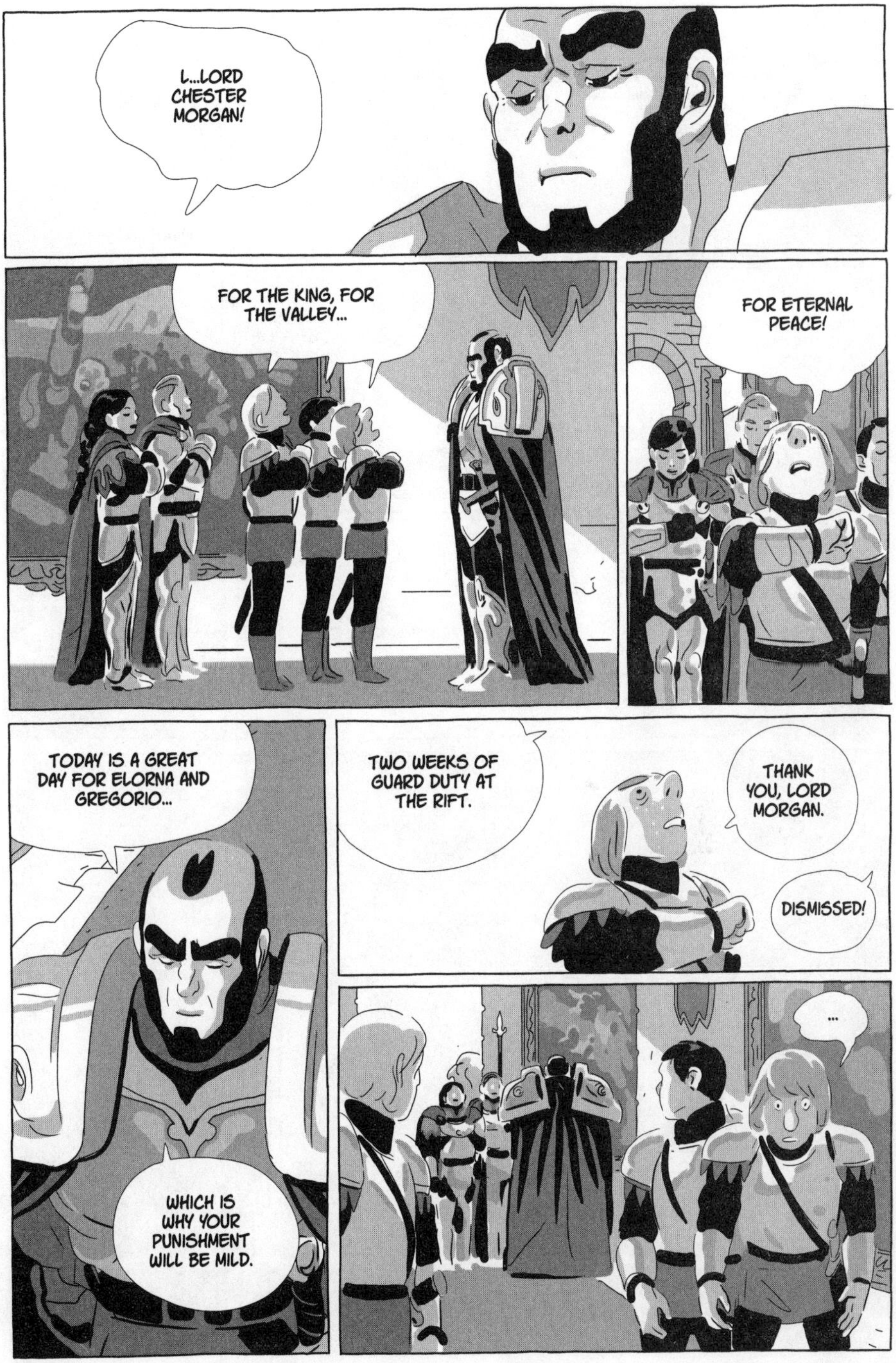
L...LORD CHESTER MORGAN!
FOR THE KING, FOR THE VALLEY...
FOR ETERNAL PEACE!
TODAY IS A GREAT DAY FOR ELORNA AND GREGORIO...
WHICH IS WHY YOUR PUNISHMENT WILL BE MILD.
TWO WEEKS OF GUARD DUTY AT THE RIFT.
THANK YOU, LORD MORGAN.
DISMISSED!
...

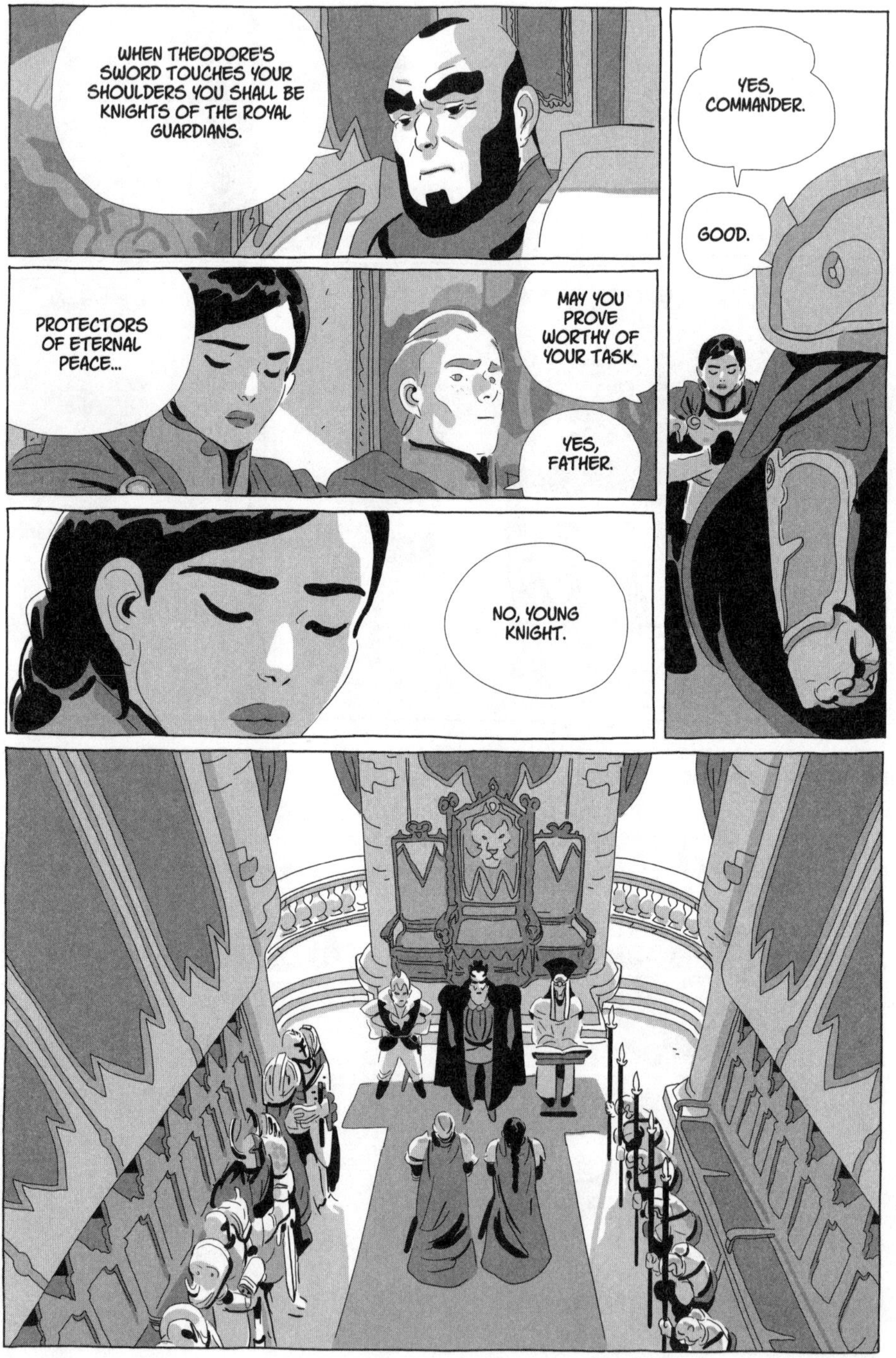
WHEN THEODORE'S SWORD TOUCHES YOUR SHOULDERS YOU SHALL BE KNIGHTS OF THE ROYAL GUARDIANS.
PROTECTORS OF ETERNAL PEACE...
MAY YOU PROVE WORTHY OF YOUR TASK.
YES, FATHER.
NO, YOUNG KNIGHT.
YES, COMMANDER.
GOOD.

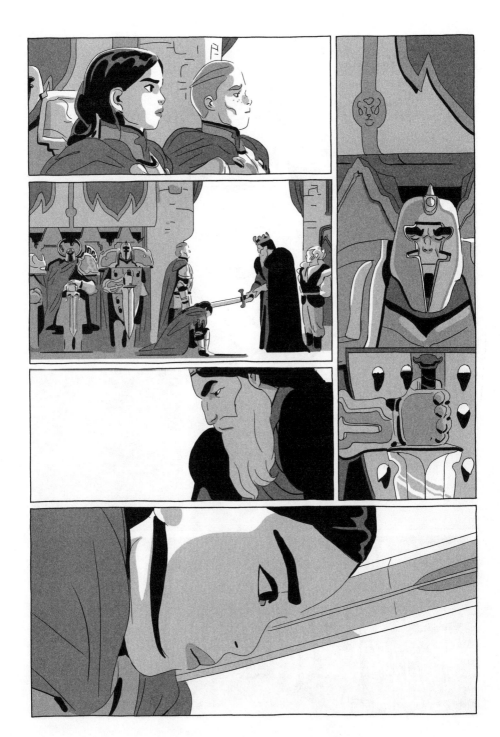

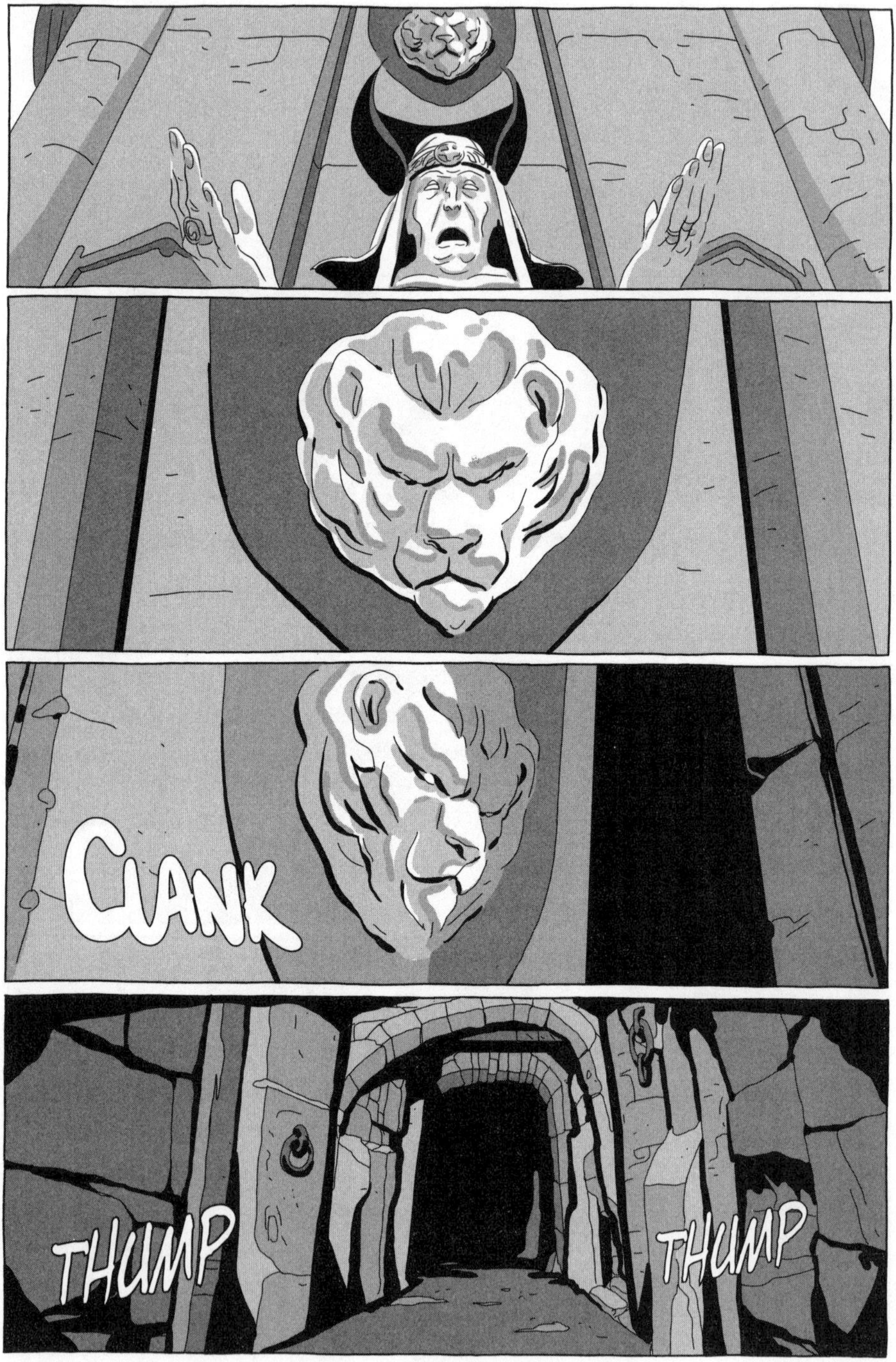
CLANK
THUMP
THUMP

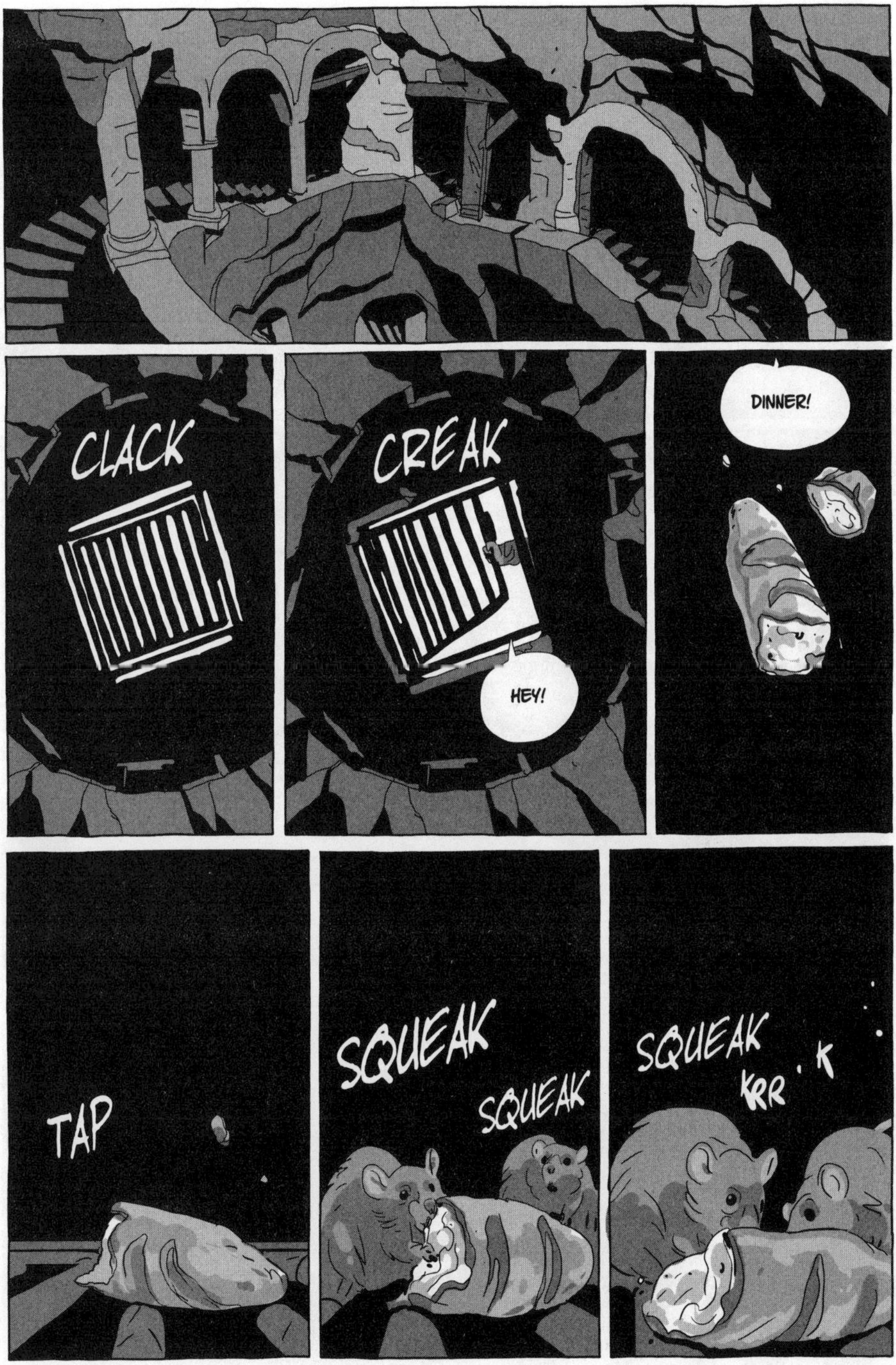

CLACK
CREAK
HEY!
DINNER!
TAP
SQUEAK
SQUEAK
SQUEAK
KRR
K

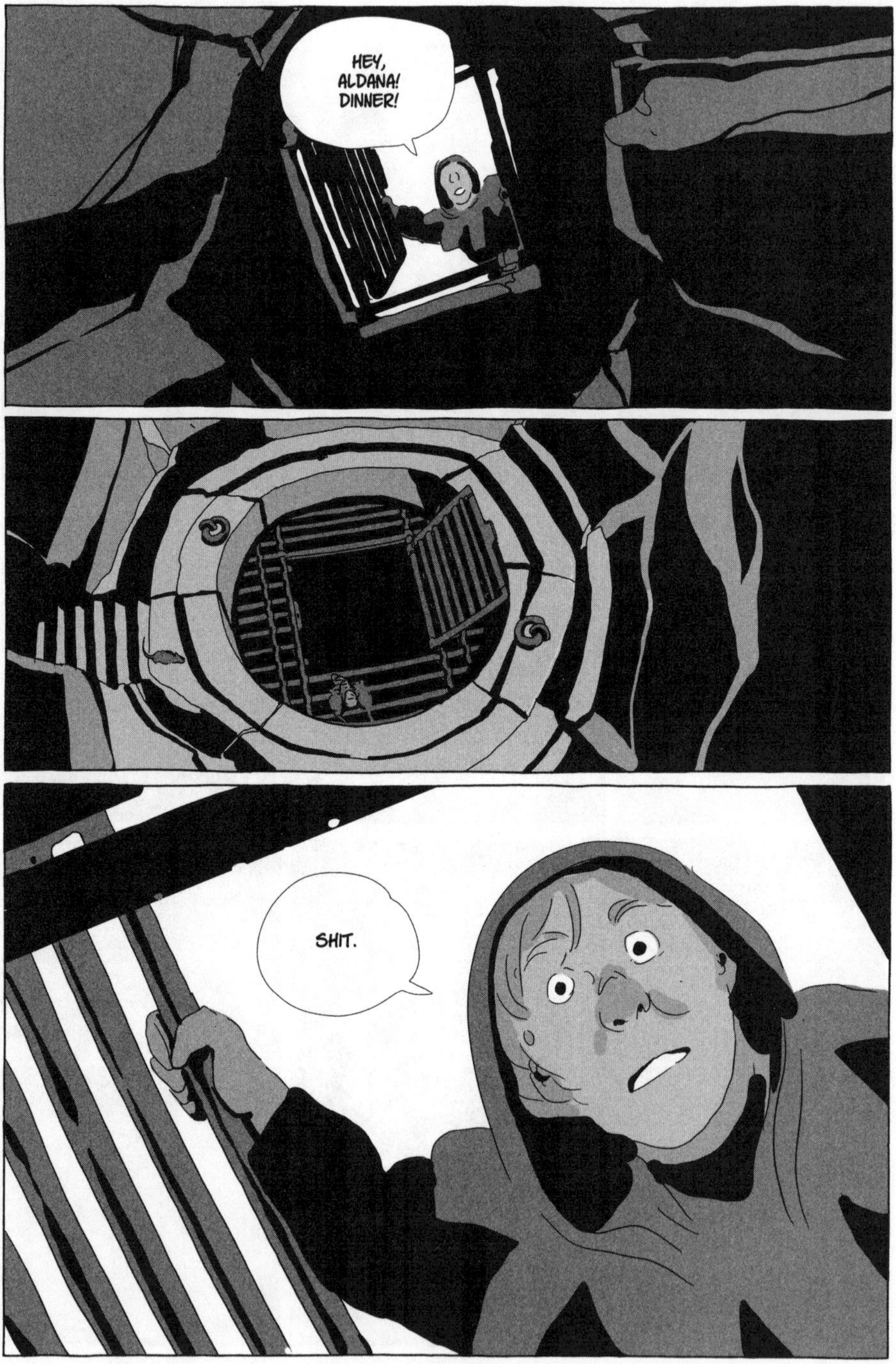
HEY, ALDANA! DINNER!
SHIT.

Don't miss any of the Last Man's earlier adventures!

In the tournament for the Royal Cup, there's a stranger who can float like a butterfly and sting like a bee, figuratively speaking. His brutal fighting style beats out any magic thrown his way, but who is Richard Aldana?

The start of an adrenaline-soaked adventure by France's top comic book stars!

Available in trade paperback

ISBN 978-1-62672-046-6

The exciting fantasy series from France's leading comic book trio continues!

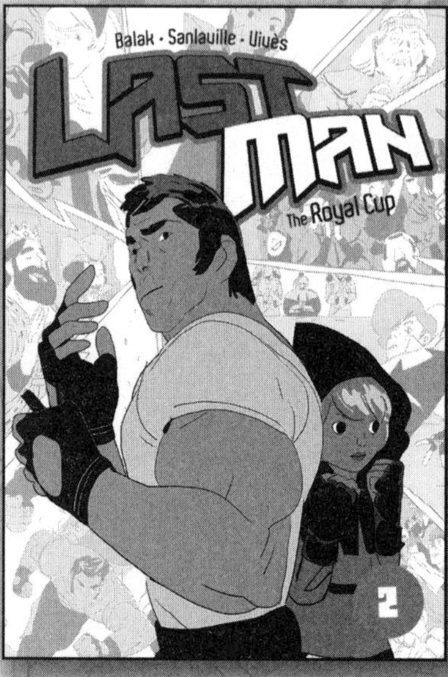
Balak · Sanlaville · Vivès
LAST MAN
The Royal Cup
2

"Last Man is irresistible. This series is a winner."
—Paul Pope

Adrian Velba knows that his fighting partner Richard Aldana is the best there is, and the Royal Cup's within their reach. But after Richard's secret origins are exposed, everything suddenly changes.

Available in trade paperback

ISBN 978-1-62672-047-3

:01
First Second
NEW YORK

"Vivès' rough-hewn but flowing art still gives the manga–influenced book a distinctive visual flavor." —*Booklist*

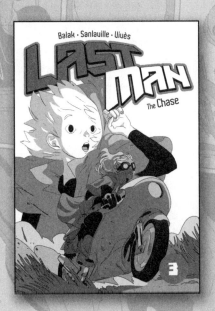

Richard Aldana vanishes from the Valley of Kings, and Adrian and his mother Marianne are in hot pursuit. But this chase leads the Velbas to an entirely different city beyond anything they can imagine, filled with motorcycle gangs, corrupt cops, and a literal legal circus. Can they escape and find Richard at last?

Available in trade paperback

ISBN 978-1-62672-048-0

First Second
NEW YORK

Last Man is a high-octane thrill ride readers won't soon forget!

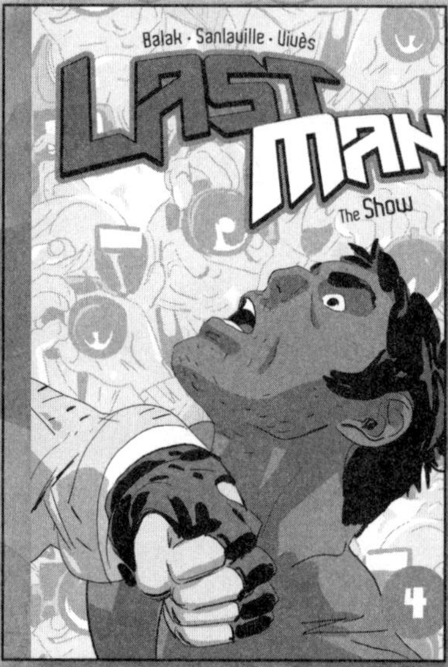
Balak · Sanlaville · Vivès
LAST MAN
The Show
4

Marianne and Adrian find Richard in Paxtown, where something sinister lurks behind the glitz and glam. To discover more answers, they enlist in the Fighting Fists Funeral Cup, that world's famous boxing tournament. But the two soon realize they are not the only travelers from the Valley of Kings with a stake in the Funeral Cup...

Available in trade paperback

ISBN 978-1-62672-049-7

:01
First Second
NEW YORK

Last Man is back with its penultimate volume!

Balak · Sanlaville · Vivès
LAST MAN
The Order
5

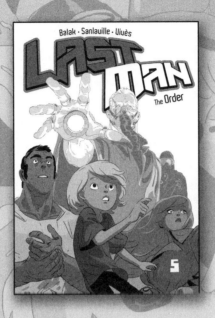

In Paxtown, Team Velba, Richard, and Cristo Canyon all duke it out in the ring against friend and foe alike. Meanwhile, in the Valley of Kings, its monarch frantically searches for the Velbas and Richard, who is now marked as a trophy thief and a kidnapper. The two worlds become linked, however, when members of a mysterious organization wielding supernatural powers arrive in Paxtown.

Available in trade paperback

ISBN 978-1-62672-050-3

:01
First Second
NEW YORK

First Second
New York

Lastman tome 6 copyright © 2014 Casterman
English translation by Alexis Siegel
English translation copyright © 2016 by First Second

Published by First Second
First Second is an imprint of Roaring Brook Press,
a division of Holtzbrinck Publishing Holdings Limited Partnership
175 Fifth Avenue, New York, New York 10010

Library of Congress Control Number: 2015951862

ISBN: 978-1-62672-051-0

First Second books may be purchased for business or promotional use.
For information on bulk purchases please contact Macmillan Corporate
and Premium Sales Department at (800) 221-7945 x5442 or by email at
specialmarkets@macmillan.com.

Originally published in France by Casterman as *Lastman tome 6*.

First American edition 2016

Book design by Rob Steen

Printed in the United States of America

10 9 8 7 6 5 4 3 2 1